THE CATHOLIC CHURCH IN IRELAND, 1914–1918

THE
CATHOLIC CHURCH
IN IRELAND
1914–1918

War and Politics

Jérôme aan de Wiel

University of Reims

IRISH ACADEMIC PRESS
DUBLIN • PORTLAND, OR

First published 2003 by
IRISH ACADEMIC PRESS
44 Northumberland Road, Dublin 4, Ireland

and in the United States of America by
IRISH ACADEMIC PRESS
c/o ISBS, 920 NE 58th Avenue, #300, Portland
Oregon 97213-3786

Website: www.iap.ie

British Library Cataloguing in Publication Data

Wiel, Jerome aan de
  The Catholic Church in Ireland, 1914–1918: war and politics
  1. Catholic Church – Ireland – Political activity 2. Religion and politics – Ireland
  3. World War, 1914–1918 – Diplomatic history 4. World War, 1914–1918 – Ireland
  5. Ireland History – 1901–1910 6. Ireland – History – 1910–1921 7. Ireland –
  Church history – 20th century
  I. Title
  282.4′15′09041

  ISBN 0–7165–2758–8

Library of Congress Cataloging-in-Publication Data

De Wiel, Jérôme aan, 1966–
  The Catholic Church in Ireland, 1914–1918: war and politics/Jérôme aan de Wiel
    p.cm.
  Includes bibliographical references and index.
  ISBN 0–7165–2758–8 (cloth)
    1. World War, 1914–1918 – Religious aspects – Catholic Church. 2. Catholic Church –
  Ireland – History – 20th century. 3. Ireland – Politics and government – 1910–1921.
  I. Title.

  D622.D34 2003
  282′.415′09041–dc21

                                    2003040729

Typeset in 10.5 pt on 12 pt Sabon by
FiSH Books, London WC1
Printed by MPG Books Ltd, Bodmin, Cornwall

To Josette and Aram who suddenly passed away.
To my parents, all my parents and my friends.
I owe them much.

Contents

Illustrations

Acknowledgements

The origins of this book are to be found in a doctorate I wrote in 1998 for the University of Caen, in Normandy. I am indebted to many people. I should like to acknowledge particularly Professor Paul Brennan of the Sorbonne Nouvelle in Paris. He has always helped me over the years and guided me in my research and has been a model supervisor. He has played a major role in the development of Irish Studies in France. I also greatly appreciate the advice given to me by Professor Catherine Maignant of the University of Lille, Professor Jean Brihault of the University of Rennes, and Professor Dermot Keogh of University College Cork. All had the patience to read a very long thesis.

The whole project and research could simply not have been possible without the help of the Benedictine community of Glenstal Abbey in Ireland. I would like to express my thanks to the following brothers. Fr Paul Nash's intervention brought me over to Co. Limerick and enabled me to begin research on this topic. Abbot Christopher Dillon and Fr Henry O'Shea facilitated access to archives in Ireland and abroad. Fr Simon Sleeman, Fr Gregory Collins and Br Denis Hooper were always very helpful when I lived in Glenstal. Br Colman Ó Clabaigh did research for me in Oxford. Fr Senan Furlong and Fr Gerard McGinty translated Italian and Latin texts into English. Fr Mark Tierney's advice on archives abroad was most helpful. Without him, most important primary sources would never have been found for this book. I particularly wish to thank Fr Brian Murphy. He was most willing to help me during my research despite his own very busy timetable. His insight and attention to detail were priceless. Finally, other staff at Glenstal Abbey School have been of invaluable help. Mr Tony Breen was always a source of encouragement. Mr Gregory Ashe and Ms Maree McCarthy patiently helped me make my way through the computer jungle; Ms Ruth Healy helped me in the administration; Mr Gerry Cronin and Br Cillian O'Shea were always ready to assist me in German; and Mr Kenneth C. O'Toole advised me on some historical aspects and especially made my style in English more fluent and readable.

In Limerick, Fr Michael Wall was most helpful during my research in the diocesan archives. In Mary Immaculate College, I could always rely on Mr John Eustace, the librarian, and Mr Tony Bonfield whose interest in the subject was stimulating and kept me thinking. Ms Sabine Egger gave me advice on titles and subtitles that were badly in need of some imagination. Mrs Maura Cronin of the Department of History at Mary Immaculate College kindly and patiently corrected the manuscript. Her advice was invaluable. Mr Michael Cusack was most supportive in this project. In Bandon, Mr and Mrs Nash were always generous in their help and hospitality when I was in Cork. In Armagh, Fr Eugene Sweeney and Fr John Gates were most obliging. In Carlow, Br Linus Walker facilitated my research in the diocesan archives. In Dublin, Mr David Sheehy advised me on Archbishop Walsh and pointed out to me other places where I could find relevant archives.

In the United States, Professor Emmet Larkin of the University of Chicago very generously read the manuscript and gave me his views. In Germany, Mr Jorg Baden indicated which archives to consult. In England, Mr Julian Putkowski did some very valuable research for me.

In Rome, Mgr John Fleming, the rector of the Irish College, gave me very useful information about the College and its history and allowed me to consult all the archives. In the College, I met Fr Oliver P. Rafferty (S.J.) who greatly helped me in deciphering the handwriting of some ecclesiastics and who offered most useful information about Church history. He also did research for me in New York. Maurice Healy kindly translated some Italian documents into English for me. In the Vatican Archives, a most fascinating place, I was helped by Mgr Charles Burns and Mgr Marcello Camisassa. Fr Liam McCarthy of the Irish Franciscans authorised me to read the archives of the most beautiful church of San Isidoro in Rome.

In the Netherlands, Mrs Erica de Roever translated documents written in Latin and Mr Peter Groot solved worrying computer problems. In France, Mr Jean-Christophe Gallet and Ms Christine Farget were most patient, despite their many commitments, in correcting my doctorate. Finally, I would like to acknowledge the patience and enthusiasm of my editor, Mr Jonathan Manley.

All of the above persons made a significant contribution to the writing of the thesis and the book. My deepest gratitude to all.

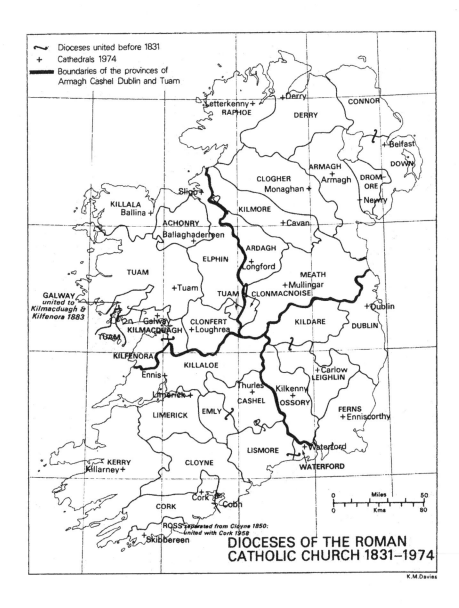

Legend:
- ∿ Dioceses united before 1831
- + Cathedrals 1974
- ▬ Boundaries of the provinces of Armagh Cashel Dublin and Tuam

DIOCESES OF THE ROMAN
CATHOLIC CHURCH 1831–1974

K.M.Davies

1. Map of ecclesiastical provinces and dioceses in Ireland, 1831–1974
(Oliver P. Rafferty, *Catholicism in Ulster 1603–1983*, Dublin: Gill
and Macmillan, 1994)

xiii

Preface

In 1989, I left Paris for Cork to do research on modern Irish history for a degree in the Sorbonne Nouvelle. Being interested in the First World War, I had decided, together with my supervisor, Prof. Paul Brennan, to study Ireland's participation in the Great War. Little did I know what lay ahead of me. Very soon my enthusiasm was dampened by the almost complete lack of secondary sources on the subject. It was, in fact, a nightmare for a young student, as the task of researching the subject seemed of gargantuan proportions. Some historians, such as David Fitzpatrick in *Ireland and the First World War*, are of the opinion that there is a lack of 'systematic study' of Ireland's involvement in the war of 1914–1918.[1] Others, like Keith Jeffery in *Ireland and the Great War*, speak of 'national amnesia'.[2] In 1998, on the occasion of the eightieth anniversary of the end of the war, Kevin Myers, a journalist working for the *Irish Times*, went as far as to declare in a documentary on Irish television: '[The war] was a colossal experience for the Irish people and yet within thirty or forty years it had been publicly removed. Not even Stalin could have been as complete in his removal of memory.'[3] These are strong words but during my research for this book I reached the conclusion that this was indeed the case. The lack of secondary sources and the scarcity of Great War memorials in public places commemorating fallen Irish soldiers are all too obvious. A few references to the war are made sporadically in books that deal with the evolution of Irish politics at the beginning of the twentieth century. Authors, however, essentially debate about the justification, or rejection, of the Easter Rising of 1916 that occurred right in the middle of the war. They analyse the causes and consequences of the Rising but neglect, or choose to ignore, the impact of the war in the country. And yet, as a mass of undiscovered or ignored archives reveal, the war definitely produced a political climate that radically changed the course of Irish history. But subsequent Irish governments, with a strong nationalist ethos, chose to commemorate Easter Rising patriotism and disregard Irish patriotism that prevailed in the trenches of France and Flanders. Back in 1989, a member of the Cumman Seanachais (history society) in Bandon, Co. Cork told me that 'the First World War is a war the Irish want to forget'. This remark was intriguing. After all, Ireland was on the side of the victors. So why this bitterness? It appeared that after a genuine pro-war feeling among Irish nationalists in 1914, the general population rapidly grew tired of the war and was disgusted by some initiatives of the British Government and blunders of the War Office. As a result, recruitment figures dropped drastically and the war became a symbol of British duplicity and broken promises. After 1918, and with the passing of the years, indifference was shown towards the commemoration of Armistice Day and remembrance of the Irish soldiers who had died for their country and for the cause they believed in defending, chiefly the freedom of small nations. In striking contrast to France, Britain and Belgium, there are no First World War memorials in the centre of towns and villages in Ireland. The monuments one finds commemorate the Rising of 1798, the Easter Rising of 1916 and the fallen soldiers of the Irish Republican Army during the War of Independence of 1919–1921. This reflects a choice in patriotism.

It is only recently that Irish participation in the Great War has been explored again. There have been initiatives to make the Irish public aware that their country did participate in the war and sent about 140,000 soldiers to the front.[4] In 1997, the Bandon War Memorial Committee declared its satisfaction when the Taoiseach (Prime Minister) announced his decision to contribute financially to the building of an Irish war monument in Messines, in Belgium.[5] Secondary school pupils now read in some history textbooks that Irishmen fought in France.[6]

If there is renewed interest in the First World War, it remains largely focused on military history and commemoration studies.[7] Other areas remain unexplored, such as the attitude of the Irish Catholic Church towards the war. Initially, research into this topic proved difficult as no books and few articles deal with the issue.[8] I wondered if there was really much flesh to put on the bones. Then fortune smiled on me. During a visit to Glenstal Abbey in Co. Limerick in 1992, I met Fr Brian Murphy, a Benedictine monk who advised me to begin my research abroad in the Irish College in Rome. In the archives of the College I read hundreds of letters of bishops and priests and found that ecclesiastical gossip was most relevant, not to mention ecclesiastical machinations. Two years later, I became a teacher at Glenstal Abbey School where Fr Mark Tierney heard about my research. He too advised me to go abroad, this time to a city I knew well, Paris. There I read reports of military intelligence officers, spies, informers and members of the diplomatic corps. It was a mine of information not only about the political situation in Ireland during the war years but also about the attitude of the Catholic Church towards recruitment and the war effort in general. At first, I assumed that the topic of my research would make me travel almost exclusively in Ireland, but in fact I did most of the travelling abroad: archives of the French Army, French diplomatic corps, Archdiocese of Paris, German diplomatic corps, Irish College Rome, Secret Archives of the Vatican, Archdiocese of Westminster and archives of the Public Record Office in London. It seemed that the belligerent powers were convinced at various stages of the war that Ireland and its Catholic Church were important players able to change or influence the course of the war in Europe. In Ireland, the diocesan archivists of Armagh, Carlow, Dublin and Limerick kindly allowed me to have a close look at their documents. What I found there completed the political jigsaw puzzle that I had begun to put together abroad. Some discoveries implied a revision of the history of the Catholic Church in Ireland between 1914 and 1918. A case in point is Bishop Edward O'Dwyer of Limerick, undoubtedly the most influential ecclesiastic of the time, and also a much appreciated bishop in Italy and a loathed one in France and Britain. His repeated interventions in favour of peace reached the ears of Benedict XV and the Curia in Rome, and upset French diplomats in the Quai d'Orsay in Paris. Although a convinced nationalist, O'Dwyer felt obliged to intervene against John Redmond, the leader of the Nationalist party and an arch-apostle of war. As the war was practically erased from modern Irish history and mostly ignored by historians, O'Dwyer's attitude and strong condemnations of Redmond and his party have been misinterpreted. Interestingly, in 1973, a Dutch professor of history, George Zeegers, wrote a preface to a novel about the troubles in Northern Ireland. He briefly mentioned the bishops' role during the war years and stated: 'Especially the name of Bishop O'Dwyer of Limerick – who before had the reputation of being a very conservative and cautious bishop but who was now speaking out very courageously against the British authorities – should never be forgotten'.[9] Not many people nowadays would know about O'Dwyer's role in the First World War or about the man himself.

The world conflict had a deep impact on the relations between the Catholic Church and the dominant political party at the time, the pro-war Nationalist party, and later the anti-war Sinn Féin. In 1914 Britain and its Empire declared war on Germany for the liberty of small nations. Ireland was thus concerned since it was struggling for Home Rule. In the House of Commons in London, John Redmond, the nationalist leader, declared that for the first time Ireland and the British Empire's interests were the same.[10] The fateful summer of 1914 provoked a political upheaval since the threat of civil war between nationalists and Irish unionists, who favoured Ireland's remaining within the United Kingdom, disappeared. Both political enemies decided to wage war on Germany instead. The Irish Catholic Church, like other national churches on the Continent, largely succumbed to war fever and jingoism. Soon, bishops and priests exhorted Catholics to do their duty in France and Belgium. Bishop Gilmartin of Clonfert said that Ireland was voluntarily giving its blood to fight German militarism while Bishop Browne of Cloyne declared that the war was meant to protect the western world from German encroachment.[11] In the early months of the war, the Church stood by the recruiting sergeants. The recruitment authorities had understood that the clergy's help could be invaluable, although the Catholic Church had not always seen the Army in a good light as the hierarchy believed it could be detrimental to soldiers' spiritual welfare. The Church was well organised throughout the country and had an important moral influence on the population. This could now be fully exploited by the Army in the fevered pro-war atmosphere. Only a handful of bishops and priests were opposed to the war effort. They did not believe in the British Government's promise to implement Home Rule in Ireland as soon as the war was over, and deemed that Irish recruits should fight for Ireland's rights as a nation first and then for freedom of other nations in Europe.

Irish enthusiasm for the war, however, rapidly cooled as the War Office, under Lord Kitchener's command, began to blunder. Very little tact was shown towards the aspirations and feelings of nationalist recruits. The 16th Irish Division, a symbol of Irish nationalism and enthusiasm for the war, was not allowed to choose its own military emblem whereas the 36th Ulster Division, composed of the nationalists' unionist enemies, had every right to do so. The different propaganda and recruitment campaigns in Ireland were poorly managed. Far worse, the courage of Irish soldiers on the beaches of Gallipoli and the fields of northern France was hardly acknowledged. As a result, opposition and indifference to the war steadily grew in Ireland. On a broader scale, political apathy took hold over the country and in April 1916, a tiny group of nationalists stormed the General Post Office in Dublin and unsuccessfully attempted to establish a republic. John Redmond was conscious of the deterioration of Irish political life and pointed his finger at the British War Cabinet. In October 1916, he declared in the House of Commons that all the Nationalist party's efforts and goodwill for the war effort and a solution to the political crisis in Ireland had been ignored and even ridiculed by the Government.[12] But Redmond was the combination of an Irish nationalist and a British patriot and continued to show his loyalty to the Empire at war by supporting recruitment in Ireland despite the Government's obviously negative policy towards nationalist sensitivities. Slowly, but surely, a domestic opponent to the Nationalist party began to emerge in the country. It was Arthur Griffith's Sinn Féin, a party resolutely opposed to the war effort and very militant in its nationalism. Although Sinn Féin was divided on certain issues, it became heavily involved in the conscription crisis of April 1918 under Eamon de Valera's leadership. This crisis determined Ireland's political future.

It remained to be seen how the Catholic Church would react to these political developments and twists. To what extent would the Church's support for the war be influenced by the national question? The clergy could simply not afford to ignore public opinion. Did the Church have to follow John Redmond in his war crusade or become more independent and radical towards Herbert Asquith and David Lloyd George's cabinets? Bishops and priests were at loggerheads on these fundamental questions. Within the hierarchy, three prelates played major roles. The ageing and conservative Cardinal Logue of Armagh feared radical Irish nationalism. He was a complex man whose social origins were rather modest since he was the son of an innkeeper in Co. Donegal. He was most generous with poor farmers to whom he distributed large amounts of money which he collected for their cause. Logue preached widely against poteen-making and loved to entertain distinguished guests with champagne and oysters. He believed in the monarchy and in the British Empire although he resolutely opposed the British Government. His response to the war effort was therefore lukewarm although he was clearly in favour of the Allies. In the last two years of the war, the Cardinal behaved like an *éminence grise*, going against the republican tide. Despite his machiavellian inclinations, Logue was himself manipulated by the British and French Governments in the dying days of the war. His personality contrasted sharply with the overcautious Archbishop Walsh of Dublin. Walsh was a man of intellectual brilliancy who possessed an encyclopaedic memory. In fact, he was a born academic who was naturally predisposed to administrative work and ill-suited to the pastoral duties of a bishop. He dreaded preaching and left his flock rather unimpressed. The Archbishop was a staunch nationalist but became disillusioned with Redmond's abilities as a leader. He pretended not to take any interest in politics any longer. Yet, Walsh's presence was felt behind the scenes where he operated as a *franc-tireur* against the recruiting sergeants in his native city. He was assisted by his secretary, Mgr Michael Curran, a man who, after the war, was involved in seeking military support for the Irish Republican Army in Rome. Together with his vulpine secretary, Walsh delivered the *coup de grâce* to the British conscription authorities and changed the course of Irish history in April 1918. Some distance away in the south-west, the fearsome and eloquent Bishop O'Dwyer of Limerick, either loved or loathed, reigned supreme in his diocese where few dared to go against his will. He was a man who possessed limited patience and believed he held the absolute truth on Irish nationalism. On more than one occasion, he fought his battles alone without any support from the rest of the hierarchy. He was described as an

'Episcopal Swashbuckler'.[13] In 1914, O'Dwyer embarked upon a personal crusade against John Redmond and the war effort. His name became synonymous with independent opposition. In his quest for national independence, the Bishop was helped by the very gifted Mgr Michael O'Riordan, also a Limerick man and rector of the Irish College in Rome. The majority of prelates, however, continued to support the Nationalist party but soon became voiceless as the Irish people grew tired of the war. Among priests, a division was gradually taking place between younger generations, against the war, and older generations in favour of Redmond. Where would these divisions lead the Catholic Church, and how would all these clerical disagreements end? Between 1914 and 1918 Church support was also the object of a struggle between recruitment authorities, the Government, the Nationalist party and the nationalist opposition. This was crucially important as it meant that the clergy could decide the national question.

In the diplomatic arena, Britain's allies in the war became seriously preoccupied with the political situation in Ireland. France, Australia and the United States understood that civil war and rebellion in Ireland could play right into Germany's hands. Neutral Catholic countries criticised British policy in Ireland. It was unwelcome propaganda for the British. The French worried most and deemed that only the Catholic Church could calm the situation and revive the moribund war effort in Ireland. Manpower was much needed after the catastrophes of Verdun and the Somme. But, would France, whose anti-clerical regime was well known, be able to convince Catholic Ireland that her interest was with the Allies in the war? Would the old historic relations between the two countries be a determining factor? Thousands of miles away in the southern hemisphere other allies involved in the war against Germany were worried. The Australians believed, indeed, that as long as nationalist Ireland's political aspirations were not listened to, she could be a threat to the stability of the British Empire at war. The Australian Government had to face a fierce opposition against conscription and the war effort, mainly orchestrated by Irish-Australian Catholic clergy. It was more or less the same problem in the United States. These countries brought pressure to bear on the British Government to settle the Irish question in a definitive way. Would Herbert Asquith and David Lloyd George be able to assuage their fears? Would they approach the Catholic Church? Finally, in Rome, the Vatican closely followed the Irish crisis. On several occasions, the Holy See had supported Protestant Britain against Catholic Ireland for diplomatic reasons. At the end of the nineteenth century, Pope Leo XIII, notably, had condemned militant Irish nationalism which had developed during the Land War, even though the Irish Catholic Church was generally favourably disposed to the struggle of Irish tenants against the landlords, mostly Protestant and of Anglo-Irish descent. Yet, the First World War radically changed the relations between nationalist Ireland and the Vatican. In fact, the Holy See would become the first real diplomatic support for modern Ireland. Mgr O'Riordan in Rome and Bishop O'Dwyer in Limerick were largely responsible for this change despite British initiatives at the papal court.

One might go so far as to say that some roots of the Northern Ireland situation lay in the Catholic Church's attitude to the First World War. Although tensions between Catholics and Protestants had existed long before 1914, the Great War widened the gap between them and in such a way that it became unbridgeable. The Catholic Church's attitude towards the war effort and Home Rule was a serious contributing factor, one that engendered the partition of Ireland, even though it was very much against the Catholic Church's will. As Sinn Féin was successful in creating an alliance with the Church during the conscription crisis of 1918, a more radical form of nationalism became irreversibly associated with Catholicism. It was the creation and evolution of the modern nationalist character. Subsequent governments such as the Cumman na nGaedheal cabinets under W.T. Cosgrave and Fianna Fáil cabinets under Eamon de Valera had a very strong Catholic ethos, unacceptable to Sir Edward Carson and James Craig who were now firmly convinced that Home Rule meant Rome rule. This objection seemed valid, although the two unionist leaders had played their own part in making the ideal of a united Ireland impossible.

At the end of my research, a new and incomplete picture of Ireland between 1914 and 1918 formed in my mind. Many documents still lie undiscovered and some will perhaps remain unread forever. Definitive answers are hard to find as history is in perpetual motion. My conclusions are the fruit of my own interpretation. This book differs slightly from the conventional chronological historical narrative. In the course of my research, I became aware of certain issues that I believed might best be served thematically rather than just chronologically. All errors are mine.

1 The Church and the War, August 1914–April 1916

December 1915
'Put on the khaki, and go out and kill the savage Hun!'
Fr O'Doherty, Co. Dublin, during a recruiting meeting

December 1915
'Relief could not be given as long as people went to football
and hurling matches, and got all the amusements out of life,
caring nothing for their kith and kin in the trenches.'
Fr O'Riordan, Co. Kerry, on the failure of recruitment

IRELAND'S REACTION TO THE WAR

Before the outbreak of the First World War, the political crisis in Ireland
had intensified as Nationalists and Unionists were confronting each
other on the issue of Home Rule. Neither side seemed willing to make
concessions to the other. The Unionists, mainly Protestants, under the
leadership of Sir Edward Carson, were opposed to any idea of
autonomy for the country. The Nationalists, mainly Catholics, and their
leader, John Redmond, had been battling for years for self-government.
In 1912, a majority alliance of British Liberal and Irish Nationalist MPs
in the House of Commons in London voted in favour of Home Rule for
Ireland despite the vehement opposition of the Conservative and
Unionist parties. The law was to become operational in 1914.
Nevertheless, the Unionists and their Conservative allies did not accept
this outcome. On 28 September 1912, Carson and his followers signed
the Ulster Covenant, rejecting any form of Home Rule for Ulster where
the majority of Protestants in Ireland lived. Shortly afterwards, they
created the Ulster Volunteer Force (UVF), a paramilitary organisation
whose goal it was to defend that part of the country against any
nationalist encroachment. The force was well organised and equipped
with German and Austrian arms. Rapidly, about 100,000 men joined its
ranks.[1] The British Liberal cabinet was justifiably worried in 1913. On
25 November, indeed, Professor Eoin MacNeill, a radical nationalist,

announced the formation of the Irish Volunteers whose aim was precisely the opposite of the UVF: to defend Home Rule for the whole of Ireland. The Volunteers soon numbered about 180,000 men throughout the country.[2] Just like their political opponents in Ulster, they received arms from Germany, but unlike them, their gun-running resulted in a confrontation with a regiment of the British Army based in Dublin, the King's Own Scottish Borderers.[3] This incident, known as the Bachelor's Walk Massacre took place only eight days before the outbreak of the war in Europe.

Redmond was aware that civil war was looming on the horizon and had been planning to take control of the Irish Volunteers in a bid to maintain political focus on Home Rule and not on militant nationalism, a force historically beyond the control of parliamentarians. On 22 March 1914, he was warned that the Volunteers had planned a parade in Derry, in Ulster, throughout a Protestant district of the town. The nationalist paramilitaries intended to demonstrate their force to the unionist population whilst simultaneously defining their objection and resistance to partition. In March 1914, the British Liberal Prime Minister, Herbert Asquith, suggested the temporary exclusion of six counties in Ulster from Home Rule, but the House of Lords, mainly Conservative, put forward the permanent exclusion of the nine historic counties of Ulster. John Redmond understood that the parade could light the powder keg and asked the Catholic Bishop of Derry, Charles McHugh, to persuade the Volunteers to change their planned itinerary. McHugh managed to do so by asking his priests to denounce their activities,[4] indicating how powerful and persuasive the Catholic Church could be. Redmond and the members of the Catholic hierarchy grasped that it was vital to moderate the nationalistic feelings of the Volunteers. Their cooperation seemed to be crowned with success. The Inspector-General of the Royal Irish Constabulary (RIC) noted that the clergy was generally not opposed to the paramilitary organisation provided it was led by responsible people.[5] Redmond feared that the Irish Volunteers might resort to violence and endanger the constitutional movement. His best option to avoid this was to take control of the Volunteers and in June 1914, he successfully managed to impose his own nominees to the Provisional Committee of the paramilitary organisation. The more radical nationalists in the committee did not seek to oppose Redmond since the Nationalist party was in a very strong position after having negotiated Home Rule in the House of Commons in London.[6]

These events brought about a rapprochement between the Nationalist party and the Catholic Church. Although the Church was in favour of Home Rule, some prelates had always been suspicious of Redmond's alliance with the English Liberals. They believed that autonomy, introduced by the Liberal party, could pave the way to the secularisation of the country.[7] If the worst had been avoided in Derry, political problems continued to plague Ireland. Events on the continent, however, would momentarily appease the tensions in the country, and generate a very temporary solution against all odds. On 28 July 1914, Austria-Hungary declared war on Serbia and only very few understood the gravity of the international situation. One of them was John Hagan, the vice-rector of the Irish college in Rome, who was on vacation in Co. Donegal. He wrote to the rector of the same College, Michael O'Riordan that 'the political situation [in Ireland] is full of uncertainties; but there is a general feeling that the end is near... and the war between Austria and Servia [sic] will tend to hasten a solution'.[8] Hagan was right. If the United Kingdom was involved in the conflict, it was imperative that the Irish question be settled in order to make clear to the rest of the world, and the great powers in particular, that she was united and strong. On 2 August, Pope Pius X asked all the Catholics in the world to pray for peace, but in vain. On 3 August Germany declared war on France. Some Irish nationalist newspapers, like the Cork Examiner, asked how Britain could possibly stay out of the conflict since she had failed in her role as a mediator.[9] The Freeman's Journal, largely representing the views of the Nationalist party, refused to admit that Ireland would be automatically involved in the war if Britain was. It stated that 'never was jingoism so little rampant in the land. If this country does take part in the conflict it will be against the wishes of almost every one of her inhabitants.'[10] On 4 August 1914, Britain declared war on Germany, which had just invaded Belgium. Maurice Headlam, an English civil servant based in Dublin, remembered that the atmosphere in the Irish capital was, that day, 'irritatingly apathetic' and that a friend of his, a member of the Guinness family surprised him by asking 'Which do you think will win?'[11] The Irish did not seem to be particularly preoccupied by the war. And yet, the same Freeman's Journal that had declared that the war would not be popular in Ireland stated on 5 August 1914: 'Whatever the issues a week ago, the event will now decide the freedom of Europe. A Teutonic triumph means the disappearance of France as a first-class power [and] the permanent crippling if not break-up of the British Empire... The fight is a fight for national and racial liberty as the issues are defined today.'[12] The Protestant Archbishop of Armagh, Charles Frederick D'Arcy, also noticed a sudden turnabout in Irish public opinion. On 5 August, he wrote: '... the war fever set in and the temperature rose rapidly. In Ireland, it seemed at first as if all our divisions had been suddenly healed... amazing change in Irish feeling – all united in support of Great Britain.'[13]

This sense of union between Protestants and Catholics due to a common danger during the mobilisation days was also experienced in

Germany where Lutherans and Catholics held ecumenical services together. It was called *Jesu-Patriotismus*, Jesus patriotism.[14] The Irish press reported this abrupt popular support for the war in Ireland and the sudden union of hearts between nationalists and unionists, in the same way their continental counterparts did with a superb touch of exaggeration. The *Cork Examiner* informed its readers that 'Rule Britannia' could be heard in Cork and that the RIC, in Glanmire Terminus railway station, had been obliged to remove an overexcited crowd who were involuntarily blocking the trains, trying to see the soldiers off. The crowd's reward was truncheon blows.[15] Nevertheless, the population in Ireland seemed to be genuinely excited about the war. In his report for August 1914, the Inspector-General of the RIC wrote to the Under-Secretary: 'All classes displayed a strong patriotic and anti-German feeling, and joined irrespective of creed and politics in giving a hearty send off to the Reservists when they left to join the Colours.'[16] In Ulster, the *Belfast Newsletter* was, perhaps, a little more objective. Reporting the departure of some Ulster Volunteers and Irish Volunteers to their respective barracks in the railway station of Cookstown, the newspaper commented: 'Free fights took place...Union Jacks were waved by one side, which the other tried to get at; in one case they succeeded but it was quickly rescued. Shouts of "Home Rule" and "Ireland a Nation" were drowned by the greater volume of sounds as the Unionists sang "Rule, Britannia!" and the national anthem.'[17] In Britain, about 8,000 foreigners were at once suspected of being spies and had to face police investigations.[18] In Ireland too, there were early symptoms of spy fever, some nearly fatal, others comical. In Castletownbere in Co. Cork, soldiers opened fire on fishermen seeking shelter with their boat and one man was wounded. In Enniskerry, near Dublin, 'a respectably dressed young man of somewhat foreign appearance' was arrested by the Dublin Metropolitan Police. The local population was convinced he was a German spy whereas, in fact, he was an English tourist who bore a French name.[19] Even the clergy suffered. In Ballina, 'two persons dressed in clerical garb were arrested...and detained in the barrack', where a large hostile crowd had gathered. It turned out that the two men were Scottish Catholic priests.[20] An angry young mob went on the rampage in Dublin and destroyed three shops owned, as believed, by Germans. The socialist *Irish Worker* denounced this display of hatred and jingoism.[21] There is no indication, however, that such behaviour was widespread in the country, and at any rate the German and Austro-Hungarian communities in Ireland were probably very small.

Why had the population changed its mind about the war within a few days?

On 3 August 1914, in the House of Commons, John Redmond had made a spontaneous statement, promising Britain the support of the 'democracy of Ireland' and adding rather optimistically: '...I say to the government that they may tomorrow withdraw every one of their troops from Ireland (loud cheers). I say that the coast of Ireland will be defended from foreign invasion by her armed sons (renewed cheers), and for this purpose armed Nationalist Catholics in the South will only be too glad to join arms with the armed Protestant Ulstermen in the North.'[22] Redmond's reaction was both predictable and shrewd. It was predictable because he believed in the British Empire and had absolutely no intention of creating more difficulties in Ireland for the British Government for this would play right into Germany's hands. His sense of Irishness was a combination of Irish nationalism and British patriotism. It was also an astute move because Sir Edward Carson and his supporters could no longer depict nationalists as being disloyal to the Crown. Redmond believed the war was a unique opportunity to prove to the rest of the world Ireland's new nationhood and also her unity. According to him, the war would have a healing effect on the Irish people. He would declare later: 'Let Irishmen come together in the trenches and spill their blood together and I say there is no power on earth when they come home that can induce them to turn as enemies one upon the other.'[23] Redmond's speech in the House of Commons was extremely well received. Only a fraction of the Unionist party, including Carson himself, did not applaud.[24] They understood what consequences this unity might have on their struggle against Home Rule. Redmond was naive in his hopes of seeing a united Ireland. Immediately afterwards, Carson and his followers began a rather sectarian recruiting campaign. They were authorised to form the 36th Ulster Division, mainly composed of UVF volunteers. Only fourteen Catholics were allowed to join the division after they had signed a formal engagement against Home Rule.[25] As for Carson, he simply declared: 'No, we are all brothers. They are our own volunteers; they are men of our own religion.'[26] There seemed to be some divisions among Protestants; the Anglican Bishop of Ferns, Dr Bernard, despite being a staunch unionist, publicly praised John Redmond and called him 'a true patriot and a wise statesman.'[27] On 11 September 1914, the British War Office approved the formation of the 16th Irish Division, mainly composed of Redmondite nationalists and Catholics. This spirit of unity as depicted by Charles Frederick D'Arcy, the Protestant Archbishop of Armagh, was only illusory or, at best, temporary. It looked more like a ceasefire between two sides in order to shoot at a third one.

On 15 September 1914, Herbert Asquith announced that Home Rule would become law but that it would be implemented only after the war, and a special solution would have to be found for Ulster. The idea pleased nobody and some unionists spoke about treason. But Redmond and Carson understood that the Irish question could only be settled when war in Europe conflict was over. On 20 September, the Nationalist leader was travelling in Co. Wicklow and stopped at Woodenbridge. There, he addressed a group of Irish Volunteers and pronounced the following fateful words: '... account yourselves as men, not only for Ireland itself, but wherever the fighting line extends, in defence of right of freedom and Religion in this war'.[28] From this moment on, Redmond and the Nationalist party would be fully committed to the war effort. However, Redmond's new departure was not to everybody's liking. Arthur Griffith from Sinn Féin clearly opposed the idea of the Volunteers being sent abroad. According to him, the war was not Ireland's business. 'What has Ireland to defend and whom has she to defend it against?' he asked.[29] James Connolly's Irish Labour party rejected any participation in the war. To Connolly, the war was in the interest of the capitalists, at the expense of the workers, a similar opinion to those expressed by Lenin and Rosa Luxemburg. He was utterly dismayed by the failure of international socialism to prevent the war.[30] As for Professor Eoin MacNeill, he did not accept Redmond's decision to use the Volunteers for any purpose other than defending Ireland. On 25 September, MacNeill denounced Redmond's speech at Woodenbridge and expelled his members from the Irish Volunteer organisation.[31] As a result, the Volunteers split into two different movements: the overwhelming majority, about 170,000 men, followed Redmond and became known as the National Volunteers, and about 2,000 of them remained loyal to MacNeill and were still known as the Irish Volunteers. These opposition nationalists, including members of the Irish Republican Brotherhood (IRB) whose aim was to fight against England by any means possible, grouped in the Irish Neutrality League and were resolutely opposed to Irish participation in the war. The opposition heaped derision on Redmond's decision. *Irish Freedom* wrote: 'No more callous spectacle could be seen than the recent bartering in Irish blood that won us King George's autograph on Redmond's Bill.'[32] Members of the Volunteers, who were now ready to fight for Ireland and Britain against Germany, were depicted as degenerates by a rather rabid anti-British press. Pamphlets were handed out on which the people could read:

> Come all ye true hearted Irish youths,
> And listen to my lay...
> I've enlisted for fame as a warrior bold,
> At ten bright pence a day [...]
> I'm one of the Empire's warrior sons,
> But I hope there'll never be a war,
> For my liver gets white when I think of a fight
> And my legs wouldn't carry me far.
>   (John S. Ellis, *Eire Ireland*, vol. XXXV: 3–4)[33]

This was the political scene in Ireland when the First World War broke out. One important question remained: how had the powerful and influential Catholic Church reacted to all these events? Its position could not simply be disregarded in a traditional Catholic country.

The Catholic Church in Ireland has always played an important role in the political development of the country. Throughout the nineteenth century it battled for Catholic emancipation and education. Towards the end of that century, it took an interest in Home Rule and apart from a few exceptions and reservations, it was fully in favour of Irish autonomy. The British Government understood this role and sometimes used it to its own advantage. The Church proved to be quite useful in maintaining law and order and in exercising a moderate influence on radical nationalist movements. During the Rising of 1798, the hierarchy advised the people not to fight against the English and again in 1848, priests were successful in dissuading rebels to take up arms.[34] It had a wide and well-organised structure throughout the country. There were four ecclesiastical provinces and at the head of each was one archbishop. The country was then divided into twenty-eight dioceses under the spiritual care of twenty-eight bishops. Eventually, the dioceses were divided into numerous parishes where priests were employed in looking after the faithful. On the eve of the First World War, there were about 3,000 secular priests in the country.[35] They seemed to have some political influence for it is estimated that between 1853 and 1892, nine Irish Nationalist parliamentarians were unseated because priests had used 'spiritual intimidation' on the voters.[36] At the local level, priests were 'a mine of information' in the sense that they knew exactly what was happening in their parishes, and knew personally all of their parishioners.

The members of the hierarchy were also involved in the political evolution of their country, some more than others. During the nineteenth century, the bishops were essentially preoccupied with the education of Catholics and most of them backed the Nationalist party. The episcopate demonstrated its political weight when it largely opposed the leader of the party, Charles Stewart Parnell in a divorce case. On this occasion, it had the effect of dividing the party in two. It would only be fully reunited some years later, in 1900, under the leadership of John Redmond.[37] The Church's position on secret societies like the IRB was unambiguous as the hierarchy did not approve of them. The bishops regularly denounced IRB members. Cardinal Michael Logue, Primate of Ireland from 1887 to 1924, would during the war ask the people of his archdiocese to be on their guard against secret societies. As for the Irish Volunteers, their case was somehow different as they were not a secret or subversive organisation. They simply meant to defend Home Rule, accepted and approved of by the British Parliament. Nonetheless, the Church was generally not in favour of their creation as it feared that the Volunteers might fall into the hands of fanatical extremists. The example of Archbishop William Walsh of Dublin is a point in case. His personal secretary, Mgr Michael Curran, noted in his memoirs:

> The Archbishop did not welcome the establishment of the Volunteers at the beginning. In fact, he disapproved, but as events developed he realised there was full justification for their formation since the arms of the Ulster Volunteers frightened and coerced the weak English Government. His opinion of the Irish Volunteers, therefore, fluctuated from time to time but he never believed that the movement would succeed in its objects. Characteristically, he always feared that some wild irresponsible element would force matters to extremes and ruin the entire national cause.
>
> (Mgr Curran's memoirs, p. 9)[38]

The British Government and its representatives in Dublin Castle had had time to analyse the political influence of the Church and rapidly understood what a determining role the Catholic clergy could play in the war effort in Ireland. The organisation and structure of the Church in the country could be of invaluable help to recruiting campaigns for there was no conscription in the United Kingdom. If the Church could be persuaded to become increasingly involved in the war effort, the effects would only be beneficial. Not only the British, but also the French and the Germans were convinced of this.[39] But, what was the traditional attitude of the Irish Catholic Church towards the Army?

At the turn of the century, the Catholic Church was quite hostile to recruiting operations. The hierarchy was of the opinion that the presence of troops, particularly in Dublin and in the cities, endangered morals. It denounced the fraternisation of soldiers and women. In 1901, the United Irish League (UIL), originally a league of farmers in support of the Nationalist party, complained about the behaviour of soldiers in Dublin to Archbishop Walsh. Walsh agreed and immediately replied in a letter entitled 'The Military Nuisance', published by the *Irish Daily Independent*.[40] He simply objected to the fact of 'soldiers being allowed to congregate in any particular thoroughfare', especially at night. Walsh's reaction was understandable. Before the war, Dublin had the worst slums in Europe and prostitution was rampant. It is estimated that about 1,677 women were prostitutes in Dublin in 1900, and sexually transmitted diseases were rife.[41] The proximity of barracks was not calculated to solve the problem. Cardinal Logue was not at all in favour of the Army. But, his reasons were historical or political rather than moral. On Saint Patrick's Day, 17 March 1901, he had made a speech in front of Armagh Cathedral in which he lambasted the British authorities. Despite the fact that he was proud to belong to the British Empire, Logue accused the Government of mismanaging Irish affairs, which had forced thousands of Irish men and women to emigrate. The irony, according to him, was that now the same authorities were looking for recruits:

> [The authorities] were warned by far-seeing men from time to time of the mistake they were making in driving into other lands the hands that make the wealth and the heads that design, driving away those who would be the strength of the Empire when assailed, getting rid of them in order to get rid of a little trouble... They might come to Ireland now for men, and men were not to be got.
>
> (*The Irish Times*, 18 March 1901)

Logue ended up by saying that the only recruits the British Army would have would be 'cripples, lame and blind'! The cardinal was a shrewd political observer and knew that the arms race in Europe would drive the recruiting sergeants to Ireland. Such declarations of the heavyweights of the Irish hierarchy were not meant to incite Irishmen to join the colours, especially at a time when Home Rule was being negotiated. For the more extreme nationalists, it simply was a form of collaboration. The political developments in Ireland and the Church's stance on military matters did deter Irishmen from joining the Army. In 1899, the number of recruits was 28,352, and in 1913, the number dropped to 20,780, a decrease of nearly 27 per cent. Only between 14 per cent and 15 per cent of soldiers were Catholics. Furthermore, the Army was regarded as a symbol of British rule by the nationalist population, striving for Home Rule. [42]

When the war broke out, there can be little doubt that the British authorities in Ireland were anxiously waiting for the reaction of the Catholic Church. Initially, they must have feared the worst since Pope Pius X and his successor, Benedict XV, had asked all the Catholics to pray and work for peace. On 1 November 1914, Benedict XV, in his encyclical *Ad Beatissimi*, had blamed the war on the loss of Christian wisdom, and the self-interest of men and nations. No country was accused in particular. If the rules of papal infallibility and spiritual authority were followed, this could mean a serious Catholic opposition to the war effort. In fact, British fears were soon assuaged. Although the Pope had condemned the onset of the hostilities, he gave no direct instructions to the national churches in Europe. It appeared that he wished to remain neutral, though at the same time working for peace. As a consequence, the national churches gave vent to their nationalistic feelings, just as their flocks did. The Catholic Church in Ireland was thus facing its own responsibilities. Members of the episcopate and priests alike were free to express their feelings and ideas about the war. As will be shown, many of them were in favour of Irish participation in the conflict, at least at the beginning. Only a handful of Irish ecclesiastics were resolutely against it, among others Michael Curran, Walsh's secretary. On 12 September 1914, he wrote a bitter letter to his friend Mgr Hagan in Rome in which he stated: 'The [Nationalist] Party are endeavouring to work the anti-German war ticket for all they are worth ... I expect we will have a great recruiting campaign after next week ... Popular and general opinion here are surprisingly jingoistic. What a change from the day of Howth and Bachelor's Quay.'[43] The British authorities were reassured. If the Army had not been too popular at the eve of the war, the conflict with Germany had changed this state of affairs as the nationalist population was behind John Redmond and his party, and the Catholic Church equally so. The clergy's help would be forthcoming.

Ireland's participation in the war and her alliance with Great Britain was the logical continuation of the Nationalist party's policies for the country. Redmond and his supporters had no intention of severing all links with England as they desired to remain part of the British Empire. The Catholic Church would give its blessing to the party's endeavours in the war effort and participate directly in this effort. In the early stages of the conflict, the Church would, on one hand, multiply declarations in favour of the British Empire and a new Irish nation, and, on the other hand, denounce Germany as a ruthless barbaric destroyer of civilisations and liberty, a condemnation exacerbated by the fact that Germany was the cradle of Protestantism. This tide of nationalistic and chauvinistic feelings was hardly surprising if one takes into account the fact that the country was on the brink of Home Rule. Just like Redmond's party, the Church believed the war was a unique opportunity to make clear Ireland's nationhood and manhood. The Irish Catholic Church was no different from most of its sister churches in Europe in exhorting its sons to fight. Generally, it had a Manichaean vision of reality as it depicted the enemies as the representatives of evil on earth and Ireland and her allies as the defenders of good.

The Bishop of Kildare and Leighlin, Patrick Foley, was one of the very first prelates to publicly express his feelings in favour of the war. In August 1914, he sent a circular letter to all the priests of his diocese whose duty it was to read it out to all the churchgoers. The Bishop also authorised its publication in the *Irish Times*. The letter was a clear example of most of the hierarchy's frame of mind regarding the conflict as it encapsulated the main pro-war ideas:

> It becomes the duty of us as faithful Christians and loyal citizens of the great God, on whom all Nations and Empires, as well as individuals, absolutely depend, to come to the aid of the armies which are fighting on the side of justice and right; and to enable them through the might of His power to triumph over their adversaries.
>
> (*The Irish Times*, 16 August 1914)

It really seemed to be a war for 'Big Words'.[44] The fatherland had become sacred and the fight for its defence and survival could only be just and lofty. In Foley's eyes, God sided with the Allies just as German and Austrian bishops were equally convinced that He backed their armies. The letter indicated the considerable gap between the Vatican and its pro-peace policy, and the national churches. The *Irish Catholic*, which regularly voiced the opinion of the Irish hierarchy, justified without any hesitation the outbreak of the war. It strongly believed that the war was the result of the personality of Emperor William II of Germany and the expansionist policies of his country.[45] It also stated that no British statesmen could be blamed for the current hostilities. From a theological point of view, the hierarchy felt that the war was fully justified. As seen above, the Bishop of Kildare and Leighlin was convinced that God was siding with Britain and her Allies. It was true that certain circumstances had helped Foley to make up his mind. Germany had violated Belgium's neutrality and the United Kingdom was bound by a treaty to protect this neutrality. Furthermore, Ireland could only sympathise and identify with the plight of small Catholic and independent Belgium. It was a case of *jus ad bellum*, right war, as defined by Saint Augustine and other eminent theologians.

During the first months of the war, John Redmond received the support of many bishops. They nearly all validated his policy regarding the Irish Volunteers. This paramilitary force could become a fertile recruiting ground for the War Office and its recruiting sergeants. They were not particularly well equipped but were already more or less drilled and used to military life and discipline. The Volunteers could rapidly be incorporated into the British Army and sent to the front. But, was their original aim not to defend Ireland only? Two bishops, Charles McHugh of Derry and Patrick O'Donnell of Raphoe, whose dioceses were in Ulster and which risked being excluded from Home Rule, were not sure about the Volunteers' role. On 8 August 1914, McHugh, like

11

Foley, sent a circular letter to his priests, justifying the war and fully endorsing Redmond's policies. According to him, the war would bring a unity between the Irish people. He spoke about Irish 'assistance in preserving the peace of nations and in restraining within due limits a Power that would set at nought the very foundations on which civilisation rests'.[46] McHugh did not specify, however, what form this Irish assistance should take. One had to wait and see what political developments were ahead for Ireland. McHugh did not have to wait for too long. On 18 September, the Government of Ireland Act promised Home Rule for Ireland after the war, with a special solution to be found for Ulster. At least six bishops sent their congratulations to Redmond for having obtained autonomy for the country. They were Harty of Cashel, O'Donnell of Raphoe, Mangan of Kerry, Coyne of Elphin, Gilmartin of Clonfert and Foley of Kildare and Leighlin.[47] O'Donnell, one of Redmond's staunchest supporters within the episcopate, sent a letter to the leader of the Nationalist party, which was later published by the *Freeman's Journal*. He wrote: 'Ireland as a whole has now the chance of taking her part in moulding the destiny of nations, as well as in shaping her own by the impress of true civilisation, and our Irish Unionist friends are relaxed from the grip of their unwise resolve to resist a reform [Home Rule] that will prove as beneficial to them as to us.'[48] O'Donnell was carried away by this spirit of unity.

The role of the Irish Volunteers was now clear. On 26 September, the Nationalist leader was at the Mansion House in Dublin, together with Herbert Asquith, in order to boost the recruitment campaign in Ireland. The Prime Minister assured his audience that it was his wish to see an Irish Brigade and that Irish recruits would not be absorbed in the British Army. It was true that the War Office had authorised the formation of the 10th and 16th Irish Divisions. In October 1914, O'Donnell wrote to the *National Volunteer* that Redmond was an enlightened and wise leader and that it would help the new Irish constitution, once the continental war over, if it had 'a seasoned army of Christian men at its back'.[49] It remains difficult to know with certainty exactly how many bishops supported Redmond and the war at the end of 1914. If one takes into account speeches, letters to the press etc., it can be estimated that twenty-one bishops out of the total of twenty-seven were in favour of the war; three were neutral (not necessarily against Redmond); one was ambivalent (Cardinal Logue) and two frankly against (Archbishop Walsh and Bishop O'Dwyer).[50] It is noteworthy that bishops never went personally to recruiting meetings. The National Synod of Ireland had set very strict rules concerning participation of members of the clergy in political events. In fact, participation was not advised.[51] As a result, many bishops confined their activities and sent letters to these meetings instead. Some allowed their words to be used in propaganda posters.

They were the Archbishop of Armagh, the Archbishop of Tuam, and the Bishops of Cloyne, Derry, Ferns, and Dromore.[52]

At the beginning of 1915, the number of men who enlisted was higher than anticipated especially bearing in mind that Ireland had been on the brink of civil war only a few months before. Between 4 August 1914 and February 1915, 50,107 Irishmen had joined the Army.[53] Maybe Redmond had hoped for more? The Nationalist leader was doing his best to promote recruiting, but the War Office and its chief, Lord Kitchener, and some British generals, were the obstacles to better recruitment figures in the country. Kitchener, although a native of Co. Kerry did not like the Irish whom he considered idle.[54] As for nationalists, he deemed that they were a danger to the stability of the British Empire for which he had fought all his life. On more than one occasion he had had serious disagreements with Redmond regarding the newly created Irish divisions. The two men argued over the emblem for the 16th Division. Redmond wanted a harp but Kitchener objected on the grounds that it was too nationalistic whereas he raised no objection to the Red Hand of Ulster for the 36th Division, composed of men ready to defy the British Parliament. Eventually, the two men agreed on the Shamrock. Later, Kitchener would tell General Friend to have nothing to do with nationalist leaders.[55] General Sir Bryan Mahon reported a conversation he had with Mrs Asquith, the Prime Minister's wife, about Kitchener. Mrs Asquith said: 'He opened his career with two incalculable blunders – he ignored the Territorial Force, and he muddled the Irish.'[56] But Kitchener's attitude was not the only factor hindering increased enlistment. The War Office disliked promoting Irish patriotism in its recruiting campaigns.[57] The recruiting authorities in Ireland never exploited the courage and bravery of Irish regiments, notably the Royal Munster Fusiliers at Etreux in France.[58] It must be said that there was no real organisation in charge of voluntary enlistment in the country. In November 1914, even the unionist *Church of Ireland Gazette* denounced this state of affairs: 'What has the [Government] done? It has stuck up a few posters, which nobody really looks at, here and there, and scattered a few more recruiting sergeants about the country. What is wanted is an organised recruiting campaign, with that spectacular side of military service which appeals to the imagination.'[59] It was only on 23 April 1915 that the Central Council for the Organisation of Recruiting in Ireland (CCORI) realised this. Until then, recruiting matters were left in the hands of people not always aware of the reality of the Irish situation.[60] General Mahon's experience is very pertinent. In 1914, he had been sent over to Ireland to assess recruitment. Mahon wrote that the '[Volunteers] were enthusiastic about the Great War... and that the prospects of recruiting for the British Army were far better than I had expected'. But the

General added: 'During the first five or six weeks of the Great War, recruiting beat all its records in Ireland. In fact, more men came forward than were wanted – and official blunders began then and there.'[61] Taking all these problems into consideration, John Redmond's task to convince young people to fight was not an easy one. It was the same for bishops. They knew Redmond's difficulties but they did not give up. On 6 December Redmond was in the west trying to boost recruitment. John Healy, the Archbishop of Tuam, felt that the Nationalist leader had to get all the support possible and sent a letter to the meeting Redmond was attending. The letter focused on Redmond's personality, for it was crucial that the people continued to believe in him. Healy stated: 'In my opinion, he is the safest and wisest guide Ireland could have and he was never more needed at the present moment. In difficult and trying circumstances he has shown himself to be a man of conspicuous courage, of prudence, and of true statesmanlike capacity.'[62] In December 1914, the RIC reported to the authorities of Dublin Castle that a few 'Sinn Féin priests', who were resolutely against recruiting, were very active but that there was no reason for alarm. The Chief Inspector wrote that 'the Catholic Clergy throughout the country in general supported the policy of the Irish Parliamentary Party [Nationalist party] in relation to the war and recruiting for the Imperial Army'.[63]

Those who believed that the war would be short were beginning to lose patience as it was more and more obvious that all the belligerent countries were willing to fight until the bitter end, in a war of attrition in which hundreds of thousands of men were being sacrificed in trench warfare. The conflict was becoming more modern also. On 19 April 1915, German Zeppelins bombarded England for the first time, and the population understood that the seas were no longer an absolute line of defence for their country. Earlier in the year, Pope Benedict XV had decreed that 7 February would be a day for expiation and prayers for peace. In Italy, 60,000 faithful gathered on Saint Peter's Square and prayed for the conflict to come to an end. The Pope's appeal seems to have had some influence on the Italians but their country was still not at war. In Germany and Austria, however, many Catholic soldiers went to mass that day.[64] In France, his appeal was badly received and Cardinal Amette, the Archbishop of Paris, had to explain the Pope's position on the war to the Government and French Catholics.[65] The Pope's initiative was bound to have had some effect on the Irish episcopate. On 14 February 1915, the bishops published their Lenten pastorals, which always provided a clue to the hierarchy's feelings on current affairs. Bishop O'Callaghan of Cork referred to Benedict XV's peace message and deemed that the war was the responsibility of all the nations involved.[66] Thomas O'Dea of Galway condemned the war without any hesitation and wrote that it was the result of the lack of brotherly love between men. He remarked that this was also the case in Ireland where two nations were at war.[67] Clearly, O'Dea did not believe in this spirit of unity so dear to Redmond. Bishop Hoare of Ardagh was of the same opinion. Bishop O'Donnell of Raphoe put forward the idea that the Pope could become a mediator between the belligerents. Other bishops, who from the very beginning had supported Redmond and his pro-war policy, now had a more cautious approach to the conflict. This was the case of Kelly of Ross and Harty of Cashel. Harty quoted large extracts of Benedict XV's appeal.

A certain number of prelates, however, continued to support the war effort despite the Pope's latest initiative. McHugh of Derry denounced 'the new philosophy of life which goes by the name of *Kultur*'.[68] Coyne of Elphin wrote about 'those beloved ones who nobly sacrificed their lives at the call of duty, and in what they believed to be a just, holy, and patriotic cause'.[69] Archbishop Healy of Tuam thought that Ireland owed Belgium a debt, dating back to the Penal Laws, and the country could not simply stand by while Belgium, 'its people and its priests were slaughtered'.[70] Browne of Cloyne implored God's protection for the Irish soldiers who fought to guarantee Ireland's liberty and safety. The most patriotic prelate was perhaps O'Neill of Dromore who stated that the brave soldiers were fighting 'against the overwhelming forces of a ruthless despot, and to strike down the tyranny of a militarism that threatened the very existence of the British Empire and other European States'.[71] O'Neill was certainly right when he declared that the very existence of the British Empire was at stake, for on 4 February 1915, the German Government had announced that British territorial waters were now a legitimate war zone and that German submarines would sink any ship in them.[72] On 22 April, chemical warfare was used for the first time at Ypres in Belgium against British and French soldiers. The authorities in Dublin Castle realised that the war would cost many lives and they had to make sure that young Irishmen did not remain only potential recruits. The authorities at Dublin Castle also understood that the recruiting and propaganda campaigns were not efficient enough. The defence of the British Empire was not a theme calculated to arouse the sympathy of Irishmen in 1915. An observer of Irish political life stated: 'Direct [British] patriotic feeling was lacking…There is no natural devotion to the Empire among the peasants and working men of Ireland.'[73] As seen above, the Central Council for the Organisation of Recruiting in Ireland (CCORI) was founded in April 1915 in order to find a remedy for these problems and inject new blood into a quite unimaginative recruiting campaign. The CCORI's main approach was to use Irish sentiments. For example, forty-six new posters were placarded in Trinity College that year, forty-four referring to Ireland. Six of those included appeals from the Catholic Church.[74] Since the onset of the war, some bishops had claimed that the conflict in Europe was not only a British matter but also an Irish one. They were aware that if recruitment was to be successful, Irishmen's interest had to be aroused and, consequently, all feeling of insularity had to be stamped out. Bishop Sheehan of Waterford and Lismore sent a message of encouragement to a recruitment meeting in Waterford town in April 1915. He wrote: 'The object of your gathering appeals, and appeals powerfully, to every man in the land. The war is not an English war alone or a French or a Belgian war. It is an Irish war to save our country and our people from ruin and misery.'[75] In the same month, Bishop Brownrigg of Kilkenny sent an almost identical message to a similar meeting.[76] It remained to be seen if the CCORI, the Nationalist party and the pro-war bishops would manage to increase recruitment.

Military and political circumstances on the Continent and in Britain would change the course of events of the war, changes that were not to boost voluntary enlistment. On 25 April 1915, the battle of Gallipoli began in Turkey. Many Irish regiments were bravely fighting on the beaches and were in a desperate situation as Turkish snipers had taken up position on the cliffs. The War Office simply did not mention their courage in its bulletins to the press. Timothy Healy, the Nationalist MP, reported to the Prime Minister that this had not only very bad effects on recruitment, but also Irish goodwill generally speaking.[77] On 7 May, the *Lusitania* was sunk off Cork by a German submarine. The CCORI immediately produced a poster on which the Irish people could read: 'Has the despair of the innocent children not sent a thrilled horror through you; are the cries of 39 Irish victims to go unheeded?'[78] Some Irish ecclesiastics were outraged by this German atrocity and stepped up their efforts in the recruitment drive. Mgr Hogan, the President of Maynooth seminary, sent a letter to a meeting, saying: 'The more men you get, and the more effectively they do their work, the better I shall be pleased.'[79] However, the sinking of the *Lusitania* was probably the last event that played into the hands of the recruiting sergeants. The summer of 1915 dissuaded many men to join up and little by little the Catholic Church would withdraw its active support for recruitment. On 25 May, Herbert Asquith announced the composition of the new coalition cabinet in Britain. Sir Edward Carson was included. This shocked public opinion in nationalist Ireland for it meant that unionism had a strong political influence on the British Liberals. John Redmond was also offered a post but he rejected the offer. He had asked the Volunteers to fight in France, hoping that in return the British Government would show its goodwill towards nationalist Ireland. By May 1915, it was obvious that this would not be the case.[80] A few days later, on 3 June, Bishop Fogarty of Killaloe openly rejected Redmond's policy and regretted that Irish soldiers on the front were fighting for Carson.[81] This letter was made public. On 25 July,

Cardinal Logue declared at Dundalk that the Government was to blame for the failure of recruitment.[82] On 28 July, Benedict XV asked all the rulers in the world 'to put an end at last to this horrible slaughter, which for a whole year has dishonoured Europe'.[83] The Pope's words were not meant to encourage the most zealous pro-war bishops in Ireland. On 4 August, Bishop O'Dwyer of Limerick asked John Redmond to follow Benedict XV in his quest for peace but the Nationalist leader refused to do so.[84] This would prove particularly significant a little later.

Undeniably all these political developments had had some serious effects on the hierarchy. From a nationalist point of view, Dr Fogarty had certainly stated the truth. Moreover, the bishops' consciences must have been weighed down by the Pope's declarations. At the end of August 1915, the Bishop of Waterford and Lismore sent a letter of support to John Redmond and a recruiting meeting.[85] Bishop McHugh of Derry followed suit in October,[86] but this kind of episcopal support was dwindling away. The bishops were still in favour of Redmond and the Nationalist party as there was no alternative, but they were keeping their distance from the Nationalist leader's pro-war policy. During a recruitment meeting in Dublin in autumn 1915, the 'bishops were notable by their absence'[87] and most of them sent no more letters of encouragement. Recruitment figures were decreasing rapidly. In January 1916, Augustine Birrell, the Irish Secretary, reckoned that there were 562,115 Irishmen fit for military service. Until 15 December 1915, a total of 94,797 men from Ireland had joined the colours.[88] If one adds the total of all the enlisted men in the provinces of Connaught, Leinster and Munster where there was an overwhelming Catholic majority, one obtains the approximate figure of 45,037 Catholic recruits, or about 8 per cent of the total of potential recruits. This figure is not exact as it remains difficult to establish with certainty the number of Catholic recruits, but it gives a rough indication. At first sight, it appears to be very low. But, bearing in mind the fact that Ireland seemed to be heading for a civil war in 1914, the way Irish recruits were treated by the War Office, the political problems concerning Home Rule and partition, and the bad recruiting organisation in the country, this figure is quite remarkable. In fact, 1914 and 1915 were the years of missed opportunities. The enlistment figures would have been far better if the British authorities had been more sensible towards Irish nationalists. On 3 September 1915, Bishop O'Donnell of Raphoe wrote a letter to the *London Irish Citizen*, reflecting this state of affairs. He was of the opinion that the Irish regiments had shown great courage and bravery on the front but he also added: 'It would be well for Ireland and well for England if the Home Rule Act had been in operation before the war. The response to Mr Redmond's appeal would then be far heartier, good as that response is now.'[89]

O'Donnell's bitterness was certainly justified. The authorities at Dublin Castle were well aware of the growing discontent and tried to invigorate enlistment by creating yet another recruiting body called the Department of Recruiting in Ireland (DRI) in October 1915. The DRI replaced the CCORI whose methods had not proved successful, and at its head was the Lord Lieutenant of Ireland himself, Lord Wimborne. If twenty-one bishops had openly supported the war effort in 1914, in April 1916 only nine were still doing so: McHugh of Derry, MacRory of Down and Connor, O'Donnell of Raphoe, Browne of Cloyne, Mangan of Kerry, Kelly of Ross, Healy of Tuam, Gilmartin of Clonfert and Harty of Cashel.[90] These prelates continued to condemn Germany and to support the Irish soldiers at the front. In March 1916, Browne, for instance, was still comparing Ireland to Belgium and Poland and paid tribute to 'the voluntary presence in the armies of the Allied nations of 150,000 daunted soldiers from this sparsely populated little island'. Pride probably explained this inflated figure. Browne added that participating in the war was 'our citizen duty'.[91] This kind of support, however, was rare on the eve of the Easter Rising and news from the front was not particularly reassuring. Since the Gallipoli disaster in 1915, rumours were rife in Ireland that British generals were deliberately sacrificing Irish regiments.[92] Bishop O'Donnell, Redmond's staunchest supporter in the episcopate, received several anonymous letters denouncing the war. One of these stated: 'Will you not ask your priests in all your churches to pray for peace and pray for the dead who died for Ireland?'[93] Those bishops who had changed their minds about recruitment were still supporting John Redmond, but they had adopted a more cautious attitude towards the war. Abraham Brownrigg of Ossory was an example. In April 1915, he had wholeheartedly embraced the war effort. In March 1916 in his Lenten pastoral, he wrote about it, instead, as a shocking war for Christians, and vehemently criticised the British Government's decision to withdraw some funds originally intended for education in Ireland. He declared that 'the millions that are saved in our country are to be spent with prodigal extravagance in pampering and enriching the people of England'.[94] There was no longer any mention of British democracy granting Ireland the right to be free or the union of Ireland and Britain against German expansionism. Clearly, the political climate and the euphoric days of August 1914 had gone. The *Tablet*, a newspaper which voiced the opinion of the English Catholic Church and regularly informed its readers on the situation in Ireland, only published the Lenten pastorals of O'Donnell, Browne and McHugh, all favourable to the war.[95]

In April 1916, Dublin Castle, the British Government and Lord Wimborne's DRI could no longer count on the unconditional support of the hierarchy. The Pope's initiatives in favour of peace, the war of attrition in Europe and the War Office's ambivalent attitude towards nationalist recruits had taken their toll. Moreover, as will be seen, Cardinal Logue's peculiar position on the war effort and his inability to unify the episcopate, Archbishop Walsh's 'political silence' and especially Bishop O'Dwyer's personal crusade against Redmond and the war, were other undermining factors. The Irish Catholic Church was far from being impressed by the British Government. On 5 April 1916, Augustine Birrell put forward a motion in the House of Commons in London to suppress certain anti-Catholic clauses, dating back to legislation of the early eighteenth century. These clauses concerned restrictions imposed upon religious orders.[96] It was undeniably more a political gesture than a sudden inspiration of religious tolerance.

If the bishops had initially welcomed Ireland's participation in the conflict and the war effort and then withdrawn their active involvement, how had their priests reacted?

PRIESTS AND THE WAR EFFORT

Priests would be key players in the recruitment campaigns. Contrary to their bishops, who never attended recruitment meetings in person, the situation was different for priests. There were about 3,000 of them in the country. In 1914, the RIC recorded only twenty-four priests who had openly criticised the war.[97] In other words, an overwhelming majority of the clergy was behind Redmond. Being local men, close to their flocks, priests could become essential components of propaganda efforts by persuading men to join the Army. They were the source of moral authority in the cities, towns and villages. As Alfred Blanche, the French consul in Ireland during the war, noted: 'The real ecclesiastical authority for the Irish Catholic farmer is the parish priest.'[98] The priests were 'prominent local figures, intimately familiar with the districts in which they lived and having regular opportunities of communicating with the great bulk of the population'.[99] Most of them had espoused the aims of Irish nationalism and supported the constitutional politics of the Nationalist party. When Redmond declared himself in favour of Irish participation in the war, the priests followed suit. The party was backed throughout the country by the United Irish League (UIL) and one of its main administrators was Bishop O'Donnell of Raphoe. Many priests were members of local branches of the UIL and organised recruitment meetings.[100] Like the population generally, they were in a political wilderness a few days before the beginning of the hostilities in F when the events at Bachelor's Quay in Dublin happened. How w‹ Irish Volunteers react? On 31 July 1914, a great Volunteer pa‹

19

organised in Cashel in Co. Tipperary. Its aim was to show nationalist Ireland's determination to obtain and defend Home Rule. Fr Innocent Ryan was invited to speak at the meeting. He told an excited crowd that the country was angry and that the Irish would no longer tolerate the 'enemy'. On that day he was referring to Britain, not Germany. He went on to say that for generations the Irish people had had to endure the bad treatment of the British rulers but that 'they [were] determined to stand it no longer'.[101]

As mentioned above, the moment John Redmond assured Britain that Ireland would be on her side against Germany, all bad feelings towards Perfidious Albion were forgotten. Priests were no different from the laity and were equally swept away by a wave of nationalism and a hatred for all things German, and fully embraced the war effort. The National Synod had very strict rules concerning the participation of priests in political events. Curates were allowed to travel outside the boundaries of their diocese to participate in meetings only if they had permission of the parish priest. The Synod also forbade the clergy to use their churches for political purposes. That is why many priests personally attended recruitment meetings. In fact, these rules were not a major obstacle since the bishops and parish priests were largely in favour of Redmond. One of the most committed pro-war priests was Fr Arthur Ryan from Tipperary. On 20 September 1914, the very same day John Redmond asked the Volunteers to fight abroad, Ryan explained to a crowd that Ireland had been denied the rights of a true nation but that Home Rule had changed this. Ireland had just won a major political battle, he continued, and all the nationalists were now united. Ryan even included the Fenians! It is more than doubtful that the Fenians would have agreed with Ryan, but the priest's words were characteristic of this euphoric and nationalist élan. He said about Britain: 'Our enemies in the past, have become our friends, and have ranged themselves on our side, made our cause their own.'[102] Ryan's statement demonstrated the unity between the Nationalist party, the Catholic Church and the majority of the population. Priests who took an active part in recruitment drives were quick to point out that Irish recruits would fight for Ireland first, then for the Empire. They had accepted Redmond's idea that the war would promote this new nationhood. Many priests supported the idea of an Irish brigade, symbolising Ireland's manhood, and were trying to operate a phenomenon of identification between Belgium, Poland and Ireland. In October 1915, at a time when recruitment figures were declining and the Irish population was losing confidence in the War Office, Fr Ryan told his fellow Tipperary men 'that it would be an everlasting shame...if the gaps in the Irish divisions were not filled by Irishmen, but by Scottish and Welsh regiments'.[103]

Another theme frequently used by recruiting sergeants, priests and the press was German atrocities. When the invading German armies destroyed part of the ecclesiastical library of the University of Louvain, in Belgium, the outrage in Ireland seemed genuine as Louvain was comparable in many ways with Maynooth. Fr Gill evoked this tragedy during a lecture in the Abbey Theatre in Dublin. Very cleverly Gill told his audience that 'one of the most interesting churches in Louvain . . . was the old chapel of the Irish Franciscan College of St Anthony of Padua'.[104] By doing so, he emphasised the link between Ireland and Belgium. Undoubtedly, the 'tragedy of Louvain' was well exploited by the recruiting authorities. Mgr Curran wrote to Mgr Hagan in Rome that 'Louvain [was] a God send to them'.[105] The Belgium theme went hand in hand with German barbarity. This latter theme was generally crude and frankly lacking in subtlety. Germans were described as 'Huns'. They were incapable of having Christian feelings towards their fellow humans. They were simply barbarians because they were Germans. The Catholic clergy did not appear to object to this kind of propaganda and occasionally even participated. On 26 September 1915, Fr O'Byrne declared during a meeting:

> The Germans were out for conquest, and they conducted the war in a most ruthless manner, stopping at nothing to achieve their nefarious designs. Age and sex were not respected, and the actions of the Germans could not be said to have been done in the heat of battle, because the handbooks given to them before the war told them to stop at nothing to achieve their ends.
>
> (*The Irish Times*, 27 September 1915)

This new theme for recruitment was often derided by nationalist opposition newspapers and republicans. Bishop O'Donnell received an anonymous letter stating: 'Please, find picture of Germans "Barbarians and Baby-Killers" [found] at Mas [sic].'[106] The opposition began to vehemently denounce pro-war priests. In December 1915, the *Hibernian* inveighed against the recruiting activities of Fr O'Doherty of Dublin. The priest had indeed depicted the German army in very unchristian terms and had asked his fellow Irishmen to 'put on the khaki, and go out and kill the savage "Hun"'.[107] These kind of declarations were systematically denounced by the opposition press. Concerning O'Doherty's outburst, Fr P.J. Walsh, one of Archbishop Walsh's secretaries, sent a humorous letter to Mgr Hagan in Rome in which he summed up O'Doherty's problems with the press. He wrote that the *Hibernian*'s main article had been entitled 'Dr O'Doherty's Dope' and that *Nationality*'s headline had been 'The Burst of the new Vicar of Bray'.[108] Walsh's letter corroborated the fact that the clergy was decidedly not united on the question of recruitment at the end of 1915. Elsewhere, pro-war priests were sometimes physically intimidated. In

October 1915, Mgr Arthur Ryan, an ardent supporter of the 16th Irish Division in France, was threatened with violence if he attended a recruitment meeting in Tipperary town. A few days before the scheduled meeting, the inhabitants were able to read posters denouncing the war and Ryan's activities. According to the *Freeman's Journal*, the town had taken umbrage and defended its patriotic priest. Ryan himself was not at all deterred and went ahead with his speech at the meeting.[109]

These situations, however, were not widespread in Ireland. The anti-recruitment forces must have realised that physically threatening priests in a devout Catholic country would be counter-productive. Arthur Griffith's *Nationality* was fully aware that at the end of 1915, recruitment was declining rapidly and that the Catholic Church was divided on the issue. It was precisely those issues that *Nationality* would exploit in order to prevent Irishmen from enlisting. Griffith decided to neutralise Mgr Ryan's influence by a very clever two-way approach. Firstly, the newspaper published extracts of Ryan's pro-war harangues. Secondly, it contradicted these extracts by using anti-war declarations of other priests.[110] By doing so, Griffith placed the Irish people in a difficult moral dilemma: did men have to join the Army and could the people rely on the advice of the Church? *Nationality* had clearly demonstrated that there was no unity of opinion within the Catholic clergy. As will be seen, it seemed that the opposition newspapers had the wind in their sails because at the same time Bishop Edward O'Dwyer of Limerick had embarked on a successful anti-war crusade against John Redmond. *Nationality*, *Spark*, *Eire Ireland*, and the *Hibernian* acknowledged the importance of the Catholic Church in their propaganda and regularly used anti-war declarations of priests. In an article entitled 'Catholics and the English Army', the *Hibernian* tried to persuade its readers that pro-war priests were definitely in a moral quandary for they were opposing the very words of the Pope. To a devout Catholic, the following passage must have been striking:

> The appearance of Irish priests on recruiting platforms in some parts of the country brings many thoughts to one's mind. Catholic priests are God's anointed – ministers of the Prince of Peace; He who said: 'My peace I leave you, my peace I give you'; and again, 'He who lives by the sword...'
>
> Our Holy Father the Pope has set a noble example for priests to follow. He has counselled peace, not war.
>
> (*The Hibernian*, 1 January 1916)

There were also other difficulties with which the pro-war priests were confronted. It has been noted that recruitment was poorly organised and that the War Office was prejudiced against Irish nationalism. But, perhaps an even worse enemy of voluntary enlistment was political apathy. In rural Ireland a very strong sense of insularity prevailed. Even in France, it appeared that the rural population was not as motivated to fight as urban people were. Farmers and villagers were stupefied, surprised and wept when they learnt about mobilisation, and patriotic fervour was not particularly obvious.[111] The *Church of Ireland Gazette*, as early as November 1914, highlighted this problem and stated: 'The military authorities have to combat two things, that sense of insular security, and, we may say, of insular isolation.'[112] Unlike Belgium and France, Ireland was far removed from the theatre of war, and life went on as usual. In September 1915, Fr Magill wrote to the *Irish Times* in this way: 'Relief [to the Irishmen at the front] could not be given as long as people went to football and hurling matches, and got all the amusements out of life, caring nothing for their kith and kin in the trenches.'[113] Fr O'Riordan from Kerry regretted that the Irish considered the present war to be England's, not Ireland's.[114] Ironically, this apparent lack of political motivation played into the hands of the opposition but only as far as the war was concerned. The Irish population were not thinking of switching political allegiance and abandoning John Redmond and the Nationalist party. Desmond Fitzgerald, the organiser of the Irish Volunteers in Co. Kerry, wrote after an anti-war meeting held in Dingle peninsula: 'There was plenty of applause, but that might mean nothing more than that the people were satisfied that we were giving them good entertainment.'[115]

This political apathy was reinforced by the fact that Ireland was experiencing an economic boost, which was very profitable to farmers, who were obliged to increase their productivity for the war effort. At that particular time, the economy under the Union had never seemed so favourable to Irish farmers.[116] The wages of farm labourers rose by as much as 70 per cent between 1914 and 1918 and work was plentiful in the countryside.[117] In rural Ireland, the reaction to the onset of the hostilities had been quite reserved. In Co. Clare, there seemed to be no real interest in the war and the agricultural boom proved to be a powerful incentive not to enlist.[118] The Inspector General of the RIC was well aware of the mercantile spirit that animated the farmers and wrote in his monthly report for January 1916: 'Farmers all over Ireland are still holding back and appear to feel no interest in the War except as a means of making money.'[119] Even in urban Ireland, there was a lack of interest in voluntary enlistment because of economic conditions. The average pay for unskilled labour in Dublin in 1913 was about eighteen shillings a week.[120] The basic pay of a British soldier could vary from one regiment to the other. A soldier serving in the Life Guards, for instance, would earn between seven and eight shillings a week. The average was one shilling a day. According to a prominent First World War historian: 'Scepticism has been expressed by some historians about the role of economic factors in the decision to enlist.'[121] In 1915, the ever warlike *Church of Ireland Gazette* welcomed the introduction of so-called 'separation allowances', money paid to the wives and relatives of soldiers at the front, as it estimated it would boost recruitment.[122]

It would seem that early Irish enthusiasm for the war had really been a question of patriotism before anything else. It remains difficult, though, to state with certainty why men joined the Army. Before the war, there had been more recruits in Dublin than in Belfast and economic considerations were probably more important than political or ideological ones.[123] Halfway through 1915, the number of enlisted men had already dropped considerably. John Redmond was conscious of the existing situation. On 10 February 1916, together with Lord Wimborne, he took part in a recruiting meeting at Mansion House in Dublin. In his speech, the leader of the Nationalist party paid tribute to the production figures of the farmers but he also added: 'It would be base ingratitude to the labouring classes of the country in Ireland and to the labouring classes in the towns in Ireland if the farmers were to throw upon them to-day the whole burden of protecting their property.'[124] Redmond's message was clear.

However, were the pro-war priests able to change public opinion and attitude towards enlistment? If, at first sight, priests appeared to be important and influential men within their communities, their real power was restricted to religious matters. It was quite different when politics came into play. They were quite close to the population as most of them had parents who were substantial tenant farmers or who came from lower middle and middle-class background in cities.[125] It was very difficult for priests to oppose the wishes and opinions of people with whom they shared the same social origins. Had they really the power to convince people against their will into joining the Army, even if they felt that the war was theologically and morally justified? Could they reproach prosperous farmers who stayed aloof from the war? These were serious questions, for if the local clergy was continuously exhorting people to go and fight, it ran the risk of finding itself isolated within its parishes. Undoubtedly, there were limits to the power of the Catholic Church in Ireland. In February 1918, Alfred Blanche sent a report about the political situation of the clergy to Stephen Pichon, the Secretary of the French Foreign Office. He summarised the political quandary of the priest:

He [the priest] in order to provide for his needs, could only rely on what he could get from the goodwill of the faithful. While possessing on them moral authority, he materially depended on them, and his living conditions have not changed much today. If he wants to retain his prestige, he must find out which way the wind is blowing, guess where public opinion is going to and even anticipate it, in short, to follow public opinion in actual fact while seemingly guiding it, lest he suffers badly in all his interests.

(Quai d'Orsay, Paris, vol. 547 Grande-Bretagne/Irlande, Blanche to Pichon 19 February 1918, pp. 19–20)

Blanche had correctly analysed the situation. What was valid a few months before the conscription crisis of April 1918, was equally valid between August 1914 and April 1916. The DRI encouraged all the recruitment committees to use priests 'where you can get him'.[126] In April 1916, just before the Easter Rising, very few priests were available. Economic prosperity, bad recruiting organisation and insularity had taken their toll. In fact, at the end of 1915 during a new recruitment campaign, not many priests were to be found on the platform together with recruiting sergeants.[127] After the Easter Rising in April 1916, Major Price declared to Lord Hardinge, who was in charge of examining the causes that had led Irish rebels to take up arms against the British Army, that the 'clergy, as a body, are, on the whole, lukewarm on the subject of recruiting'.[128]

Price's answer was correct. This lukewarm attitude would become rather cold after the execution of the rebel leaders.

THE CHURCH, BELGIUM, POLAND AND THE WAR ECONOMY

If recruitment for the Irish Divisions or the British Army was the main criterion in measuring the Catholic Church's participation in the war effort, the clergy was also involved in other areas related to the conflict. These principally concerned help to Belgium and Poland and support for the war economy.

When the German Army violated Belgium's neutrality, recruitment authorities, newspapers in favour of the Nationalist party and various politicians realised that it was a theme that could be easily exploited for propaganda reasons. In 1914, the comparison between Ireland and Belgium could strike the Irish population's imagination since they were two small Catholic countries. The phrase 'poor little Catholic Belgium' would be often heard or read during the first years of the war. The aim of the phrase was simple: Irishmen had to identify themselves with the Belgians so that recruitment would be stimulated. Some of those who used the Belgian theme were honest and acted without ulterior motives. The Church was among them. One of the very first to 'connect' the Irish to the Belgians was Bishop Hoare of Ardagh. In a letter published by the

Irish Catholic on 12 September 1914, Hoare reminded his people that both countries were historically related. He evoked the Penal Laws and told his parishioners that they would be 'guilty of black ingratitude if they [Irish] were unmindful of the services of Catholic Belgium in educating priests during the Penal Days, in giving welcome and hospitality to [the] brave Irish Brigade'.[129] He finished by asking the Irish to donate money to Belgium. The Bishop tried to convince the population that it had a moral obligation towards Belgium, a 'historic debt'. The letter proved that most of the Irish prelates carefully followed John Redmond's political progress for Hoare had only spoken of a financial aid to Belgium, not of a military one which the Nationalist leader had not yet promised at that time.

This was to change soon. On 13 September 1914, Cardinal Mercier, the Belgian Primate, was in London. The Irish living in Britain took the opportunity to give him a message of sympathy from the Irish people to the Belgians. T.P. O'Connor, the only Irish MP elected in England, had instigated this initiative, fully backed by Redmond and the party. Had the leader realised a few days before the decisive vote on Home Rule that his country would be involved militarily in the conflict and that an unqualified support for Belgium was on the way? Cardinal Mercier, in his reply, indicated that the two countries would be allied in the war. After all, was not the conflict about the existence and independence of small nations? Mercier thanked the Irish people and added that if there was one country that could understand what Belgium was going through it was Ireland. He explained: 'Your admirable history is a perpetual stimulus for the generations which have seen you at work, and your perseverance in preserving the Catholic Faith and defining liberty is a powerful support to our own hopes for the future.'[130] At the end of his speech, the Cardinal blessed all the members of the Nationalist party. After Redmond had asked the Volunteers to fight abroad, the clergy began to denounce German occupation and atrocities in Belgium. The various recruitment organisations and pro-war press used many comments made by priests and bishops on the matter. Some priests declared that it was the Irishmen's duty to go to the front in Europe before Prussian militarism reached Ireland and committed the same atrocities as in Belgium.

The Church especially helped Belgian refugees and organised collections for their country. On 13 October 1914, the hierarchy met in Maynooth and all bishops present agreed to support Belgium in her dark hours. The prelates adopted two resolutions. Firstly, they denounced the destruction of the university of Louvain and decided to add their voice to the protests, which had occurred throughout the world. The hierarchy reminded the people that one of the colleges in Louvain had been founded by Irish Franciscans, and that many

Irishmen had found a refuge there during the Penal Laws. It was the same position as Dr Hoare's a month before. Secondly, a collection was to take place in every parish in the country. Every bishop was to ask his priests to work for Belgium. The churchgoers would be asked to donate money, which would be given to Cardinal Mercier or to committees in charge of helping Belgium.[131] The generosity of the Irish population and the excellence of Church organisation were proven. Robert Browne, Bishop of Cloyne, responsible for the Belgian Relief Fund, declared in February 1915 that £28,352 had been collected.[132] Archbishop Walsh paid tribute to the people's generosity. Walsh, as will be seen, did not want to have anything to do with the war effort and refused categorically to allow the churches in his diocese to be used for recruitment purposes. Therefore, his letter, published by the press, insisted purely on the humanitarian aspect of the collection. He wrote: 'I cannot refrain from saying that the response to my appeal on this occasion has been in excess of anything that, with all my experience of the generosity of the people of Dublin, I had ventured to anticipate.'[133] The Bishops of Dromore, Cloyne, Raphoe and Tuam equally praised the efforts of the Belgian Relief Fund but, unlike Walsh, they included passages denouncing German barbarism and implicitly asked Irishmen to enlist.[134] In May 1915, Cardinal Mercier wrote a long letter, thanking the Irish people and its Church, and sent it to the four Archbishops of the country. Belgium, however, was not the only Catholic country to be treated so generously. In October 1915, the hierarchy decided to support Poland in the same way. In the previous month, the Polish episcopate had asked all the Catholics in the world to pray for Poland, divided between Germany, Russia and Austria-Hungary, and to contribute money in order to help the country and her refugees. The Pope had fully approved of this appeal. A collection was organised and once more the generosity of the Irish population was evident. In 1916 Bishop Kelly of Ross, the smallest diocese in Ireland, wrote to Mgr O'Riordan in Rome that his parishioners had donated £250 for Poland.[135] More strikingly, in 1917, the Roman newspaper *Osservatore Romano* informed its readers that Ireland had given FFr290,000 (approximately £11,600) to Poland,[136] this at a time when Ireland was in a political turmoil and when the war had become very unpopular in the country.

Perhaps the most visible sign of the war in Ireland was the arrival of Belgian refugees. These were people who had lost everything. There were even Benedictine monks who founded a monastery in Enniscorthy in Co. Wexford.[137] These refugees were generally warmly welcomed. Buildings were given to them and money and clothes' collections were organised for them. The *Freeman's Journal* believed that the exiles would be well treated. Dr Harty of Cashel was even clearer on this

2. John Redmond and the National Volunteers (courtesy of the National Library of Ireland)

subject. The Archbishop wrote a circular letter meant to be read in every church of his diocese. Once more, the familiar theme of identification between Ireland and Belgium, and the Penal Laws, was evoked. Harty stated: 'Today, Belgium is the sufferer, and Ireland is called to pay the debt of gratitude, which has accumulated during centuries'.[138] Harty and the *Freeman's Journal* had no reason to worry. During the first months of the conflict, the War Refugees' Committee acknowledged this. It worked in favour of the Belgians and helped them to integrate into Irish society. On 19 January 1915, the bishops paid tribute to the committee and asked the people to continue to support it.[139] But in March 1916 a remarkable incident took place. Some refugees had settled in Ulster in the archdiocese of Armagh. In one of the towns, where eight Belgian families were living, three had suddenly converted to Protestantism. It was obvious that the taking care of refugees was not exclusively a Catholic affair. Nevertheless, Cardinal Logue severely criticised what had happened. He wrote in his Lenten pastoral that these conversions happened because of Protestant proselytism and that they constituted 'a betrayal of trust and a violation of the laws of charity and hospitality'.[140] He also accused the committee of insufficient vigilance and regretted that Catholic money supported Protestant efforts. Logue's words were harsh, for the committee did its best to ensure that Belgians were well cared for. Furthermore, there is no evidence that proselytism was widespread in Ireland and Logue probably attached great importance to an isolated case. It is more of an

3. Lord Kitchener, head of the War Office, did not handle Irish patriotism well
during the war (courtesy of *The Illustrated London News*)

4. A group of Irish soldiers returning after the capture of Ginchy, 9 September 1916. Taken from *Ireland's Unknown Soldiers* (Denman)

indication that tensions between Catholics and Protestants remained alive despite the so-called union of the hearts between nationalists and unionists, which some people claimed had taken place in the country because of the war against Germany.

There was another area in which the Catholic Church was to play an important role, the war economy. The clergy was generally not much involved in economic matters except, to some extent, in economically related problems such as working conditions and social conflicts. In 1913, the Church had supported the employer William Martin Murphy against Jim Larkin, the leader of the Irish trade unions, during the 'Dublin Lockout'. On this occasion, the hierarchy had decided that socialism was a serious threat to the interests of the country despite the fact that workers' conditions were bad and that Dublin had one of Europe's worst slums.[141] It was obvious from the onset of the hostilities in Europe that the war would have important repercussions on the economy. The first prelate to evoke this problem publicly was Laurence Gaughran, the Bishop of Meath. In the beginning of August 1914, Gaughran preached in the cathedral of Mullingar and advised his parishioners not to panic and not to withdraw their money from the banks. His sermon was later published by the *Irish Catholic* under the title 'Danger of Panic'.[142] Gaughran would later be involved in 'economic operations' in Ireland. The country was enjoying a major economic boom at that time. Mgr O'Riordan reported to Bishop O'Dwyer that the country's prosperity had really struck him.[143] Other bishops encouraged

30

5. John Redmond as a recruiting sergeant for the British Army, *Gaelic American* (26 September 1914)

REDMOND IN HIS LATEST ROLE.

The Irish Political Charlie Chaplin, With Apologies to the Real Charlie.

6. John Redmond as Charlie Chaplin, *Gaelic American* (18 September 1915)

7. The socialist *Irish Worker* rejects John Redmond's support for England in the war (7 November 1914)

8. Anti-war cartoon in the *Irish Worker* (14 October 1914). Notice the Catholic priest walking with a rifle on his shoulder

9. John Redmond working for Britain's interests, *Irish Worker* (6 September 1914)

10. John Redmond (left) bringing a reluctant Irish Volunteer to Lord Kitchener, *Irish Worker* (26 September 1914)

11. The socialist *Irish Worker*'s opinion on the real state of affairs on the Western
Front (19 September 1914)

farmers to increase their production in order to meet the future demands
of the population and to be ready for a possible famine caused by the
war. In February 1915, Dr O'Donnell stated in his Lenten pastoral that
'not half enough acreage is turned up by plough or spade. Now is the
time to make a new start.'[144] It was very unlikely that Irish farmers had
waited until the seventh month of the war to do as the Bishop of Raphoe
said. On 12 May 1915, David Lloyd George, Minister of Munitions
then, asked the British population to save their money and to cut down
expenditure. He told the people that 'it [was] not a question of meanness,
but of patriotism'. Finances were necessary to continue waging the war
under the best possible circumstances and Britons had to make their
money available to the Government. In July 1915, the Irish authorities
decided to form a new committee that would inquire into the war
economy. It was called the Irish War Savings Committee (IWSC), chaired
by The O'Connor Don and Sir Walter Nugent, member of the Ancient
Order of Hibernians, an organisation devoted to defending Catholic
interests and supporting the Nationalist party. The aim of the IWSC was
to implement Lloyd George's ideas throughout Ireland. Nugent and The
O'Connor Don quickly understood that the Catholic and Protestant
Churches could play a crucial role in propagating their ideas throughout
the country. On 16 July 1915, the committee sent a circular letter to all

the Catholic and Protestant bishops in order to explain its aims and ask for their help and advice in the matter: 'One of the objects of that Committee is to inculcate exceptional national thrift during the present crisis.'[145]

The IWSC's appeal shows once again the importance that the Government attached to the Church's role in the global war effort. Everywhere and in every area the clergy's help was looked for. Many bishops responded positively to the appeal. Among the first were Abraham Brownrigg of Ossory, Robert Browne of Cloyne, James Browne of Ferns and John Healy of Tuam. All agreed with the IWSC and promised to advise their priests and vicars to persuade their flocks of the need for thrift in time of war. Daniel Cohalan, the auxiliary Bishop of Cork, replied negatively. Cohalan was not convinced of the utility of the IWSC because he deemed that the rural population was not spending superfluously. As for the urban population, it had no money to spend anyway: 'And here in the part of the city that I have to deal with many should spend more if they had it, and the only waste that I know of is drink, and with that waste I will deal very soon.'[146] Cohalan did not even mention the war in his reply and seemed to be essentially preoccupied by social problems in his diocese. His reaction came just after the public confrontation between John Redmond and Bishop O'Dwyer of Limerick, who was arguing in favour of the Pope's latest peace initiatives, and at a time when recruitment figures began to drop seriously because of the War Office's disastrous Irish policy. It is worth noticing that in July 1917, Cohalan spoke about Sinn Féin in relatively neutral terms and thought that the emerging nationalist party was 'on its trial'.[147] Even more relevant perhaps was the fact that Cohalan had been educated in Germany before the war[148] and that, as a result, his sympathy might have been with the Triple Alliance. The Bishop's cousin, also called Daniel Cohalan, was a judge in the United States and was in league with Sinn Féin, Clan na Gael and other Irish republicans. Later in the war, in 1917, the British intercepted and decoded a message from Count von Bernstorff, the German ambassador in Washington, to the German Foreign Office in Berlin. Von Bernstorff advised his Government to convince the Vatican to appoint Daniel Cohalan as Bishop of Cork.[149] The Vatican had been persuaded on that occasion. It seemed that Cohalan was becoming an 'opposition bishop', like O'Dwyer, had pro-German feelings and, therefore, declined to attend a public meeting on thrift in Cork.

Bishop Kelly of Ross in West Cork accepted the invitation to the meeting held on 10 September 1915. Kelly had the reputation of being the economist of the Irish hierarchy. When asked to speak, the Bishop was frank with his audience and did not hide the fact that he fully approved of the IWSC's aims. According to him, the main objective was to help Ireland in the recession that would come after the war. He also reiterated his support for the countries of the Triple Entente:

> Tonight we propound from this platform distasteful doctrines. We insist on the need of economy and savings for the double purpose of enabling the Government to carry on the war to a successful issue and to enable ourselves, when the war is over, to meet, as best as we may, the bad times that will come. To guard against misunderstandings, I must declare at the outset that I assume that the Allies will win the war (cheers) and my opinions are governed by that assumption.
>
> (NLD, Brennan papers, MS26166, speech of the Bishop of Ross, 10 September 1915)

Kelly ended by quoting Lloyd George's speech on thrift in the House of Commons. The Bishop's words were subsequently published and 10,000 pamphlets were handed out to clergy and various people in favour of the IWSC.[150] The committee had decided not to do things by halves. Two important prelates, however, reacted quite differently.

At the end of July 1915, Cardinal Logue was invited to speak at the Oireachtas, a meeting of the Gaelic League in Dundalk in Co. Louth. Douglas Hyde, the President of the League, welcomed Logue and officially asked him to open the meeting. The Cardinal began a long speech in which he commented on the economic situation of the country. He was of the opinion that Ireland's industrial under-development was the result of gross English mismanagement. The latter had been responsible for the emigration of hundreds of thousands of Irish men and women over the decades. He also regretted that agriculture was not more productive which, according to him, explained why there were not ten million inhabitants in Ireland, for the country had simply no means to nourish them. All this was the British Government's fault. Logue's speech must have delighted the republican and nationalist opposition which, ironically, he had regularly denounced as being dangerous for the political stability of the country. But, the Primate of All Ireland went even further. He accused the British war industries of squandering Irish money and suggested that very little of it would return to Ireland.[151]

The Cardinal had probably a good insight into financial matters for Britain was experiencing some serious economic problems at precisely that time. The British Government had lent huge amounts of money to her allies, £1,741,000,000 had gone to Russia and France alone. As a consequence, Britain was now forced to borrow some £1,365,000,000 from her dominions and neutral countries.[152] Moreover, the Liberal Government had been obliged to control and regulate the United

Kingdom's economy and put an end to the free market system. Because of those changes, there was some disorganisation in the national production. It would seem that Logue was alluding to this state of affairs. The Cardinal also said that the Irish should refuse to borrow English money. He estimated that between £60,000,000 to £100,000,000 in Irish banks had still not been used and that Ireland should not get into debt for nothing. And yet despite all his criticisms, Logue was still in favour of the British Government, or rather British Empire, to which he was proud to belong. His opinions were in fact not at all contradictory. He approved of Home Rule and thought that Ireland could prosper in the Empire's economical and political system if she was given the chance to do so. He added: 'If Irish industries had been encouraged in the past and the Irish people kept at home, that would be a great thing, not only for Ireland, but for the whole Empire.'[153] Logue bore resentment to the Government, not the Empire, which was totally different in his mind. It is therefore not surprising that he did, after all, approve of the IWSC's initiatives. He strongly advised the population to save their money, which would be borrowed by the Government and paid back with interest to them. He ended by saying that there was no other choice but thrift and economy. The unionist *Irish Times*, and the *Freeman's Journal*, published the speech under the title 'The Great Need for Thrift'. In December 1915, the IWSC decided to use certain extracts of Logue's speech to spread their ideas. A poster was conceived and placarded throughout the country. The Irish could read:

> The Cardinal's advice
> I agree thoroughly with a number of people who are moving at present to induce the people to practice thrift and economy... When money is plentiful it is time we should lay up something for the rainy day... If the people waste now, there will be a terrible reckoning hereafter. This is a thing which cannot be too prominently kept before the minds of the people at the present time.
> His Eminence Cardinal Logue at the OIREACHTAS, Dundalk, 26 July 1915.
> (NLD, Brennan papers, MS26166, IWSC to Augustine Birrell, 31 December 1915.)

The poster had been cleverly conceived as the signature of the highest Catholic ecclesiastical dignitary and the Gaelic word 'OIREACHTAS' endowed it with a certain nationalist meaning.

On 4 August 1915, a second member of the hierarchy reacted to the economic problem in Ireland. He was Bishop O'Dwyer of Limerick. O'Dwyer had sent a long letter to John Redmond, which was published by the press and created a sensation in the country. The prelate asked the Nationalist leader to act on the Pope's peace appeal. In a very logical and eloquent argument, he alluded to Ireland's economy in time of war. But contrary to Logue, the Bishop demanded the immediate cessation of the hostilities in Europe, not only to save lives, but also to save Ireland from an unprecedented economic and financial catastrophe, which was waiting to happen. O'Dwyer explained that Redmond knew well of the enormous debt that was accumulating in Ireland, which would paralyse the country in the years to come. He estimated that the first post-war British budget would probably be around £400,000,000 and that Ireland would be obliged to contribute £20,000,000. The Bishop asked Redmond if he thought that the country could possibly prosper with such a financial burden. Eventually, he concluded the economic paragraph of his letter by mentioning the difference between England and Ireland:

> Then, the moment the war ceases, there will be a sudden collapse of prices, and woe betide the man who will not have made provision for that day. Strong men will be hard set to keep their heads over water; but the ordinary farmers will find it enough to do to pay their annuities much less to meet an unheard-of load of taxation. England, too, will feel the strain, but she has great resources. She can weather the bad times for some years, and whatever way the war goes, will recover her prosperity. It will be very different with us. Win or lose, the war already spells poverty for us for a generation, and, if it goes on for another year, it will sink us in irretrievable ruin.
>
> (*The Tablet*, 21 August 1915)

O'Dwyer had astutely used the economic theme in his presentation. He had thus caught the population's attention by predicting a financial crisis, which would hit both the pro and anti-war sides. The farmers, especially, must have been impressed by O'Dwyer's arguments. They had not joined the colours en masse and were enjoying an economic prosperity thanks to the war, but which the war could also soon wreck, according to O'Dwyer at least. It came as no surprise that Redmond tried his best to persuade farmers to enlist a few months later in February 1916 at the Mansion House in Dublin. 'Big words' and great ideals like the independence of small nations and fighting for religion and civilisation were no match for O'Dwyer's arguments that hit farmers hard. In August 1915, most of the farmers were indifferent to the war and had little interest in world politics. The economy seemed to have become a political battlefield between O'Dwyer and Redmond, but also between O'Dwyer and Logue as the Bishop's letter appeared in the press very shortly after the Cardinal's speech in Dundalk. One is inclined to reach the conclusion that O'Dwyer had also tried to neutralise Logue's influence. There was definitely no unity about the war within the hierarchy. As for Redmond, he decided to reply negatively to O'Dwyer's letter. This matter will be studied in more detail later. Briefly, Redmond's public letter was not appropriate to the situation. It was short and did not even try to prove O'Dwyer's economic arguments wrong. The Nationalist leader simply stated that the Bishop's ideas were not 'calculated to promote the cause of peace'.[154] This was an incredible political blunder for it seemed to the people that the Bishop had a number of pertinent questions that Redmond did not wish to answer publicly or to which he had no precise answer. O'Dwyer's letter had a huge impact. The nationalist opposition press immediately got hold of the story and denounced Redmond's pro-war policy. Eoin MacNeill praised the Bishop in the *Irish Volunteer* and outlined the Nationalist leader's weaknesses: 'Mr. Redmond has not ventured to controvert the Bishop of Limerick's forecast of £20,000,000 a year to be levied on Ireland – if Ireland submits. He has avoided the disagreeable subject, and blinked the Bishop's questions.'[155] MacNeill also compared O'Dwyer's financial estimations to those made by a member of the Nationalist party, J. Horgan, in a book entitled *Home Rule: a Critical Consideration*, published in 1911. Horgan had actually almost reached O'Dwyer's figures.[156] In economic matters, however, Redmond and the IWSC still had the support of most of the bishops until the end of 1915. Dr Gaughran, the first to have warned the people in 1914 against a possible financial setback, wrote a letter to all the churches of his diocese in which he favoured the idea of thrift.[157]

It remains difficult to establish with certainty the Church's influence on the war economy in Ireland. One cannot say to what extent a bishop or a priest was instrumental in encouraging an individual to save money or to invest in war bonds. Nevertheless, it is possible to show that the Catholic Church, apart from some notable exceptions, did approve of the IWSC's aims and fully participated in its propaganda campaigns. On 1 March 1916, Mathew Nathan, the Irish Under-Secretary, sent to his chief, Augustine Birrell, a report of the IWSC. It mentioned that various newspapers like the *Irish Times*, the *Freeman's Journal*, the *Daily Express* and the *Northern Whig* had generously helped the committee in its efforts. But, the Catholic and Protestant Churches' support was also acknowledged: 'Thrift has been preached from numerous pulpits of all denominations whereby it is hoped an effective appeal has reached a large section of the community.'[158] The report mentioned in particular Bishops Kelly and Gaughran. Nathan added: 'One definite success of the Committee has been to get a number of the Catholic clergy to preach on the duty of thrift.' If at the end of 1915 and the beginning of 1916 the Church no longer actively supported recruiting, it was still convinced of the necessities of an economy geared to win the war.

SUMMARY

The first years of the war, from August 1914 to April 1916, resulted in a weakening of the alliance between the Catholic Church and the Nationalist party. This was not because of a radical change of opinion within the Church regarding Home Rule but rather as a result of a difference of opinion on the manner of achieving autonomy for Ireland. To John Redmond, there was no doubt that the way to resolve the Home Rule crisis and to avoid partition was nationalist Ireland's full participation in the war effort, which would eventually bring Catholics and Protestants together. This explained why the Nationalist leader continued to call for recruits despite the obvious negative policy of the War Office, the various recruitment organisations and the British cabinet. Bishops and priests, even those still in favour of the Nationalist party, began to have doubts about Redmond's pro-war policy. They simply could not run the risk of forcing Irishmen to join the Army against their will and find themselves, as a consequence, isolated within their communities and dioceses. The population generally seemed to be politically apathetic, was enjoying some economic prosperity and had become largely indifferent to the conflict in Europe. Unless the new coalition cabinet took some serious steps in favour of the Nationalist party and against partition, a change in public opinion could hardly be expected. These problems would become even more critical after the Easter Rising of April 1916 and would almost put an end to recruiting in the country. Members of the hierarchy, like Bishop O'Donnell, and priests, like Fr Arthur Ryan, still publicly supported Redmond and his war policy but had to have the courage of their political opinions and operate alone. Most Redmondite clergy had become practically voiceless by April 1916.

  Three prelates, however, who were to dominate ecclesiastical political life during the war years, were quite dissatisfied with Anglo-Irish relations and decided to voice their opinions and make their presence felt. Their interventions were to have a major impact on Irish history.

2 The rogue bishops

March 1915
'And so far our interests the Government seems quite indifferent to them, provided it gets plenty of recruits.'

Cardinal Logue on British policy in Ireland
in a letter to Bishop O'Donnell

May 1915
'Our recruiting geniuses in Dublin got a bad slap in the face from his Grace.'

Mgr Curran informing Mgr Hagan in Rome on Archbishop
Walsh's intervention against the Central Council for the
Organisation of Recruiting in Ireland

December 1915
'Home Rule has been kept for many years dangling before his nose like the carrot before the donkey; he gets a sufficient sniff of it occasionally to keep him draughting for the English Government.'

Bishop O'Dwyer in Nationality *on Redmond's*
refusal to work for peace

The different opinions expressed by bishops concerning recruitment and the economy reflect the internal dissensions within the hierarchy about the war in general. Between 1914 and 1918, three prelates, in particular, distinguished themselves by their attitudes towards the conflict. Their actions and reactions influenced the course of politics, recruitment and the war effort in Ireland. They were Cardinal Logue of Armagh, Archbishop Walsh of Dublin and Bishop O'Dwyer of Limerick. Their cases will now be examined individually.

CARDINAL LOGUE: FOR THE EMPIRE, AGAINST THE GOVERNMENT!

Throughout the duration of the war, Cardinal Logue seems to have had an ambivalent attitude towards the war effort. On various occasions, he gave contradicting impressions. On the one hand, he clearly supported the countries of the Triple Entente but on the other hand, he repeatedly told the British Government that it would not find recruits in Ireland. It was what he called 'the revenges which time brought about',[1] a phrase that would not particularly help the recruitment organisations. He spoke of the necessity to defend the British Empire but stubbornly refused to encourage his Church to participate more rigorously in recruitment operations. Logue is generally considered to be a quintessential nationalist, in favour of John Redmond's party.[2] He was also one of the patrons of the Gaelic League and fully approved of Ireland's cultural renaissance.

Yet, if he was a convinced nationalist, his political opinions were more complex than those of his fellow bishops. Logue became Primate of All Ireland after Cardinal Daniel McGettigan's death in 1887. He had been coadjutor for nine months during McGettigan's illness when Archbishop Walsh effectively led the hierarchy. Logue, in fact, replaced Walsh and McGettigan at the same time.[3] It seems that the Vatican gave the red hat to Logue in order to diminish Walsh's influence on Irish political affairs. The Curia deemed that the Archbishop of Dublin was too nationalistic and did not trust his judgement.[4] The new Cardinal was essentially preoccupied with spiritual and moral matters. He supported, among others, movements to combat alcoholism in Ireland. Logue would have been pleased to read the Inspector General of the RIC's report for January 1916 in which he stated that 'throughout Ireland drunkenness [is] declining', but would have been worried when the Inspector added that 'some excessive drinking unfortunately [occurs] amongst soldiers' wives and dependents [sic]'.[5] During the war the Cardinal did his best to ensure that Catholic chaplains accompanied Irish regiments.

Regarding politics, Logue was rather cautious. Nevertheless, in March 1901 on the occasion of King Edward VII's coronation, the Cardinal made an important speech in which he stated his opinions on the British Government's politics in Ireland and on recruiting in the country. This coronation sermon was quite controversial. The new British monarch had been obliged to take an oath against the Catholic doctrine of transubstantiation and the same oath mentioned that the cult of the Virgin Mary was idolatrous. In his speech, Logue mingled the religious issue with political matters by using two main lines: the relations between Ireland and the British Empire, and the relations between Ireland and the British Government. This distinction, made in 1901, helps to explain Logue's ambivalent attitude towards the war effort years later. He began by assuring his audience that the new King was not to blame for the controversial coronation oath, so insulting for 'the Catholics of the Empire', but that Edward VII had been

12. Cardinal Michael Logue: For the Empire, against the Government! (with kind
permission of the archdiocese of Armagh)

13. Archbishop William Walsh played a vital role in defeating conscription (with kind permission of the archdiocese of Dublin)

14. Bishop Edward O'Dwyer, the most implacable enemy of the war effort in Ireland (with kind permission of the diocese of Limerick)

DONKEY REDMOND AND THE HOME RULE CARROT.

"But Mr. Redmond, at the back of his mind, cares, I dare say, just as much as the average Irishman for Anglo-Saxon domination; but the exigencies of politics compel him to simulate feelings that he cannot possibly entertain. Home Rule has been kept, for many years, dangling before his nose, like the carrot before the donkey; he gets a sufficient sniff of it occasionally to keep him draughting for the English Government and he fears now that, if he attempted to show any independence as an Irishman, or any spirit as a Catholic, his English allies, or masters, would gladly find their excuse for throwing him over, and evading their promises on Home Rule. To my mind, that is the explanation of his attitude towards the Pope."— From Bishop O'Dwyer's article on "The Pope's Plea for Peace" in *The American Ecclesiastical Review* for December.

15. John Redmond depicted as a donkey in the *Gaelic American* (18 December 1915); the Irish-American newspaper was inspired by a letter of Bishop O'Dwyer found by Thérèse Fitzgerald, Mary Immaculate College, Limerick.

obliged to do so because of 'the remnant of a barbarous code'. He was alluding to the penal legislation of the late seventeenth and eighteenth centuries. Logue was of the opinion that the King, when he was Prince of Wales, had always been well disposed towards the different peoples of the Empire. He also felt that many British Protestants were against the oath. As for the late Queen Victoria, he was sure that the Irish were deeply touched by her death. She had been 'the model of a good Christian matron'. It seems that Logue had strong royalist feelings. Like Redmond, he rejected the idea of an Irish republic and favoured the idea of Ireland being a British dominion within the Empire. But the Cardinal was not willing to turn a blind eye to certain problems between Catholics and Protestants. He simply would not accept that Irish Catholics were considered as second class citizens within the United Kingdom. According to him, if the Government did not fully recognise the rights of Catholics, they would not come to the defence of the Empire. The *Irish Times* reported his very prophetic statement, just thirteen years before the onset of the Great War:

> There was one thing, for instance; those very men [Irish Catholics] who were branded as idolatrous in the present lamentable war [the Boer War] shed their blood like water in South Africa for the welfare of the Empire in which they were insulted and calumniated, and would be asked to do so again. Europe was now arming and gathering men for the field, and as a matter of necessity England must arm also. She would send her emissaries over to Ireland with oily tongues to wile their young people into the Army, and if his countrymen took his advice they would say to these recruiting sergeants...that as long as an insulting declaration remained on the Statute Book of England they would never enrol themselves under her flag.
>
> (*The Irish Times*, 18 March 1901)

The British Government did not pay heed to Logue's warning. It would bitterly regret it in the years to come.

On 20 August 1914, three weeks after the beginning of the hostilities, Pope Pius X died. Logue immediately left for Rome to take part in the funeral and in the election of a new Pope, who would be Benedict XV. On 28 September, he was on his way back and was interviewed by a journalist of the *Irish Independent* in Plymouth. He was asked how he felt about Herbert Asquith's latest visit to Dublin where he had launched the recruitment campaign in company with John Redmond. Logue was aware that the *Irish Independent* was not among Redmond's staunchest supporters and replied that it was not at all surprising, for Ireland had always demonstrated her loyalty. He was emphatic that 'Irishmen throughout the world would stand by the Empire' and denounced the 'barbarities of the Germans and the destruction of Louvain and Rheims Cathedral'.[6] In view of Logue's declarations in 1901, his views were very consistent. And yet, on his return to Dublin, he categorically denied having said this. He explained to a journalist of the *Freeman's Journal* that he had 'only said a few words to the correspondent at Plymouth...denouncing the barbarism of the Germans in burning Rheims Cathedral'.[7] The Cardinal accused the journalist of having given his own interpretation rather than what he had really said. Was his denial of condemning Germany out of hand a retraction of what he had declared in 1901? In fact, Logue was not contradicting himself. At the end of September 1914, the political situation in Ireland was not that clear. The British Government had not yet put forward a definite proposal concerning Home Rule and the danger of excluding six north-eastern counties, in which Logue's archdiocese lay, was still in the air. Consequently, Logue was consistent and cautious, and would not directly advise Irishmen to enlist as long as the Government did not guarantee nationalist Ireland that partition was not on the cards. The Cardinal was not as optimistic as Redmond regarding Home Rule and the war. He explained to the *Freeman's Journal*: 'I don't trust your politicians in England very much. They have an Amending Bill to bring in. What that will be I don't know'.[8] Logue was prudent and had adopted a wait and see policy. Contrary to Archbishop Harty and Bishops O'Donnell, Mangan, Coyne, Gilmartin and Foley and others later on, Logue did not congratulate Redmond when Home Rule was put on the statute book but suspended until the war was over.

Throughout the war, Logue never appealed to Irishmen for recruitment. Yet, he was far from being indifferent to the conflict. The only time he was explicitly involved in a recruitment campaign was in January 1915 when he sent a telegram to the *Freeman's Journal*, criticising the German occupation of Belgium. His words were used at once for a poster entitled 'The Cardinal and the War'.[9] He generally avoided making public pronouncements on recruitment, but there was no doubt, however, that he strongly favoured the Allies. In October 1914 Bishop Keating, of Northampton in England, was invited to speak at the annual conference of the Catholic Truth Society, presided over by Logue. Keating made a long speech in which he denounced German barbarism and Prussian militarism, two very fashionable topics in those days, but also referred to the Pope's importance in the future peace negotiations and argued in favour of equality between Catholics and Protestants within the Empire. Logue approved of these ideas but added that Catholics throughout the world had to stick together in order to forget their differences and work for God.[10] Unlike many Irish, British and French bishops, and apart from his statement in Plymouth, Logue never evoked German barbarism. To use such a theme would play directly into the propaganda machine's hands. In his Lenten pastoral of February 1915, the Cardinal spoke about barbarism caused by the war and the sufferance endured by the Belgian people without mentioning Germany in particular. The only time he directly referred to Germany was to denounce its arrogant cultural hegemony, which endangered other nations.[11]

On 24 June 1915 during a meeting of the Maynooth Union, Logue denounced the power of the press in Ireland and Britain. He charged that journalists were able to publish important information on the military situation, which would benefit Germany, and, referring of the munitions crisis in Britain: 'I think the publication of our weakness in the matter of munitions and in other things in the Press has given more information and more courage to the enemies of the country than even spies had been able to do.'[12] Phrases such as 'enemies of the country' and 'our weakness', prove that Logue was unquestionably a nationalist. His declaration was more important than it appeared at first glance. It came one month after Herbert Asquith's new coalition cabinet in which Sir Edward Carson and James Campbell, two prominent unionists, were members. These two men were distrusted in Catholic Ireland.[13] Despite his reservations about the Government, Logue was not inclined either to castigate it, for the war had to be won. Therefore, his support was intentionally limited. In March 1916, he refused to condemn the Central Powers after the massacres of the Armenian population became known, and simply said he found it strange that Christian countries were allied to Turkey, responsible for the mass killings of Christian Armenians. But, he did not explicitly name Germany or Austria-Hungary.[14] In fact, Logue had been denouncing barbarism in the war for quite some time without mentioning any of the belligerent countries in particular. On 18 October 1914 in Dundalk, he declared that modern warfare no longer took into account those rules that were supposed to make war more humane.[15] In his Lenten pastorals of 1915 and 1916, he reiterated his opposition to 'instruments of destruction' killing people indiscriminately, and 'the abuse of mines'. He called them a 'crime against humanity'. He was also of the opinion that the *jus in bello*, the theory of right conduct in war devised by Christian theologians, was not respected and that men were, therefore, 'relapsing to primitive barbarism'.[16] Amidst the horrors of modern warfare, Logue did not forget to pay tribute to the courage of Irish soldiers, French soldier-priests and Belgium but his Lenten pastoral was far from being a pro-recruitment statement. The Cardinal's words were in stark contrast to the *Church of Ireland Gazette* which suggested that chemical warfare was necessary since the Germans had initiated it and that principles of international law could no longer be implemented.[17]

Since the onset of the hostilities, Logue had worried about the spiritual welfare of Irish soldiers at the front. According to Catholic doctrine, dying or dead soldiers had to receive extreme unction. In October 1914, the *Freeman's Journal* reported that the Cardinal did not believe that many priests accompanied soldiers into battle. He also denied having received from the War Office the authorisation to appoint chaplains to the new Irish Army or Irish regiments in the British Army. He issued a strong warning to the War Office, saying that if it wanted more recruits in Ireland, it would have to remember that Irish Catholic soldiers did have specific religious needs.[18] It was the beginning of a long and complex bureaucratic battle between the Irish and British hierarchies, involving the Vatican and the War Office, about the right to appoint chaplains to Irish regiments. Briefly, it is quite clear that the Irish hierarchy resented the interference of the British Cardinal, Francis Bourne of Westminster. On this occasion, the Irish received support from Pope Benedict XV.[19] In February 1915, Logue declared that he hoped the spiritual needs of Irish seamen serving in the Royal Navy were now better looked after. He reminded his diocesans that the British Admiralty had often ignored the religious demands of those 28,000 Catholic sailors and that an anti-Catholic bias was still very much alive. He maintained that if things did not get better, few would volunteer for the Navy. Finally, the Cardinal made a comparison between Anglican and Catholic seamen: 'This discrimination against Catholics is neither fair, just, patriotic, nor politic . . . Sailors, belonging to the Church of England, have their own chaplains in nearly every ship . . . Both patriotism and good policy urge this reform.'[20] This posed a serious threat to the British Government, the same as he had made in 1901. The authorities seemed to have listened to him, for a few months later, in June 1915, the Cardinal admitted that both the War Office and the Admiralty were doing their best to solve the problem.[21] Logue would later declare to the *Irish Catholic* that the War Office had been quite cooperative in the chaplaincy issue but that there was an evident lack of priests for the task.[22]

Despite this, tensions between Irish Catholics and English Protestants, all subjects of the Empire, were regularly fuelled. Logue was very touchy about relations between the two Churches. In June 1915, he made a speech for the Maynooth Union in which he shared his concerns about Home Rule with his audience. He said that Irish autonomy was as yet only a promise of the British Government and that the people had to wait and see. He then severely criticised the creation of a council for the registration of teachers. According to him, this council would be composed of a majority of Protestants who would have the power to freely appoint Protestant teachers in Catholic schools. He detected in this council 'the old spirit of ascendancy'.[23] Herbert Asquith's cabinet did not appear to be able to assuage or dissipate all these fears and tensions, and consequently Logue had adopted a very cautious approach to the war effort in general. As early as 11 March 1915, only seven months after the beginning of the war, the Cardinal wrote to Bishop O'Donnell about his distrust of the Liberal Government:

> It is pretty clear that the Government pay very little attention to the remonstrances of the Bishops, and I think they pay just as little to the representations of Mr. Redmond. They feel they have us stalemated by keeping Home Rule, or at least the form which

Home Rule may take, hanging in the balance; and so far [*sic*] our interests they seem quite indifferent to them, provided they get plenty [*sic*] recruits.

(ACA, O'Donnell papers, Logue to O'Donnell,
11 March 1915)

Logue's letter also seemed to be an indirect warning to John Redmond since he knew well that O'Donnell was fully in favour of the Nationalist leader's policies, and that the Bishop of Raphoe would probably bring the Cardinal's opinions to Redmond's notice.

Logue's position was essentially the same as Archbishop Walsh's or Bishop O'Dwyer's except that he continued to argue in favour of the Empire. It was, therefore, not surprising at all that he delivered a *coup de grâce* to the CCORI's hopes of collaborating with him for recruitment some four months later at the Oireachtas in Dundalk, on 25 July 1915. On that occasion, Logue predicted that 'these people that were driven out were going with vengeance in their hearts, and in the weak days for England, as weak days came for every Empire, the *coup de grâce* would be given to England by those people they were driving out of the country'. His words were rather prophetic, pronounced just nine months before the Easter Rising in April 1916. Clearly, the Cardinal had sensed some major discontent among the more radical fringe of Irish nationalism. He noted that there were still many potential recruits in the country, especially among farmers but 'they could not deplete the country of men. They wanted someone to till the land. They could not all turn out and go to the front.'[24] Despite all the current political problems, however, he believed that recruitment in Ireland had been among the best within the Empire. While Logue defended the farmers' lack of participation in the war effort, the president of the Protestant synod of Tuam condemned it. The *Daily Express* reported his words a few days after Logue's speech at the Oireachtas: 'The farmers, except in one or two districts, have hardly responded at all [to recruitment]. I dislike dividing our people into social grades, for as a Church we recognise no social distinctions, and yet I am bound to call attention to this fact.'[25] Voluntary enlistment was declining rapidly in Ireland, a fact recognised by both the Catholic Church and the Church of Ireland.

On 8 September 1915, a meeting took place in Dublin between Lord Wimborne, the Lord Lieutenant, General Friend, the Commander-in-Chief of all the forces in Ireland, and Sir Mathew Nathan, the Under Secretary. The three men were discussing the recruitment crisis as Irish enthusiasm for the war had become practically non-existent.[26] Wimborne intended to organise a huge recruitment meeting in the city on 1 October 1915. He told Friend and Nathan that Redmond had promised to come and that Joseph Devlin, the Nationalist leader in Ulster, would probably also give his consent. The Lord Lieutenant's idea was to give the people the impression of a national and sacred union, the equivalent of the *Union Sacrée* in France, for he also had invited Mr Sharman Crawford who would represent the Unionist party, and Lords Londonderry, Barrymore and Meath, who would represent the landlords. To Nathan's surprise, Wimborne also proposed to invite Cardinal Logue! Clearly, Wimborne had not fully grasped Logue's policy on the war effort, or he had not read his *coup de grâce* speech in Dundalk. Wimborne's suggestion indicates how poorly the chairman of the CCORI and future DRI was informed about Irish public opinion. Nathan, of course, advised the the Lord Lieutenant not to invite him: 'I told Lord Wimborne that it was most unlikely, judging from his public utterances and from what I had heard as to the attitude of the Catholic Church, that Cardinal Logue or any of the Catholic Bishops would take part in a recruiting conference.'[27] This meeting did eventually take place on 10 February 1916 with Redmond and Wimborne, but without Logue. In January 1916, the newly created DRI sent a Captain Kelly to Armagh in order to ask Logue to neutralise all hostility from his priests towards the Army. This indicated that the authorities recognised the influence of the Catholic Church in this matter. Kelly suggested that the Cardinal should circulate a letter to those fractious priests, asking them to pray for the men serving at the front. Logue simply replied that Kelly had to put his request in writing and that he would think about it. The Captain informed Nathan that he doubted very much that the Cardinal would cooperate. The Under Secretary advised him not to go any further.[28] A last attempt to acquire Logue's help was made in April 1916, shortly before the Easter Rising. Once more, Kelly was involved and had sent a circular letter to all the Catholic bishops, asking for their permission to organise recruitment meetings near their churches. Not all prelates replied but Kelly received favourable answers from all except Logue and one or two others. Unfortunately, the Captain did not give their names.[29]

It was clear that the Cardinal supported the British Empire and her Allies but because of the national question he refused to give any substantial help. His policy was logical and dated back to Edward VII's coronation ceremony. The various recruitment bodies had not paid heed to his warnings and, consequently, had to work without an important ally who would definitely have cooperated with them. It must also be said, however, that Logue was on his own within the hierarchy. He never tried to unite the bishops and elaborate a common policy towards recruitment and other aspects of the war effort in Ireland, or towards the British Government. He lacked the charisma of Edward O'Dwyer and the organisational abilities of William Walsh. Logue was shrewd and stubborn but did not have the intelligence of some of his colleagues.[30] In April 1915, Mgr Curran, Walsh's secretary, wrote to Mgr Hagan in Rome stating that the Archbishop of Dublin was exasperated with the poor work of the Standing Committee of the Irish hierarchy, chaired by Logue. Walsh had spoken of 'waste of time, disorder and ill advised [action]' and had been 'worn out listening to the Cardinal endeavouring to make himself heard in order to regale the Committee with a grievance he had against Moyne Park from which four of his fourteen nuns were expelled without reference to him'.[31] One may wonder, then, whether Logue would have proved either an efficient ally for the CCORI and DRI, or capable of neutralising Walsh and O'Dwyer's anti-war activities. Perhaps the two organisations somewhat naively believed that his title of highest Catholic dignitary in Ireland would have been sufficient to incite men to join up in large numbers. Yet, it cannot be said that Logue was a poor analyst either, because his judgement about recruitment and Irish nationalist discontent since 1901, had proved to be remarkably accurate. Despite his imperial tendencies, he had been forced to adopt a very nationalist attitude towards the war in Europe because of poor British policy in Ireland. He was neither republican, nor Sinn Féiner, nor even Nationalist party supporter since he disagreed with John Redmond's pro-war inclinations. In fact, Michael Logue had become an independent nationalist.

ARCHBISHOP WALSH'S DEAFENING POLITICAL SILENCE

Before becoming Archbishop of Dublin, Walsh had been Professor of Moral Theology and later president of Maynooth Seminary. He was noted for his intellectual brilliance and his analytical faculties. As a teacher he did not seem to have much patience for weak pupils and perhaps this indicates a slightly arrogant side to his character. Walsh had a gift for languages and was particularly good at German, which he spoke fluently. He regularly went on vacation to Germany where he enjoyed Wagner's operas at Bayreuth.[32] He was consecrated archbishop in 1885 despite British diplomatic initiatives in the Vatican to prevent his consecration. The British Government believed that he was 'a dangerous and violent man'.[33] This analysis was exaggerated but it was true that Walsh had strong views on Home Rule and he fully backed the Nationalist party's endeavours to obtain autonomy. His statements on current affairs were regularly published by the press. In 1886 William Gladstone thought that Walsh was the voice of the hierarchy and it was clear that he was the main 'politician' in the hierarchy.[34] When, in 1887, Michael Logue became Primate of All Ireland, there was a feeling that Walsh should have had the red hat, but because of his outspoken views on the national question he had compromised his chances. It was thought that Logue would counterbalance Walsh's political weight within the hierarchy for he was more moderate in his views on Home Rule.[35]

At the turn of the century, however, Walsh became disillusioned with the Nationalist party and its new leader, John Redmond. He denounced the party's reliance on the British Liberals to grant Home Rule to the entire island and was of the opinion that this alliance would bring about secularisation in the educational system in Ireland.[36] In 1905, the Archbishop decided to break all links with the party. In 1912, Redmond, aware that he had lost an important ally and on the brink of obtaining Home Rule, tried to involve Walsh again but the Archbishop would have none of it and wrote to the Nationalist leader: 'As to the matter about which you have written, I can only say that it is now some years since I made up my mind to have nothing more to do with Irish politics and that nothing in the world could now induce me to change my mind in the matter.'[37] Fr Patrick Walsh, one of his secretaries, confirmed that he no longer wished to take an active interest in Irish politics but that privately he still followed the Home Rule crisis.[38] As this crisis dragged on and opposition in Ulster to Home Rule became more and more forceful and well organised, Walsh, apparently, was losing all faith in the Irish Parliamentary Party but was not convinced either by the creation, in 1913, of the Irish Volunteers. The main reason for this was the personality of their chief, Prof. Eoin MacNeill, whom he knew well. Mgr Curran wrote about the Archbishop that he 'had no belief in Eoin MacNeill as a political and much less as a revolutionary leader'.[39] Furthermore, Walsh had always feared that the Irish Volunteers might be controlled in the long term by extremists and use violence in their fight for Home Rule. In this, he was not mistaken.

In the daily administration of his diocese, the Archbishop was supported by Mgr Michael Curran and the two men often spoke about politics. Curran was a strong nationalist who feared that socialists like James Connolly and Jim Larkin might jeopardise Ireland's struggle for Home Rule. During the Dublin Lockout of 1913, he sided with the employers.[40] He had a regular correspondence with the republican-minded Mgr Hagan, vice-rector of the Irish College in Rome. In 1920, when Curran was himself appointed vice-rector of the same College, he became involved in an arms-traffic in favour of Irish republicans in the War of Independence.[41] It seemed that the secretary had a taste for cloak-and-dagger work. He was also a close friend of Seán T. O'Kelly who was a member of the Irish Volunteers and who would later become

President of Ireland. In his memoirs, Curran stated about Walsh: 'recognising that I took a keen interest in public affairs and that my nationalist views largely corresponded with his own, we frequently discussed the political events of his own earlier career as well as those of the time'.[42] One might ask to what extent Walsh was influenced, or allowed himself to be influenced, by Curran. Whatever the case, in 1905, the year he broke all links with the Nationalist party, Walsh began to take an interest in Arthur Griffith's newspapers which he and Curran analysed. It was certainly an indication that Walsh was beginning to think of a nationalist alternative to Redmond's party, although he did not express this publicly. Had he done so, he would have broken his vow of silence regarding Irish political affairs and put himself in opposition to most of the Irish bishops. But it was the Archbishop's nature to be extremely cautious and prudent before taking any significant decision. Subsequent events would prove this to be the case. In August 1914, when the war broke out and Redmond promised Britain Ireland's support, Walsh was disgusted and believed that the Nationalist party was no longer serving Ireland but their masters, the English Liberals. On 25 September 1914, he deplored the fact that John Redmond, John Dillon and Joseph Devlin, together with Herbert Asquith, had all participated in a recruitment meeting at Mansion House in Dublin. Early recruitment figures showed that Ireland was in the grip of war fever and that Redmond was in the driver's seat. How could Walsh help his 'own' nationalist Ireland without being in the limelight? He decided to act off his own bat and to hinder all recruitment campaigns within his diocese. In his work against the war effort, he received invaluable help from Mgr Curran.

William Walsh had never seen the Army in a favourable light. As has been seen, well before the outbreak of the hostilities in Europe, in 1901, he had openly expressed his disapproval of soldiers roaming in night-time Dublin. He feared that the presence of soldiers would lead his city to depravity. In February 1914, the Archbishop refused to bless the flag of the military cadets.[43] Yet, despite Walsh's well-known anti-militarism, the recruitment organisations would regularly appeal to him for help. The reason for their apparent inconsistency was logical. In their eyes, Walsh was the most important member of the hierarchy, for he was at the head of the diocese that had the largest number of Catholics in the country and also was the most industrialised one, excluding Ulster. It was among the working classes and the most underprivileged sections of the urban population that recruits would be forthcoming. Walsh was too clever a politician not to know that the recruiting sergeants would focus their attention on him and try to enlist his collaboration. The Archbishop, therefore, tended to adopt a policy of systematic refusal no matter what was asked of him. The first to approach him was Lord

Aberdeen, the Lord Lieutenant of Ireland. In October 1914, Aberdeen organised a charity meeting meant to improve the material conditions of soldiers at the front and wondered whether Walsh would kindly participate. Walsh simply and curtly replied: 'For reasons with which it is not necessary for me to trouble Your Excellency, it will not be possible for me to be present at the meeting.'[44] Shortly afterwards, Walsh received a letter from Wilfrid Ward, representing the Government, in which he asked him to sign a petition stating that the United Kingdom had been forced to declare war on Germany in order to protect Belgium's neutrality. Ward added that it had already been signed by several English Bishops and Cardinal Bourne, Primate of the English Catholic Church, and that John Healy, the Archbishop of Tuam, was about to sign it. According to Ward, 'it would add very much to the weight of the document to have among our signatories some Irish Bishops and especially Your Grace'.[45] Walsh refused to sign it and said that he was not sure of England's sincerity.[46] Contrary to the majority of the Irish prelates, Walsh had not been submerged by this wave of popular nationalism in favour of Britain although Curran described him as being 'mildly anti-German'.[47] This tends to suggest that Walsh might not have had much sympathy for great powers in general and for authoritarian regimes like Kaiser Wilhelm II's in particular, but that he had not forgotten his interest in all things German either, hence his 'mildness'.

In March 1915, the Redmondite recruitment authorities displayed considerable and disconcerting naivety. Colonel Maurice Moore, in charge of training the pro-Redmond National Volunteers, asked Walsh to organise an open-air mass in Phoenix Park in Dublin for his Volunteers! The Archbishop replied immediately:

> I fear I have to say to you that the project of a mass in the Phoenix Park on Easter Sunday is hopeless. There are many difficulties in the way. But the real source of all the difficulty in the case is the extraordinary way in which a project such as that organised, if I can call it organised by your Committee, involving complicated religious arrangements in our churches, either throughout the city or elsewhere in its neighbourhood was sprung upon the diocesan administration without even a formal notice to me or to any diocesan authority as to what was in contemplation.
>
> (DDA, Walsh papers, 387 I, Walsh to Moore,
> 14 March 1915)

Walsh had realised how badly organised the recruitment authorities were and used this as an argument to refuse Moore's request. In this way, Walsh's refusal was based on 'technical' grounds and did not appear to be politically motivated. Even if Moore's approach had been subtler, the Archbishop would have found another pretext. Some time later, Fr

Mooney, the chaplain at Beggar's Bush barracks, received a very dry letter from a Lieutenant Colonel Owens who wrote that he intended to organise a military parade followed by a religious ceremony on Easter Sunday in the Pro-Cathedral. The press also announced this, four days before the ceremony was due to take place. Fr Bowden, the administrator of the cathedral, warned Walsh and Curran about this. Walsh wrote a letter that Mooney had to sign and send to Owens. It stated: 'The matter has been brought to the notice of His Grace, the Archbishop, who directs me to express his surprise that the military authorities, without having even applied for permission to make use of that church, announce their "intention" of holding a Parade Service there, and I am obliged to add that no such service can be held.'[48] On this occasion too, Walsh seemed to indicate that it was not feasible because of technicalities. In April 1915, 25,000 National Volunteers paraded in front of John Redmond and Colonel Moore but the paramilitary force never made it to mass. To Walsh it was obvious that the methods of the military and recruitment authorities were completely chaotic and amateurish. The CCORI had to wait for a better opportunity. German warfare provided a good incentive when a U-Boat sunk the liner *Lusitania* off Cork. The Irish public was shocked because it brought the war, for a brief moment, very close to home. Walsh publicly condemned the torpedoing and spoke about a 'horrible massacre'. The new council jumped at the opportunity. They wanted to know whether the Archbishop of Dublin would at long last condemn Germany and incite Irishmen to join the colours. On 12 May 1915, the CCORI informed Walsh on behalf of General Friend, the Commander-in-Chief of the British forces in Ireland, that it had taken the liberty of using his words for a recruitment poster and asked Walsh's approval. The poster read:

> His Grace the Most Rev. W. Walsh Archbishop of Dublin and the [*sic*] sinking of the Lusitania described it as 'That Horrible Massacre'. Germany says she will do it again! Will you do your part to prevent her of so [*sic*] – join an Irish Regiment.
> (ICR, Hagan papers, 1915, letter no. 72,
> Curran to Hagan, 17 May 1915)

Walsh at once severely condemned the council's initiative and replied drily:

> I have received your letter informing me that your Council 'has taken the liberty of producing, and proposes to distribute, a poster' containing some words spoken by me last Sunday. In reply I have only to say that, in my opinion, your Council, in producing the poster, a copy of which you have forwarded to me, has taken a very great liberty indeed, and that I reserve the right of taking

such action as I deem fit if I find the poster 'distributed' in the manner which seems to be contemplated.

(DDA, Walsh papers, 387 I, Walsh to CCORI, 12 May 1915)

Mgr Curran wrote sarcastically to Mgr Hagan that 'our recruiting geniuses in Dublin got a bad slap in the face from His Grace'.[49] Curran was right since it was the CCORI's first and last attempt to enlist Walsh's help. Recruitment had reached a dead end in the country.

Walsh seemed to be on the offensive against the war effort in May 1915. On 20 May, he ordered Curran to write to Abbot Marmion, an Irish Benedictine monk, to warn him that he would not invite Mgr de Wachter, Cardinal Mercier's coadjutor, to his residence. He thought that his invitation could be used by the recruitment authorities. Furthermore, according to Curran, Walsh did not hold most of the Belgian refugees in high esteem 'and regarded them as the least deserving of support'. Curran himself agreed with the Archbishop and wrote in his diary that these Belgians were, 'in most cases, worthless and worse than worthless'.[50] Walsh was not guilty of a lack of Christian charity, for his actions in favour of the poor and the underprivileged are well-known and documented. It was more a temperamental reaction to the fact that the Belgian refugee theme was used for propaganda activities. Back in January 1915, Walsh and Logue had refused to write an introduction for Cardinal Mercier's Lenten pastoral entitled 'Patriotism and Endurance'. The pastoral had been translated into English and 500,000 copies were to be distributed throughout the United Kingdom.[51] On 17 May 1915, Denis Gwynn, who worked for the British Ministry of Information, asked Walsh to become a subscriber to his new nationalist newspaper called *New-Ireland*. On 25 May, the Archbishop, true to form, turned the offer down by saying: 'I regret that, as one result of a radical change that has gradually been effected in Irish political affairs through the establishment of a working alliance between the "leaders" of the Irish Parliamentary Party and the late Government, I have now, for a considerable time, found it impossible to take any further interest in Irish politics.'[52] This apparently quite innocuous correspondence sheds light on the Archbishop's nationalist frame of mind. Walsh clearly stated that he had repudiated the leaders of the Nationalist party. Mgr Curran believed that his reply to Gwynn was in fact meant for his father, Stephen Gwynn, who was a member of the party, captain in the British Army and greatly in favour of recruitment. Undoubtedly, John Redmond was made aware of this letter. Moreover, Walsh's strong statement was well calculated and premeditated. Indeed, on the very same day, 25 May 1915, Herbert Asquith announced his new coalition cabinet including Sir Edward

Carson. Although Redmond refused to become a member, he still supported Britain in her war effort. To Walsh, this was only the confirmation of the party's servility and lack of independence towards the English Liberals and the Government. At the beginning of 1915, he had told Timothy Healy, one of Redmond's enemies in the party, that he feared the formation of such a cabinet and Healy had noted that 'he [was] evidently no swallower of Redmondite promises'.[53] But Walsh's disgust and anger must have intensified when it became known, a few days later, that James Campbell, an intransigent Unionist, would also become a member of the new coalition cabinet. In 1912, Walsh had had a serious argument with him concerning the interpretation of a papal bull entitled *Quantavis diligentia*. Campbell's attacks on Walsh had often been sarcastic.[54] Herbert Asquith's latest political move did much to exacerbate Walsh's nationalism and, as a result, he persevered in his efforts to hinder as much as possible all recruitment campaigns in Dublin. Walsh, like Logue, had become an independent nationalist.

The new Lord Lieutenant of Ireland, Lord Wimborne, head of the recently created Department of Recruiting in Ireland (DRI), had run out of ideas. In August 1915, he invited Walsh to his residence in order to discuss the recruiting crisis and ask the Archbishop's advice. Walsh, of course, refused the invitation.[55] The British persisted in their efforts to ensure the help of members of the Catholic hierarchy despite recent political developments and the declarations or actions of prelates like Logue, O'Dwyer, Fogarty and Walsh. In this light, Wimborne's approach seems very naive to say the least. It would be too simple, however, to attribute everything to the lack of organisation and naivety of the recruitment authorities. After all, bishops such as McHugh, Healy, O'Donnell, Harty, Kelly and Gaughran were still in favour of the war effort in Ireland, which gave the CCORI and later the DRI a glimmer of hope. But Walsh was far more important than these other bishops because he administered a diocese, which numbered the most Catholics, 434,586 men and women.[56] Moreover, underprivileged inhabitants in Dublin would be more inclined to join the Army in Dublin than anywhere in the country, especially in rural areas. One can therefore assume that Walsh's influence on the population was perceived by the DRI and Wimborne as determining and crucial, and that their recent appeal for Walsh's advice was in fact a desperate one. Recruitment was in the doldrums for the Irish had lost nearly all interest in the war in Europe. Fr P.J. Walsh wrote to Mgr Hagan: 'I will say nothing about the war…We are sick and tired of it here and likely to be still sicker.'[57] By December 1915, P.J. Walsh's statement was certainly not an exaggeration.

The DRI, however, did not give up all hope and tried a new approach. In April 1916, Captain Kelly was once again involved in a slightly subtler approach in that Walsh was not asked directly to participate in a recruitment campaign. Kelly instead asked Walsh whether he would object to any recruitment meeting held near churches in his diocese. Wimborne was convinced that this would stimulate voluntary enlistment. Undeniably there was a practical side to this idea as recruiting sergeants would be very close to places frequented by the crowds attending mass. Walsh's reply was very 'technical' as he invoked administrative rules to refuse Wimborne's request. He replied that the National Synod at Maynooth in 1900 had considered such questions and taken the decision that the churches and their grounds should only be used for religious purposes and that collections and other activities would be allowed only in so far as they did not 'in any way obstruct the freedom of access' of the faithful. He ended his letter with an indirect warning: 'I do not consider that the clergy would have any right to object to [your plan] except in so far as it might interfere with reasonable access to the Church.'[58] The Archbishop did not use personal or political motives to justify his refusal, which would have put an end to his political silence. But it was fairly clear that he continued to operate as a *franc-tireur* against all recruiting sergeants. It was not the first time that this specific issue of recruiting meetings being held near churches had been raised. In November 1914 when recruitment was still at its peak, *Eire Ireland*, a nationalist opposition newspaper, had denounced the British Army's initiative to hand out pamphlets at the entrances of churches. According to the newspaper, people were hindered or prevented from going to mass.[59] On 15 April 1916, Kelly informed Walsh that Wimborne thought the whole matter was a misunderstanding.[60] The Lord Lieutenant had no desire to provoke Walsh into publicly denouncing recruitment activities such as Logue and O'Dwyer had done recently in a most devastating way.

From August 1914 until April 1916, Walsh had shrewdly thwarted all the CCORI and DRI's efforts without breaking his political silence. Nevertheless, he had not encouraged more extreme nationalists and republicans either. In fact, in his Lenten pastorals of February 1915 and March 1916, he reminded his flock that the Church had condemned all membership in secret societies, in other words the Irish Republican Brotherhood (IRB) whose aim was to establish a separatist Irish republic by using physical force if necessary. In 1915, he wrote that successive popes had denounced these societies in the interest of law, order and religion, and that helping or belonging to them could lead to excommunication.[61] Walsh feared that a rebellion due to nationalist discontent with British policy was on the cards. His fear that the Irish Volunteers would challenge the British Army suddenly became very real in the early days of April 1916. While sapping the war effort in Dublin, Walsh also adopted Pope Benedict XV's peace efforts. He was convinced of the Roman Pontiff's infallibility.[62] In August 1915, he had written a circular letter to all the churches in his diocese, asking Catholics to pray for the restoration of peace.[63] By April 1916, Wimborne and the DRI knew they had lost the battle for the archdiocese of Dublin. Walsh had been very consistent in dealing with the war. Nationalist Ireland had been badly treated by the British Government and was not well represented by her parliamentary politicians; in return, it was totally out of the question that he would help Redmond and the recruiting sergeants. It was, after all, the continuation of the political silence that he had adopted since 1905 and even a world war would not change his mind.

BISHOP O'DWYER'S ANTI-WAR CRUSADE

Edward O'Dwyer was consecrated Bishop of Limerick in 1886 and quickly acquired notoriety for his devastating attacks on Irish public life. He often acted alone and attached great importance to his independence. His only friend among the prelates was Bishop Fogarty of Killaloe, a diocese next to his own. Although he was never a member of any political organisation, he had supported Isaac Butt, the founder of the Irish Parliamentary Party, in the 1870s and was convinced that Home Rule would bring prosperity to Ireland. O'Dwyer sided with Butt in the first Home Rule campaign during the general election of 1871. On that particular occasion, he was the only priest present on the platform.[64] When he became a bishop he did much for the neglected working class of Limerick. His relations with the Nationalist party, however, were to be quite tumultuous since he did not agree with the Plan of Campaign in 1886. The Plan sought to enforce a decrease in rent that farmers paid to landlords; if the latter refused, farmers would pay no rent at all. John Dillon, one of the strategists behind the Plan, spoke in strong terms on how to obtain this decrease and some farmers were physically intimidated in order to encourage their participation in the Plan.[65] Unlike the majority of the bishops and the priests, who were often involved in organising the Plan locally, O'Dwyer was convinced this was morally wrong and, furthermore, was on friendly terms with Lord Emly, Sir Stephen de Vere and the Earl of Dunraven. All had the reputation of being good or improving landlords and were converts to Catholicism.[66] O'Dwyer described boycotting and intimidation, the main tactics of the Plan, as 'hell' and spoke publicly against it. Soon, he became embroiled in a bitter controversy with Dillon. The press published extracts of their speeches and their letters. Dillon wrote that the Bishop '[represented] a small minority of the Roman Catholic Church in Ireland who are on the side of the oppressor against the oppressed'. The two men met on one occasion and the Bishop told the politician that the Plan was nothing less than 'highway robbery and plunder'.[67] The *Roscommon Herald* thought O'Dwyer was 'an Episcopal Swashbuckler'. The *Freeman's Journal* believed that O'Dwyer was unfair to Dillon. Others thought that the Bishop was a 'shaky kind of patriot'.[68]

Within the hierarchy, O'Dwyer became isolated and acquired the reputation of being a maverick. In a letter to Archbishop Walsh, who was much in favour of the Plan, he warned of 'the spirit of general resistance to Civil Authority which has been growing in Ireland and if encouraged will produce the same results to religion that the revolution has produced in every country in which it has triumphed'.[69] The two men were at loggerheads with one another on the issue and became rivals. O'Dwyer's position was soon vindicated as Pope Leo XIII condemned the Plan of Campaign. Logue and Walsh were utterly amazed by this decision. In fact, nationalist Ireland had been the victim of diplomacy between Britain and the Vatican. The British Government had promised its help against the Italian State concerning certain papal domains and property if, in return, the Holy See would help Britain in her Irish policy.[70] The Pope's decision did much to strengthen O'Dwyer's ultramontane tendencies. He became an absolute ruler in his diocese and forbade his priests to absolve anybody who was involved in the Plan. The Pope was hated in Ireland. In 1888, Archbishop Croke of Cashel wrote to Mgr Tobias Kirby in Rome: 'The Pope is cursed in every mood and tense from Donegal to Baltimore; and wherever his picture was found in private houses it has either been displaced simply, or torn to bits.'[71] John Dillon and John Redmond denounced Leo XIII's intervention. In Wexford, Redmond said: 'If Home Rule were to mean Rome Rule, I for one would not be a Home Ruler.'[72] The Irish hierarchy found itself in a very critical position and widespread anti-clericalism was a genuine threat. O'Dwyer obtained the reputation of being a 'Castle Bishop', a bishop working for the authorities, or a 'Landlord Bishop'. Soon afterwards, he refused to condemn Charles Stewart Parnell, who had been against the Plan and who was then involved in the divorce case which ended his political career. The Bishop feared Dillon taking over the leadership of the Nationalist party as he was an 'immediate danger to the faith and religious spirit of the people, and their loyalty to Rome'.[73]

Before the outbreak of the First World War, O'Dwyer was mainly concerned with education. Up to that point, he had always been suspicious of the Nationalist party's alliance with the English Liberals in the House of Commons in London. He suspected that the Liberal party was trying to suppress religion in schools and that this would eventually pave the way for secularisation in Ireland if Home Rule was put into operation. When John Redmond, and not John Dillon, was appointed leader of the party in 1900, O'Dwyer was reassured since Redmond had been campaigning for the creation of a Catholic university. The Bishop's opinion of the party fluctuated according to political events, for he questioned Redmond's wisdom in trusting the Liberal party and their promises on Home Rule. A few months before the war, however, the Bishop of Limerick began to seriously doubt the Government's sincerity towards nationalist Ireland even though Home Rule was to become effective that same year. On 6 March 1914, he wrote to Mgr O'Riordan in Rome that he was waiting to read Herbert Asquith's proposals regarding autonomy. His concern was the possible partition of the country: 'There is the [illegible], immediate exclusion, with right [of the six northern counties] to come in afterwards. The Unionists might agree to this; and possibly the Irish Party.'[74] The Bishop was right. He was, of course, well aware of the Unionists and Conservatives' opinions on Home Rule and had felt that the Liberals could no longer be trusted on partition when in 1912 in the House of Commons T.C.R. Agar-Robartes had put forward a proposal to exclude counties Down, Antrim, Armagh and Derry and had declared: 'I have never heard that orange bitters will mix with Irish whiskey.'[75] Publicly, he did not comment on partition but closely followed the debates and, on 21 May 1914, he sent another letter on the issue to O'Riordan:

> We are still in great uncertainty as to the measure of Home Rule that we are to get, but it seems to me that the greater part of Ulster falls out, in as long as it wishes to stay out, that we shall have two Irelands and the government and the Irish Party are simply turning down opinion in the country [illegible]. How Cardinal Logue and the Catholics will like their new nationality is another thing.
>
> (ICR, O'Riordan papers no. 15, letter no. 123,
> O'Dwyer to O'Riordan, 21 May 1914)

Clearly, O'Dwyer had lost some faith in the Nationalist party's ability to find a solution to partition, to which O'Dwyer was opposed. He also held the view that Redmond was no longer taking into account public opinion about the crisis, and predicted that the northern Catholics and their bishops would strongly oppose it. His words were prophetic. If he did not air his views on Redmond's leadership, perhaps he was waiting for a more opportune moment. His confrontation with Dillon during the Plan of Campaign days would tend to indicate that it was only a matter of time before he would do so.

In August 1914, the world was at war. As has been seen, the majority of Irish bishops did not heed Pope Pius X's peace appeal and indulged in warlike speeches. Two of them, Fogarty and O'Dwyer, did not remain indifferent to this appeal. The Bishop of Limerick's reaction was slow in coming for he had become a master in timely interventions.[76] He understood how Home Rule was postponed and how Redmond encouraged Irishmen to join the Army. The war fever in Ireland had set in and he must have been bitterly disappointed and intrigued by the behaviour of the people. On 28 October, Turkey declared war on Russia and on 5 November, France and the United Kingdom declared war on Turkey. Only a few days before, the new Pope, Benedict XV, observed in his encyclical *Ad Beatissimi* that the belligerents had to work for peace. It was there that O'Dwyer decided to intervene publicly. At the annual meeting of the county nurses, he denounced the war and spoke of a 'wild fury'. But his speech was really an indirect warning to John Redmond and his pro-war policy. Although the Bishop did not name the Nationalist leader, it was clear that he included him when he denounced the diehard attitude of rulers: 'People talk lightly of the war going on for years; some public men speak of carrying it on until their enemies are beaten to their knees.'[77] This was, according to him, contrary to the Christian religion. Not once did he mention Germany's responsibility or the just cause of the Triple Entente, unlike Bishops McHugh and O'Donnell. Still, in November 1914, Bishop Fogarty wrote an interesting letter to Hagan in Rome, summing up the political situation in the country:

The Irish papers are much a mass of English garbage. As to the people of Ireland, they, as far as I can see, are as a body for England to win, not I believe for love of England but they are doing well now and don't want to be disturbed by Germans or anyone else. But the recruiting is unpopular and factors for it are 1) because there is no one there to be spared for recruiting; 2) they don't want to die in the present cause.

(ICR, Hagan papers 1914, 1–202, Fogarty to Hagan, 27 November 1914)

Fogarty must have been referring to recruitment in rural areas where his own diocese was. In November 1914, voluntary enlistment was doing well but mostly in urban areas. The people in the countryside were becoming more prosperous so that materialism and financial prosperity engendered by the war had replaced political interest and ideals. Farmers had plenty of work and no time for the Army. Fogarty went on to write that he did not wish Germany and Austria-Hungary's defeat and dismemberment for they were, in his opinion, the bulwark against aggressive Russian-Orthodox expansionism. At the same time, though he had no real reason to like Britain, he did not wish its defeat either despite the fact that it was allied to Russia. In December 1914, O'Dwyer, like Logue and Walsh, refused to sign an anti-German petition, which came as no surprise in view of his recent comments in

Limerick on the war. Benedict XV's encyclical was a source of inspiration for O'Dwyer's Lenten pastoral of February 1915. Like the Pope, he denounced the war in general without blaming any country in particular. The reason for the present war was militarism and the consequent arms race. Alluding to the assassination in Sarajevo which led to the hostilities, he remarked: 'The horrible crime which was the immediate occasion of the outbreak, was merely the spark that fired the magazine, but the explosives had been accumulating for years.' As to the merits of international diplomacy, the Bishop wrote that 'there was nothing formally in the dispute that any reasonable men could not settle in an hour but what no one could settle was the latent distrust of one another on the part of the Governments and the determination on all sides, sooner or later, as the opportunity offered, to crush their opponents'.[78] Redmond and his colleagues did not pay any attention to O'Dwyer's fulminations. On 7 March 1915 in Ulster, the northern Nationalist leader, Joseph Devlin, harangued a crowd during a recruitment meeting and said: 'We have young men of strength, of courage, of brains who would not...play a man's part in the freedom of the fatherland.'[79] Devlin tried to instil a sense of shame in Irishmen by comparing them to very brave young Englishmen who had left their comfortable and sometimes even luxurious homes to fight for the freedom of their nation. In April 1915, T.P. O'Connor told an American journalist that John Redmond hoped 'we would have no talk of peace as long as there was a single German soldier left on the soil of Belgium, France or Alsace-Lorraine'.[80] It was this kind of diehard pro-war attitude that Edward O'Dwyer would attempt to contain.

In the meantime, O'Dwyer's Lenten pastoral had struck a chord in Rome and was to have very important consequences on nationalist Ireland's relations with the Vatican. The Bishop sent a copy to Mgr O'Riordan in Rome. The rector of the Irish College was impressed by O'Dwyer's eloquence and forceful writing, and also noticed that his ideas were the same as the Pope's. O'Riordan decided to translate the pastoral into Italian and gave a copy to Benedict XV, with whom he had regular audiences, and to several Italian cardinals. In a letter to the Bishop, the rector explained that he thought Benedict XV would approve of it for it was a neutral pastoral, denouncing the war in general.[81] On 8 April 1915, O'Riordan informed O'Dwyer that the Pope and the cardinals of the Curia had expressed their great satisfaction and he included an extract of Archbishop Sbaretti's letter, praising O'Dwyer for 'his excellent pastoral...which could be read with benefit and enlightenment in all the countries, neutral and belligerent'.[82] Why did the Bishop of Limerick's letter strike such a chord in Italy? The answer to this question lies in the international situation. Italy was not yet at war but was secretly negotiating with Britain. The Vatican, not yet a fully independent state, was doing everything it could to keep Italy out of the conflict. The Roman Curia feared that the Vatican would be isolated once Italy joined the Triple Entente. Consequently, O'Dwyer's letter was also a very useful tool for anti-war propaganda in Italy because it emanated from a belligerent country. On 6 June 1915, two weeks after Italy had entered the war, O'Riordan wrote to O'Dwyer that his pastoral was a sensation and that he had sent four more copies to Cardinal De Lai. The Archbishop of Florence wanted to congratulate O'Dwyer whereas the Cardinal of Naples was using it in his seminary.[83] It was the beginning of the Bishop of Limerick's increasing popularity in Italy and at the Vatican, and it did much to strengthen O'Dwyer's resolve against militarism.

The first severe blow to John Redmond and his party came, however, from the Bishop of Killaloe, and it was the more significant because Fogarty had been an enthusiastic Nationalist party supporter. In fact, he had done much to bring the Irish Volunteers in Co. Clare under Redmond's control in 1914.[84] Fogarty realised that the war was getting more inhumane every day and, whatever one's political opinions were, one could no longer morally support it. But what really upset Fogarty was Herbert Asquith's new coalition cabinet. The fact that Carson and Campbell were members meant that the English Liberals recognised the political weight of the Unionist party and that there was every chance that Ulster would be excluded from Home Rule. Fogarty no longer trusted Redmond's political judgement and sent him a very angry letter on 3 June 1915. He called the new cabinet 'a horrible scandal and intolerable outrage on Irish sentiment'. According to him, the Liberal Government had only demonstrated hypocrisy towards Irish nationalist aspirations: 'The English having got all they wanted from Ireland, don't care two pence about her feelings. Such is our reward for her profuse loyalism and recruiting... The [Nationalist] Party, to my mind a great mistake, have taken the whole thing lying down, without a bit of fight.' Fogarty concluded with some very bitter remarks about Ireland's participation in the war: 'And it almost makes me cry to think of the Irish Brigade fighting, not for Ireland, but for Carson and what he stands for, Orange ascendancy here. Home Rule is dead and buried and Ireland is without a national Party or a national Press.'[85] The Bishop had broken all links with Redmond and, for the time being, found himself in a political vacuum since he had no alternative to the Nationalist party. Redmond reacted immediately and sent Fogarty's letter to Asquith, saying that the prelate had always been a staunch supporter of his party, but that he now represented a new spirit of discontent in the country.[86] The leader wanted to give the Prime Minister a clear indication of what was happening in Ireland. Despite all the bad news, Redmond continued to support the Government. It was true that he was in a most difficult position. He still believed that Ireland's support for the British Empire would be beneficial in the long run. But, above all, it seems that he did not wish to take into account the admonitions of a Catholic bishop regarding the war and Home Rule lest Unionists and Protestants interpret this as a clear indication that the Catholic Church would play a vital part in running an autonomous Ireland. Unfortunately for the Nationalist leader, the opportune moment O'Dwyer had been waiting for arrived a few weeks later.

The Pope appealed for peace on 28 July 1915, just one year after the onset of the hostilities. Only a few days before, John Redmond had written to Dublin Corporation that although the war was, at present, the most important thing nothing could prevent Home Rule from becoming law. He asked the people to trust the Nationalist party and claimed that they were on the threshold of autonomy. Redmond had felt that his followers were no longer so sanguine about the war and that the War Office's inept handling of recruitment in Ireland was taking its toll on voluntary enlistment. The new coalition cabinet, moreover, did not improve relations between nationalist Ireland and Britain. Redmond had to assure public opinion that his policy was the right choice and that was why he asked Ireland 'to do everything in her power to support the cause of the Allies'.[87] Benedict XV's appeal was quite different. His message, *Allorchè fummo*, emphasised that the war was completely futile and that the belligerents had to cease fighting immediately and work for peace. This was the duty of Christians. In Ireland, however, radical nationalists were growing more impatient and restless. To them, the war was delaying Home Rule and the coalition cabinet presaged an inevitable partition of the country. On 29 July 1915, Douglas Hyde, President of the Gaelic League, resigned, feeling that the organisation was becoming more and more politicised under Patrick Pearse's influence. On 1 August, the same Pearse made his funeral oration in honour of Jeremiah O'Donovan Rossa, the old Fenian revolutionary, in which he defied the authorities and declared that 'Ireland unfree shall never be at peace'.[88] In this light, Redmond's letter to Dublin Corporation became even more understandable, from his point of view at least. It was at that moment that Bishop O'Dwyer decided to intervene publicly. He wrote a long letter to Redmond, which was a model of eloquence and Machiavellian ingenuity. O'Dwyer was well aware that the Nationalist leader was in a tight corner and that the country had lost nearly all interest in the war. Therefore, he must have known in advance that his letter in favour of the Pope's latest peace initiative was going to have a sensational effect and that republican and nationalist opposition movements would take it over for their own benefit. Perhaps O'Dwyer wished to control this new nationalist élan before it degenerated into violence. Archbishop Walsh feared the same thing. O'Dwyer left no chance to Redmond. He had already warned him indirectly on a couple of occasions and was too shrewd a politician himself not to know that he would put Redmond in an awkward and difficult situation. The Bishop begged him to listen to the Pope's appeal and throw the 'weight of [his] influence strongly on the side of peace'. O'Dwyer wrote that he failed to understand why political leaders carried on with this senseless war while the Pope simply asked them to stop fighting and go to the negotiation table. He also denounced the diehard attitude of some politicians, willing to keep on fighting until Germany was thoroughly routed. Clearly it would have been difficult for Redmond not to identify with those politicians. O'Dwyer then tried to create serious doubts in Redmond's and the people's minds by remarking: 'But is there a competent man in England this moment who is confident of being able to crush Germany?' The Bishop of Limerick ended his long letter with a direct appeal to Redmond:

> The prolongation of this war for one hour beyond what is absolutely necessary, is a crime against God, and humanity... Therefore we may hope that you will use your influence to get a fair hearing for the noble and Christlike proposal of the Pope... Whatever they may say or do in England, we Irish Catholics have no excuse for disregarding the appeal of our Holy Father. ... Before this disastrous war, by your wise and upright statesmanship, you deserved well of your country, and brought her to the threshold of Home Rule. It may be in God's Providence, that you, a Catholic Irishman, are destined to render her, and the whole world, a still greater service, by leading the English government to take the first step, at the word of the Pope, towards the re-establishment of peace on earth.
>
> (LDO, O'Dwyer papers, file H, O'Dwyer to Redmond, 4 August 1915)

O'Dwyer implied that Redmond would naturally accept his and the Pope's appeal as the Nationalist leader was a good Irish Catholic, which would only further dramatise Redmond's future refusal. O'Dwyer's intervention would make the leader's position very precarious. Indeed, on the one hand, if Redmond listened to O'Dwyer, he risked breaking his alliance with Herbert Asquith and forcing the Prime Minister to lean more on the Unionists. He also must have been aware that if he followed O'Dwyer and Benedict XV on this path, he would make clear that the Catholic Church had incontestably great power in the country and that Home Rule meant Rome rule. Not only would he have accentuated the existing divisions with the Protestants, but also within his own party as John Dillon resented the Church's interference in politics and had had several clashes with O'Dwyer before the war. On the other hand, if he refused, he knew that he would probably lose some of his grip on public opinion and on some nationalist opposition movements. O'Dwyer, as has been seen, had also included a paragraph on the future economic catastrophe that was to follow in Ireland if the war continued. Financial issues were always likely to impress the population. Undoubtedly O'Dwyer knew beforehand all the dilemmas Redmond would have to face after the publication of his letter in the press.

Redmond decided to reply negatively but his answer was too short and not at all appropriate to O'Dwyer's letter. He simply stated that he had 'read it with the utmost care' but that peace was out of the question and that he felt that he could not morally influence the Government at this particular time: 'Nor do I think that that I would be justified in endeavouring to bring pressure to bear upon the Government to enter into any negotiations for peace at a time when the German Powers, who have been the aggressors in this war, show no sign of any disposition to repair the wrongs they have inflicted upon Belgium and our other allies'.[89] Not discussing O'Dwyer's economic arguments was a serious mistake. On 13 August 1915, the Bishop wrote to Mgr O'Riordan in Rome that he had received from Redmond 'a simple refusal' but he was confident that 'the popular fear of taxation and poverty [would] soon bring pressure to bear on himself'. He added sarcastically: 'He and the Irish Party are afraid to do anything. The Home Rule carrot keeps the Irish donkey moving.'[90] The nationalist opposition press applauded the Bishop and severely criticised Redmond. Eoin MacNeill understood that the Nationalist leader's reputation had been damaged and published a savage attack on Redmond in the *Irish Volunteer*. He also criticised the *Irish Times* for having published O'Dwyer's important letter in between the cricket and racing reports, whereas Redmond's reply appeared in the first column entirely devoted to the war.[91] On 8 September 1915, the Bishop wrote to Mgr O'Riordan that he was surprised at the number of letters of support he had received from people. His hopes of seeing Nationalists and Catholics denouncing the war and opposing Redmond's policies, however, were short-lived. He told O'Riordan: 'The helplessness from our people is deplorable. They have given up the habit of thinking. That is done for them by the "Machine".'[92] He had fallen out with the Nationalist party, which he had nicknamed 'The Machine'. O'Dwyer's comment on the Irish people might have been severe, but it was undeniably true for it reflected Ireland's political apathy at the end of 1915 which, ironically, Redmond was also experiencing for his cause.

Shortly afterwards, O'Dwyer noted that 'the English don't seem to like the idea [of peace] and the Irish patriots boil over with indifference at the mention of it'.[93] The Bishop's letter had caught the eye of the nationalist opposition but not yet of the people. This would change in the months to come. Mgr O'Riordan, as usual, lost no time in translating O'Dwyer's letter into Italian and presented it to the Pope who was extremely pleased with it.[94] It was the second time that O'Dwyer was much in favour at the Holy See. Between 1914 and 1917, the Bishop, in his correspondence with O'Riordan, would continuously deplore this war that had no end in sight. On 20 August 1915, Italy declared war on Turkey, and on 15 October, Ireland also found itself at war with Bulgaria since the Government of the United Kingdom had declared war on the Balkan State. On 18 October 1915, Redmond declared at a conference on recruiting in Dublin that 'the Irish [were] entitled to their full share of the compliments paid to the rest of the United Kingdom for their hitherto magnificent response to the appeal for men'.[95] Redmond did not mention that the number of recruits was already dropping sharply in the last months of 1915. In the meantime, O'Dwyer received a letter from a member of the hierarchy who had remained quite silent in the aftermath of his correspondence with Redmond. Thomas O'Dea, Bishop of Galway wrote that it was O'Dwyer's disposition 'to stand alone' and that it could not possibly be a bishop's modus operandi: 'It would take from the dignity of the position if I were to join you.'[96] Clearly, O'Dea had very little time for 'episcopal swashbucklers' and preferred that the hierarchy acted as a body on the political situation in the country. Dr Fogarty saw no wrong in O'Dwyer's anti-war crusade and wrote ironically to the Bishop of Limerick: 'Our "Allies" are doing badly. If the Germans get to Constantinople they will make John Bull's head turn grey in one night.'[97] O'Dea and Fogarty illustrated how much the hierarchy was divided on the war issue, and that the people and the recruitment authorities could not expect a common statement either in favour of or against the conflict.

In November 1915, however, a second confrontation between O'Dwyer and Redmond took place and this time the Nationalist leader's hold on Irish public opinion was seriously impaired. In October, the DRI and Lord Wimborne had initiated a new recruitment campaign. The losses of the 10th Irish Division at Gallipoli in Turkey had been huge and public opinion in Ireland was led to believe that Irish recruits were deliberately used as cannon fodder.[98] Some even maintained that Wimborne had sent a circular letter to men fit for military service. According to New Ireland, a secret list of potential recruits had been drawn by the RIC.[99] Panic took hold of some Irishmen who believed it was the beginning of conscription. They tried to emigrate to the United States and wanted to embark in Liverpool. Some maritime companies like White Star and Cunard refused to take them aboard as they deemed they should be at the front. About 700 Irishmen tried to leave Britain and were harassed by a hostile English mob. The Manchester Guardian denounced this chauvinistic incident. The Press Association interviewed

John Redmond about it. The leader awkwardly tried to reassure British public opinion, declaring that the whole matter was limited to the west of Ireland only and that some people wrongly believed they would be conscripted. He added: 'That, of course, is no excuse. It is very cowardly of them to try and emigrate.'[100] This last sentence was probably the beginning of the end of Redmond's political career and ambitions. O'Dwyer was very indignant about Redmond's remark on his own compatriots. He published a long and vitriolic letter, which created a sensation throughout Ireland. It was an attack on the Nationalist party and its leader. The letter was not published in Dublin but it appeared on 11 November 1915 in regional newspapers such as the *Limerick Chronicle* and the *Cork Examiner*:

> The treatment which the poor emigrant lads have received at Liverpool is enough to make any Irishman's blood boil with anger and indignation . . . They do not want to be forced into the English Army, and sent to fight English battles in some part of the world. Is that not within their rights? . . . It is very probable that these poor Connaught peasants know very little or nothing of the meaning of the war. Their blood is not stirred by the memories of Kossovo, and they have no burning desire to die for Serbia. They would much prefer to be allowed to till their own potato gardens in peace in Connemara. Small nationalities, and the wrongs of the Rheims Cathedral, and all the other cosmopolitan considerations that rouse the enthusiasm of the Irish Party, but do not get enough recruits in England, are far too high-flying for uneducated peasants . . . But in all the shame and humiliation of this disgraceful episode what angers most is that there is no one, not even one of their own countrymen, to stand up and defend them. Their crime is that they are not ready to die for England. Why should they? Mr Redmond will say that a Home Rule Act is on the Statute Book. But any intelligent Irishman will say a simulacrum of Home Rule, with an express notice, that it is never to come into operation. . . . Yet the poor fellows who do not see the advantage of dying for such a cause are to be insulted as 'shirkers' and 'cowards', and the men whom they have raised to power and influence have not one word to say on their behalf.
>
> (*The Cork Examiner*, 11 November 1915)

O'Dwyer may not have been very tactful when he spoke about 'uneducated peasants' who were not interested in 'cosmopolitan considerations' but he had told the truth. There can be little doubt that for farmers, enjoying some degree of economic prosperity and having a strong sense of insularity, the war was only of secondary interest. Not even Redmond himself would have disagreed on this point. Unquestionably, O'Dwyer's letter was extremely nationalistic and had an anti-British tone. But more importantly, he succeeded in identifying with popular public opinion, especially in rural Ireland. For farmers who feared conscription, O'Dwyer had become their 'episcopal swashbuckler'. Nevertheless, he had not yet declared what was to be the alternative to the Nationalist party.

Once again, Redmond decided to ignore O'Dwyer's attack, which confirmed in many minds that the Nationalist leader had no solutions to the pertinent questions it raised. Instead, on 23 November 1915, he exhorted the Irish living in London to join the Army and a few days later he went to France where he reviewed several Irish regiments.[101] It must be noted that John Dillon, strangely enough, had remained silent during Redmond's confrontations with the Bishop. His more radical nationalism and his latent anti-clericalism would tend to suggest that he would have condemned O'Dwyer's attacks out of hand. Probably for party discipline and unity's sake, Dillon had decided not to voice his feelings. But, the irony is that he probably agreed with O'Dwyer on certain points. The difference between the Bishop and Redmond was that O'Dwyer took into account the evolution of public opinion and that Redmond still believed he could manipulate or change it to his benefit. It is true that O'Dwyer had far more room to manoeuvre than his opponent who was constantly obliged to deal with the coalition cabinet and the Unionists. As might be expected, the nationalist opposition newspapers crowned O'Dwyer king of their cause. *Nationality*, the *Irish Volunteer* and the *Hibernian* published his letter.[102] The Bishop's ideas spread rapidly not only among the public, but also among the nationalist opposition. He was no longer the Landlord Bishop or Castle Bishop of years ago. His popularity extended well beyond the limits of his diocese. In 1915, the RIC noted that fifty-five priests had been reported for seditious activities and opposing recruitment whereas only twenty-four cases had been observed in 1914. Three priests from counties Tyrone, Kildare and Limerick had read O'Dwyer's letter in their churches. Fr Thomas Wall from Limerick encouraged the youth to join the Irish Volunteers and to oppose conscription with a pitchfork if necessary.[103] In December 1915, the Inspector General of the RIC had noticed that some priests were openly preaching against recruitment: 'The activity of Irish Volunteer organizers [sic] in spreading disloyalty and discouraging recruitment for the Army was maintained during the month [December], particularly in the counties of Cork, Kerry, and Limerick, where the movement is supported by some Roman Catholic clergymen.'[104] Undoubtedly, O'Dwyer's influence was felt in the south-west. If the pro-war clergy was becoming apathetic, the anti-war clergy was becoming louder and louder even if it was a small minority. The RIC found copies of O'Dwyer's letter in at least seventeen counties.[105] The Inspector General wrote in his monthly report: '... printed copies of the Bishop of Limerick's letter on the War and the treatment of Irish emigrants at Liverpool are freely distributed at the Chapel doors and elsewhere by Irish Volunteers in uniform, and others'.[106] On 25 November 1915, Sir Mathew Nathan, the Under-Secretary, wrote a report based on the findings of the Special Branch. He advised that the Government ought not to take any measures against people acting against recruitment in Co. Kerry and who were quoting O'Dwyer's letter because he believed it would give the Bishop even more publicity.[107] On 2 December, Nathan informed Augustine Birrell, the Irish Secretary, that a Patrick Hegarty from Derry had been distributing copies of the letter in Co. Donegal, and that posters of the letter had been posted up in Carndonagh on the morning before a recruitment meeting. Birrell replied: 'I do not think in view of the circulation the letter has had already we can usefully try and stop its further circulation.'[108] Dublin Castle was powerless and not one bishop complained that O'Dwyer's letter had been circulated in his diocese. Fogarty wrote to O'Dwyer: 'The whole body of the people have rallied to you and your letter on the Emigrants. It has opened their eyes.'[109] O'Dwyer's letter was a source of deep inspiration for anti-war nationalists and the opposition. Indeed, three months laster the Inspector General of the RIC wrote in his monthly report for February 1916: 'The Bishop of Limerick has unfortunately rendered immense assistance to these seditious writers in their propaganda against recruiting by his letter, reproduced in circular form by the thousand, in which he states that this war is England's war and that Irishmen have no interest in it.'[110]

In December 1915, the Bishop of Limerick took up his pen once again. He knew that his recent letter had favourably impressed the Irish at home, but it was also of vital importance to impress those Americans of Irish descent. The United States was still neutral and could be an immense source of help either for the Nationalist party or for the nationalist opposition. The journalist and author Shane Leslie was in America where he was representing Redmond and his party. Leslie was on friendly terms with the Irish-American Cardinal of New York, Dr Farley, and informed Redmond that the Cardinal approved of Home Rule and his ideas, but that he had to remain neutral because of the international situation. Leslie wrote that Farley had been obliged to refuse Redmond's request to distribute copies of Cardinal Mercier's Lenten pastoral at the entrance of all the churches in his archdiocese for he had also forbidden the distribution of *Fatherland*, a German-American newspaper in favour of Germany in the war.[111] Redmond replied to Leslie by noting that he was fully in favour of a new newspaper that would represent the views of the Nationalist party in the

United States.[112] Shortly afterwards, the newspaper *Ireland* was published.

Redmond understood that America had always been a haven for many radical Irish nationalists who were determined to use force to liberate Ireland from Britain, and that it was crucial to circulate the opinions of the constitutional cause. It is not known whether O'Dwyer knew of Redmond's correspondence with Leslie, but the Bishop knew that the United States would become a battleground for propaganda, and that it was important to spread the opposition's message across the Atlantic. He wrote a long article for the *American Ecclesiastical Review*, in which he stated that he did not at all believe in German atrocities in Belgium, and that he did not trust the Bryce commission that had been inquiring into those alleged atrocities simply because all its members were British. According to him, the aim of the Government was to instil hatred for the Germans. As to the freedom of small nations, he thought that it was all hypocrisy and that a nation could not be indefinitely occupied. The more injustice was done to that nation, the more violent its rising would be. The allusion to Ireland was obvious and it seemed that O'Dwyer was warning the British authorities. Finally, he severely criticised Redmond's refusal to listen to the Pope's peace appeal:

> He cannot find one word of courtesy or deference for the head of the Church, but puts aside his solemn and fatherly appeal, made in the name of Christ Our Lord, as if it were a resolution passed by some pettifogging political clique... Home Rule has been kept for many years dangling before his nose like the carrot before the donkey; he gets a sufficient sniff of it occasionally to keep him draughting for the English Government.
>
> (*Nationality* 25 December 1915)

The Bishop deplored Redmond's lack of independence towards the English Liberals. Arthur Griffith's *Nationality* also published O'Dwyer's letter. It is difficult to know what impact it had on Irish-American opinion in 1915. There is no mention of it in Leslie's correspondence with Redmond. It cannot have failed, however, to impress Clan na Gael and other such organisations. What is most relevant in this episode is the Bishop's tactical sense. He knew exactly when and where to attack. His friend, Bishop Fogarty, wrote that he had rebuked Redmond 'with deadly force'.[113] The Nationalist leader again decided to ignore the letter. Mgr O'Riordan thought otherwise and translated it into Italian and entitled it *L'Appelo del Santo Padre per la Pace*, the Holy Father's appeal for peace. The rector's intention was to counter the views of some members of the English hierarchy in Rome, who had set out to influence Benedict XV's friendly feelings towards Ireland.[114] Halfway through December, the 16th Irish Division left Ireland for France and, the same month, O'Dwyer denounced the war in Saint John's Cathedral in Limerick.

What was the people's opinion in January 1916? The question remains difficult to answer. In Limerick, public opinion still seemed to favour the Nationalist party.[115] But, if one takes recruitment numbers in order to measure the party's success and influence, it is clear that Redmond's policies had not fully convinced Irishmen.[116] What was O'Dwyer's opinion on the matter? In a letter to Mgr O'Riordan, he observed that 'it [was] very hard to gauge opinion in Ireland now'. According to him, 'Redmond and the *Freeman* [spoke and wrote] like British Gingos [*sic*]'. He believed that Catholics had been roused by alleged German outrages on nuns and priests. But he was also convinced that there 'still [was] a good survival of nationality' and that the Gaelic League had done some good work.[117] O'Dwyer was certainly right when he said that the *Freeman's Journal* was pro-British. The national press, especially in Dublin, was largely in favour of Redmond and Irish participation in the war. Consequently, it is difficult to give a precise and objective assessment of the situation. In February 1916, Redmond and Wimborne joined together on a recruitment platform in Dublin. In March, O'Dwyer once more wrote a strong anti-war Lenten pastoral in which he reiterated the same ideas as in his article for the *American Ecclesiastical Review*.[118] He added that the Triple Entente's victory was far from certain, contrary to what Bishop Kelly of Ross firmly believed. *Nationality* acclaimed the pastoral and the *Spark* noted: 'It is sad to see Bishops accepting as gospel the lurid world pictures of the hydrophobiac Press regarding the German campaign. But in some matters Bishops are quite simply men... Of course, the Bishop of Limerick, as usual, shows a right appreciation of the whole situation.'[119] In March, the *Catholic Bulletin* edited by John J. O'Kelly, who would become president of Sinn Féin in 1926, made a common cause with O'Dwyer.[120]

In April 1916, Ireland seemed to be heading towards an uncertain political future. The Nationalist party had unquestionably lost in popularity. But to whose benefit? Arthur Griffith's Sinn Féin and James Connolly's Labour party were not yet in a position to rival Redmond's party and organisation in the country. Their political programmes remained obscure or not credible to most Irishmen. These nationalist opposition movements had found a surprising ally in Edward O'Dwyer. His political evolution from the Plan of Campaign days to the First World War had been extraordinary. It appeared that he had become the key figure of a new emerging nationalism: a nationalism that refused to collaborate unconditionally with the British Government and that did not wish to see the Home Rule for their country subordinated to the war in Europe.

SUMMARY

The three rogue prelates, Logue, Walsh and O'Dwyer had become independent nationalists. Each of them had their own motives, but it was clear that they felt the Nationalist party was not taking decisions in the best interest of Ireland. John Redmond was thus deprived of the possible help of three ecclesiastics whose positions, abilities and eloquence could have made a major contribution to the war effort. But it was, above all, Bishop Edward O'Dwyer's impressive presence on the political scene that was the main force during this period. He had unquestionably unsettled the Nationalist party and won over some important elements of public opinion to his cause. It remained to be seen how the Bishop would use his new found popularity. The mistake of Redmond's party was to have been too timid with O'Dwyer. It would be more difficult to slow down his political progress now, wherever that was leading. O'Dwyer's ultramontane tendencies had naturally made him follow the Pope in his quest for world peace. In fact, he had found an important 'cover' in Benedict XV to oppose the war effort in Ireland. It is obvious that the Pontiff's repeated appeals for peace must have disturbed some pro-war bishops. In the years ahead, O'Dwyer would continue his collaboration with the Vatican. The first years of war had also proven that the British authorities, the CCORI, the DRI, the Nationalist party and the nationalist opposition movements attached great importance to the Catholic Church's opinions and that its support could be decisive. This would be the case until the very end of the war in November 1918.

In January 1916, the Supreme Council of the Irish Republican Brotherhood (IRB) had decided to stage a rebellion against the British in Ireland. The chosen date was Easter 1916. Once again, two ecclesiastics would play major roles: the Bishop of Limerick and the Archbishop of Dublin.

3 The summer of 1916: Rising, conscription and partition

October 1938
'I was much struck with the Pope's familiarity with the Irish cause, and with the arguments put forward by England.'
Count Plunkett on his secret mission to the Vatican, in a letter to unknown addressee.

1916
'God has left us yet one hero, His pen is like a sword of fire,
Ireland loves him, Ireland thanks him,
God watch o'er you, Bishop O'Dwyer.'
Anonymous, after the Easter Rising.

The events of the Easter Rising in Dublin in April 1916 put the Catholic Church in the limelight. Firstly, it appeared that the rebels genuinely feared the Church's power. So much so, that the rebel leaders decided to send George Plunkett, a papal count, to the Vatican to seek the Pope's advice or even approval. Among the nationalist opposition movement, a debate took place about the theological justification of an armed rebellion against the British authorities in Ireland. The general population and the British Army appealed directly to priests to put a halt to the rebellion. Then, the consequences of the Rising provoked a clear radicalisation in the attitude of the clergy towards the British Government and Ulster Unionists who were accused of being the real culprits of the Easter Rising. These accusations came from members of the hierarchy who had strong nationalist feelings like Bishop Fogarty, Bishop O'Dwyer and Archbishop Walsh, but also from prelates who were usually more reserved and cautious in their political statements such as Dr Gilmartin of Clonfert and Dr Mangan of Kerry. The younger clergy also succumbed to political radicalism. This evolution within the Church did much damage to John Redmond and his party. They had been severely criticised by Walsh and O'Dwyer whose popularity was rapidly increasing. Whether the Bishop of Limerick liked it or not, he had become the moral leader of a nationalist opposition movement that was temporarily without a leader since they had been either shot or imprisoned in the aftermath of the Rising. The Church's radicalisation intensified as Herbert Asquith took the decision to permanently exclude certain counties of Ulster from Home Rule. Bishops and priests of the dioceses that would not become autonomous fiercely opposed the British plan and vehemently criticised Redmond, badly let down by his Liberal allies. Cardinal Logue and Bishop O'Donnell, both from Ulster, had difficulties in accepting the radicalisation of their clergy and wondered where it would eventually lead.

In Europe, the war had entered its third year and there was still no end in sight. The front was a quagmire and a stalemate, and very costly in human lives. The French Government and its Prime Minister, Aristide Briand, were quite worried about the turn of events in Ireland. They knew that British policy in Ireland was far from successful and that it could have important repercussions: the possible destabilisation of their main ally, Britain, and the complete failure of recruitment. Soldiers were much needed on the Allied side, especially in the context of the battles of Verdun and the Somme.

COUNT PLUNKETT'S SECRET MISSION TO THE VATICAN

At the beginning of 1916, the IRB planned a rising against the British authorities. The Irish republicans had decided to follow the old saying 'England's difficulty is Ireland's opportunity'. The Irish Volunteers and James Connolly's Irish Citizen Army (ICA) were also involved. Perhaps never before had the republicans been in such a favourable situation. Britain was fighting for her very survival in France, and Germany had promised Sir Roger Casement, a republican then based in Berlin, 20,000 rifles, 4,000,000 cartridges and German soldiers in support of the Rising.[1] The German High Command, just like the French and the Spaniards in previous centuries, realised the advantage of a successful rebellion or liberation war in Ireland: Britain would have a weak western flank. The British themselves, of course, were well aware of it. The Act of Union between Britain and Ireland in 1801 during the Napoleonic wars was, above all, a strategic necessity.[2] The Conservative and Unionist parties, which opposed Home Rule three times in 1886, 1893 and 1912, had argued that an autonomous Ireland would be the Achilles heel of the British Empire. The future German help and also French propaganda missions proved Ireland's geopolitical importance.

The IRB, a secret organisation, did not have many members and understood that it was vital to infiltrate the command structure of the

16. Mgr Michael Curran had a penchant for cloak-and-dagger work (with kind permission of the archdiocese of Dublin)

GEORGE NOBLE COUNT PLUNKETT, F.S.A.

(Father of Joseph Plunkett, who was Executed, and of George and
John Plunkett, Sentenced to Penal Servitude).
Arrested May 1st, 1916, and detained in Richmond Barracks
till June 5th, and now Deported to Oxford.

17. Count George Noble Plunkett, on a secret mission to the Vatican (courtesy of
the National Library of Ireland)

Sinn Fein Rebellion, 1916.
Sackville Street, Dublin.

18. British soldiers in Dublin after the Easter Rising (courtesy of the National Library of Ireland)

Irish Volunteers who were under Professor Eoin MacNeill's command. MacNeill, however, only approved of physical force if the British authorities tried to suppress Home Rule or the Volunteers. He had a defensive view of the paramilitary force. The IRB decided to neutralise MacNeill's influence and secretly recruited Patrick Pearse, a Volunteer within its ranks, to do so. In 1915, Thomas Clarke, who was a member of the supreme council of the IRB, founded the military council. Pearse, Joseph Mary Plunkett, Eamonn Ceannt, Sean and Clarke MacDiarmada and Thomas MacDonagh were also included in the new council. They decided to use the Irish Volunteers for a rising planned on Sunday 23 April 1916. On 19 January 1916, the military council informed James Connolly about its plan.[3]

One crucial question remained: how would the Catholic Church react to such a rising? The leaders of the IRB knew that the Church had a very strict theological interpretation concerning the use of violence against a legitimate government. Given that the overwhelming majority of those about to fight were Catholics, it was vital to persuade them of the just cause of the Rising. If unconvinced, the Volunteers might simply not obey orders. One should not underestimate the religious aspect of this matter. The hierarchy had always been a serious obstacle to the IRB, even if it had not always been successful in dissuading people to join this illegal organisation in the 1860s and 1870s.[4] Bishops regularly denounced the existence of secret societies and their members were threatened with

O'DWYER AND MAXWELL.

———:0:———

"Come, join me in my dirty work," wrote England's
  butcher bold,

"You've rebel priests within your See, who love not us
  I'm told ;

Remove these men where never more they'll threaten
  England's sway,

And England's love and gratitude shall be your own
  for aye."

Then answer made the brave O'Dwyer : " My laws are
  not as thine,

For *yours* condemn in ruthless haste—it is not so with
  mine.

Ere I condemn, I'll know the charge, the witness, place,
  and time,

And ere I punish, I'll have proof that there has been a
  crime."

And swiftly came the bogus charge, in humbler accents
  framed,

" Methought it needed not to prove the guilt of those
  I've named :

They've hearkened to the rebels' words, they've blessed
  the rebels' cause,

By voice and pen they've taught their flocks to spurn
  the Empire's laws."

Our Bishop true, no longer now, his anger can restrain,

His words are cutting as the scythe that reaps the
  harvest grain :

" Those men you name are godly men, in act and thought
  guilt-free,

They serve their God and love their Land, *that* is no
  crime to *me*.

And were their guilt as black as Hell, you think, at your
  behest,

I'd join with those whose hands are dyed with blood
  from Ireland's breast ?

Full many a ruthless English cur has held our land in
  thrall,

But History, sure, will write you down, the blackest of
  them all.

And do you think that I forget my country's martyred
  dead—

The brave, the pure, the high-souled lads, whose blood
  you've foully shed.

But here's your answer, I may share the fate of those
  who died,

But I'll not be the first O'Dwyer to take the tyrant's
  side !"

Descendant of a noble clan, may you be left us long,

Fearless and true to uphold our cause 'gainst tyrants
  cruel and strong.

They thought that every voice was stilled, that hearts
  were cold with fear,

No coward threats *your* heart could chill, nor make your
  voice less clear.

And oh ! thank God that there are men, to speak with
  love and pride,

Of those who lie in prison cell, and those that nobly
  died.

And when the glorious tale is told of Irelnd's latest
  fight,·

In letters golden shall be writ " O'Dwyer upheld the
  right !"

TO THE MEMORY OF THE O'RAHILLY.

———:0:———

He's dead, alas ! Peace to his gentle soul ;
  For he was loving, kind, sincere, and true,
His noble spirit ever sought the goal
  Of native freedom, dearest land, for you.

He loved the mellow accents of thy tongue,
  As links that bound him to a brighter past,
When lay of love or warlike song was sung,
  In that sweet speech he cherished to the last.

He fain would free thee from the cruel yoke
  Of Saxon law, misrule, and studied wrong :
But died—not unavenged—ere yet the stroke
  Had snapped the bands of thraldom's binding thong.

He's dead ; but now his spirit brighter reigns,
  Inspiring hope to the desponding breast,
Death hath no terrors, after-death no pains
  For patriot souls—the noblest and the best.

Be brave, ye children ; braver be his wife,
  Who mourn him, sleeping now, beneath the sod :
His native land he cherished more than life,
  And only loved it less than he loved God.

To save the waning manhood of our race,
  His blood he shed, his very life laid down :
By sacrifice complete, he won the grace
  Of patriot's brightest wreaths—the martyr's crown.

Revere his mem'ry ; think not 'twas in vain
  He strove for freedom—ev'ry nation's right :
We count not cost, nor reckon loss or pain,
  When 'tis for God and Country that we fight.

19. Booklet 'Poems and Songs of Easter Week'; poem relating the confrontation
between Bishop O'Dwyer and General Maxwell (PRO, London, CO 904/161)

excommunication or refused absolution. Around the turn of the century the Church seems to have been very effective since the number of IRB members dropped from 80,000 in 1860 to 1,500 in 1911. Religious motives for not joining the IRB appear to have been genuine.[5] In the archdiocese of Dublin, the archbishop always insisted that a paragraph denouncing the activities of Fenians, Ribbonmen and Freemasons be included in his Lenten pastoral.[6] The rebel leaders simply could not afford to ignore this 'religious problem'. If the Irish hierarchy was not going to cooperate with them, it would be necessary to find ecclesiastical support elsewhere. The military council decided to send an envoy to the Holy See before the fateful date of 23 April to explain the theological justification of their planned rising. If Benedict XV was convinced by their just cause, it could galvanise the rebels and also possibly pre-empt the hierarchy's condemnation. It is likely that the military council of the IRB was aware of the Pope's favourable attitude towards nationalist Ireland, otherwise the risk of a stern rebuke would have been too great. Perhaps Bishop O'Dwyer and Mgr Curran played a part in informing the rebels about Benedict XV's favourable opinion of Irish nationalism. The two men corresponded respectively with Mgr O'Riordan and Mgr Hagan in Rome. O'Riordan often met the Pope and related his audiences to O'Dwyer, whereas Curran exchanged ideas with Hagan, a more radical nationalist. Curran knew Patrick Pearse and Seán T. O'Kelly, a childhood friend. Archbishop Walsh's secretary had always suspected that O'Kelly was a member of the IRB. The two men frequently met at the Gaelic League's office in Parnell Square in Dublin to discuss the latest political developments in the country.[7] It is, therefore, conceivable that Curran informed Pearse and O'Kelly about Vatican policy.

The rebels agreed to send Count Plunkett to the Holy See. Plunkett's son, Joseph Mary, was involved in the military planning of the rising. The Count's mission was to inform Benedict XV about the planned rising in Ireland. Plunkett had received his papal award in 1884 and seemed to be the obvious choice for this mission. In April 1916, he became a secret member of the IRB and was sent to Switzerland where he met the German Ambassador, *Herr* Gisbert von Romberg, to whom he gave a message for Sir Roger Casement, outlining the plan of the rising.[8] Plunkett told the Ambassador that he was on his way to the Vatican and that he had considered travelling to Germany to meet Casement in person but that he feared it might endanger his mission to the Holy See, which he deemed to be 'extremely important'.[9] Romberg sent a report to the Auswärtiges Amt, the German Foreign Office in Berlin, in which he informed the Kaiser's Government that the Irish rebels wanted German officers to assist them in the rising and a submarine to block Dublin harbour.[10] Shortly afterwards, around 8 April 1916, Plunkett had a private audience with the Pope. Years later, this meeting aroused a public controversy concerning the people at the origin of the Roman mission. In 1938, Plunkett wrote to Fr Rope, an Irish Franciscan based in Rome, that he had been 'commissioned by the Executive of the Irish Volunteers (the Provisional Government) to communicate their intention to Pope Benedict XV'.[11] Eoin MacNeill, the head of the Volunteers, had always claimed that he had not actively prepared the rising. A public row between the two men had taken place in 1933. In the *Irish Press*, MacNeill denied the existence of the so-called Provisional Government and refuted the fact that an envoy had been sent to Rome.[12] Plunkett claimed that it was MacNeill in person who had signed the order of his mission. In 1961, *Irish Historical Studies* published two memoranda written by MacNeill, one shortly before the Rising and one shortly afterwards. Nowhere in those two documents does MacNeill refer to the Count and his Roman mission. Nevertheless, he wrote that two days before the rising, on Saturday morning 22 April, Joseph Mary Plunkett had paid him a visit and: 'told me that he had received a message direct from Rome to the effect that the Pope had sent his blessing to the Irish Volunteers and to myself in particular'.[13] The impression given by these two memoranda is that MacNeill did not know about the Count's mission.

It would be outside the scope of this study to elaborate on MacNeill's role in the events leading up to the Easter Rising, but one may wonder what his exact role had been. At the beginning of 1916, he had felt that Pearse and others were possibly planning a rebellion and had explained to them that it would not be morally justifiable. Pearse had then agreed with MacNeill.[14] Seventeen years later, Plunkett implied that MacNeill had known at least from the very beginning of April about the future Rising and that he had wanted to know exactly what the Pope thought. After all, MacNeill was professor of Celtic studies, not of theology. It seems hardly plausible that Plunkett, personally knighted by Leo XIII and a practising Catholic, lied to Benedict XV. The Count's audience with Benedict XV lasted for about two hours and nobody else was present. Plunkett gave the Pope a letter, written in French, announcing and justifying the future rising in Ireland:

Dear Holy Father,
I have been sent as an envoy to Your Holiness, on behalf of the President and the Supreme Council of the Irish Volunteers (national troops). Mr President (Prof. Jean MacNeill) gave me a document addressed to Your Holiness that the present circumstances forced me to leave in Ireland.
[Plunkett then wrote that the Supreme Council unanimously supported the liberation of the Holy See and the restoration of its ancient rights and he explained that the Council had asked him to explain to the Pope the present political crisis in Ireland; the Count wrote six paragraphs justifying the future rising]

7) It cannot be doubted that we are oppressed. It is obvious that we run the risk of being massacred. We believe that the war taxes will naturally engender famine; we have no more resources. So, we are forced to rebel. It is because of all these conditions that there is not one parish without volunteers. We have an effective force of 80,000 trained men; and the people, the Catholic nation, is with us. The American Irish are going to send us a big shipment of arms; and the German Government has promised us its help. It is during the war that we have the greatest chance of success to obtain the freedom of rights and of worship for our Catholic country.

8) The insurrection should begin in the evening of next Easter day.

(Archives of Holy Congregation of Extraordinary Ecclesiastical Affairs, Vatican)[15]

In a letter dated October 1938, the Count related his audience with Benedict XV and wrote: 'I was much struck with the Pope's familiarity with the Irish cause, and with the arguments put forward by England.'[16] In fact, this was not surprising. Herbert Asquith had had an audience on 31 March 1916 to explain Britain's war policy in general and her policy in Ireland in particular.[17] It is also further proof that Mgr O'Riordan, the rector of the Irish College in Rome, was equally active in defending nationalist Ireland's cause at the papal court. Finally, the Count asked the Pope to bless the rebels, which, according to Plunkett, he did. In 1917, Sean Fitzgibbon, an old Irish Volunteer, was told by the Count: 'I could say that [the Pope] approved [of the intended rising] – after a certain measure of success had been achieved'.[18] Plunkett also explained that on that occasion the Pope had refused to bless the future Rising but that he did bless the Irish Volunteers. Although there was no third party present at the audience, able to confirm Plunkett's claims, it is likely that Benedict XV had given his blessing. Concerning the envoy to Rome sent by the Provisional Government, and the Pope's knowledge of Irish affairs, Plunkett had not lied. His personal letter to the Pope, and O'Riordan's activities in Rome corroborate his claims. It is not very likely that a papal count and practising Catholic would have distorted the Holy Father's words. Furthermore, the international diplomatic situation must be taken into account. The Vatican was secretly financed by Germany and had found out that its diplomats would be excluded by Britain and Italy from the future peace conference.[19] The Holy See, therefore, had no reason at all to support Britain.

Another interesting issue raised in the letter is Plunkett's mention of '80,000 trained men', ready to participate in the planned rising. It is difficult to work out where and how he got this figure. Indeed, in January 1916, the Military Council of the future rebels calculated that they could rely on 3,000 Irish Volunteers in Dublin, 13,000 in the provinces, about

200 members of Connolly's Irish Citizen Army and about 2,000 IRB men.[20] This is a total of approximately 18,000 men. Was the Count relying on an extra 62,000 men that would spontaneously help the rebels once the Rising had begun? This is hardly likely for he would not have described them as 'trained', although James Connolly had told MacNeill and Patrick Pearse in January 1916 'that once the fighting began, the country in general would rally to the insurgents'.[21] MacNeill had begged to differ with Connolly's views during their meeting. It seems rather that Plunkett wanted to make sure that the Pope was convinced the rebels had a chance of succeeding and, therefore, inflated the figure. This was crucial as rebellion against oppression is justified by Catholic theology provided there is a reasonable chance of success.[22] Plunkett's statement to Fitzgibbon in 1917 tends to indicate that this had been the Count's intention. When Plunkett left Rome, four people knew about the future Rising: Mgr O'Riordan, Mgr Hagan, Benedict XV and a journalist of the *Melbourne Advocate*.[23] The Count was back in Dublin on Friday 21 April 1916 and sent a full report to the Provisional Irish Government. When the rising began, Plunkett claimed that he saw an extract of his report, relating his audience with the Pope, in the General Post Office in Dublin.[24]

In Dublin, events began to move faster. Since February 1916, the Irish Volunteers had let it be known that if the Government tried to disarm them, a bloodbath would occur. On 19 April, Alderman Thomas Kelly announced to his colleagues that he was in possession of a document emanating from the Ministry of Irish Affairs. It stated that the authorities had issued orders to confiscate all arms belonging to the Volunteers.[25] This document was a forgery conceived by Joseph Mary Plunkett, meant to neutralise MacNeill as he did not agree with the rising. Bearing in mind Plunkett's letter to the Pope, MacNeill's role in the unfolding events becomes rather ambivalent. Perhaps he did agree, at first, with Patrick Pearse and Joseph Mary Plunkett and then changed his mind afterwards. MacNeill got a copy of the document which he immediately sent to Bishop O'Dwyer in Limerick.[26] It is not known how O'Dwyer reacted but it was clear that he had become a main actor within the nationalist opposition. The evening newspapers published the document with a formal denial of the military authorities. Archbishop Walsh did not accept their denial. Mgr Curran lost no time and went to Dawson Street where the headquarters of the Volunteers were located. He had a discussion with MacNeill, who was convinced that the document was genuine, and that it had to be handed out at all costs to the Volunteers. Curran offered to help and distributed copies, notably in Parnell Square.[27] That same night, Curran wrote to Mgr Hagan in Rome and narrated the events of the day. Curran had been duped by the document and linked it to a rumour that the Germans were about to land in Lough Swilly, in Co. Donegal. According to him,

'Liberty Hall [headquarters of James Connolly's Irish Citizen Army] and some of the wilder of the Sinn Féin people would certainly join the Huns'. But he was equally convinced that 'neither John MacNeill nor the National Volunteers would [join the Germans]'.[28] On Saturday morning, 22 April, Fr John McArdle informed Curran that an officer of the Irish Volunteers had told him that the rising was to take place the next day, Sunday 23 April. Curran then told Archbishop Walsh about the latest rumours in town, and also about Sir Roger Casement who had just been arrested near Tralee, in Co. Kerry, having come over in a German submarine to tell MacNeill to cancel the rising.[29] He had lost all confidence in his German allies who would not send over their soldiers but only a boat with old guns.[30] The Archbishop was seriously ill at the time and took the news very calmly, 'like a man who saw the inevitable but who had no power to alter events'.[31] On Saturday night, Eoin MacNeill learnt that the document was a fake and that the *Aud*, the German ship carrying the guns and ammunition, had been scuttled by her captain in Irish waters. MacNeill tried to inform the Irish Volunteers and cancel all manoeuvres due to take place the next day at 4 p.m., the chosen time for the Rising.

On Sunday morning 23 April 1916, Curran eagerly read the headlines of the *Sunday Independent* and was relieved to learn that all volunteer manoeuvres and parades had been cancelled even though he felt that the rising was only a matter of time.[32] He was right. That very morning, the military council of the rebels met in Liberty Hall and decided to begin fighting the next day at 12 p.m. because of MacNeill's intervention. At 2.30 p.m., a worried Miss MacNeill, the professor's sister, called at the Archbishop's house and asked for help. She had brought copies of a letter, written by Eoin MacNeill, confirming the cancellation of all manoeuvres. These copies had to be distributed in Dublin. Curran thought about using priests in the city and asked for Walsh's permission. The ill and tired Archbishop did not object, although he reiterated that he would not personally intervene.[33] Curran left immediately and was successful in his task as most Volunteers obeyed MacNeill's orders. There was, momentarily, no further risk of a badly planned rising. Curran and McArdle could be satisfied but it was only the calm before the storm. The same night, Curran wrote to Mgr Hagan in Rome and described in detail the volatile situation in Dublin. He feared a split between moderate and extreme Irish Volunteers and was of the opinion that MacNeill was losing his grip on the movement. Curran was firmly convinced that the British Army had adopted a provocative attitude but that the Volunteers were equally pushing things seriously. According to him, they were out for war and were sending arms all over the country and he added that the Army could get no recruits whereas the Volunteers were getting many. He personally feared that 'it [might] end in an attempt at conscription'.[34] The

Archbishop's secretary had correctly analysed the situation. The tensions between the Irish Volunteers and the British Army were palpable and the internal divisions within the Volunteer movement made things very complicated and confusing. But one important fact emerged: the power of the Catholic Church. All the major political forces tried to get its support: the rebels in trying to win over the Pope to their cause; the British in their war effort; the MacNeill family in asking Archbishop Walsh for help. Amidst all these events, it appeared that Mgr Curran was not only a witness but also an important participant. He would prove it again during the Easter Rising and later during the conscription crisis of April 1918.

ARCHBISHOP WALSH, THE CLERGY AND THE RISING

The events of the Easter Rising and its consequences are well known and it would be beyond the scope of this book to describe them in detail. Briefly, Eoin MacNeill's counter-order confused the volunteer movement and as a result the rising mainly took place in Dublin and a few other isolated places in the counties of Dublin, Wexford, Louth and Galway.[35] In the city of Cork, there were some skirmishes and Bishop Cohalan played a major role in the surrender of the rebels. The main fighting happened in Dublin between Monday 24 April and Saturday 29 April 1916 when the rebels laid down their weapons. During that week, the Catholic clergy was directly involved in the fighting by attending the wounded and dying on both sides. The British and French Governments realised the gravity of the situation and the disastrous repercussions the rising could have on the course of the war. They recognised the importance and influence of the Catholic Church on the actual political situation.

On Monday 24 April at 12.05 p.m., Count Plunkett met Mgr Curran at the Archbishop's House and asked to speak to Walsh. Curran informed the Count that Walsh was seriously ill and could not be disturbed. Plunkett then asked the secretary to convey a message to him and gave Curran a rather detailed account of his audience with Benedict XV. Plunkett claimed that Benedict XV was extremely worried and had asked him if there was any other solution apart from a rebellion. The Pope had asked Plunkett if he had met the Archbishop of Dublin. Plunkett admitted that the Archbishop had not been consulted and promised the Pope that he would meet Walsh 'as soon as he arrived home'. An important detail can be noted here. Plunkett himself stated that he was back in Dublin on Friday 21 April.[36] At that moment, the rising was still planned for Sunday 23 April. It is clear that Plunkett did not seek to meet Walsh immediately on his arrival, perhaps because of the difficulties with MacNeill and Casement. Even

Curran wrote in his memoirs that 'it was noteworthy that he came on the Monday and not on the Sunday'.[37] In fact, Plunkett presented Curran with a fait accompli for the Rising was due to begin at noon. One may wonder if the rebel leaders feared Walsh's intervention. They knew that the clergy had been instrumental in cancelling all manoeuvres the previous day. Plunkett also told Curran that he had asked for the Pope's blessing. Unfortunately, Curran's memoirs do not give a definitive answer on that matter. In the middle of his conversation with the Count, Curran was informed that a man wanted to speak to him urgently on the phone. It was a jeweller from the city centre who told Curran that the rising had begun and that the General Post Office (GPO) had just been taken by the rebels. The man asked if Walsh could not stop all this. Curran rushed off to see Walsh and told him about the rising and the Count's visit. The Archbishop was dumbfounded. Curran recorded that he 'thought less of the poor Count than of Eoin MacNeill. He looked on the Count as a simple soul and could not conceive a man like him being at the head of a revolution as it really was.'[38] Curran went at once to the GPO. The first rebel he recognised was James Connolly, 'in uniform with a huge colt revolver'. When the atheist Connolly saw Curran he shouted: 'All priests may pass!', confirming the importance of religion for the rebels, even atheistic ones. A few moments later, Curran was inside the GPO, just before the fighting began. He asked to speak to Patrick Pearse:

> [The Volunteer] went off and got Pearse whom, of course, I knew well. He was flushed but calm and authoritative. I at once said that we had just got word by telephone of this attack, that I had informed the Archbishop of the position and told him I was coming down to ascertain the facts and that, if there was anything that could be done, I would do it. 'But', I said, 'I see now that nothing can be done'. 'No', he said, 'we are going to see it out'. 'You know my feelings; if there is any possible thing I can do, I will be very glad to do it', I said. I thought there might possibly be some message or other. 'No', he said, 'but some of the boys would like to go to confession and I would be delighted if you would send over word to the Cathedral'.
>
> (NLD, O'Kelly's papers, MS 27728(1),
> Curran's memoirs, pp. 41–2)

Curran promised Pearse he would do so and left the GPO. During the rising, the Catholic clergy behaved courageously and took care of the wounded and dying rebels and civilians, and also of British soldiers. Priests were heroic, notably around the Pro-Cathedral, in Church Street, Haddington Road and Whitefriar Street.[39] *The Freeman's Journal* paid tribute to them: 'In every area of the city where there was fighting the priest was at the call of either party.' The nationalist newspaper equally added that the 'High military command [spoke] in terms of unstinted appreciation of the great personal risks which the clergy underwent in fulfilment of their mission.'[40] Many priests acted as negotiators between the Army and the rebels. It seems that the majority of the Dublin clergy was against the rising but that just before the fighting broke out, the number of priests in favour of Sinn Féin, the IRB and the Irish Volunteers was very small but increasing and that these had been very active.[41]

On Wednesday 3 May 1916, General John Maxwell, whose forces had put down the rebellion, and his aide-de-camp, Lord Stuart de Decies, called in on the Archbishop just after the execution of Pearse, Clarke and MacDonagh. During the conversation, Maxwell told Walsh that the Capuchins of Church Street had behaved bravely but that a certain number of priests had participated in the rising. Incredible as it may seem, Maxwell believed that those seditious priests had to be deported immediately and that Walsh would help him in this. British naivety had reached its zenith. Did Maxwell not know about Lord Wimborne's difficulties with the Archbishop? The General gave a list to Walsh, containing the names of subversive priests. Walsh remarked that he could do nothing as not one of them was in his archdiocese and advised Maxwell to consult their respective bishops. According to Curran, who was present during the meeting, Walsh 'had a little malicious pleasure in anticipating the reply he would receive from Dr O'Dwyer'.[42] The General would indeed bitterly regret it. Walsh had been quite silent during the Easter Rising. It was true that he had been seriously ill but two of his letters were published by the press. One concerned public safety, in which he asked the population to follow Lord Wimborne's instructions. Another one was a reply to Maxwell who had written to him on 8 May, asking him to give him the names of priests who had distinguished themselves by their courage. The General's letter reached Walsh at a time when public opinion changed in favour of the rebels after their leaders had been shot. A man named Cleary from Dublin wrote to Mgr O'Riordan in Rome that everywhere there was 'very intense feeling over the Dublin executions and over the panicky deportations – even strong opponents of the Sinn Féiners [felt] strongly'.[43]

Also on 8 May, John Redmond warned the Government in the House of Commons in London that the executions were changing public opinion in favour of the insurgents whereas it had been against the rising.[44] Walsh was well aware of the latest developments when he wrote back to Maxwell on 11 May. He stated that '[he had] been much struck by [his] request to be furnished with names of the clergy in cases of special gallantry or devotion' and simply stated that they had done their duty as priests and that there was nothing exceptional in that.[45] In the light of Maxwell's recent visit to the Archbishop and the sudden change in public opinion, this letter was very significant. If Walsh had agreed to work with the General, the Irish public would have interpreted this as an act of collaboration with the British authorities. In fact, Walsh subtly told Maxwell that he would not collaborate with him and that he was not disposed to play into the hands of the unionists who demanded that the Catholic Church denounce the rebels. Furthermore, he knew that Church denunciations of republicans had provoked bitterness and divisions in the past, and he remembered how much people had been against him when he had publicly denounced Charles Stewart Parnell some twenty-five years before.[46] It was simply the continuation of his 'political silence'. Curran also believed that 'the silence of Archbishop Walsh . . . [was] a fact of enormous importance that ought to be noticed'.[47]

Behind the scenes, however, William Walsh struck twice. On 24 April, the first day of the Easter Rising, James O'Connor, a Catholic solicitor working for the British Crown, begged Walsh to put an end to the rebellion. The Archbishop had run out of patience with the authorities and simply told the solicitor that it would have been completely ridiculous since the rebels had not taken up arms in order to lay them down again. He added, in a bellicose manner, that O'Connor and the Government with which he was associated should resign. Walsh had told Fr P.J. Walsh, one of his secretaries, that he detested the British Government's idea to put down rebellions with 'spiritual arms'.[48] The Archbishop's conversation with Maxwell and, shortly afterwards, the General's correspondence with Cardinal Logue and Bishop O'Dwyer show that Walsh had guessed the authorities' tactics right from the beginning. It was on 27 May 1916 that Walsh privately revealed his political frame of mind. He received Justice Shearman and Sir MacKenzie Chalmers, members of the commission investigating the causes of the rising, at his residence in Dublin. He told them that the main cause of the recent fighting was 'the breakdown of the constitutional movement', in other words Redmond's party, and severely criticised the clause on 'concurrent legislation' in the Home Rule Bill. This clause meant that the British Parliament had the right to cancel any act passed by the Irish Parliament. Chalmers did not know about this particular law and believed that Home Rule 'was bound to break down'. Walsh deplored the fact that 'Irish members of Parliament misrepresented the bill as "the greatest charter of liberty" '.[49] As far as the causes of the rising were concerned, the Archbishop pointed his finger at British and Irish constitutional politicians.

The difference of opinion between the Nationalist party and Walsh had reached its peak. But the Archbishop still refused to intervene publicly in Irish affairs for Herbert Asquith, on 23 May, had entrusted the Minister for Munitions, the talented and nimble David Lloyd George with the delicate mission of finding a solution to the Irish question.[50] At the end of the same month, Cardinal Farley of New York founded the Irish Distress Fund (IDF) meant to help the victims of the rising. The Irish-American prelate asked Walsh to become the president of the executive committee, which he accepted. In Ireland, the IDF became known as the Irish National Aid Association (INAA) and later on as the Irish National Aid and Volunteer Dependants' Fund (INAVDF), managed by the young Michael Collins, also head of the IRB.[51] The INAA started under favourable auspices since Walsh wrote to the treasurer that he had just received £1,000 from the United States and that a Thomas Hughes Kelly would soon cross the Atlantic to discuss the distribution of the money throughout Ireland.[52] The British authorities looked unfavourably on this new collaboration between Ireland and Irish America especially since the USA had not yet entered the war. Irish Americans were an important political lobby, capable of influencing the White House. It is, therefore, not surprising that the British immediately tried to harm the INAA. Curran informed Mgr Hagan in Rome that the fund had collected more than £10,000 but that Hughes Kelly had been forbidden to land in Ireland. He was of the opinion that he would 'raise murder' on his return to America and that Cardinal Farley was a powerful support.[53] This Irish-American collaboration was significant because Irish America began to support Sinn Féin rather than Redmond's Nationalist party,[54] even though this support was called into question the moment the United States declared war on Germany in April 1917. Walsh never doubted his participation in the INAA and when on 16 August 1916 the very nationalist INAVDF replaced it, Walsh agreed to become its honorary president.[55]

The British were not alone in being worried about Ireland. The French Government focused its attention on the United Kingdom and its rebel colony. André Géraud, a civil servant in the French embassy in London, sent a report to the Quai d'Orsay in Paris, the French Foreign Office. He wrote that the INAVDF was an organisation that backed Sinn Féin and that Farley and other Irish American prelates had written pastoral letters, recommending sending money to the fund. He indicated that more than £20,000 had been sent from the USA.[56] The French had been shell shocked by the Easter Rising. They knew that if their Allies got bogged down in Ireland, negative repercussions would undoubtedly occur in their military strategy. This was all the more worrying since the French Army was at that time involved in the greatest battle the world had ever seen, Verdun, and that the outcome of this unprecedented large-scale struggle, so costly in lives, was far from certain. Some of the British troops would have had to be withdrawn from the front if the rising had been entirely successful.[57]

The Germans had thought about destabilising the British Empire before the war.[58] Their arming of both the Ulster Volunteer Force and the Irish Volunteers in 1914 suggests this policy.

On 25 April 1916, Colonel de la Panouse, the military attaché of the French embassy in Britain, informed the French War Secretary, that law and order had been re-established in Dublin. According to him, the Nationalist party and the Catholic clergy were satisfied that this rebellion allowed them to publicly denounce the socialist Irish Citizen Army and the Sinn Féiners.[59] De la Panouse was right because a majority within the clergy had condemned the rising but this was before the execution of the rebel leaders. Not only did the rising catch the French and the Americans' attention, but also the Vatican's. On 30 April, Benedict XV ordered Cardinal Pietro Gasparri, the Secretary of State, to enquire on his behalf into the situation in Ireland. Firstly, Gasparri sent quite a peremptory telegram to Cardinal Logue in Armagh, asking him to cooperate in order to restore law and order in the country and not to hinder the British authorities in their task.[60] It is not clear how Logue reacted to this first telegram but taking into account his severe criticisms of the British Government since the beginning of the war, it is very unlikely that he was pleased with the Cardinal's tone. This telegram was later published by the Italian newspaper *Corriere della Sera*. Strangely enough, however, Gasparri sent a second telegram to Logue, written in French and, this time, it was far more sympathetic. He simply asked to be informed about the current situation and prayed that Ireland would be spared bloody conflicts. Logue replied that the insurgents had surrendered unconditionally and that peace had been restored.[61] On 3 May 1916, Sir Henry Howard, head of the British mission in Rome, told Gasparri that the tenor of the two telegrams was remarkably different. Gasparri replied that they both conveyed the same idea.[62] The Italian Cardinal's explanation was not very convincing. Benedict XV knew about the future rising in Ireland. His Secretary of State did not. It would have been completely incomprehensible, if not criminal, if the Pope had waited for the fighting to begin in order to ask for the restoration of peace. Consequently, Gasparri, not being au fait with the exact situation, sent this first peremptory telegram. Benedict XV, aware of Gasparri's initial message, probably asked his Secretary of State to send a more sympathetic one. The French embassy in Rome had followed the whole affair and informed its Prime Minister, Aristide Briand, that the Pope's telegram had been spontaneous and that the British mission had absolutely not intervened. The embassy was of the opinion that the telegram was 'an indirect appeal to Irish submission'.[63] Of course, the French author of the report knew nothing about Count Plunkett's audience with Benedict XV. It could be assumed that Aristide Briand was by now reassured about the turn of events in Ireland: the British authorities were controlling the situation and the Vatican had also intervened. Nothing could be further from the truth.

One day before the French embassy in Rome had sent its report, the Président du Conseil had received, on 3 May 1916, a letter from Paul Cambon, the French Ambassador in London. Cambon had carefully studied the rising, its causes and its consequences and had outlined the future position of the Irish Catholic Church. He explained to Briand that France had been very popular in Ireland in the past, as she had been England's enemy. The present war had changed this and now, ironically, Germany had taken over France's role. Furthermore, French pre-war anti-clerical policy had shocked Catholic Ireland and had allowed the Germans 'to create support in the clergy of the island'. Cambon recognised that these pro-German priests were not only very active but also quite successful as recruitment had practically ceased to exist. But even more important, the ambassador had understood that the British authorities had lost all control over Ireland and that the Nationalist party's influence had diminished. He wrote 'that the [British] Prime Minister's Irish policy had completely failed', notably in Ulster when the UVF was created. Cambon believed that the Sinn Féiners were still in a small minority but that they were active and determined, and that it was very likely that 'from the bottom of their hearts, the majority of the population was with them'. He wrote his report before even the execution of the rebel leaders began. Concerning the clergy, he remarked: 'This association [of Sinn Féin] with the enemies of the Church [the Irish socialists, ICA] forced the clergy to adopt a kind of neutrality in the recent rising but it is to be feared that under the pressure of popular passion, cleverly assisted by the Germans, that the clergy will be lenient towards the partisans of a complete independence for Ireland.'[64] Cambon's words were prophetic. They implied that the Church would not go against the wishes of the population. As has been seen, priests were not in a position, or did not wish, to morally force the Irish people to join the Army lest they became isolated within their own parishes. It seemed that Cambon had discerned a difference between the theoretical power of the Church and its real power. If the people had decided for a new political departure, the Church would not oppose it, unless it was definitely against its interests. Future events would prove this to be the case.

THE HIERARCHY'S REACTION TO THE EASTER RISING

Wherever there was a risk of fighting between the Army and the Irish Volunteers, the clergy tried to disperse the insurgents.[65] In some cases, priests acted like mediators. The most striking example was the auxiliary Bishop of Cork, Daniel Cohalan. The situation in the city of Cork was confused. On Sunday 23 April, the rebel leaders, Terence

McSwiney, Thomas MacCurtain and Sean O'Sullivan had orders to join forces with the Irish Volunteers in Co. Kerry. But the same day they also received Eoin MacNeill's counter-order, cancelling all manoeuvres. They decided to stay in Cork. On Monday night 24 April, a message signed by Patrick Pearse ordered them to begin the rising. Bad weather conditions, however, forced the leaders to begin on Tuesday, the very day General Stafford and the Army entered the city.[66] A peculiar situation developed as the two forces took up positions and watched each other. Cohalan and the Mayor knew that the military authorities had given the rebels an ultimatum, demanding their unconditional surrender before Saturday at noon. On Friday night, the Bishop and the Mayor crossed the Volunteer lines and tried to persuade the leaders to surrender. The negotiations were protracted and difficult as emotions ran high but Cohalan, nevertheless, managed to convince the Volunteers not to fight in the city. At 3 a.m., the Bishop and Mayor returned to the British and Stafford agreed to defer the ultimatum until Monday at noon. The rebels then demanded, somewhat incongruously, 'to give up all their arms and ammunition *to the Bishop personally* [in italics in original text] on the condition that he would not allow them out of his possession and would return them on demand'.[67] Of course, the British General refused but guns remained silent and the rebels eventually surrendered. It is to be noted that Cohalan was one of the first members of the hierarchy to state publicly that Sinn Féin could become a credible alternative political party.

One of the striking facts in the aftermath of the rising was the silence of most of the bishops. Of thirty-one prelates, auxiliary bishops included, only seven unreservedly condemned the rebels. They were Kelly of Ross, Higgins of Tuam, Harty of Cashel, Mangan of Kerry, Logue of Armagh, Hoare of Ardagh and Gilmartin of Clonfert. According to them, the Easter Rising was completely unjustifiable from a theological point of view. The rebels had therefore committed a serious crime and under no circumstances should another rebellion take place in Ireland. Dr Hoare invoked the theories of *jus ad bellum*, just war, and carefully explained when it was legitimate to revolt against a government. He wrote that two factors were essential: 'A) there must be a righteous cause, so that the resister will not, by his resistance, do more harm than good – there must be a real grievance and clear oppression; B) there must be a strong probability of success, otherwise harm will preponderate'. His views were published in the *Irish Catholic*.[68] Hoare, however, hoped that reconciliation would soon come and that the Government would be clement. The Bishop of Ardagh had understood that the executions were changing public opinion. Dr Higgins agreed with Hoare and spoke 'of the insanity and utter madness of any body of men...rising up against the English Army, which amounted to five millions of men'.[69] Higgins subsequently refused permission to celebrate a requiem mass for the executed rebels.[70] Dr Gilmartin said that the Irish people's duty 'was to support law and order, to show no sympathy in word or fact with any uprising against authority'.[71]

Explanations and causes of the rising were also put forward by these seven bishops. The most severe critic of the rebels was unquestionably Kelly of Ross. On 9 May 1916, the Redmondite *Freeman's Journal* published a long text from Kelly. The Bishop expressed his disgust for the rising and did not take into account the effects of the executions. He believed 'it was a war made in Ireland by Irishmen themselves'. But he went further and decided not to take into account Redmond's current difficulties with the British cabinet and the disastrous decisions of the War Office which had generated so much frustration among nationalists. He simply stated: 'Mr Asquith said in Parliament that this rising in Ireland was a clear indication of German influence... If all this be true, and Mr Asquith has of course information I have not got, this rising hasn't even the claim to be an Irish rising'.[72]

Kelly's idea that Ireland was but a pawn on the international and military chessboard was correct. The French and the Germans had long recognised the island's geopolitical importance. Mangan of Kerry asked a congregation in the cathedral of Killarney why the Irish supported revolutionary movements: 'Was it to fight the battles of Germany?' But Mangan was less severe in his condemnation of the rebels than Kelly. He said that he had never had any sympathy for the 'Volunteer movements, North or South'. According to him, Carson was really the man to blame for the whole situation: 'The responsibility rested on Sir Edward Carson and his supporters and... it was a mistake that nationalists should have imitated their example. The evil was accentuated when the nationalist Volunteer body split into two parties.'[73] Dr Gilmartin had also pointed his finger at Carson. According to both bishops, Carson had been the architect and initiator of organised militarism in Ireland, which sooner or later had to degenerate into violence.

These statements and perceptions were later confirmed by Mgr Touchet, the French Bishop of Orléans, during the first French mission to Ireland. In a letter to Aristide Briand, Touchet wrote that some Irish prelates were convinced that 'there was German money and Orange money involved in the matter'.[74] Unfortunately, Touchet did not give the names of the bishops who had put forward these explanations. It seemed that Sir Roger Casement's predictions had come true. A few months before the rising, Casement had become disillusioned with his German allies and friends, and rightly believed that their help to the Irish republican cause would be minimal. As a result, the rising would fail hopelessly, Germany's popularity in Ireland would wane overnight and the Church would sternly condemn the rebels. While in Berlin he confided to his diary: 'Once the Bishops...are moved to denounce a "German plot" against the internal peace of Ireland, then we may find public feeling in Ireland change to the complete detriment of Germany and leave her with no shred of Irish goodwill. The British recruiting sergeant will get the reward – not the German military machine.'[75] Only the subsequent executions of the rebel leaders, including Casement proved him wrong.

Once the causes had been explained, the bishops had to think of the possible consequences of the Easter Rising. Archbishop Harty of Cashel reiterated his support for John Redmond's constitutional policy and asked his diocesans to continue trusting the Nationalist party.[76] Harty had sensed that Redmond was in trouble. The rising and the bad recruitment figures showed that the party had lost some support. A few months later, he would be involved in a French propaganda mission to boost the war effort in the country. The Archbishop knew the rising was a golden opportunity to denounce Sinn Féin and the Irish Volunteers as dangerous troublemakers, as Colonel de la Panouse had indicated in his report to the Quai d'Orsay. The moment had come to strengthen the ties with the party. Regrettably for Harty, military short-sightedness did not take into account the capacity for Irish rebels to turn into martyrs and the rebel leaders were summarily shot, provoking public outrage. General Maxwell was clearly operating in an unfamiliar territory but should have remembered Napoleon's maxim: 'There are two powers in the world, the sword and the spirit. In the long run, the sword is always defeated by the spirit.' Imprisonment of the rebel leaders should have been the obvious option. The opportunity was thus lost for the Archbishop of Cashel. Kelly was of the same opinion as Harty and tried to use, perhaps, more persuasive economic arguments to stamp out the nationalist opposition movements and dissuade the population from supporting them:

> There is no doubt about it that you will suffer and suffer very severely for this insane outbreak. As you all know, the taxation that has so far resulted is enormous, but I am compelled to say that in the distribution of it over the Kingdom the Englishmen and the Scotchmen showed a disposition to treat this country leniently... Will they continue such treatment? Will the English people on whom every day the war continues, fresh taxation falls, be prepared to let us off lightly any longer, when they see us in this deliberate outbreak in Dublin doing all we can to continue the conflict that is so disastrous for them – because the Dublin rising will prolong the war. It is probably so intended.
>
> (*The Freeman's Journal*, 13 May 1916)

Kelly had become a financial scaremonger but his alarmist predictions were clever for they could not fail to impress the Irish people in this period of economic prosperity. As a matter of fact, he countered the arguments put forward by independent nationalists who, in February 1916, attempted to protest against overtaxation due to the war. These nationalists had condemned the Nationalist party's attitude towards the issue.[77] What the Bishop said was that the rising would make things even more disastrous. Higgins also alluded to the problem and mentioned the farmers in particular: 'Although they had not yet got all the land for which they were fighting in Ireland all their lives, they had got the greater part...and if the rebellion had succeeded to any extent all would have been taken from them.'[78] He had correctly analysed rural Ireland's reaction to the rising for the Inspector General of the RIC mentioned in his report that the farmers feared that the rising might put an end to their prosperity. The Inspector General was also of the opinion that they preferred John Dillon to John Redmond.[79] If this was the case, some political radicalisation had taken place among the farming community as Dillon wished the party to be far more independent in its dealings with the British cabinet than Redmond.

But, how did the highest ecclesiastical dignitary in Ireland react? Cardinal Logue waited for the annual meeting of the Maynooth Union, which he chaired, to make a public statement. He had been able to follow the correspondence between Archbishop Walsh and General Maxwell, and also between the General and Bishop O'Dwyer, as will be seen. Lord Hardinge's commission had made inquiries about the rising and had found that young priests had sided with Sinn Féin and had been guilty of subversive activities. It is true that eight reports from the RIC, coming from counties Donegal, Dublin, Laois, Longford, Louth, Clare, Galway and Leitrim, had highlighted the fact that the young clergy had expressed sympathy for Sinn Féin.[80] Logue, who detested Arthur Griffith's party, was very upset by the conclusions of Hardinge's commission. In his long speech for the Maynooth Union, he rejected these conclusions and accused the Government of slandering young priests. As to the evidence of the RIC, he said it had no foundation: 'I believe that these reports upon which these gentlemen – County Inspectors and others – based their accusations of the priesthood on the occasion of this Commission are simply gathered up from suspicions...and these suspicions are founded on the most futile and the most absurd grounds'.[81] Logue refused, at once, to accept the undeniable fact that there was indeed an increase of Sinn Féin priests. It is difficult to establish with certainty the exact number of seditious priests but it would have been around thirty-five.[82] There is, however, an explanation of the Cardinal's staunch denial. At the end of the nineteenth century during the Land War, Logue had complained to Arthur Balfour, then Irish Secretary, about the methods used by the RIC to track down anti-British priests. He had not trusted the RIC ever since.[83] If it was Logue's aim to separate the clergy from Sinn Féin, he got off to a bad start because his stubborn refusal to admit certain facts could not possibly help to purge the Church from revolutionary elements.

Like Mangan and Gilmartin, Logue criticised the creation of paramilitary forces in the country but did not mention any politician in particular. This reflected his usual cautious approach. He added that when he learnt about the rising in Dublin, he immediately knew that 'the public authorities [would] muddle this, as sure as the sun shone'. Logue seems to have anticipated some form of reprisal action that the Army might take. Indeed, shortly after the executions General Maxwell had met the Cardinal for a discussion about the rising. Logue had told him frankly: 'You put your foot in it! In shooting those fifteen rebel leaders, you made martyrs out of them. Since then, the small Sinn Féin group has considerably increased: the majority of the country is favourable to them'.[84] The *Irish Times* and the Church of Ireland had approved the executions.[85] Logue persisted in his systematic denunciation of Asquith's cabinet. He criticised the Government's decision to round up men as suspects and take them away from their families before it 'sent them away to England, either to jails or to concentration camps'. According to him, the Government 'should have let this die out like a bad dream...without going to these extreme measures'.[86] The British cabinet had indeed taken the decision to send rebels and all suspects to internment camps in Britain. By 1 May 1916, 400 men were detained in England.[87] In total, 3,340 men and 79 women were taken into custody and sometimes their arrest was arbitrary.[88] It is hard to resist the temptation to think about what would have happened if the Government had not shot the leaders and simply released the rebel prisoners shortly after their surrender, as Logue suggested. Although the Cardinal had analysed the problem well, he did not propose any solution. It seemed that he was not able to put forward any constructive policy. Perhaps he believed that it was not incumbent on ecclesiastics. However, despite the fact that he had lost all faith in Herbert Asquith and his ministers, Logue could not refrain from mentioning a theme that was dear to him: the support to the Empire in time of war. The *Freeman's Journal* reported his words:

> He did not see why patriotism should stand between the duty of Irishmen to the higher powers and their attachment to their country and their religion. On the contrary, they had the strongest proofs that when, unfortunately, this lamentable disturbance [the rising] arose, the Irish were rallying round the state and the

Empire and sending their best and dearest to shed their blood on the battlefields of Europe and Asia.

(*The Freeman's Journal*, 22 June 1916)

It could appear that Logue was not at all realistic in June 1916 and that he had no idea of the evolution of public opinion towards the war. Between February and August 1916, voluntary enlistment had only attracted a mere 9,323 men.[89] But, in view of his declaration to General Maxwell, it appears that Logue was in fact well aware of the political situation. His imperial declaration was meant to impress the Irish Catholic population and prevent them from taking sides with Sinn Féin. That is why he said that the Irish were courageously participating in the war. Since his speech at the Oireachtas in Dundalk in 1915, he had known that recruitment was declining in Ireland. The Cardinal agreed with Mangan and Gilmartin, but contrary to these southern bishops, he did not point his finger at the unionists but at the Government instead. Logue's archdiocese was in unionist territory and his imperial speech suggests that he still hoped that Carson and his supporters would eventually trust an autonomous Ireland within their cherished Empire.

One bishop who dissociated himself from the rest of the hierarchy was Michael Fogarty of Killaloe. Fogarty was patiently waiting for an opportunity to publicly intervene in the discussions regarding the Easter Rising. The opportunity presented itself on 12 May 1916 when the British Prime Minister arrived in Ireland to assess the situation for himself. Asquith stayed until 18 May. This visit was described as the beginning of a new area in Irish history. It was a triumph for Sinn Féin because the Prime Minister focused all his attention on the rebels and the nationalist opposition rather than on those who had remained loyal to the British Crown, in other words John Redmond and his party. Asquith visited prisoners in gaols who understood that they had not been beaten in vain since the Prime Minister himself seemed to recognise their importance. Those prisoners shouted 'victory' the moment their prominent guest left. The rising had become 'the most successful failure in history'.[90] Asquith must have been seriously worried to leave England and his war cabinet. On Sunday 14 May in the Church of Quin in Co. Clare, a combative Fogarty decided to speak out, explain the origins of the rising and warn Herbert Asquith. He began by saying 'he was not going to trouble [the congregation] with a denunciation of the unhappy young men who were responsible for that awful tragedy. There [were] enough and plenty in Ireland to do that.' Unlike Bishops Kelly, Higgins, Gilmartin and Mangan, he believed that the rebels had sacrificed themselves for their country even if they had committed a serious crime. But like them he singled out Carson, his *bête noire*: 'Sir Edward Carson has been the root cause of all this trouble. He it was who schooled our unfortunate country into ideas and practices of rebellion.' He added ironically: 'He has been allowed to go free; he has been honoured with a seat in the Cabinet.' Fogarty referred to the setting up of the Provisional Government in Ulster and the creation of the Ulster Volunteer Force in 1913, meant to resist Home Rule which had been democratically approved by the British Parliament. He denounced the fact that James Campbell was a member of Asquith's new coalition cabinet: 'Mr. Campbell was one of the ringleaders in the projected revolt in Ulster. He is now Attorney-General of Ireland, whose office it is to advise on the punishment of the Irish insurgents who in all probability would never have handled a rifle but for his example.'[91] Fogarty appeared to be referring to an article written by Eoin MacNeill in 1913 entitled 'The North Began'. In this article MacNeill had written that the Irish Volunteers had followed the example of the UVF. Fogarty concluded his sermon by warning Herbert Asquith:

> The Prime Minister, whom we all respect, and who is kindly disposed towards this country, is, I see, now in Ireland. I hope, before he leaves, he will put an end to these most operative causes of discontent and angry feeling. He will be well advised if in his treatment of Ireland at this juncture he is guided by the kindly words of Mr Birrell [Irish Secretary], whom I regret ... and not by the cruel and Cromwellian spirit that still haunts the gloomy spaces of Dublin Castle ... You cannot exterminate the national spirit of Ireland.
>
> (*The Freeman's Journal*, 17 May 1916)

Fogarty regretted Birrell's resignation as he had been one of the best Irish secretaries.[92] The Bishop of Killaloe's words were published by the *Freeman's Journal* on 17 May 1916 under the title 'Sir Edward Carson the Root Cause of all this Trouble'. This article must have caught Asquith's attention because the previous year, on 3 June 1915, John Redmond had sent him a letter from Fogarty, denouncing the Nationalist party's blind alliance with the English Liberals and breaking all links with the Nationalist leader.[93] Some newspapers were inspired by the Bishop's arguments. The *Catholic Bulletin* of August 1916 stated in its editorial that Irish Volunteers prisoners '[were] sent to break stones, pick oakum, sew sacks or indulge in some similar convict luxury peculiar to Portland and Dartmoor [prisons]' whereas the Unionist leaders who had openly planned a rebellion against the British authorities in 1913 'were rewarded with the most coveted posts open to men of their profession in England or Ireland'.[94] Bishop Cohalan had also expressed his horror when he learnt about the executions and the massive deportations. On 12 May 1916, on behalf of the inhabitants of Cork, he sent a telegram to John Redmond, Lord

Wimborne and Herbert Asquith, explaining that the Government's actions were alienating the population and 'if persisted in, ...may seriously imperil the future friendly relations between Ireland and England'.[95] A few days later, Cohalan sent another telegram to Wimborne, Asquith and General Maxwell, reiterating his previous appeal,[96] but to no avail. The Prime Minister was by now fully aware of a political radicalisation not only among the nationalist population but within the Catholic Church as well.

If these bishops had voiced their feelings openly, no less than twenty-two other prelates had not made any significant declaration. They can be divided into two distinct groups. The first had decided to follow more or less Archbishop Walsh's attitude, to wait and see how events would develop. These bishops knew that the Nationalist party was in a tight corner. The second group still continued to support Redmond but was too cautious to make any major public pronouncement. Their attitude can be summed up in a letter written by Bishop MacRory of Down and Connor in Ulster to Mgr O'Riordan in Rome: 'The Dublin affair is a shocking and idiotic tragedy. It was engineered by a few desperate socialists and a few sincere but silly patriots. Of course it had no chance whatever of succeeding. The danger is that it may have succeeded in gravely injuring Ireland's constitutional cause.'[97] The letter goes on to prove that Paul Cambon, the French Ambassador, had been right when he had written that the Church was somewhat embarrassed by the presence of atheist socialists in the rising. It is likely that these prelates were in a majority position within the hierarchy. Among those was, surprisingly the staunch Redmondite Patrick O'Donnell of Raphoe who made no criticism of the events in Dublin. This is in itself very relevant as it indicates a state of confusion amidst the bishops who still favoured the Irish Parliamentary Party. It is equally noteworthy that there seemed to be a difference in the arguments used by the northern bishops and the southern bishops. The northerners did not accuse the unionists of being the real cause of the rising. Logue had carefully avoided the subject. Perhaps were they afraid of a flare up of sectarianism in their respective dioceses. However, some of the southerners did not hesitate to voice their feelings.

John Redmond and his party realised that things were no longer going according to plan. On 11 May 1916 in the House of Commons, the energetic John Dillon lambasted the Government in a bitter speech. He denounced the stupidity of its policy in Ireland and said that it would mean the destruction of his party: 'It is the first rebellion that ever took place in Ireland where you had a majority on your side. It is the fruit of our life work ... and now you are washing out our whole life work in a sea of blood.'[98] His words were prophetic. Dillon also demanded explanations concerning the reputedly bad and unjustifiable behaviour of some British soldiers during the rising. Asquith answered that he would open an enquiry. General Maxwell told a journalist of the *Daily Mail* that Dubliners had complained about British military brutality, notably in North King Street, and was willing to punish the culprits if these accusations were founded.[99] Dillon was right, for some innocent civilians had been killed by soldiers.[100] When Asquith returned from Ireland, he informed members of his cabinet that British troops had indeed shot defenceless people.[101] Shortly afterwards, he asked David Lloyd George to settle the Irish problem. But it was too late. Never again would the British Government find favourable circumstances in Ireland. The only hope for British interests and the Nationalist party was the immediate implementation of Home Rule in all of the country. On 29 May 1916, Mgr Curran sent a letter to Mgr O'Riordan in which he described, not without humour and irony, the current situation in Dublin:

> Things are settling down here but by no means in the old way. The effects of the rising are indescribable and incalculable. The national soul is roused; scoffers of Sinn Féin are now sympathisers and after all the military outrages and looting and despotism, the position of the British Government here is not an enviable one. Even all the good ladies who cheered the English soldiers entering from Kingstown have turned rebels since these gentlemen have taken their rings as souvenirs and used their toy dogs or pet Persians as targets.
>
> (ICR, O'Riordan papers no. 17, letter no. 37, Curran to O'Riordan, 29 May 1916)

Curran spoke justly about a 'national soul' that the executions had provoked. The question was whether this new nationalist élan would last or not. But one thing was certain: Bishop O'Dwyer had played a crucial role in arousing the nationalist soul.

BISHOP O'DWYER'S RISE IN THE NATIONALIST OPPOSITION

The relations between the Bishop of Limerick and John Redmond were at a low ebb when the rising occurred. O'Dwyer had not made any public declaration on the issue until General Maxwell asked him to take disciplinary action against two of his priests who, the General thought, had been guilty of subversive activities. On 6 May 1916, O'Dwyer was in Kilmallock on a pastoral visit when he received Maxwell's letter.[102] The General wrote that Fr Thomas Wall from Drumcollogher and Fr Michael Hayes from Newcastle West were 'a dangerous menace to the peace and safety of the Realm' and that he would have arrested them had they not been priests. The General asked O'Dwyer: 'In this case I would be glad if

Your Lordship could obviate the necessity for such action by moving these Priests to such employment as will deny their having intercourse with the people, and inform me on your decision.'[103] The Bishop took a few days to think about it and, on 9 May 1916, he ordered Fr James O'Shea, the parish priest of Kilmallock, to send an answer on his behalf. This first letter was courteous and O'Dwyer simply stated that the General's demands were quite severe. He was willing, however, to open an enquiry if Maxwell could give more details on what kind of subversive activities Wall and Hayes were involved in. He added that he would strictly follow ecclesiastical procedures in this matter, not military rules.[104]

On 12 May, Maxwell sent a second letter to the Bishop. He wrote that Fr Hayes was the president of the local Irish Volunteers and that he had distributed pamphlets, inciting young people to join the movement. Concerning Fr Wall, the General was far more precise. He remarked that on 14 November 1915, this priest had blessed the flags of the Volunteers and had spoken out against conscription. This was correct since the RIC reports, on which Maxwell must have based his accusations, confirmed Wall's activities.[105] But, what the General was implying was that Wall, that very same day, had read O'Dwyer's letter regarding the Irish emigrants in Liverpool in his church in Drumcolloher. Maxwell concluded his letter by saying: '. . . it should not be difficult for Your Lordship, under such disciplinary power as you may possess, to prevent at any rate priests from mixing up with and inciting their flock to join an organisation such as the Irish Volunteers have proved themselves to be'.[106]

O'Dwyer reigned supreme over his diocese and unquestionably knew about Wall's action in his church. In the light of this fact, Maxwell's second letter was like a warning to the Bishop after he had refused to take immediate disciplinary measures against Hayes and Wall. It must not be forgotten that at that particular time, Maxwell had been brushed aside twice by Cardinal Logue and Archbishop Walsh. The General's patience with ecclesiastics was running out. He knew about O'Dwyer's anti-war crusade but now the Bishop had to fall back into line. Before answering, the Bishop questioned the two priests and Wall admitted that he was indeed a member of the Volunteers.[107]

He carefully thought over the contents of his letter and took into consideration the latest political developments in the country. On 1 May, the first Irish prisoners had arrived in England. On 9 May, in the House of Commons, Sir John Lonsdale had put forward a proposal that conscription should be enforced in Ireland. Sir Edward Carson had approved.[108] On 12 May, James Connolly and Sean MacDermott had been the last rebel leaders to be shot. On 14 May, his friend, Dr Fogarty, had publicly denounced Carson and the British Government. When, on 17 May, O'Dwyer sent his reply to Maxwell he was in a bellicose mood, to say the least. His letter created a tremendous sensation in Ireland and the date was timed to perfection since Herbert Asquith was still in the country. He began by saying that he could not find any fault with the behaviour of Fr Wall and Fr Hayes and described them as 'excellent priests, who hold strong national views'. He then made a personal and humiliating attack on Maxwell, whom he called a 'military dictator':

> You remember the Jameson raid, when a number of buccaneers invaded a friendly State, and fought the forces of the lawful Government. If men deserved the supreme punishment it was they. But, officially and unofficially, the influence of the British Government was used to save them, and it succeeded. You took great care that no plea of mercy should interpose on behalf of the poor young fellows who surrendered to you in Dublin. The first information we got of their fate was the announcement that they had been shot in cold blood. Personally, I regard your action with horror and I believe that it has outraged the conscience of the country. Then the deporting of hundreds and even thousands of poor fellows without a trial of any kind, seems to me an abuse of power as fatuous as it is arbitrary; and altogether your regime has been one of the worst and blackest chapters in the history of the misgovernment of the country.
>
> (*The Capucin Annual*, 1942, pp. 335–6)

An important distinction must be made here. The extent of the British Government's involvement in the 'Jameson Raid' in the Boer War in South Africa was never fully revealed.[109] According to popular belief, one of the British soldiers who had been taken prisoner by the Boers was John Maxwell himself.[110] Apart from the fact that Maxwell had taken command of British soldiers and was later commandant of a laager, concentration camp, in the Transvaal, there is no evidence to substantiate this.[111] It was the end of the General's 'spiritual arms' tactics. O'Dwyer's letter rallied all nationalist public opinion behind him. Mgr Curran wrote that it was published in Dublin by the *Evening Mail* and that the newspaper sold all its copies despite the warnings of the authorities.[112] The letter was also handed out as a pamphlet.

O'Dwyer's action has been criticised by historians who believe that his letter was meant to make a consensual declaration of the hierarchy on the Easter Rising impossible and that he had behaved in a typical opportunistic way.[113] This analysis is simply not justified if the war is not taken into account. Firstly, Home Rule had been granted and then suspended because of the hostilities in Europe, and the British Government was eagerly waiting for Irish recruits to show the new nationhood of their country as well as their gratitude to British democracy. When the recruits showed up, they were not particularly well treated by the War Office, a fact that David Lloyd George himself had recognised.[114] It was also clear that Lord Kitchener preferred UVF recruits and gave preferential treatment to the 36th Ulster Division. He had thought about keeping them in Ireland to crush a possible nationalist rebellion.[115] Only O'Dwyer, Fogarty and occasionally Logue had publicly denounced this state of affairs. Secondly, as we have seen, the Bishop did not intend to harm the General in the first place. Thirdly, it is highly unlikely that the hierarchy would have reached a consensus of opinion on the Easter Rising. It is not conceivable that prelates such as Logue, Walsh, O'Dwyer, Fogarty, Kelly, O'Donnell and Higgins, all at loggerheads on a range of issues, would have agreed on a common declaration. Nevertheless there can be little doubt that O'Dwyer was indeed a political opportunist. O'Dwyer had opposed the Plan of Campaign during the Land War. And yet, in October 1916, he told an amused Archbishop Walsh who had supported the same Plan: 'When did we ever get anything by constitutional means? We won the land laws by shooting landlords. We won emancipation by the threat of civil war!'[116] When André Géraud, the civil servant of the French embassy, visited O'Dwyer in Limerick in June 1916, the Bishop told him that if France wanted to recover Ireland's friendship she could easily do so.[117] The Bishop probably implied that if the French Government could persuade the British to implement Home Rule at once for the entire island, the war effort would receive a serious boost. Yet, in October, Mgr Hogan, President of Maynooth, told Géraud that he overheard O'Dwyer saying: 'If the allies win, we will lose.'[118] But it is not surprising that O'Dwyer took this attitude. He was an individualist who operated within a hierarchy that did not want to denounce obvious negative British policy in Ireland. Even the handful of active pro-war bishops could hardly deny that nationalist Ireland had been unfairly treated. O'Dwyer was also a realist and knew that the rebels had not been defeated totally in vain. The executions had stirred up indignation throughout the country, which, until then, had become quite apathetic. On 18 May, he wrote to Mgr O'Riordan: 'There is hardly a second opinion in Ireland as to the savagery with which the Government has been acting. But it will do good. The country was being hypnotised by the politicians, but it is being revived these days.'[119]

But how had the Irish public and various political forces reacted to O'Dwyer's correspondence with Maxwell? It remains quite difficult to measure public opinion in the aftermath of the rising as the objectivity of many newspapers and reports could not be trusted in these years of war and propaganda.[120] In August 1916, the Inspector General of the RIC noted in his monthly report that there was no 'reason to believe that the majority of the people [were] pro-German' but that the population had lost nearly all interest in the war, even in Ulster where recruits were no longer forthcoming.[121] Many opposition newspapers had been censored by the authorities, although it would be easy to guess that they fully approved of O'Dwyer's victorious swashbuckling with the General. The Nationalist party and John Redmond did not comment on the matter. The *Freeman's Journal* remained silent, as it did not want to give even more publicity to the Bishop of Limerick. The hierarchy did not voice any opinion either. As for the *Irish Catholic*, published with Cardinal Logue's imprimatur, it simply continued to denounce the rising, quoting Saint Paul and Saint Thomas, which considerably annoyed the nationalist opposition.[122]

In June 1916, O'Dwyer went to Maynooth to participate in a ceremony. When he left the seminary, he was given a long ovation by the students.[123] This happened only a few days after Logue's speech for the Maynooth Union in which the Cardinal had denied that the young clergy were in favour of Sinn Féin. It would seem that the population generally held O'Dwyer in high esteem. To the nationalist population, he was no obscure revolutionary but a respected member of the venerated Catholic hierarchy. The people had lost interest in the war. The poor recruitment figures confirmed this. But, they also knew that the British Parliament was about to debate on the issue of conscription. Many in the country were against compulsory military service, be it on moral or financial grounds. In October 1916, André Géraud had noted in his report for the Quai d'Orsay in Paris that the economic prosperity in Ireland played deviously into Sinn Féin's hands as it did not encourage young Irishmen to join the colours.[124] They had all the reasons to stay safely at home rather than to fight for a shilling a day. Had O'Dwyer not publicly said, in 1915, that Irish farmers were more interested in cultivating their potato fields in peace? For many Irishmen, the Bishop had become the champion of their cause. On 25 June 1916, Mgr O'Riordan received a letter from Ireland which clearly indicated O'Dwyer's position: 'On every side the letters of Bishop O'Dwyer are accepted as exactly the right word in the right place and time – he was frantically cheered at Maynooth, singled out above all the other bishops.'[125] Various organisations and committees such as the Boards of Guardians of Limerick, Tipperary and Croom, Limerick County Council, and Rathkeale Town Council praised the Bishop.[126] Irish Volunteers and other republican prisoners also paid tribute to him. A few of these prisoners wrote poems in which O'Dwyer was depicted as a national hero:

> Who shall write the Easter story
> Who is worthy to relate
> All its romance, hopes, and glory
> How our leaders met their fate?

[followed by thirteen stanzas evoking Pearse, McDonagh, McDermott, Clarke, Daly, Connolly, MacBride, Kent, Mallin, Colbert, Heuston,

Plunkett, O'Hanrahan, William Pearse, Thomas Kent, O'Rahilly and Shaun Connolly]

> God has left us yet one hero
> His pen is like a sword of fire,
> Ireland loves him, Ireland thanks him,
> God watch o'er you, Bishop O'Dwyer.
>
> (LDO, O'Dwyer papers)

This poem highlighted a serious problem: who was going to lead the nationalist opposition in the political arena? Its anonymous author seemed to think that O'Dwyer was the ideal man. It must be remembered that most opposition leaders and intellectuals had been either shot or imprisoned, whether they belonged to Sinn Féin, the Irish Volunteers or the Irish Labour party. Arthur Griffith had been arrested on 3 May 1916 and sent to England where he was joined, later on, by Seán T. O'Kelly.[127] Eamon de Valera, still relatively unknown in public life, had also been deported to England, as was Eoin MacNeill.[128] On 15 June 1916, O'Dwyer wrote to O'Riordan: 'Nothing could equal the stupidity of the Government...Now the old spirit is bubbling up again, and will probably end by squelching Redmond and his gang.'[129] He was worried about the possible 'division of the country' and accused the *Freeman's Journal* of deceiving the Irish people. On the war he remarked: 'The great powers...have great faith in the power of lies.' If he had condemned Redmond, he had not put forward any alternative to channel this new nationalist energy. But this would soon become one of the main issues of the summer of 1916. At the end of June, some opposition newspapers could see ahead. The leaders were no longer there to take up the pen and write anti-British and anti-Remond articles but these newspapers found that O'Dwyer was decidedly a worthy source of inspiration. The *Irish Opinion* decided to publish a speech made by O'Dwyer in 1910 in which the Bishop had stated that Ireland would need 'educated men', capable of shaping a constructive policy for the country. The editorial said: '[O'Dwyer's] words are so appropriate to the present situation in Ireland that it would be a public loss not to recall them and give them the widest possible publicity'.[130] What the *Irish Opinion* implied was that Redmond and his party were no longer these men. In July 1916, the *Irish Nation* published an article entitled 'The Party must go' in which it developed exactly the same ideas as the Bishop's: 'The present Parliamentary Party must be got rid of and immediately...They must be replaced by new men, righteous men, upright, honourable and EDUCATED men [capital letters in original text].'[131] Nationalist Ireland was momentarily leaderless, at least according to the opposition.

Herbert Asquith had sensed the Irish people's growing anger after the executions and the deportations. He knew it was in Britain's interest to adopt a generous policy of conciliation.[132] Some prisoners were indeed released. But, it was, above all, a political move. On 1 July 1916, the major British offensive on the Somme in France had been launched. The 'Big Push' proved very expensive in human lives. There were no less than 60,000 casualties in one day's fighting. The 36th Ulster Division lost 5,500 men in two days.[133] The whole operation was a disaster. Conscription had already been introduced in Britain at the beginning of 1916. It was only a matter of time before Ireland would have to face compulsory military service. In this case, it was important to win back popular support in the country. Releasing prisoners was perhaps a good way. But the Government was careful in choosing prisoners for release. Leaders like Griffith, MacNeill and de Valera were too dangerous. The first one would be liberated at Christmas 1916,[134] and the other two in June 1917.[135] The British authorities had at long last realised that their allies in Ireland were still the Nationalist party and that they had to help John Redmond before it was too late. The longer imprisonment of some of the nationalist opposition leaders was a clear indication of their policy. One of those nationalists who had avoided the attention of the British authorities, managed to send a message to Count von Bernstorff, the German Ambassador to the United States, and wrote that the Irish Volunteers and the opposition had no more leaders of significant calibre.[136] This situation could only favour the Government and perhaps Redmond.

The ever watchful Mgr Curran had not been duped by Asquith's move. He wrote to Mgr Hagan in Rome that many prisoners had been liberated but that some would have to wait longer, 'particularly to prevent the rise of literary activity of an inconvenient kind'.[137] Despite the fact that the opposition was deprived of its intelligentsia, it was to be expected that someone would take the initiative. On 4 August 1916 in Omagh in Ulster, George Murnaghan and F.J. O'Connor founded the Irish Nation League (INL) against partition. They had been bitterly disappointed with Redmond's policy on the issue. Laurence Ginnell quit the Nationalist party and wrote the political manifesto of the INL. Ginnell asked Stephen O'Mara, a politician from Limerick, to help him in setting up a new party throughout the country. He stated that 'Limerick would for many reasons be the best place to launch such a project'. O'Dwyer was in turn contacted and had no objections to the plan but refused to give a 'public episcopal approval'.[138]

The Bishop's reasons for approving, yet refusing at the same time were logical. He knew that the opposition could soon be completely disorganised and that something would have to be done rapidly before it was too late. This problem was haunting him. On 31 August, he wrote to Mgr O'Riordan: 'If O'Brien and Healy had not discredited themselves we should have an alternative, but as it is, I do not see who are to displace the 'Party', unless as is not improbable, the Sinn Féin men gather strength enough to rout them'.[139] This allusion to Sinn Féin answers the question as to why he refused to publicly support the INL despite his sympathy. O'Dwyer feared that the nationalist opposition would soon be broken up in various rival factions, which could only favour the Government, the unionists and John Redmond. The summer of 1916 had seen the creation of other parties apart from the INL. There was the Repeal League of Michael Judge and the 'Sinn Féin party' of Herbert Pim, an old unionist now nationalist.[140] Judge did not agree with the INL and Pim. William O'Brien had founded the All for Ireland League (AIL), but O'Dwyer did not trust him as his letter to O'Riordan shows. It is, therefore, not surprising that the Bishop began to take a strong interest in Sinn Féin. The party had existed since 1905, had not yet an organisation throughout the country that could rival with the Nationalist party, but O'Dwyer could only approve of Griffith when he repeatedly denounced Redmond for being the puppet of the British Government. Furthermore, Sinn Féin belonged to this new nationalist élan, together with the Gaelic League and the Gaelic Athletic Association, which O'Dwyer fully endorsed. Griffith and Sinn Féin had also denounced Irish participation in the war. One question remained: how could he effectively help Sinn Féin?

An opportunity presented itself in September 1916 when Limerick Corporation decided to grant O'Dwyer Freedom of the City. The decision had not been unanimous as some members of the corporation were of the opinion that the Bishop had insulted the Nationalist party and that he had identified himself with the nationalist and popular cause only on certain occasions.[141] Clearly, these members were referring to his attitude during the Plan of Campaign. The Bishop accepted the honour and set out to write a long acceptance speech in which he justified his political evolution since his arrival in Limerick in 1886. Shortly before the ceremony, he asked for Dr Fogarty's advice on his speech. The Bishop of Killaloe recommended him to be more cautious in his explanation of the Easter Rising and the legal use of armed force: 'The ordinary reader may, and is likely to, take it as an approval on your part of the right of rebellion in Ireland until we get back our Irish Parliament. It may also be that some be objected to by high ecclesiastics in Ireland.' He also warned him that the English Government might make a formal protest at the Vatican. More relevant was the fact that Fogarty told O'Dwyer not to use the word 'Hebrew' in front of the Irish Under Secretary's name, Sir Mathew Nathan. 'Insult no man's race', wrote Fogarty.[142] O'Dwyer's writings seem to reveal an intolerant side to his character, or else the war and the rising had exacerbated his nationalism. As a result, he may have run out of patience with anything foreign. O'Dwyer took into account Fogarty's suggestion but could not resist using the word 'Jew' instead. It is to be noticed, however, that the Bishop had boycotted the Redemptorist Order in 1904 after some of its priests had been involved in anti-Jewish demonstrations in his home town.[143]

On 14 September 1916, the Bishop made his acceptance speech in Limerick. He began by acknowledging his popularity, which was unquestionably real, but stated that '[he felt] somewhat strange in these surroundings of public favour'. It was a dramatic change from the Plan of Campaign days. Then he justified the position he had adopted during the Land War and denied that he was a demagogue or an opportunist. O'Dwyer eventually broached the tricky part of his pronouncement: the Easter Rising. Very astutely, he made a comparison between Ireland and Belgium to give, at the very least, mitigating circumstances to the rebels without justifying the rebellion:

> In the very height, or depth of this juggling [the Home Rule crisis], the great European war broke out, and the political leaders of Ireland took up the cry from their masters in England, that it was a war for small nationalities...No appeal could go deeper into the Irish heart...One cannot be surprised if the Irish Volunteers said: if all this is true of Belgium and Serbia, and Poland, and all the other small nations of Europe, does it not hold good for Ireland?... When Lord Wimborne and Mr. Devlin and Mr. Redmond called on our young Irishmen to go to Flanders and give their lives for Home Rule in Belgium, was it not natural in view of the state of their own country that they should ask themselves if it was not all British cant and hypocrisy and in their anger and indignation break out into rebellion?
> (LDO, O'Dwyer papers, file 'Irish politics 1912–1922', Freedom of the City speech, 14 September 1996)

In this way O'Dwyer summed up his attitude towards the war since the early days of August 1914. He did not believe Britain's promises on self-determination, or that the rising had been entirely in vain since it had forced Herbert Asquith to come to Ireland. The Bishop's old enemy, John Dillon, would hardly have disagreed with him. He then made a ferocious attack on the individuals in the administration: 'No people in the world, that could help it, would stand being governed by strangers, men like Wimborne and Birrell and Nathan, a gang of carpet baggers, who came here for their personal interest at the behest of their party.' Clearly, O'Dwyer had adopted the meaning of Sinn Féin, 'ourselves alone'. He also said that French anticlerical politicians like Combes and

Viviani were 'Continental infidels'. The Bishop criticised the Imperial system and, contrary to Cardinal Logue, he could see no advantage in belonging to it. There was no solidarity between Ireland and England, and there was no independent government in his country, but it was governed by 'some English barrister from Bristol or Manchester or some Jew from Shoreditch [district in London]'. He was alluding here to Birrell, Lloyd George and Nathan. The war and the rising had taken their toll and led O'Dwyer to adopt separatist language. It was only at the end of his long and vitriolic speech that O'Dwyer made known his vision for Ireland: 'I will state my alternative to the Party, who trust the Liberals, and are now reduced to the statesmanship of Micawber – waiting for something to turn up... Sinn Féin is, in my judgment, the true principle, and alliance with English politicians is the alliance of the lamb with the wolf; and it is at this point precisely that I differ from present political leaders, and believe that they have led, and are leading the National Cause to disaster.'[144] The main victims of his diatribe were the Nationalist party and the British Government but not once did he point his finger at the Unionists. The danger of partition was in the air and, like Logue, he did not want to alienate Protestants.

But what exactly did support for Sinn Féin mean? This party was in disarray after the Easter Rising. Its leaders had been imprisoned and its newspaper, *Nationality*, suppressed by the authorities at Dublin Castle. According to the RIC, Sinn Féin was not well organised except in the counties of Laois, south Tipperary, east Galway, Sligo, Cavan, Louth, Cork, Clare and Limerick. Significantly, O'Dwyer and Fogarty's dioceses were in the last two counties. As to the ideology of Griffith's party, it remained somewhat obscure but it would become more precise in the years ahead. Many people declared themselves to be Sinn Féiners although they were not always aware of what it really meant.[145] The party was, above all, synonymous with opposition. Eamon de Valera would define the politics of Sinn Féin after his return to Ireland in 1917. It is difficult to be sure of the impact of O'Dwyer's speech on the population. Nevertheless, if one takes into account his popularity from which Sinn Féin must have benefited, he had given the party a solid foundation on which it could build up an organised opposition. Subsequent events would prove this to be true. The Bishop of Limerick had impressed some people. Walter McDonald, a professor in Maynooth seminary, wrote that O'Dwyer was 'one of the greatest and most courageous and most patriotic Irishmen of all time'.[146] On 17 September 1916, Dr Fogarty sent him the following letter: 'You have your critics amongst "the sober brows" but the great body of the people, especially the young, male and female, are in boundless admiration of you.'[147] Fogarty's reference to young people, and males in particular, was relevant for they would have been threatened by conscription. On 23 September, the *Irish Opinion* published extracts of O'Dwyer's address and, on the same day, *New Ireland* ran a headline: 'The Bishop of Limerick – An Historic Speech' and added that: 'Nothing could be more admirable than this statement of the Irish case, which will be endorsed by all Irish Nationalists worthy of the name.'[148] On 29 September, O'Dwyer wrote a letter to O'Riordan in which he stated that the Irish Volunteers had been wrong in rebelling and that he had condemned him, although 'all [his] sympathy [was] with them'.[149] The Bishop identified himself so much with the rebels' cause that he began a long correspondence about a possible theological justification of the rising with, of all people, Patrick Foley of Kildare and Leighlin who was publicly in favour of the war![150] Nonetheless it appeared that O'Dwyer had much respect for Foley's knowledge of the theories of just war.

Another man who was convinced of the causes of the sudden turnabout in Irish public opinion was the British Prime Minister. On his return to London from his stay in Ireland, Asquith quoted these causes to the members of his war cabinet and mentioned the Bishop of Limerick's letter to General Maxwell.[151] By now it was clear that O'Dwyer had become the 'moral leader' of the nationalist opposition. If the origins of Irish discontent had been established, what were the political initiatives of the Government in the summer of 1916?

THE CONSCRIPTION AND PARTITION CRISES OF 1916

On the morrow of the Easter Rising, the British cabinet realised that it was imperative to find a solution to the Irish problem as soon as possible, before it had serious repercussions on the war. The situation could not have been more complex. On the one hand, the Unionist party was opposed to Home Rule but was in favour of the war and supported Asquith's Government. On the other hand, the Nationalist party, the allies of Asquith's Liberals, also supported the war effort but demanded that Home Rule be implemented in the whole of Ireland, Ulster included. Asquith knew that Redmond was facing serious difficulties after the executions of 1916. It was important that he maintained his alliance with the Nationalist party for they were the only valid and acceptable nationalist force with whom the British could envisage negotiations. Asquith could simply not imagine negotiations with Sinn Féin or people of the same calibre as Patrick Pearse and James Connolly. However, O'Dwyer's increasing popularity, the public's largely indifferent attitude to the war, the rising and the executions were not the only factors responsible for the Nationalist party's decline.

In June 1916, André Géraud had been sent to Ireland by the French embassy in London to make a full report on the state of political affairs. He wrote to the Quai d'Orsay in Paris that John Redmond was partly to blame for the weakening of his position. Géraud believed that nobody could know with certainty who was still supporting the party. There were organisations that backed Redmond in theory, like the United Irish League (UIL), the Ancient Order of Hibernians (AOH) and the National Volunteers, but the Frenchman believed the 'party had carefully avoided to count up those who really belonged to them and those who belonged to the revolution'. What he implied was that Redmond was losing touch with the grass roots. According to Géraud, all the indications were that the Nationalist party would continue these tactics. Finally, he stated that the Catholic Church was the only powerful organisation left in the country.[152] The Frenchman was right when he stated that the Nationalist party refused to criticise itself as the RIC reports in 1916 confirmed his analysis. The Irish police had concluded that the UIL was no longer as active as it used to be throughout the country. Only in Belfast, where Joseph Devlin reigned supreme, and in counties Longford, Tipperary and Wexford, where Redmond came from, was there still some activity.[153]

Lethargy seemed to have taken over the party. Besides, some divisions in the party were appearing. John Dillon had sensed the danger and wanted the party to become more radical in its dealings with Asquith whereas Redmond was still willing to compromise with the British Government.[154] The Nationalist party's opponents took advantage of its disarray to attack it. At that particular time, conscription was being debated in the House of Commons in London. It had already been introduced in Britain in March 1916 for enlistment figures had seriously dropped but Ireland had been exempted.[155] On that particular occasion, there had been a difference of opinion between Redmond and Dillon. Both men were against the Compulsory Military Service Bill but Redmond wanted the party to abstain during the vote in Parliament, not wanting to hinder Asquith, whereas Dillon wanted it to vote against the bill, showing solidarity with anti-conscriptionists. Redmond won the argument. Dillon, however, showed his anti-clerical feelings by opposing an amendment to exclude priests from the bill.[156]

The French Consul in Dublin, J. de Longchamps, reported to Paris that the party was afraid of alienating its rural support in Ireland if it supported conscription. The consul was of the opinion that Irish farmers had got some of their land back since the Wyndham Act of 1903. Consequently, their anti-English feelings were no longer as intense as they used to be and the war had been a serious financial boost for them. De Longchamps added, interestingly, that the remembrance of the Land Wars was, however, still very much alive and younger people would seek to emulate their elders in opposing the British authorities, if conscription went ahead.[157] It was a perfectly plausible explanation. The war was squandering human lives and was not going in the Allies' favour. The Gallipoli fiasco, the battle of Verdun and the recent surrender of the British forces to the Turks at Kut were only striking examples of a general picture.[158] So, conscription loomed on the horizon in Ireland.

On 9 May 1916 in the British Parliament, Sir John Lonsdale, a staunch Unionist, said that compulsory military service should be implemented in the country. Sir Edward Carson, also present during the debate, saw there an excellent opportunity to test John Redmond's commitment to the idea of Home Rule and his loyalty to the Empire. He declared that under the Home Rule Act, all decisions concerning defence were to be taken by the Imperial Parliament of Westminster.[159] Redmond refused and said that his power was rapidly decreasing in Ireland. What were Carson's hidden motives for this rather untimely and opportunistic intervention? By now, it was exceedingly clear that Redmond was a loyalist in favour of the Empire, something the Unionist leader also claimed to be. The Nationalist leader was totally committed to the war effort and refused to give in to O'Dwyer. He cannot possibly be accused of being a Catholic clerical politician. Almost thirty years before, during the Plan of Campaign days, he had openly said that he rejected 'Rome Rule'. In 1904, he had strongly and publicly condemned the Jewish pogrom which occurred in the city of Limerick. The attack on the Jews had been led by a Catholic Redemptorist priest and Redmond had said on that occasion that the 'good sense and the spirit of toleration of the Irish people' would prevail.[160] Carson's lasting distrust might be the answer. But plain prejudice against all things nationalist and Catholic is more likely. His intervention, indeed, looked as if he wanted to destabilise and discredit Redmond even more and provoke a further radicalisation of nationalism, this time in the constitutional arena, which would have justified and strengthened his Ulster separatism. Whatever the Unionist politician's intentions were, Herbert Asquith understood that it was not in the United Kingdom's interest to alienate even further Irish nationalism and opted not to impose conscription.

Colonel de la Panouse, the French military attaché, had closely followed the debate. In his report to the War Secretary in Paris, he explained that many Irish MPs were against conscription and that the Prime Minister had not taken the risk to bring about 'a conflict between Irish and English on the one hand, and between Irish and Irish on the other hand'. This conflict 'would be far too dangerous at the present moment'.[161] De la Panouse must have been wondering about the course of events in Ireland. He knew that Asquith had made the best possible decision but also stood to lose thousands of potential recruits. From the summer of 1916 onwards, the threat of conscription would be like a sword of Damocles over Ireland, especially after the disastrous Somme offensive. In August 1916, the *Freeman's Journal* accused the Government of preparing a new military service bill.[162] In September, Mgr Curran wrote to Mgr O'Riordan: 'There is renewed talk of conscription. I am sure they will make efforts to introduce it. If they do, they will taste the real feeling of the country and will be glad to let sleeping dogs lie. It is one question on which we will all unite as a man at once and strongly.'[163] Curran's words were to prove prophetic in April 1918. On 15 October, he told Mgr Hagan that bishops from the rural areas of the country were of the opinion that the military authorities would only conscript 'dead bodies'. He wrote the same about Dublin.[164] Clearly, farmers had really no interest at all in the war. Curran had probably obtained his information from Walsh for a few days before the bishops had met in Maynooth. Their meeting had proved how divided the hierarchy was about its support for the Nationalist party. Archbishop Walsh had insisted that the bishops declare their unanimous opposition to conscription and partition. Some prelates, still in favour of Redmond, had thought that they also had to declare their support for the party and its constitutional policy, which some of them refused to do. Because of all these internal divisions, there was never a consensual declaration.[165] The *Irish Independent*, owned by the anti-Redmondite William Martin Murphy, managed to gather enough information about this discreet meeting. In an article entitled 'Conscription opposed', the newspaper informed its readers why the bishops had not reached a common declaration but that they were united against compulsory military service.[166] The authorities had been warned. The hierarchy, however, did not worry about conscription at this stage. In September 1916, Henry Duke, the new Irish Secretary who replaced Augustine Birrell, told the British cabinet that conscription in Ireland was simply not feasible.[167] But, the Catholic Church demonstrated its power and determination during the partition crisis in the summer of 1916. Asquith's disastrous handling of Redmond would lead the latter to a political deadlock, which played right into the nationalist opposition's hands.

In Ulster, as elsewhere in the country, the Easter Rising was resented by both nationalists and unionists. The executions radically changed the nationalist frame of mind. A RIC inspector from Armagh stated in his report that 'after the execution of the rebel leaders a malignant spirit manifested itself by indifference to Allied successes, falling off in recruiting, and indifference to supplying comforts to the wounded'.[168] On 10 May 1916, Joseph Devlin, the leader of the Nationalist party in the north of the country, wrote to John Dillon that he found it amazing that 'everybody in Ireland [had] not been driven into the Sinn Féin movement'.[169] Devlin, like Dillon, believed that the party had to become more radical in its dealings with the British cabinet but Redmond still favoured the idea of supporting the Government in these times of international crisis. Devlin made no secret about his apprehensions: '[We] will lose all we have gained by our attitude towards the war.'[170] The conflict in Europe had become a fatal obsession for Redmond. Asquith wanted to clear the political atmosphere in Ireland and appointed David Lloyd George as negotiator in Irish affairs. Little did the Prime Minister know that from this moment onwards, Irish politics would become even more opaque. Lloyd George had been a brilliant Minister for Munitions and had done much to make British industry adapt itself to the demands of total war.[171]

The Welsh politician began negotiations on 26 May and took the unusual step of talking separately with the Unionists and the Nationalists. To the former, he promised that counties Armagh, Antrim, Down, Fermanagh, Tyrone and Derry would definitely be excluded from Home Rule. With the latter, he encouraged the impression that partition would only be temporary. Home Rule would be immediately implemented in Ireland except in the above mentioned counties. It is difficult to know exactly what Lloyd George was planning. If one takes into account his role as Minister for Munitions, he must have known that there were major war industries concentrated in Ulster, and little in the rest of Ireland.[172] Harland and Wolff in Belfast, for instance, supplied ships to the Royal Navy.[173] The Navy had always been central in British strategic conceptions. Therefore, it can be reasonably assumed that he was extremely careful in not alienating the unionist population, which may have disrupted the crucial war industry. At the end of May 1916, Lloyd George made public his proposals for Home Rule. They were so cleverly worded that both Unionists and Nationalists could interpret them as being favourable to their respective causes.[174]

Very rapidly, the bishops and the clergy whose dioceses were inside the proposed exclusion zone mobilised their forces against Lloyd George. Cardinal Logue wrote to Bishop O'Donnell that he feared bishops would be considered as traitors in the history of the country, if they accepted Lloyd George's scheme.[175] The Catholics of Ulster were outraged by the latest British initiative. Throughout the six excluded counties protest meetings were organised. Many priests participated. On 8 June, Fr John O'Doherty read out to the crowd in Omagh four letters of four Ulster bishops, all denouncing partition, be it temporary or permanent. Only Logue had not sent any letter. Charles McHugh of Derry deplored the cabinet's decision and wondered how responsible statesmen could have come up with such proposals. According to him, they would 'incite a new rebellion more disastrous than the one [they had] unfortunately witnessed a short time ago'.[176] McHugh remarked that there was a Nationalist parliamentary majority in the nine historic counties of Ulster. It was a clear warning for Redmond. The Bishop of

Derry had always supported the party in its efforts in general and in its war policy in particular. He indicated that he would not blindly follow the party on the road to partition. Dr MacRory of Down and Connor was even more direct in his warning: 'True statesmanship ought to be able to find some means of healing instead of perpetuating our unhappy differences.'[177] MacRory demanded that democracy decide about partition. The Bishop of Clogher, Dr McKenna, compared Ulster's fate to Alsace-Lorraine, unjustly torn from France's bosom. He declared that partition was the 'grossest insult to the spirit of Irish nationality', and concluded prophetically: 'It would, in my opinion, exasperate and embitter for all future time the Irish race throughout the world.'[178]

After an initial prudent reaction to the Easter Rising, the northern bishops had now thrown all caution to the winds. Only one Ulster prelate had a different reaction, Patrick O'Donnell of Raphoe. O'Donnell still trusted Redmond and his party. In February 1914, he had declared that he approved of partition only if it was Sir Horace Plunkett's plan. This plan implied that certain areas in Ulster would have the right to be included in the Home Rule zone by plebiscite.[179] In his letter, O'Donnell wrote that the Omagh meeting was fully justified but that an assembly of northern nationalists had to decide on 'unity of action'. Finally, the Bishop of Raphoe made the following guarantee: 'The Irish Party in a matter of this kind, when it is fully discussed, will not agree to anything that would be against the mature judgement of the clergymen and laymen who can speak for the Nationalist population whose exclusion would be sought.'[180] O'Donnell had sensed that if the new partition crisis was tackled badly, it would be fatal to the Nationalist party. It must be noted that O'Donnell's own diocese, Raphoe, was in Co. Donegal, outside the planned exclusion zone. On 10 June 1916 in Dublin, John Redmond publicly announced that he agreed with David Lloyd George's proposals.[181] Archbishop Walsh had not yet reacted.

Generally, the southern bishops did not make much comment on the issue. They might have felt that this was a problem that could best be solved by the northern bishops alone. Bishop O'Dwyer had been prudent and waited for the opportune moment to intervene. On 15 June, he wrote to Mgr O'Riordan: 'The immediate issue is the division of the country to conciliate the Orangemen, or rather to please the nonconformists. Ruse and falsehood that the *Freeman[s Journal]* can think of are being used to deceive the country, but whatever else our countrymen are, they are no fools.'[182] He seemed to think that partition could be implemented but that if it proved unsatisfactory, the country would reunite. On 16 June, Redmond met all the northern bishops in Dublin, including Cardinal Logue. The Nationalist leader found that all the prelates were hostile to Lloyd George's plan. MacRory suggested a democratic vote but Redmond refused.[183] The party's northern ecclesiastical support was waning.

In the meantime, Joseph Devlin had accepted David Lloyd George's proposals and had the delicate task of convincing Ulster Nationalists. On 17 June, he managed to convince the majority of 1,800 delegates by insisting that partition would only be temporary. However, an important part of the clergy in counties Tyrone, Derry, Fermanagh and Armagh was against him and these priests were very active in organising anti-partition meetings.[184] On 20 June, Devlin assured northern Nationalists that the six counties temporarily excluded from Home Rule would be defended by the party in the House of Commons in London, as Lloyd George had guaranteed. The next day, Dr McHugh sent a letter to the *Derry Journal*, expressing his worries on Catholic education in a state controlled by Protestants.[185] It was an old Catholic fear. On 23 June 1916, the great meeting of Ulster Nationalists, suggested by Bishop O'Donnell, took place in Belfast. The atmosphere was strained and the debates were stormy. A courageous John Redmond tried to dissipate all worries and said that if partition was permanent he would be totally opposed to the British proposals. Some people shouted: 'Is the Bishop of Derry a liar?' and 'What about the Cardinal and the Ulster bishops?'[186] Redmond stayed calm and told his unruly audience that if they did not agree with him, he would resign as chairman of the Nationalist party. It seemed that Redmond had still some power of persuasion despite all his recent setbacks for 475 delegates voted for the new Home Rule bill and 265 against.

Lloyd George's proposals were to become a reality. The *Freeman's Journal* acclaimed the leader's victory in Belfast and denounced the *Irish Independent* which was of the opinion that Devlin had betrayed the northern Nationalists.[187] The reaction of the Ulster bishops was negative. Only two days before the Nationalist meeting in Belfast, Cardinal Logue had declared to the *Derry Journal*: '[it would be] infinitely better to remain as we are for fifty years to come than to accept these proposals'.[188] Bishop O'Dwyer was very shocked by the Nationalists' decision. He wrote to O'Riordan that it was a form of patriotic suicide but added: 'We shall have two countries: the Orange Free State; and the three provinces. But I shall be surprised if the thing becomes law.'[189] The French Consul in Dublin had also analysed the partition debate. In his report to Aristide Briand, he explained that the Irish resented the fact that industrial Ulster was cut off from the agricultural south. He also stated that Cardinal Logue supported the northern bishops and added that some prelates in the south were also supportive. De Longchamps' remark is relevant because it implied that not all bishops were equally concerned by the Ulster crisis. The Consul was of the opinion that since the clergy was in favour of Home Rule, its opposition to partition would only be 'platonic'.[190] He was badly mistaken here for the Ulster clergy did not give up that easily. In July, for instance, Dr McHugh attempted to set up a new party called the Anti Partition League, an alternative to the Nationalist party.

The Belfast decision to accept partition on a temporary basis was strongly resented by Bishop O'Dwyer. It was not so much the Nationalists' acceptance of Lloyd George's plan that he could not fathom, but rather their persistence in following the Nationalist party. He wanted the people to become more independent in their judgement. In 1906, he had talked about the 'intellectual decay' of the Irish, too absorbed in the party's constitutional politics.[191] On 27 June 1916, he wrote bitterly to Mgr O'Riordan about his incomprehension of his compatriots, just after the Belfast meeting. According to him, the Nationalist party thought for them: 'T'is [sic] a queer country: but the 'Machine' nowadays is universal. The [Irish] Times is in great delight at Devlin's triumph over clericalism. That's our [underlined in original text] thanks for our loyalty in the war.'[192] The Bishop's patience with the political evolution was wearing thin. He denounced a lack of radical nationalism, and believed political apathy had settled in the country. O'Dwyer also deplored British hypocrisy towards Ireland in the war. His attitude was hardly surprising by June 1916. The nationalist population, however, did not seem willing to switch allegiances because of the economic prosperity in the country, which had lulled them into passivity and indifference. Under these circumstances, Redmond did not need to worry too much about radical nationalists as their very radicalism might affect this prosperity and upset public opinion. Certainly, his Belfast victory would point towards this. In September 1916, the Irish Nation lost patience with the Irish and published an article entitled 'Are the Irish People gullible?'[193] Frustration had taken hold over the opposition. Both O'Dwyer and the Irish Nation could not believe their luck when they suddenly learned about John Redmond's political assassination by Asquith's war cabinet. Was fortune changing sides?

On 11 July in the House of Lords, Lord Lansdowne declared that partition had to be permanent. On 22 July, Lloyd George informed Redmond that the cabinet considered his Home Rule proposals were final, including the permanent exclusion of six Ulster counties.[194] These statements outraged nationalist Ireland. Everybody understood that Redmond had been discredited and manipulated. The Freeman's Journal was terribly embarrassed as it had stated only a few days before: 'The country regards the proposals of Mr. Lloyd George as offering an opportunity for a definite step in advance to the realisation of the aims of the constitutional movement'.[195] On 12 October, Frank Barrett informed Redmond that the newspaper's circulation in Cork city was about eighty copies whereas the *Irish Independent*, its great rival, was about 1,500 copies. Barrett deemed that it was the same throughout the whole country.[196] The decline of the *Freeman's Journal* had begun. Later, in June 1917, Mgr O'Riordan wrote that 'the *Freeman* [was] like an old wasp that [had] lost its sting'.[197] The Nationalist party was losing its voice in the country.

The Government's approach to the Irish question was catastrophic, for the people would progressively support Sinn Féin. Lloyd George had been a disastrous negotiator but brought success for the war effort in the north of the country. His reward was to become Prime Minister a few months later. But that was not all. On 29 June 1916, British justice had condemned Sir Roger Casement to death. Not only Redmond and Dillon had protested but also Cardinal Logue, a vehement anti-Sinn Féiner. The Cardinal believed that Casement's pardon would bring some stability to the country.[198] He was right but it was in vain. The republican prisoner was executed in August. It seemed that everything was done to increase nationalist resentment. The incompetence of the war cabinet in Irish affairs was all too obvious. On 20 July, a huge anti-partition meeting was held in Derry. About a hundred priests participated. One of the organisers read out a letter from Dr McHugh. He lambasted the British Government, Sir Edward Carson, and the Conservative party, and broke all links with the Nationalist party. He wrote: 'But what seems the worst feature of all the wretched bargaining that has been going on is that Irishmen calling themselves representatives of the people are prepared to sell their brother Irishmen into slavery to secure a nominal freedom for a section of the people.'[199] It was not only the repudiation of Redmond by one of his most loyal supporters within the hierarchy, and one who had declared himself in favour of the war in 1914, but also a denunciation of Home Rule itself. What degree of freedom did Home Rule actually offer? McHugh's point of view was identical to Archbishop Walsh's: not much. This meeting brought about the creation of the Anti Partition League, mainly based in counties Derry, Tyrone and Fermanagh. Later, it changed name and became known as the Irish Nation League.[200] Ulster had become the cradle of radical nationalism.

One of the main events of July 1916 was Archbishop Walsh's return on the political scene. After more than a decade of 'political silence', Walsh had decided to give voice to his feelings about the Nationalist party. In a letter to the press, he outlined Redmond's disastrous policy in the House of Commons. But what he regretted mostly was that the people 'had become hopelessly possessed of the disastrous idea that "the Party", or, to use the new-fangled term, its "leaders", could do no wrong'. On this point, he shared O'Dwyer's opinions. Walsh deplored the fact that Redmond and his followers had become untouchables and that anybody criticising them was branded 'a traitor'. The lack of independent parliamentary policy had been ruinous. The consequences of all this was that the country '[was] now face to face with a truly awful prospect'. Walsh was alluding to partition. He concluded his letter with a warning for the people:

> The Home Rule Act is still on the Statute Book. Will Irish Nationalists be any longer fooled by a repetition of the party cries that this fact makes them master of the situation; that the Act cannot be modified without Nationalist consent; and that Ireland awaits only the end of the war to find the portals of Old House in College Green automatically opened for the entry of the members of a Parliament greater than Grattan's?
>
> (*The Tablet*, 5 August 1916)

In a postscript, Walsh expressed his amazement that the nationalist public had never asked themselves if the Home Rule Parliament would be a 'Parliament in any sense worthy of the name'. It was exactly what he had told Sir MacKenzie Chalmers immediately after the Rising. Walsh and O'Dwyer had the same opinion on the apathy of the people and wished them to be more aggressive and active on the political front. It seemed to be happening in Ulster: it had to happen throughout the rest of the country. Mgr Curran hastened to congratulate the Archbishop and said people hoped that Walsh 'would give the lead in a call back to the old lines of independent opposition'.[201] On 29 July, the *Irish Nation* also complimented the Archbishop and tried to persuade its readers that Walsh's position was also the newspaper's. The *Irish Nation* was edited by Michael Judge who had recently founded a new radical party called the Repeal League.[202] Walsh and O'Dwyer had become the hopes of the nationalist opposition. At the end of July, the Anti Partition Committee [*sic*] of Belfast asked for the most popular ecclesiastic's support. O'Dwyer's answer was negative and harsh. He had run out of patience with nationalists and replied: 'I can well understand your anxiety and indignation at the proposal of your own political leaders to cut you off from your country, and hand you over to the Orangemen of the North. But I have very little pity for you. For years you have acquiesced in a kind of political servitude in which your most important function was to shout the shibboleths of what they call "The Party". You gave up willingly the right to think and became puppets.'[203] The Bishop added, though, that he did not believe that the partition scheme would become law.

O'Dwyer's answer has been described as 'a characteristic torrent of abuse', and it is thought that he had no interest in the issue of partition, in fact that he saw partition as an excellent way to get rid of

Protestants.[204] It is difficult to agree with this interpretation. It is right that O'Dwyer was an enthusiastic Catholic and that he could be very intransigent at times. In the light of his correspondence with Mgr O'Riordan in Rome, however, there is no doubt that he was definitely interested in the partition issue. Had he not written on 24 June 1916, that the decision of the Nationalist meeting in Belfast was 'shocking'? Had he not also written ironically about the future 'Orange Free State'? Finally, on 14 September 1916 in his acceptance for the Freedom of the City of Limerick, he had asked publicly: 'Does [Herbert Asquith] think that partitioning a country by religions is the way to emancipate it?'[205] At the height of his popularity, O'Dwyer could simply not afford himself to approve openly or tacitly of partition. This attitude would have been quite inconsistent and would have made the nationalist opposition wonder about his motives. It is probable that his harsh answer to the Anti Partition Committee was meant to radicalise Irish nationalist public opinion and to rid it of its torpor.

The partition crisis had to come to a head and had to bring about a radical change. According to O'Dwyer, Sinn Féin was the best option and every nationalist had to unite behind this party. On 24 July, John Redmond declared that the Government's attitude paved the way for Irish radical nationalism. In 1918, John Dillon admitted that the negotiations of 1916 had 'struck a deadly blow at the Irish Party'.[206] This is true but the rapid mobilisation of the northern clergy had also been a crucial factor. In August 1916, O'Dwyer was once again embroiled in a public controversy. This time, his victim was Mrs Starkie, wife of the Resident Commissioner, who had just written a brochure entitled 'Patriotism'. This brochure emphasised the merits of the British Empire and exposed how Serbia and Belgium had been unjustly invaded by Germany and Austria-Hungary. It was to be distributed throughout schools in Ireland. O'Dwyer, not unreasonably, deemed it was a manifesto in favour of recruitment. He promptly circulated a letter to all the principals of the schools in his diocese in which he denounced British policy in Ireland since 1914, and wrote: 'In my opinion, [the Resident Commissioner] himself has been quite enough for us for many years without inflicting upon us the activities of an educational Mrs Proudie... The whole history of our country is one lesson in Patriotism. The Yellow Ford, Benburb, the Curlew Mountain, Limerick, Fontenoy – these are the memories that thrill the heart of every young Irishmen.'[207] All were the names of battles that the Irish won over the English and the Scots.

Not all the bishops, however, were as radical and many still remained very cautious. Some had not abandoned John Redmond. In fact, they seemed to be in a majority in October 1916. But they lacked a charismatic 'spokesman', like O'Dwyer, Walsh or Fogarty. Cardinal

Logue, in the hypothesis that he continued to support the Nationalist party after its recent debacles, did not take any initiative to unify the hierarchy. He had understood that this task was virtually impossible. It is difficult to see how Logue could have managed to conciliate the northern bishops, the southern bishops and prelates like Walsh, O'Dwyer and O'Donnell. On 10 October, the semi-annual meeting of the hierarchy took place in Maynooth. Little is known about this meeting but it was eagerly awaited, as it was the first one after the Easter Rising. Mgr Curran, clearly informed by Walsh, wrote an informative passage in his memoirs:

> On 10 October 1916, at the semi-annual meeting of the Bishops in Maynooth the statement drawn up for and passed by the Standing Committee was an appeal for constitutional methods and was of a strong Redmondite tendency. During the discussion by the general meeting on this statement, the Archbishop of Dublin secured the insertion of a demand for amnesty, but opposed the document in general on account of certain additions. He also objected on account of the absence of any reference to conscription, which omission would be noted and misconstrued. Accordingly despite the efforts of the Chairman to force it through and to rule out all amendments, he voted against it. During the discussion which was developing against the statement, the Archbishop of Dublin proposed leaving the whole matter to the northern Bishops who strongly objected to it because it could be construed as favouring partition. As a result of the lack of general agreement, the whole matter was dropped. The Bishop of Limerick (Dr O'Dwyer) declared that he did not care whether the statement was passed or not, so long as it was clear that it was not passed unanimously... The most effective opponent of the proposed declaration was Dr McHugh, Bishop of Derry, who was most emphatic that any approval of constitutional agitation would be construed as approval of Redmond's constitutionalism.
>
> (NLD, O'Kelly papers, MS 27728(1),
> Curran's memoirs, p. 171)

This passage accurately reflected all the divisions within the hierarchy. Logue, who chaired the meeting,[208] demanded that the bishops demonstrate their support for the Nationalist party. This did not mean that he still approved of Redmond's political tactics but that in his eyes there was simply no nationalist alternative. O'Dwyer had become even more militant. His remark regarding a unanimous declaration was very astute for it made the Redmondite bishops take full responsibility for their political convictions whereas he would have plenty of room for political manoeuvring. It should be noted that no declaration was signed, not even by O'Donnell, Harty, Kelly and Coyne for instance, still in favour of the Nationalist party. Their attitude was far too cautious as Redmond badly needed support. Mgr Hogan, the President of Maynooth, confirmed this state of affairs when he told André Géraud that the meeting '[had] a complete lack of moral courage'.[209] Finally, the hierarchy unanimously agreed to send a Catholic mission to China, which spoke volumes about its interest in the war in Europe.[210] Géraud wrote a report for the Quai d'Orsay in Paris, summarising the situation. The French civil servant deemed that 'the Catholic Church was reserved and that it still had an ambiguous attitude'. He had had a discussion with Archbishop Bernard of the Church of Ireland, who had told him that 'the Catholic Episcopate was the strongest body in Ireland'. According to Bernard, 'it had never had so much power before'. It is true that the Church seemed solid and well organised, especially when compared to the nationalist opposition and the decaying Nationalist party. Géraud, however, rightly wrote 'that this power was not used'.[211] According to the Frenchman, the Church was all-powerful.

SUMMARY

After the summer of 1916, the Catholic Church began a slow political transformation for undoubtedly some of its members, particularly the young clergy, had taken offence at British policy in Ireland, largely conditioned by the war. Moreover, it had become weary of the efforts of the Nationalist party that did not seem able to find credible solutions to several crises. The nationalist and Catholic population shared the weariness of the Church. It saw in Edward O'Dwyer its representative but he refused to officially take the head of the nationalist opposition and rather declared his support for Sinn Féin whose leaders had been imprisoned and whose politics had yet to be defined. This ecclesiastical radicalisation was also symbolised by William Walsh's return to the political arena. Unlike the Bishop of Limerick, Walsh did not endorse Sinn Féin. Although the two men shared a certain number of ideas, notably that the Irish people were too passive in political matters, they did not combine their efforts. Perhaps there was still some old rancour between them dating from the Land War days. In a sense, the relations between these two prelates reflected the divisions and the lack of unity within the hierarchy. Michael Logue stubbornly refused to admit this radicalisation as he did not trust Sinn Féin and was in favour of the Empire, despite his repeated criticisms of the British Government. Only a concerted effort could have eradicated this radicalisation and assuaged his fears but, in 1916, that was impossible. The majority of bishops still favoured John Redmond. They were conservative, prudent and feared drastic changes in Irish society. Their support of the Nationalist leader, however, was tacit and voiceless. The Catholic Church was little by little adapting itself to a new political environment. The question was where this political transformation would lead. Nevertheless, one thing was sure: the clergy had, by and large, stopped its active help in recruitment. The Easter Rising and British war policy had made two victims in Ireland: the Nationalist party and the war effort. Had John Redmond paid heed to John Dillon's warnings and threatened to stop any collaboration with Herbert Asquith, maybe the Nationalist party would have had a chance to win over nationalist public opinion and the Catholic Church. Unfortunately for them, they did not do so.

The political climate in Ireland seriously worried the French Government as it could have repercussions on Britain's war strategy. Persuaded of the importance of the Catholic Church by their various diplomatic services, Aristide Briand's cabinet decided to send an ecclesiastical propaganda mission to Ireland in order to operate a rapprochement between the two countries and boost recruitment.

4 The first French mission

March 1915
'If ever German troops should set foot on Irish soil, these soldiers will have to be Catholics.'

Captain Hans Boehm, Department IIIb,
German General Staff

April 1916
'Is propaganda in our interest? Most certainly yes if we think about the danger that represents now for the British Government, and subsequently for us, the existence of hostile elements in Ireland.'

J. de Longchamps, French Consulate Dublin,
to Quai d'Orsay Paris

At the onset of the hostilities in Europe, the old Franco-Irish friendship theme was in the limelight again. John Redmond was quick to evoke the historic and military relations between the two countries for propaganda reasons in order to boost recruitment. By 1915, however, France focused her attention on the political situation in Ireland. Politicians in Paris wondered how Irish nationalists would react to the British war effort at a time when their country was involved in the struggle for Home Rule. Unlike France, conscription did not exist in the United Kingdom and everything depended on the goodwill and motivation of the public. At first, the French could be reasonably satisfied with the amount of recruits in Ireland but their initial optimism gave way to frank concern. The French Government knew that relations between Ireland and France had always been conditioned by France's attitude to Britain, her traditional enemy. Since the French and British were now allies in the war, would nationalists not seek an alliance with Germany and create a weak flank for the British, threatening to destabilise operations on the western front? To the French, this geopolitical question was of crucial importance.

The French diplomatic corps notified the Quai d'Orsay, the Foreign Office in Paris, that the war effort in Ireland had enemies. In the French embassy in London, Ambassador Paul Cambon was informed by Timothy

Power O'Connor, an Irish MP, that the nationalist opposition was denouncing French anti-clerical policy, which might influence Catholics in the country. Moreover, some bishops had also spoken against the French for the same reasons. Cambon correctly believed that the Irish Catholic community was larger than Ireland itself and expanded to the USA, still neutral, and to the British Empire. In France, ministers, civil servants and officers were of the opinion that Irish Catholicism could be a threat to the stability of Britain. The Ambassador was equally worried about German propaganda activities that emphasised this French anti-clericalism. At a time when the number of Irish recruits had seriously dropped, the French Consul in Dublin, J. de Longchamps, explained that the Catholic Church could give a significant boost to the war effort in Ireland. According to him, it was necessary to strengthen the relations between French and Irish Catholics.

The Easter Rising of April 1916 amply vindicated French worries. Had Patrick Pearse and his troops been successful, there can be little doubt that Germany would have enjoyed a diplomatic and military advantage. In Paris, in his office at Matignon, the French Prime Minister knew that it was time to take actions that would ensure better cooperation between the Allies. If relations between Ireland and Britain were tense, a rapprochement between Ireland and France should be encouraged to make sure of Irish participation in the war. But, at what level? A French political mission was excluded from the beginning since the Nationalist party was in trouble. Such propaganda would be too blatant. The French could not negotiate with the nationalist opposition either since it was against the war. Little by little, the idea of an ecclesiastical mission took shape. To the French Government, the powerful Irish Catholic Church was the only valid negotiator left despite the fact that some of its members were openly against recruitment. How would anti-clerical France approach Catholic Ireland?

IRELAND'S IMPORTANCE IN THE WAR

Throughout the centuries, Ireland has been of major geopolitical interest to continental powers. The Spanish and then the French in 1798, tried to 'liberate' and control the country with the aim of delivering a knockout blow to Britain. British Conservatives and Liberals argued whether an independent Ireland would be a direct threat to England's security.[1] The British were justified in their concerns. In the nineteenth century, Louis Napoleon's Second Empire became the ally and protector of Irish nationalists and republicans. Paris was a refuge for the IRB and Fenians. The best known Irish republican in the French capital at the time was James Stephens. The author Victor Hugo supported Ireland's claim to independence and French consuls in Ireland reported to the Quai d'Orsay that people were still hopeful that France would intervene on behalf of Ireland against England. During the Franco-Prussian War of 1870, Ireland expressed massive support for France. Many Irishmen enlisted in the French Army, money was collected and sent to Paris, anti-Prussian protests took place in Irish towns, the Irish College in Paris became a hospital for French soldiers and some republicans tried to revive the Irish Brigades which fought for France in past times.[2] However, the French were no longer the only continental power to express serious interest in Ireland. Shortly before the outbreak of the First World War, the Kaiser had been advised to wait for further developments in Ireland before striking against France, Russia and Britain.[3] To some generals of the Central Powers, like Conrad von Hötzendorf of the Austro-Hungarian Army, the Home Rule crisis was a factor to be reckoned with. In 1893, Otto von Bismarck was reported to have said: 'England counts for nothing in European politics unless the Irish question has been settled.'[4] In Germany, military strategists realised how much a civil war in Ireland between nationalists and unionists or a nationalist revolt against the British authorities would play into their hands. In September 1914, Count von Bernstorff, the German Ambassador to the United States, sent a very explicit coded message to another German diplomat in Stockholm:

> It seems to me that the most important point is whether there is any possibility of coming to an agreement with England or not, or if we must prepare ourselves to fight until death. In the last case, I recommend granting Irish wishes provided there are really Irishmen prepared to help us. The setting up of an Irish Legion, composed of Irish prisoners of war, would be a fantastic idea if it really can be conceived.
>
> (Auwärtiges Amt, Bonn, Germany, Foreign Office Archives, Den Krieg 1914 file R211153, von Bernstorff to Reichenau, 25 September 1914)

The idea was quite simple: if the Irish rebelled, the British Government would be obliged to withdraw some troops from the western front and send them to Ireland before the situation was totally out of control. It seems that the French had anticipated this scenario. In 1920, a French review called *La Documentation Catholique* stated that shortly before the war the American ambassador to Germany had been of the opinion that the Kaiser was absolutely convinced that Britain would remain neutral because of the situation in Ulster. According to the review, Berlin had sent a special envoy named von Kühlmann to Ulster to assess the political situation.[5] If *La Documentation*

Catholique's information was correct, it would appear that pre-war German diplomacy was partially based on political unrest in Ireland. The fact that Germany had supplied arms to the UVF and to the Irish Volunteers in 1914 would tend to confirm the review's statement. Von Bernstorff also said in his message that the Irish in America had assured him that 'Catholic Ireland [would] provide no voluntary recruits for England'.[6] The Ambassador's mention of Catholicism was to prove important, as their plans to 'liberate' Ireland would take into account the religious factor. Very rapidly in the war, the German High Command and its military intelligence toyed with the idea of setting up an Irish brigade made of Irish prisoners of war, and envisaged the possibility of a landing in Ireland. Sir Roger Casement was in Berlin and was prepared to help them with their plans. On 20 November 1914, the German Government issued an official statement, declaring that Germany would not invade 'Ireland with a view to its conquest or the overthrow of any native institutions in that country'. It added that German soldiers would not be invaders and that their Government desired 'only NATIONAL PROSPERITY and NATIONAL FREEDOM' [capital letters in original text] for Ireland.[7]

At the end of December 1914, von Bernstorff sent another coded message from America, this time to the Auswärtiges Amt, the German Foreign Office, in Berlin. The Ambassador gave an estimation of the strength of the British Army, Ulster Volunteers and National and Irish Volunteers in Ireland. He suggested that no less than 25,000 German soldiers should be involved in the invasion of Ireland. Interestingly, he added that there were tensions between English and Irish soldiers in Northern France. Unfortunately, he did not give more details on this subject. Von Bernstorff added that when the Irish soldiers in the British Army learnt about the successful German liberation of Ireland, they would cooperate with the Germans.[8] In this, however, he was mistaken. It remains difficult to know with certainty exactly how Irish soldiers in the trenches in France reacted to the news of the Easter Rising, which happened two years later in 1916. According to jingoistic newspapers and their rather subjective notion of objectivity, the soldiers were disgusted with the Irish Volunteers. The *Freeman's Journal* published a letter of a private who wrote that the 16th Irish Division should 'go over to Dublin to settle things'. He called the rebels 'poor misguided fools'.[9] Apparently, German soldiers put up notices opposite the trenches of Irish regiments on which soldiers could read that 'English guns [were] firing on [their] wives and children'. Captain William Redmond, John Redmond's brother who was fighting in France, confirmed this story and maintained that the Irish replied by 'singing "Rule Britannia" to the accompaniment of mouth organs and melodions'.[10] Back in 1914, Casement was eager to set up this liberation brigade and sent a secret message to Eoin MacNeill in Dublin, promising him German help and asking him for Catholic priests to act as chaplains in the brigade. Casement wanted men of the calibre of 'Father Murphy of Vinegar Hill',[11] who had led a section of the Wexford rebels in the rebellion of 1798. Ironically, on that particular occasion, the rebels had waited for the French to arrive in Ireland. The Kaiser's Government approached the Vatican and a Fr Crotty was sent to the Irish prisoners of war camp in Limburg in Germany.[12] Casement went on to explain that the Germans would sow discord in Egypt and India, trying to destabilise the British Empire. It is true that before the onset of the hostilities in Europe, the Kaiser and some of his generals had talked about instigating uprisings in India and had thought of backing the Muslim world.[13] These plans depended, however, on the defeat of the Royal Navy, not a foregone conclusion. It was in France's interest that Ireland remained politically stable. In the first seven months of the conflict, recruitment got off to a good start and the war effort was supported by John Redmond and the Nationalist party, and also by the Catholic Church. All was quiet on the Irish front.

THE FRENCH WORRY ABOUT IRELAND

As early as 1915, Paris became quite anxious about the evolution of the war effort in Ireland. As has been seen, recruitment figures dropped, the War Office made blunders, the CCORI and DRI were not always well organised and the Catholic Church's active support steadily declined. In April 1916, the French Consul in Dublin made an analysis of the situation for the Quai d'Orsay in Paris:

> But the remedy to a frame of mind [anti-war spirit of the Irish] that exists above all because of ignorance would be a well-organised propaganda which does not limit itself to appealing to Irishmen in order to incorporate them into the British Army, and which would really inform the whole population of the real causes of the war, of Ireland's interest to participate actively, of the useful aims for her social and economical development that she must look for in this participation. This propaganda was never seriously attempted by the British Government.
>
> (Archives of Quai d'Orsay, Paris vol. 545 Grand-Bretagne/Irlande, letter no. 7, de Longchamps to Ministre des Affaires étrangères, 18 April 1916)

De Longchamps was not inclined to look on the bright side regarding the success of a possible propaganda mission simply because he felt that the Irish deeply distrusted Britain. According to the Consul, another reason was that the Irish had gradually lost touch with the European continent and that a strong sense of insularity prevailed. However, he emphasised that the Irish had never forgotten the historic ties between their country and France even though Franco-Irish relations were not as strong as they used to be. On the political front in Ireland, other developments worried the French. Various political forces were opposed to the war and were quite militant. Arthur Griffith's Sinn Féin, James Connolly's Labour party and Eoin MacNeill's Irish Volunteers all grouped together in the Irish Neutrality League.[14] On 28 November 1914, the *Sunday Independent* published an agreement between Sir Roger Casement and Count von Bernstorff regarding the formation of an Irish brigade composed of prisoners of war detained in Germany.[15] The agreement stated that in the case of military operations overthrowing the British authorities in Ireland, 'the Imperial German Government [would give] the Irish Independent Government so established its fullest moral support'. The RIC had noticed that some 'Sinn Féin priests' in their anti-war propaganda had asked the people not to forget the 'anti-clerical policy of the French Government'.[16] These priests were alluding to *la querelle religieuse* in France, the bitter conflict between the State and the Catholic Church before the war, which had given France an anti-clerical reputation.

It is difficult to assess precisely what influence these various political forces had on the Irish Catholic and nationalist population and the war effort between 1914 and 1915 but their sole existence was enough to worry T.P. O'Connor, the only Irish Nationalist MP to represent a constituency in England. O'Connor was on friendly terms with Cambon who was concerned about British policy and commitment to France in the war. In 1912, the French Ambassador had been told that the Liberal cabinet would not last long, that it was pacifist and that the Conservatives would be better. As late as July 1914, he was still not sure how Britain would react if Germany attacked France.[17] Cambon had also closely followed the Home Rule crisis and was not particularly impressed by the British Government's handling of Irish affairs. In May 1916, just after the Easter Rising, he wrote to Aristide Briand, the French Prime Minister, that Herbert Asquith's Irish policy had 'completely failed' and that he had been apathetic when the UVF threatened to resist Home Rule in Ulster with arms if necessary.[18] T.P. O'Connor and Paul Cambon had met on several occasions to discuss German influence on Ireland. The diplomat was worried about the effects of German propaganda, which stressed French anti-clericalism, on 'Catholic countries, on Italy, on Spain, on South America and on Ireland'. According to Cambon, the Germans had been very subtle. He firmly believed that Irish communities in Britain and in the United

States would be targeted soon, and since these communities were powerful political lobbies, German efforts had to be nipped in the bud.[19]

On 5 December 1914, Cambon wrote to Cardinal Amette, the Archbishop of Paris. He explained that the young Irish clergy were either pro-German or anti-British, and said that he had been contacted by O'Connor who begged the French Cardinal to make a strong statement. If Amette accepted, the statement should emphasise that his Church was not being discriminated against by an anti-clerical government, and that all the French, Catholics included, were fully united in the defence of their nation. Cambon added that Amette should mention the number of priests in the Army, since they were conscripted, and say how many had been killed on the battlefield. Cambon was convinced that this would be the best possible answer to German propaganda. Amette's message would be given to 'the Irish people throughout the whole world in order to shed light for them on the feelings of French Catholics'.[20]

T.P. O'Connor had grasped that the nationalist opposition and the republicans were trying to break off and deny that old Franco-Irish friendship to hinder recruitment in Ireland. On 6 December 1914, he sent a report to Cambon entitled *Mémorandum sur l'état d'âme en Irlande* (memorandum on Ireland's frame of mind). He wrote that the vast majority of the Irish people were behind John Redmond and that 'some trends without influence but noisy were against them; partly because of the remainder of the old Irish animosity towards England due to well known historical reasons'.[21] O'Connor was right. Redmond still was master of the situation but it was important to eliminate immediately any movement that could harm the war effort. He also brought up the fact that the opposition movements used the French Government's pre-war anti-clerical policies to their advantage and that 'those incidents were used to deceive the real and honest Catholics'. O'Connor added that these nationalists had not taken into account the fact that the war had 'erased all internal differences [in France] and had led French Catholics to be among the bravest defenders of their nation's existence'. O'Connor certainly spoke the truth concerning this new rapprochement between the Church and the Government in France. President Poincaré had appealed for a *Union sacrée* (a sacred union), of all the French against the Germans. A Catholic revival in the country was noticeable as church attendance increased dramatically and pilgrimages became very popular.[22] Even the international press reported this sudden French conversion, notably the *Tablet*.[23] However, the Irish nationalist opposition much preferred to stick to the pre-war situation. O'Connor concluded his memorandum with a suggestion to counter the opposition. He told Cambon that Ireland was ready to send over a delegation to France, composed of various Irish parliamentarians and members of the

Ancient Order of Hibernians (AOH), the defenders of Catholicism par excellence. The aim of this delegation would be to demonstrate to the Irish people that traditional Franco-Irish relations were very much alive.

The Ambassador sent this plan to his Government, which promptly approved of it. Paris had become extremely worried about German propaganda, denouncing the 'anti-clericalism of the eldest daughter of the Church'. On 5 February 1915, the Quai d'Orsay asked Mgr Baudrillart, the rector of the Institut catholique de Paris, to become head of the Catholic Committee of French Propaganda Abroad.[24] France's concern was fully justified. On 2 March 1915 in Berlin, Captain Hans Boehm sent a detailed report to the Auswärtiges Amt, regarding the Irish Catholic Church. Boehm maintained that the clergy knew that the Kaiser's Government was still on very good terms with the Vatican and that the Germans received support from some cardinals of the Curia.[25] Boehm was a member of Department IIIb of the General Staff in charge of military intelligence abroad. He had lived in the United States and returned to Germany when the war broke out. His speciality was Irish affairs. He later returned to America in 1915 and kept in touch with Irish republicans.[26] Boehm wrote about how useful the Irish Catholic Church would be if German troops landed in the country: 'If ever German troops should set foot on Irish soil, these soldiers will have to be Catholics. The sight of practising Catholic German soldiers would be so different from what people are used to see from English soldiers, that the priests would rapidly make cause with them and the people would blindly follow the priests' advice.'[27]

Boehm's optimism was exaggerated. It is very doubtful whether Irish people, farmers especially, would have welcomed the 'liberation force' at a time of unprecedented economic prosperity as the arrival of German soldiers might mean the disruption of the economy and the end of their profitable incomes. In Paris, the French noted that their Government had enemies among the Irish hierarchy. In February 1915, the bishops made public their Lenten pastorals. Generally, the prelates still were in favour of the war but two of them mentioned the religious problem in France. Cardinal Logue acknowledged the Catholic revival in that country although he called its Government 'infidel' and praised the courage of priests conscripted in the French Army. Bishop O'Dwyer wrote in the same vein and denounced the war.[28] It was high time the Irish delegation left for Paris.

The visit took place from 30 April to 1 May 1915 and among the delegates were Joseph Devlin, President of the AOH, and T.H. Gallagher, Lord Mayor of Dublin. John Redmond was to be at the head of the delegation but illness kept him in Ireland. He was replaced by T.P. O'Connor. Fr John Mullan was the only ecclesiastic present and the absence of any member of the hierarchy might seem surprising on such an occasion. It must be remembered, however, that Cardinal Logue had given no precise instructions to the episcopate on recruitment and the war effort in general, and that the resolutions of the National Synod of 1900 in Maynooth did not encourage active political involvement of members of the clergy. The distinguished visitors were received by M. Georges-Leygues, president of the *Comité d'Action et d'Information à l'Etranger*, a committee in charge of propaganda in foreign countries. After discussions with their French counterparts, the Irish went to the *Palais de l'Elysée* where they were welcomed with great pomp by the President of the French Republic, Raymond Poincaré.

Everything went according to T.P. O'Connor's memorandum. Over a period of two days, speeches highlighted the old Franco-Irish friendship and, of course, the religious revival in France. Politicians and clerics mastered the art of exaggeration. O'Connor, on behalf of Redmond, explained to Poincaré Ireland's admiration for France, 'the greatest of the Celtic countries', and evoked the Irish brigade and France's hospitality for the Irish exiles in times past: 'they instinctively fled to France . . . She took our children, as children of their own, to her bosom'. To which the President replied: 'I am happy to welcome you on this soil of France which has never allowed to wither, beneath the rich flowering of Latin civilisation, the strong sap of our common race, and the inhabitants of which have preserved intact like you through the ages the essential features of the Celtic character.'[29] Poincaré and O'Connor had made blood brothers of the Irish and the French. The delicate religious aspect was of course left to Joseph Devlin who told Cardinal Amette: 'We know that this hour, in which the existence of France is menaced, has closed the era of domestic strife in your country . . . We have read how thousands of priests of your Church and ours are proud of occupying a place in the fighting ranks for the defence of their beloved country'.[30] Devlin was clearly not aware of the shortage of Irish priests to serve as chaplains or did not wish to mention it on this particular occasion. His remarks were meant to neutralise Logue and O'Dwyer's statements on the 'infidel' French Government. Amette, in turn, told Devlin that the two countries were united by 'a certain resemblance in character, in chivalrous spirit, generosity and bravery . . . and above all the identity of their religion'. The Cardinal also mentioned the old Irish College in Paris 'where for centuries the sons of Ireland and the elite of clerical youth [had] come to prepare themselves for the priesthood'.[31] Amette left out the fact that Logue had once been a pupil there. Perhaps he had been advised not to do so given Logue's repeated criticisms of the British Government. What the Archbishop of Paris chose not to say was that the very existence of the College had been threatened only a few years before by Aristide Briand's law on the separation between State and Church.[32] Finally, the master stroke of this propaganda mission came on the morning of the

Franco-Irish banquet. A number of personalities made speeches on similar lines to those of Poincaré, O'Connor, Devlin and Amette, but among the speakers was none other than René Viviani, France's most notorious anti-clerical politician. In fairness to Viviani, he was reserved in his remarks as he only evoked the ancient military relations between France and Ireland and wisely opted not to say a word about the religious question. But his presence alone symbolised France's *Union sacrée*.

The Irish delegation's visit to Paris did not go unnoticed in Berlin where Sir Roger Casement was doing his best to set up the Irish brigade. He sent a long and angry letter to his German friends, calling the members of the delegation 'political nonentities' and begging the Kaiser's Government to act more energetically in favour of an independent and republican Ireland. On the French, he remarked:

> The Cardinal Archbishop of Paris probably never found himself in worse company in his life. The President of the Republic certainly never delivered a more untruthful utterance, both in spirit, intent, and form, than that addressed to this bogus Irish deputation, representing assuredly not the national feelings of Ireland, but the wishes of the British Government. And yet this fraudulent attempt to capture the support of the 'small nationalities' and to make appeal to Irish-American sympathy is splendidly stagemastered.
> (Auswärtiges Amt, Bonn, Den Krieg 1914, file R21160, letter of Sir Roger Casement, 7 May 1915, p. 46)

Casement had correctly guessed the propaganda nature of the visit and its importance to the Irish-American world, just as Paul Cambon had thought of a few months before. Even T.P. O'Connor told the *Daily Chronicle* frankly that the aim of the delegation had been to counter German propaganda and to impress the Irish throughout the world, especially in the powerful United States.[33] But, Casement also showed an increasing frustration while in Berlin as the Germans were simply not in a position to effectively help Irish republicans as long as they had not made a significant breakthrough on the western front and, even more importantly, beaten the Royal Navy. There were other problems also. Casement and his aide-de-camp, the Irishman Robert Monteith, were no longer convinced by Germany's goodwill towards Ireland. By June 1915, Captain Boehm had asked the Auswärtiges Amt and the German High Command to be more energetic in their Irish policy. He believed that if German promises were broken, the consequences on Irish-German relations in Ireland and the United States might be disastrous.[34]

On 30 March 1916, Casement decided to sail to Ireland and warn Patrick Pearse to call off the intended rising. Casement had noticed that Rudolf Nadolny, the head of Department IIIb, had lost interest in Ireland.

He wrote Nadolny's words in his diary: 'We have no idealistic interest in Ireland and no revolution, no rifles. If it were not that we hope for a military diversion we should not give the rifles.'[35] Moreover, Robert Monteith's humble social background seemed to form an obstacle to good cooperation between the Irish and Germans.[36] Officers of the Kaiser's Imperial Army were exceedingly conscious of their upper-class standing and did not hesitate to remind Monteith of their origins. But it was not just the Germans who were to blame. Some Irish republicans, especially in America, had gargantuan notions about the capability of the German Navy, Army and Airforce. As late as April 1916, a few days before the Easter Rising, they had grandiose plans to blockade Dublin harbour with U-boats, to set up bases for German submarines in Ireland and cut off food export to England. Soldiers, officers and ammunition would reach Ireland by Zeppelin, no less! This commando-like action would, according to them, rapidly end the war. The Auswärtiges Amt must have been flattered by this motion of confidence but had the good sense to simply reply that it was impossible.[37] Although the Zeppelin operation was far-fetched, to say the least, the Germans also refused to send submarines, invoking technical reasons.[38] This reason remains quite obscure as it was obvious that Ireland would be an ideal base of attack on British shipping.

If the French and the Irish could be fairly satisfied about the Irish delegation's visit to Paris, the question was whether recruitment in Ireland would benefit from it and whether the anti-war propaganda in the country was now silenced for good.

ANDRÉ GÉRAUD TOURS THE COUNTRY

Unfortunately for the French, the delegation's visit to Paris did not increase recruitment figures and did not put a halt to anti-war activities in Ireland. On the contrary. As has been noted earlier, certain decisions of the Government, such as the inclusion of Conservative and Unionist politicians in the cabinet, had angered nationalists including moderate ones, which in turn had harmful consequences on voluntary enlistment. Between February and August 1915, 25,235 men had joined the colours and between August 1915 and February 1916, 19,801 had enlisted, as opposed to 50,107 men between August 1914 and February 1915.[39] After more than one year waiting, the 16th Irish Division eventually embarked for France.[40] The long delays had been discouraging and frustrating for many an eager Irish recruit. From September 1915 onwards, some nationalist opposition newspapers began to denounce the attempt of certain politicians to operate a rapprochement between Ireland and France for purely military purposes. The *Hibernian* published anti-French articles, alluding to the religious question. According to an article entitled 'French Catholics, their anti-German propaganda', 75 per cent of the Irish did not want to be involved in the war against Germany. It also stated: 'French Catholics are not satisfied with this state of affairs, and, to improve matters, they are now circulating in Ireland a book of German horrors and iniquities compiled by a number of leading French Catholics'.[41] The *Hibernian*'s information was correct. Suddenly, many brochures and books dealing with French Catholicism or Franco-Irish friendship had become available in Ireland.

In August 1915, the *Freeman's Journal* published the review of a book entitled *The German War and Catholicism*, edited by Mgr Baudrillart.[42] The book's aim was to disprove the fact that France had 'ceased to be a Christian and Catholic nation', which the Germans were trying to prove to neutral countries. The authors depicted 'with touching pathos...the German war against the churches' and gave as an example the destruction of the cathedral of Rheims. The *Hibernian*, however, commented sarcastically that the book was not effective as 'a special edition should have been prepared for Ireland and revised by the Lord Mayor of Dublin or some intelligent Catholic'.[43] The newspapers believed that Spanish and Italian Catholics might have been impressed by Baudrillart's arguments but not Irish Catholics. It appeared that the French had not made any obvious effort to show a distinction between the national churches in Europe and their differences. In September 1916, just after the Easter Rising, the Irish population could read in a another French book called *Ireland and France* by Alfred Duquet how the Irish had helped the French during the Franco-Prussian war in 1870.[44] This was propaganda emanating from the Quai d'Orsay.

In the meantime, in London, Paul Cambon became seriously worried about the latest political developments in Ireland. On 6 June 1915, he sent a letter to Théophile Delcassé, the French Foreign Office Secretary, in which he explained the anger of Irish nationalists. Cambon wrote that Irish soldiers on the front were in a rather dangerous frame of mind. Catholic regiments had fought bravely and lost numerous soldiers, but in Ireland the population believed that they had been deliberately sacrificed by English generals. Concerning relations between Irish Catholic regiments and Protestant regiments, the Ambassador informed Delcassé that they were not on speaking terms and that 'Orange soldiers... forced the War Office to remove a colonel when they learnt that this colonel was a Catholic.'[45] The French were well informed. The officer in question was a Catholic Dubliner whose task it was to look after the camps of the 36th Ulster Division. The officer was doing a good job but when his religion became known, the Ulster Club immediately contacted an English general and asked for his transfer.[46] In 1915, some soldiers of the 36th Ulster Division even found time at the front to burn an effigy of the traitor Lundy and continued to observe certain Orange traditions despite the proximity of the enemy.[47] Clearly, John Redmond's unity of spirit was not always alive in the trenches. Cambon concluded his letter by warning Delcassé that wounded nationalist soldiers had declared that they had fought for France and Belgium, not for England, and that 'they would be happy to fight one day for their country to ensure its independence'.[48] It seemed that Cambon was thinking of a possible nationalist rebellion as early as June 1915. In this case, there would be consequences for the British war effort. To the French, religion was linked to a threat to political stability in the United Kingdom, their main ally in the war.

In Dublin, Consul de Longchamps believed it was high time to change the recruitment campaigns in Ireland. He was ideally placed to study the evolution of Irish public opinion closely. The Consul was endowed with a great imagination and was the originator of the first French mission to Ireland. On 18 April 1916, only a few days before the rising in Dublin, he wrote to the Quai d'Orsay stating that the British had no hope of implementing a successful recruitment propaganda in the country because 'there remained, indeed, in every Irishman an incurable mistrust towards everything that came from England'. However, according to him, the French might be in a position to increase voluntary enlistment in Ireland for the Irish delegation's visit to Paris had been acclaimed in the country. France's interest was obvious:

> Is propaganda in our interest? Most certainly yes if we think about the danger that represents now for the British Government, and subsequently for us, the existence of hostile elements in Ireland. Let alone the possible spirit of rebellion of those elements, their influence is incessantly felt on the recruitment campaigns in Ireland where, except in the reserve, hardly 140,000 men have enlisted voluntarily, whereas, even while taking into account the farming necessities for the island itself and for England, an army of at least 100,000 men could be easily raised. An Army whose actions would undoubtedly be felt on the outcome of the war.
> (Quai d'Orsay, Paris vol. 545, Grande-Bretagne/ Irlande, letter no. 7 de Longchamps to Ministre des Affaires étrangères, 18 April 1916)

Britain and Ireland had become a serious strategic concern for the French. In those days, the French were involved in the biggest battle mankind had then seen: Verdun, where a force of tens of thousands of men was decimated by a deluge of artillery. General Philippe Pétain was hoping for British reinforcements, which did not arrive. The British

Expeditionary Force (BEF) was then busy reorganising itself after the Mons retreat in 1914. As a result, the French Army harboured a lot of resentment towards their allies. German propaganda was quick to exploit this state of affairs.[49] It also appeared that the United Kingdom had been guilty of procrastination in preparing for the future conflict and was, therefore, of little assistance to the French in the early stages of the war. The British officer corps was not the best, there was a serious crisis in the production of ammunition and efforts to modernise the Army were resisted.[50] In Dublin, de Longchamps put forward a practical plan. According to him, the Irish Catholic Church was most important because it had the power to control and influence not only public opinion but also decision-making. If France was to send a mission to Ireland, the Church should be at the centre of it. He reported to the Quai d'Orsay that French Catholic committees 'might well reform the ideas of some members of the Irish clergy', in other words of those who were behind Archbishop Walsh and Bishops O'Dwyer and Fogarty. De Longchamps had the same idea as Lieutenant Boehm of the German High Command in 1915. There was a political reason also to involve the French Catholic Church directly: ecclesiastics would get more Irish sympathy than representatives of an anti-clerical government. Finally, the Consul wrote that French priests should go to Ireland and also Alsatian priests who 'would inform the Irish on enforcement of German rule on the small nationalities of Deutschland [Germany]'.[51]

On 24 April 1916, French fears materialised as the Easter Rising began in Dublin. To the authorities in Paris, it was clear that Britain was no longer in a position to boost the war effort in Ireland. The initiative belonged to them and they decided to send André Géraud, of the French embassy in London, to Ireland in order to evaluate the possibilities and chances of success of a propaganda mission. Géraud crossed the Irish Sea and stayed in the country from 3 to 20 June 1916. His report for the Quai d'Orsay was highly informative about the Catholic Church in paticular and Ireland in general. The Frenchman wrote that Dublin Castle no longer had any authority in the country and that the once powerful Nationalist party was in a political wilderness. He correctly analysed that it was difficult to establish with certainty who still actively supported the party as it refused to take into account the evolution of public opinion. According to him, the party would not change tactics whether it stayed in Westminster Parliament or governed the country from Dublin.[52] Géraud's opinion was accurate since Redmond and his followers would never change their support for the war effort, for instance, although it was crystal clear that the Irish had lost nearly all interest. It was gradually losing touch with changing realities.

Géraud had an interesting discussion with Lord MacDonnell, the head of the Irish Civil Service and who formerly taught French and

German at Galway University. MacDonnell had an original explanation of the motives, which led the rebel leaders to take up arms. He was convinced that people like Patrick Pearse and his brother William became involved in extreme nationalism because their school, Saint Enda, had gone bankrupt. Nationalism was in fact a form of escapism for the two men. MacDonnell went even further and explained that Sir Roger Casement had left the Foreign Service and had become a republican because the Government wanted to decrease his annual salary by £400![53] The head of the civil service appeared to be suffering from selective memory as he said nothing about Casement's interventions in the Congo and in South America on behalf of the natives, for which he had been awarded a knighthood and that ill health had forced him to retire.

Like de Longchamps, Géraud believed that the clergy was in the best position to boost recruitment and therefore set out to meet various members of the hierarchy, including those who were absolutely opposed to the war. He mustered enough courage to meet the formidable O'Dwyer in Limerick, who told him: 'The English only yield to force. They will satisfy our demands only when they are constrained and forced to do so.' But, the Bishop added surprisingly: 'In order to win back the old popular sympathies, France would only have to lift her finger.'[54] What did he mean by this extraordinary declaration? Géraud knew about O'Dwyer's confrontations with John Redmond. He had described him as being 'the Bishop who [was] the most hostile to the Allies.' The shrewd O'Dwyer had, of course, guessed the purpose of Géraud's visit to Ireland. It is very likely that the Bishop's sense of opportunism had resurfaced and that he had in mind French pressure on the British Government in order to solve the Home Rule and partition crises in the nationalists' favour.

In Cork, Géraud met Dr Cohalan who told him that he could not say whether the Irish would rebel or not if the Germans landed in the south and west of the country. In Maynooth, Géraud eventually found an ecclesiastic who was wholeheartedly committed to the Allies' cause, Mgr Hogan, the President of Saint Patrick's College. Hogan said frankly that there were many Sinn Féiners among his young seminarians. According to him, 'the name Germany could not be pronounced in a lecture without clamours'. This pro-German feeling among young intelligentsia was also palpable in the University of Galway where Professor Anderson informed the French civil servant that the students were in favour of Germany, women even more than men.[55] Anderson related a conversation he had with an employee in a hotel during a vacation, who had assured him that a German victory would benefit Ireland from an economic point of view. This employee was adamant that the Germans would set up toy and glass factories in Ireland after the war.[56] German propaganda seemed to be rather effective. A professor of Queen's College in Cork told Géraud: 'The Entente's cause is not for small nations. They tell us about Belgium. We have it here, Belgium!'[57] These observations were made in the aftermath of the Easter Rising when passions were running high. Nevertheless, Mgr Hogan had been right, for the number of seditious priests was definitely on the increase. In 1915, the RIC had reported that fifty-five priests had openly expressed hostile feelings towards Britain and her allies, twice as many as in 1914.[58]

At the end of his eventful stay, André Géraud rightly discerned three groups of bishops within the hierarchy. Firstly, there were a few 'extremists' who followed O'Dwyer. They hated Protestant England and atheist France, and were opposed to the Allies. He included Cohalan and Walsh among them. Géraud was perhaps right about Cohalan but not about Walsh who was described by Mgr Curran as being 'mildly anti-German'.[59] Walsh had his own reasons for opposing the war effort. Instead of the Archbishop of Dublin, Géraud should have mentioned Fogarty of Killaloe. Secondly, there was a group behind Cardinal Logue. They were mainly devoted to religious matters although they had no sympathy at all for Germany. Logue had told Géraud: 'Her [Germany's] influence always seemed to me to be harmful to a Christian community. One of the good results of the war will be to get rid of it.'[60] The third group was 'composed of bishops who [had] political opinions very much in favour of the Allies'. The Frenchman quoted Harty of Cashel, O'Donnell of Raphoe, Kelly of Ross and Mgr Hogan. They still supported Redmond and with other bishops formed the majority in the hierarchy.

Géraud estimated that the Germans had been quite successful in their propaganda campaigns in Ireland. First of all, it appeared that before the war many Irish ecclesiastical students had spent brief vacation periods in Germany, while studying the language. Even Irish professors had been favourably impressed by German hospitality. Then some German professors, like Kuno Meyer, had specialised in Celtic studies and had become the leading experts in that field. Many Irish university textbooks dealing with Celtic studies were printed in Germany. Finally, Géraud described the relations between Maynooth and Germany. He explained that the majority of young seminarians liked to go to Bonn, Freiburg and Munich. One of the consequences was that some teachers in the College and bishops had been partly educated in Germany, like Dr Cohalan of Cork, and could influence their students or parishioners in their decision as to which side to support in the war.[61]

Géraud concluded his report with a proposal to counter the influence of German sympathisers in Ireland with a threefold action. To begin with, and most importantly, the Catholic Church had to declare itself openly in favour of France. Mgr Hogan was willing to collaborate with Géraud and would invite a delegation of French ecclesiastics to Maynooth, which would explain the Catholic renaissance in France and also describe German atrocities. Hogan knew Cardinal Amette of Paris well and knew that the sending of such a delegation should pose no major problem. Géraud was of the opinion that the delegation should not be in contact with any leading politician of the Nationalist party lest the visit appeared to be politically motivated. His decision seemed to be sensible enough. In the summer of 1916 indeed, John Redmond was losing his grip on nationalist Ireland whereas Sinn Féin was still largely a minority party against the war, so that the Catholic Church was the only real option left for the French. At that time negotiations between nationalists, unionists and David Lloyd George on Home Rule and partition were going on. Amette would send a telegram of congratulations to Logue if Home Rule was granted to Ireland. Logue would then publicly reply and thus show a rapprochement between France and Ireland. This idea came from Archbishop Harty, Bishop Kelly and Mgr Hogan. Harty would encourage Logue to do this.[62] Then relations between French and Irish universities had to be improved. Various exchanges between French and Irish students should take place and French professors were to counter Kuno Meyer's influence. Finally, an action on the Irish press was necessary. The French authorities were to give information on 'religious life in France, the anti-Christian and particularly the anti-Catholic aspect of Prussian warfare'. This last action should be undertaken together with the British Government.[63]

Shortly after Géraud's visit, the *Freeman's Journal* published extracts of French newspapers. On 9 October 1916, the Irish people could read an extract of *L'Opinion*, which paid tribute to T. M. Kettle, a prominent nationalist who had just been killed in the battle of the Somme. *L'Opinion* spoke about 'the imperishable glory of our brother Celts of Ireland' but felt compelled to add that Ireland would 'tomorrow rule itself as a self-governed British dominion'.[64] The Celtic blood brothers remembered not to leave their Anglo-Saxon friends out the equation.

Géraud's plan was approved by the French cabinet, and no doubt was sanctioned by the British whose interest was that Ireland remained stable even if the French had to be stabilising agents. As the Home Rule negotiations failed miserably and Bishop O'Dwyer publicly declared his support for Sinn Féin, the French had to leave rapidly for Ireland.

THE FIRST FRENCH MISSION TO IRELAND

As André Géraud had suggested in his report in June, the French delegation was entirely composed of ecclesiastics, except for Géraud himself: Mgr Touchet, Bishop of Orléans, Mgr Lenfant, Bishop of Digne, Mgr Battifol, Canon of Notre-Dame in Paris and Fr Patrice Flynn of Suresnes who was a chaplain in the French Army.[65] Flynn would be very useful since his parents were from Cork and had emigrated to France, and he was fluent in English. Before their arrival in Ireland, the delegation was met by Paul Cambon in London to be briefed on the exact nature of their mission. The new French propaganda offensive had begun, however, on a false note. On 5 October, the *Freeman's Journal* announced that the band of the Garde Républicaine, the French Republican Guard, was on its way from London to Dublin in order to give a series of concerts. The band would play at the Mansion House but also in Phoenix Park.[66] The object of the exercise was to remind the Irish of the traditional Franco-Irish friendship and grip the imagination of young men. The next day, the *Freeman's Journal* informed its readers that the Garde Républicaine had been called back to France. It published a letter from Cambon to the Lord Mayor of Dublin in which the French Ambassador declared that he was deeply sorry and that 'it [was] a question of military duty, and that the War Minister [found] it impossible to grant them any further leave'.[67] This was the official version but the truth was very different. On 4 October, the Ambassador had written to the Quai d'Orsay and explained where the real difficulty lay:

> In order to favour recruitment, the military authorities had intended to accompany recruits with their regimental music. Since the new soldiers, as is customary, go to Saint Patrick's Cathedral before their departure, it has been laid down that musicians enter at the same time. Therefore, [there was] great excitement; the Archbishop of Dublin forbade [the band] to set foot in the church. [It gave rise to] many passionate controversies. On seeing a French military band, people would be inclined to think that it is a move of the War Office to boost recruitment. With such an impressionable population in Dublin, it would not be wise.
>
> (Quai d'Orsay, Paris, vol. 540 Grande-Bretagne, letter no. 133, Cambon to Ministère des Affaires étrangères, 4 October 1916)

It was a bad omen for the French mission. The ecclesiastics arrived in Dublin on 7 October 1916 and went immediately to Maynooth. The date of their coming had not been left to chance for on the very same day the entire Irish hierarchy met for their second general meeting of the year. At first sight, Hogan had chosen a judicious moment to invite the French ecclesiastics. In fact, it was a serious mistake as the Irish bishops were completely taken aback by this visit. Géraud wrote in his report that Hogan had told nobody about it, not even Cardinal Logue.[68] On

8 October, Archbishop Walsh sent Curran to Logue to ascertain the aim of the French delegation. The secretary noted: 'This visit was unexpected and surrounded with much mystery. It was rumoured that John Redmond had prevailed on an Irish Archbishop to invite them to Ireland in the hope of promoting a more friendly feeling with France.'[69] The lack of clarity had aroused suspicions.

Redmond was not involved but from the very beginning the mission was doomed as the propaganda effort was all too obvious. On 9 October 1916, the French were introduced to the seminarians in the McMahon Hall.[70] The first one to speak was Mgr Touchet who had the reputation of being the most brilliant orator of the French episcopate. He evoked the devotion of the Irish people to their religion and paid tribute to the soldier priests in France. He described at great length how French soldiers were fighting for their Church. This was fully in accordance with Géraud's instructions to present the Germans as being militaristic and Protestant. The Bishop went on to praise Catholic France's help to Ireland during the Famine years and Catholic Ireland's help to France during the Franco-Prussian War of 1870. He remarked on the Irish soldiers on the front: 'Those Irish soldiers who had fallen in France in the present war had held high their beautiful flag, and had excited the greatest admiration of the people of France.'[71] It was now exceedingly clear what the real intention of the French delegation was. The second speaker, Mgr Lenfant, declared: 'Ireland and France were sisters... They were sisters by their fidelity to the Catholic Church...In spite of Saracens, in spite of Protestants, in spite of terrorists..., France, heart and soul, always belonged to Christ and the Church.'[72] Lenfant was trying to impress bishops like O'Dwyer who regularly criticised atheist France and those who had run out of patience with Protestant unionists in the aftermath of the rising. The speeches were well received and the *Irish Catholic Directory* recorded that the two Frenchmen had been 'vigorously applauded'.[73] This is rather surprising as Mgr Hogan had pointed out that Germany was very much in favour in Maynooth. One may wonder about the objectivity of the *Irish Catholic Directory*. Perhaps the audience was enchanted by the beauty of the language as Touchet and Lenfant had addressed the students in French. The *Freeman's Journal* gave translated versions of their speeches.

The same day, a banquet took place in the Gresham Hotel with Lord Wimborne as one of the main guests and speakers. The Lord Lieutenant delivered an important address on conscription, which was already enforced in Britain. It was a crucial issue for the war was not going well for the Allies, whether it was on the Somme, in the Dardanelles, in Mesopotamia or at Verdun. Although Herbert Asquith's cabinet had decided not to introduce compulsory military service in Ireland lest the population rebelled, it had to listen to British public opinion which resented the fact that the Irish had been left out. The question could not be easily ignored, and sooner or later, the Irish would have to participate more actively in the war effort, be it voluntarily or compulsorily. Wimborne explained that there was an evident crisis since recruitment was failing in Ireland and that conscription could not be implemented although there were between 100,000 and 200,000 men fit for military service.[74]

During the mission, Géraud had a meeting with Wimborne who assured him that the French delegation had aroused much sympathy in Ireland. The Lord Lieutenant believed that France could solve the crisis by setting up Irish brigades commanded by French officers and envisaged negotiating with John Redmond on the 'mass recruitment of the National Volunteers'.[75] If Wimborne's plan succeeded, the conscription crisis would be solved and British public opinion would be fairly satisfied even if it meant that the Irish would fight in the French Army and that the British self-esteem might be wounded. As for the Irish, their nationalism and susceptibilities would be spared. The Franco-Irish brigades seemed an ideal way out. The press eagerly welcomed the arrival of the French ecclesiastical delegation. The *Freeman's Journal* wrote: '[The visit] will give these French bishops an opportunity of ascertaining for themselves the extent to which Catholic Ireland sympathises with France in this hour of her sorest need.'[76] The *Irish Times* commented that the French had come to ask the Irish to enlist on a larger scale and play their part in the greatest conflict the world had ever seen.[77]

Contrary to what had been planned, the mission was quickly defined as political by the two most pro-war newspapers in Ireland. Mgr Curran wrote to Mgr Hagan in Rome: 'It was most amazing to see the desperate anxiety of the *Irish Times* to learn all about [the delegation's] objects.'[78] Géraud did not appreciate this publicity and was obliged to formally deny the *Irish Times*' statement.[79] On 10 October 1916, the French were introduced to the Irish hierarchy. Their speeches were more or less the same as those made before the seminarians of Maynooth the previous day. According to Curran, the visitors 'got nothing in reply but soft talk of welcome'.[80] Mgr Touchet gave, however, a relevant interview to the *Freeman's Journal*. Not once did he evoke the historical relations between France and Ireland. He strictly confined himself to religious themes and insisted on the fact that his country was involved in a just war according to Catholic theology. On the mission he remarked that it was within the scope of a rapprochement between the French and several other European Churches and as an example he quoted the cordial relations between French and Italian Catholics.[81] It was obvious that Géraud had given Touchet precise instructions after the *Irish Times*' untimely intervention.

Géraud's conclusions on the mission accurately reflected the Irish hierarchy's frame of mind. The visit had been quite successful in gauging that there was still some sympathy in Ireland for France. Only two prelates had not agreed with Mgr Hogan's initiative to invite French ecclesiastics to Maynooth: Walsh and O'Dwyer. Géraud had asked Touchet and Lenfant to mention the Allies' future victory so as to make the Irish bishops realise that their country would be in a weak position regarding Home Rule and partition if it had only half-heartedly participated in the war effort. On the other hand, of course, a nationalist Ireland fully committed to the cause of liberty and civilisation would significantly increase her chances of achieving self-rule at the future peace conference. The Frenchman's argument was subtle for it forced the hierarchy to make an important political decision and be answerable to some degree for its country's destiny. Until then the bishops had never stood united on the issues of Home Rule, partition and war effort. Géraud thought that there was a 'lack of political courage, a lack of cohesion and a lack of leadership' amongst them.[82] He was quite hard-hearted in this statement. After all, the bishops were entitled to their own opinions and the looming danger of partition made the position of the northern bishops even more complex. Moreover, the prelates could not afford to ignore the evolution of Irish public opinion towards the war. Thus, cohesion within the hierarchy in October 1916 was almost impossible. It was a fact, however, that many bishops preferred to be prudent and adopted a low profile.

Géraud was certainly right when he spoke of the lack of leadership. It would have been difficult for Cardinal Logue to make the hierarchy adopt a general positive attitude towards recruitment after all the dramatic events. As has been noted, the Cardinal had his own particular views. Nevertheless, it did seem that he was somewhat stubbornly out of touch with political developments. He refused to admit that Irish nationalism was becoming more radical and was gradually following Sinn Féin. Mgr Touchet had met Logue in Armagh, who had told him that he 'ignored the seriousness of Irish affairs and...said that if the British Government had talked frankly to him before the meetings in Maynooth, he would certainly have vanquished the opposition of those bishops favouring passivity'.[83] It is doubtful that Logue would have welcomed a direct confrontation with Walsh and O'Dwyer, and even more doubtful whether he would have succeeded in convincing them to abandon their opposition to the war effort and tacit approval of the growing nationalist opposition. It merely confirmed that Logue was at that moment overtaken by events. Afterwards, on 25 October 1916, Touchet wrote a letter to Aristide Briand, blaming the British

Government for not trusting the Irish hierarchy and for not having persuaded the bishops that seditious elements were active in Ireland.[84] Touchet implied that the Irish bishops could have disciplined those elements with spiritual arms, an argument that Walsh had strongly objected to when the Easter Rising occurred in Dublin.

André Géraud concluded his report for the Quai d'Orsay by saying that the French delegation had been successful in persuading the Irish of the Catholic renaissance in France. There was indeed a renaissance in the country but old anti-clerical feelings remained, all the more since there was a widespread belief in France that Pope Benedict XV was pro-German.[85] This was not entirely exaggerated as will be seen. In Paris, Aristide Briand, the Président du Conseil, refused to go to a requiem for fallen Italian soldiers as he deemed that masses were not his business.[86] Géraud had some grounds to be reasonably optimistic as Mgr Touchet had informed him that Irish bishops had said to him 'that they would not oppose recruitment, that they would favour it even, but privately'.[87] Concerning the British Government, Géraud was rather harsh and did not mince his words. He was of the opinion that since the Easter Rising, Asquith's cabinet had followed 'the least intelligent approach' to the Irish question. He believed that the Prime Minister should have imposed Home Rule immediately after the rising and taken advantage of the fact that both Nationalists and Unionists had been shell shocked by the events in Dublin. Instead, Asquith asked David Lloyd George to negotiate with both parties to find a compromise. Géraud thought that it had been a mistake, although he recognised that the Nationalist party had done its very best to reach an agreement with the Unionists. The Frenchman deplored the fact that as a result of the failure of the negotiations, the authority of Dublin Castle had been re-established with 'mediocre ministers and mediocre civil servants' at its head. If one considers the organisation of recruitment, Géraud's last remark was not far from the truth. He wrote that there was some rivalry between the Lord Lieutenant and the Chief Secretary and finally informed the Quai d'Orsay that Sir William Byrne had been appointed Irish Under Secretary, and that Byrne had been in charge of lunatic asylums when he was working for the Home Office. Géraud commented sarcastically: 'There is perhaps more humour than political wisdom in this nomination.'[88] General Sir Bryan Mahon, Commander in Chief of the British forces in Ireland between 1916 and 1918, shared Géraud's opinion of the British Government and its administration at the time and wrote of the Coalition Cabinet that it was 'weak...dishonest and incompetent'.[89]

The question now was, did the first French mission stimulate the war effort in Ireland again?

THE RESULTS OF THE FRENCH MISSION

The first French mission failed inasmuch as the number of recruits for the British Army continued to drop. During his meeting with Lord Wimborne, a secretary told André Géraud that 'voluntary enlistment only produced about 300 men a week'.[90] Two years later, General de la Panouse, the military attaché of the French embassy in Britain, informed Georges Clemenceau, the French Prime Minister, that in 1917 only 14,123 men had joined the Army, 5,930 from Ulster and 8,193 from Connaught, Leinster and Munster.[91] What were the reasons behind this failure?

Firstly, the date of the delegation's arrival was badly timed. It happened just after or during crucial political developments such as the Easter Rising, David Lloyd George's partition plan, the battles of the Somme and Verdun, and the conscription crisis of the summer of 1916. The Irish hierarchy, and also the press, knew immediately what the delegation's real intentions were. A letter from Bishop O'Dwyer to Mgr O'Riordan in Rome, written on 27 November 1916, proved that from the very start the mission could not possibly have been successful:

> We had two French Bishops...at Maynooth last week. They spoke a great deal about the old sympathy between France and Ireland, and comparing this with an enquiry which Lord Wimborne made a few weeks ago as to whether a brigade might be raised in Ireland to fight not for England but for France, I can make a good guess as to the purpose of their visit.
> (ICR, O'Riordan papers, letter no. 176, O'Dwyer to O'Riordan, 27 November 1916)

Secondly, the idea of an Irish brigade fighting for France was unworkable. France had become Britain's ally in the war and was no longer regarded as a haven for Irish nationalists and republicans. The war in Europe had put an end to the traditional Franco-Irish military relations. An Irish brigade would have been considered as a substitute for conscription. Géraud himself, who was still under the impression that the mission would slowly bring about a rapprochement between the two countries, advised against it on the grounds that it could seriously endanger French sympathies still surviving in Ireland.[92] The Bishop of Digne, Mgr Lenfant, explained to Aristide Briand why he believed an Irish brigade was not a feasible project:

> I asked if the Irish were able to enlist directly for France, would they not do it on a large scale? I was told: no! Our perfidious adversaries [the Germans] did everything possible to destroy the

old and deep Irish sympathies for our dear country; above all they have shown how France broke her concordat with Rome. France has insulted our Father.

> (Quai d'Orsay, Paris, vol. 545 Grand-Bretagne/Irlande, rapport d'André Gérard, Bishop of Digne to President du Conseil, p. 184)

Thirdly, the Bishop of Digne's observations were right as the relations between France and Ireland were not that good. From August to October 1917, Fr Flynn was sent to Ireland in order to assess Irish sympathy for France. Flynn met several prelates, among others Bishop Coyne of Elphin, who told him without any hesitation whatsoever: 'Since 1870, our sympathy for you has greatly diminished; the reason is religious persecution.' It appeared that the pre-war *querelle religieuse* in France had considerably damaged traditional Franco-Irish relations. Coyne's reaction was understandable. The Franco-Prussian War of 1870 had been immediately followed by the Commune in Paris. In those days, French revolutionaries had shown how hostile they were to the Catholic Church. When the Third Republic came into being, tough anti-clerical measures were introduced. In Ireland, France was seen as an anti-Catholic country and it had disastrous effects on the traditional Franco-Irish friendship. The authorities in Paris, furthermore, fully intended to avenge the defeat of 1870 and win back the lost provinces of Alsace and Lorraine. As France drew closer to Britain in order to fight Germany in the future, Ireland was no longer one of her main concerns. A most damaging blow to Franco-Irish relations occurred when the republican Government of Jules Ferry expelled the old and harmless Fenian James Stephens to Switzerland.[93] On 19 August 1917, Flynn met Cardinal Logue in Armagh. The French priest reported their conversation and certain remarks of Logue to the Quai d'Orsay:

> 'The Irish Catholics like the French Catholics but not their Government'; this obsessive sentence is heard everywhere and is completed by another one, easily understandable from a people who struggled for three centuries for its faith: 'Do you ignore', said the Cardinal, 'that in the United States, twenty million Irish, or at least of Irish descent, had decided to protest against the blasphemer [René Viviani] sent over from France? It is therefore very useful to talk about the good that exists in France since we know only the evil'.
>
> (Quai d'Orsay, Paris, vol. 546 Irlande, December 1916–January 1918, rapport du Père Patrice Flynn)

Under those conditions the idea of an Irish Brigade fighting for

France was simply no longer feasible. The French had lost their propaganda battle in Ireland. In the Quai d'Orsay, the diplomatic corps realised the importance of the Irish-American world, just as Paul Cambon had pointed out to them in 1915. Logue too understood this French preoccupation and his remark to Flynn was like a threat. In 1917, French diplomacy would not insist on a rapprochement with Ireland lest Irish public opinion might be upset in any way, all the more because the powerful United States had at long last entered the war. The French hoped to see American soldiers on the front line very soon and Ireland became less of a worry. So it appeared at least.

The political situation in Ireland had taken precedence over the historical relations between the two countries and the French and Irish hierarchies were not able to change this. Ireland was too concerned with her own problems to be worried about world affairs, especially with France who was only interested in how many infantry divisions she could supply. If France had been Ireland's old friend she should have helped her politically in her struggle for Home Rule by bringing pressure to bear on the British Government. Only then would Ireland perhaps have sent those 100,000 or 200,000 men to the front. The war had changed the nature of diplomatic relations and geopolitical considerations between France, Britain and Ireland. And yet, surprisingly enough at the very end of the war, the British and French Governments would send a second mission to Ireland in the summer of 1918. In Washington, Count von Bernstorff realised that the Germans had missed a genuine opportunity in Ireland to change the course of the war. In May 1916, he sent a coded message to Theobald von Bethmann Hollweg, the German Chancellor. In it, he stated that England had made itself many enemies in the United States during and after the Easter Rising and that the American peace movement was gaining in strength daily. He wrote that all the Irish-Americans were now in favour of Germany.[94] Perhaps, but it was only a matter of time before American public opinion, including Irish-American, would change its mind and turn largely against Germany as its unrestricted submarine warfare was claiming more and more American lives.

As for the Irish Catholic Church, it was about to enter the last two years of the war, which would shape Ireland's political destiny.

5 The Church, the War and radicalism, 1916–1918

November 1916
'For liberty and civilisation and the rights of small nations Ireland had made great sacrifices in the war, though, until the other day, the record of Irish bravery was studiously ignored.'

Bishop O'Donnell of Raphoe on Ireland's war effort in the Freeman's Journal

June 1918
'I could never understand how so many of the Bishops – practically all, indeed, who took part in public affairs – went on supporting such a set of renegades.'

Archbishop Walsh on the Nationalist party to Mgr O'Riordan in Rome

The French bishops in Ireland had rapidly become aware that the country had begun a slow political mutation and that the Irish clergy were divided on the national question. The British Government was taking decisions dictated by the war in Europe, which alienated Irish nationalist public opinion more and more. This in turn had serious repercussions on recruitment in the country. Under these circumstances, the Catholic Church was not willing to support voluntary enlistment and persuade its flocks to join the colours even if some of its members were still in favour of the Allies. This not only worried France but also Australia and the United States, which had just declared war on Germany. These countries realised that Irish Catholic opinion could have serious consequences at home and throughout the British Empire. The Easter Rising and the partition crisis had provoked a clear political radicalisation among the population and the clergy. Their anger was directed at the Government and the unionists. Where would this radicalisation lead? How would it affect the war effort? What would the nature of the relations be between the Catholic Church and the Nationalist party on one hand, and what would they be between the Church and Sinn Féin on the other hand? The situation was complex and full of uncertainties.

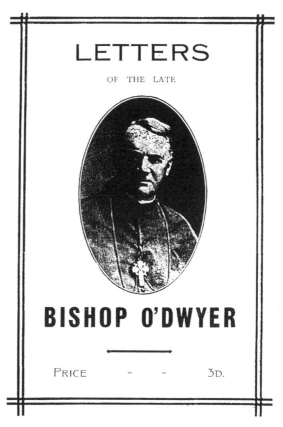

20. Booklet 'Letters of the late Bishop O'Dwyer', a compilation of Bishop O'Dwyer's anti-war writings (PRO London, CO 904/161)

Done to Death

Behind the walls of Mountjoy

————❖❖————

Letter of the Bishop of Killaloe.

————————

It is horrible that the country has to stand silently by listening to the moans of the decent young Irish boys who are being slowly done to death behind the walls of Mountjoy Prison by brutal tyrants ; or to see them thrown in their last gasp out to die like dogs outside the jail door.

They may die as poor Thomas Ashe has died, but with other results than Dublin Castle has dreamed of. Their deaths will sanctify them in the memory of Ireland and surround their heartless torturers with inextinguishable hatred and ignominy.

This is the sort of cruelty we were accustomed to hear of as possible only in the ancient Bastille, or the dungeons of Naples, or the black prisons of Russia ; but as altogether impossible under English rule. We have no need to wait for the future to inform us ; the world sees already in these hideous atrocities what the triumph of English culture means for small nationalities.

+ M. FOGARTY,

Bishop of Killaloe.

21. Leaflet 'Done to Death', written by Bishop Fogarty (PRO, London, CO 904/161)

5 Reasons

Why Irishmen should join the British Army.

1. Because Englishmen WON'T.

2. Because it is the best way to exterminate the DIRTY Irish and to finish the GOOD WORK which England began so well.

3. Because the King's Own Scottish Borderers butchered your people on the 26th of July, 1914.

4. Because Carson wants to march on Cork when the War is over and imitate Cromwell, by the way (as arranged at the Curragh).

5. Because Germany broke the Treaty of Limerick (?) and will break the Home Rule Treaty too.

IRISHMEN

Save the Bloody British Empire—and let Ireland be damn'd —Forget Irish history— Forget your Nationality—Forget the Bachelors' Walk Atrocity.

JOIN THE GURKHAS.

22. Anti-war leaflet (PRO, London, CO 904/161)

Within the hierarchy, Cardinal Logue was against the cabinet but still supported the Empire. Archbishop Walsh, Bishop O'Dwyer and Bishop Fogarty supported the nationalist opposition, then the newly unified Sinn Féin. The clergy in Ulster wanted a new party, one resolutely against partition. The Nationalist party was continuously attacked by the popular O'Dwyer and did not seek to counter the Bishop of Limerick. Sinn Féin, under the new leadership of Eamon de Valera, played the 'Catholic card' to win over the Church to its cause. Sinn Féin was anxious to shed its revolutionary and bloodthirsty image. The Irish people, so nationalistic after the executions of the rebel leaders, were gradually overcome by apathy and neither de Valera, nor Redmond, nor the recruiting sergeants were able to turn this apathy into political activism. As for the Catholic clergy, a division appeared between younger priests, more radical and supporting Sinn Féin, and older ones still faithful to the Nationalist party. Would the more conservative bishops be able to change the revolutionary temperament of the younger clergy?

Two events directly related to the war would bring answers to these questions and accentuate the radical attitude of the Catholic Church towards David Lloyd George's cabinet and the unionists, which played right in Sinn Féin's hands. Those events were the United States' entry in the war, which incited the British Government to set up the Irish Convention to find a definitive solution to the Irish question, and the peace agreement between Germany and Bolshevik Russia, which precipitated the conscription crisis in Ireland in 1918.

THE SEARCH FOR NATIONALIST UNITY

At the end of 1916, Ireland was in a political cul-de-sac. John Redmond's dominance was melting away. The various opposition movements were divided, lacked consistency and a clear political programme and above all badly needed a charismatic leader. The Church was not in an enviable position either for the twenty-eight bishops were not able to find a common and concrete policy regarding Home Rule, partition and the war. Priests did not agree between themselves as to who was the best representative of nationalist Ireland. The nationalist population was equally confused. Its initial hostility to the rebels followed by a volte-face in public opinion after the executions of the rebel leaders did not mean that it was ready to support physical force. In fact the economic prosperity that people were enjoying meant that Irishmen were not interested in taking up arms against the British forces. There had unquestionably been a nationalist élan but it remained difficult to define. It was obvious to everybody, however, that all nationalists had to be united against the British Government, the unionists and the threat of conscription. The Military Service Bill had not been implemented in Ireland in the summer of 1916 but it remained a threat. On 13 November 1916, indeed, the offensive on the Somme in France came to an end and it was a catastrophe. The Allied armies had a total of 620,000 casualties of which 420,000 were British and 200,000 were French.[1] As for the Irish, they had suffered heavy casualties too. It is difficult to assess precisely how many Irish soldiers were either killed, wounded or taken prisoner. There are some striking figures though. On 1 and 2 July, the 36th Ulster Division suffered no less than 5,500 losses and during the battles of Ginchy and Guillemont between 3 and 9 September, the 16th Irish Division suffered 4,314 casualties.[2] The Germans had lost 450,000 men and there was no significant change on the front. It was easy to see that it was a war of attrition and that all these fallen soldiers would have to be replaced soon.

On 12 November 1916 in London, an enraged and exasperated John Dillon gave a lecture entitled 'Ireland and the war in Europe'. He reminded his audience that he had advised Lord Kitchener, as early as 1914, on recruitment in Ireland and how to boost the war effort. He declared: 'Well, now, what do you think? Every single proposal that was made was turned down. We were repulsed. We met with no response for the first six months of the war.'[3] Dillon criticised the fact that recruitment campaigns had been entrusted to unionists who had no consideration for nationalist fervour. It would be hard to criticise Dillon for his outburst. As for conscription, he believed that it could not be put into operation in Ireland without implementing it in Australia, Canada and South Africa, all countries belonging to the British Empire. He concluded his long and angry speech by warning the Government: 'They want to apply conscription in Ireland. I say it would be absolute madness and I tell you this; that you can lead the Irish people – they are a people very easily led – but you cannot drive them, and if you attempt to do so you will gain no strength.'[4] Asquith, Lloyd George and others had been cautioned. Dillon's lecture was meant to clarify the party's pro-war policy and to stop Redmond's political decline. His very nationalistic and anti-governmental statements undoubtedly reflected his personal frame of mind but were also intended to win back public opinion to the Nationalist party's cause and prevent it from evolving towards the opposition.

Certain members of the hierarchy were not impressed by Dillon's latest efforts and began looking for a new political alternative. This alternative had to meet three criteria: firstly, it had to be against armed violence; secondly, it had to respect the Church's interests; thirdly, it had to have the full trust of the Irish people.[5] Bishop McHugh of Derry had tried to put forward such an alternative with the Irish Nation League, which was essentially against partition. The INL, however, was not successful for it was not sufficiently established across Ulster and was non-existent in the other provinces. Bishop O'Dwyer had appealed for the people to follow

Sinn Féin. But there were some difficulties in the way. Its leaders were still in prison and there was nobody in Ireland to take over. Furthermore, the population was not entirely aware of Arthur Griffith and Sinn Féin's ideology. It was known that it supported cultural nationalism. But, was it in favour of a republic or a double monarchy, for instance? Was it really in favour of an armed struggle as the authorities were claiming? If this was the case, would Sinn Féin not be condemned out of hand by the Catholic Church? O'Dwyer would have to answer all these questions and assure the Irish that this party was 'respectable'. Perhaps his popularity could help Sinn Féin in making a significant breakthrough. For the time being, despite all the setbacks, the majority of the people was still behind the Nationalist party, which was the only party to be organised throughout the whole country.[6]

The same could be said about the hierarchy. One of the first bishops to openly declare his support for John Redmond after the Easter Rising was Patrick O'Donnell of Raphoe. Like Dillon, he had understood that all support given to Redmond was crucial at this stage before it was too late. The *Freeman's Journal* published a long letter from O'Donnell, which was intended not only for Ireland but also for the United States, where Shane Leslie would publish it in *Ireland*. The Bishop wrote that unity between nationalists was crucial in order to obtain Home Rule. He began by paying tribute to Redmond's qualities as a leader and stated that he had acted honestly during the recent partition crisis, which was entirely true, and that he had been unjustly discredited during the negotiations. O'Donnell said that Redmond, like anybody else, could make mistakes. But the real mistake, according to him, was to destroy unity among nationalists:

> For a nation struggling to be free substantial unity is so essential that it must always be a primary concern with every National leader, to keep together the people from whom he derives his strength. Yet, now and then, no matter how capable he be, he can scarcely avoid creating opposition for himself. He may have to push on and take a line that will alienate some of his supporters. He may not be able to show his hand. He may make a mistake, or sustain a reverse. Then, men with various grievances are tempted, or think it a public duty, to offer themselves and their rival programmes for acceptance on the constitutional platform.
>
> (*The Freeman's Journal*, 14 November 1916)

This was an implicit criticism of Bishop O'Dwyer, who had declared his support for Sinn Féin, Bishop McHugh, who had been an originator of the Anti-Partition League, and of George Murnaghan, who had founded the Irish Nation League. O'Donnell rightly pointed out that only the Nationalist party was solidly implanted in the country and that only its politicians could bring about Home Rule for Ireland. Concerning the partition crisis, he stated that Redmond did not want to impose Home Rule on any area in Ulster that did not wish it immediately but that the leader would not tolerate that any area should be forced into the exclusion zone. As examples, he quoted the city of Derry, where there was a majority of nationalists, and Co. Armagh, where there were more unionists. Nevertheless, regarding those counties with a unionist majority, he emphasised that nationalists were in an overwhelming majority in the country and at Westminster Parliament. His remark was meant to reassure the northern bishops, like Logue and McHugh. Then, O'Donnell expressed the view that Ireland was paying too much tax at the moment for 'Imperial purposes', in other words the war, and that if the whole of Ireland obtained Home Rule, '[it] should be able to strike a bargain for some tolerable annual contribution'. Clearly, the economic theme had become a battleground and O'Donnell was trying to play down O'Dwyer's interventions. This was a crucial issue since taxation would be the cause of the differences between Redmond and O'Donnell in 1918. The Bishop of Raphoe ended his long letter on Irish participation in the war. He personally believed it should continue but, like Dillon, he put the Government on their guard against any inconsiderate action:

> Conscription is no more relished by the Unionist than by the Nationalist farmer. Both have been short of labourers to gather in the harvest; and if the Irish Divisions at the front are to receive strong support from rural Ireland a new and powerful inspiration will be needed. The feeling commonly entertained in Ireland is that England is on the right side in this war just because her interest happens to be there. The Irishman's interest is on the same side. But it is a small affair that has little to do with the lordship of half the earth on the commerce of all the oceans. For liberty and civilisation and the rights of small nations Ireland has made great sacrifices in the war, though, until the other day, the record of Irish bravery was studiously ignored.
>
> (*The Freeman's Journal*, 14 November 1916)

O'Donnell was alluding to the blunders of the War Office and his referring to 'a new and powerful inspiration' meant the immediate implementation of Home Rule to the entire country. On 14 December 1916, Archbishop Harty of Cashel also warned the Irish that unity was essential: 'If we don't get our Parliament again it will be our own fault. Disunion in our ranks has ever been the ruin of our hopes.'[7] Harty was, of course, thinking about Redmond's party. He had condemned the rising and still supported the Allies. Against, perhaps, all expectations, significant political developments were slow in coming in Ireland. The aftermath of the Easter Rising had produced a nationalist élan but it was not translated into political action for the reason that the opposition was largely disorganised. The West Cork by-election in November 1916 was a perfect illustration. The Nationalist party won the election simply because there was no opposition candidate.[8] Consequently, the party continued its pro-war policy, although Dillon thought that this was a mistake that could lead to the destruction of the party.[9]

At the end of November, Archbishop Walsh was brought to the attention of the recruiting authorities once again as he had been invited to a banquet given by the Lord Mayor of Dublin in honour of Lord Wimborne. According to Mgr Curran, the banquet had been organised by the Nationalist party to boost recruitment. The Lord Mayor had spoken of 'the representative nature of the gathering'.[10] Indeed, the Navy, the Army, the university, the bar, the civil service, the Protestant Archbishop of Dublin and Dr Donnelly, the very pro-war Auxiliary Bishop of Dublin, were present. True to form, Walsh refused and sent a letter to the Lord Mayor saying: 'I feel certain that my going to meet His Excellency the Lord Lieutenant at dinner in the Mansion House just now would be seriously misunderstood.'[11] Still, at the end of 1916, Germany put out peace feelers but the Triple Entente had no interest. This incensed Bishop O'Dwyer who wrote to Mgr O'Riordan that England was in a bad position and was gambling heavily, hoping that luck would turn. Concerning the economy, he wrote: 'With the national debt at over £3,000,000,000, food getting scarce, "our" allies, France and Russia, almost exhausted, it is not easy to see how much better things will be by December 1917.'[12] Pessimism had taken hold of the Bishop of Limerick.

On 7 December 1916, however, a significant event for the future relations between Ireland and Britain took place as David Lloyd George was appointed Prime Minister. It is difficult to know with certainty how the Church reacted to this change at the head of the cabinet. To many, Lloyd George was the man who had deviously manipulated John Redmond. The different nationalist groups must have viewed his arrival with serious concern, including Logue, Walsh, O'Dwyer and especially the northern bishops. Lloyd George must have been aware of nationalist public opinion and one of his first initiatives was to invite Redmond for a discussion on 9 December, during which he announced that rebel prisoners, who had not been officially condemned, would be liberated and that martial law would be suppressed.[13] The Prime Minister's decision to release prisoners dealt a blow to the opposition's propaganda machine, suddenly deprived of its Irish martyrs detained in Perfidious

Albion's internment camps. But his haste to meet Redmond was important on two accounts. Firstly, Lloyd George wanted to point out to nationalist Ireland that Redmond was still its leader and that he needed support before a more radical nationalism took power in the country. Secondly, he had at long last understood that Redmond was his most precious ally, still favouring Irish participation in the war. Lloyd George desperately needed more recruits after the latest military disasters in the Dardanelles and on the Somme. Furthermore, on 29 December 1916, the Prime Minister came to realise that the Irish world was deceptively large and by no means confined to a small island, lying west of Britain. On that day, he received a telegram from William Hughes, the warlike Australian Prime Minister, who urged him to find a solution to the Home Rule crisis, which, according to him, would boost recruitment. Hughes argued: 'A disaffected Ireland not only makes the ideal of imperial unity impossible but gravely imperils existing imperial relations.'[14] It was true that Hughes had to face the Australian hierarchy's opposition to conscription. Many Australian bishops were of Irish descent, like the formidable Archbishop Mannix. How would Lloyd George tackle this problem, as nationalist public opinion was becoming more radical at that time.

On 16 December, Mgr Curran had noticed a change of mood in Dublin. He had perceived that a rapprochement was taking place between the Redmondite National Volunteers and the Irish Volunteers. According to him, the National Volunteers 'were disgusted by John Redmond' and his politics.[15] Curran believed that a convention between the two paramilitary forces would happen soon and that it would get rid of the pro-Redmond elements. He was right, for seven months later, on 18 July 1917, Colonel Maurice Moore, head of the National Volunteers, declared that he rejected Redmond's authority and that he adhered to the original aims of the Irish Volunteers.[16] In a letter to Mgr O'Riordan, Curran remarked on Irish public opinion: 'The general spirit is firm but though the organisation is improving, it is still poor and confused and at sixes and sevens.'[17] Archbishop Walsh's secretary was a shrewd observer for British military intelligence confirmed his analysis.

After the Easter Rising, the Army had decided to put into operation a new intelligence network throughout Ireland with the aim of analysing the country's political evolution. Ireland was thus divided into three regions: the Southern District, the Northern District and the Midlands and Connaught District. At the head of each region was a senior officer whose task was to carefully examine the information gathered by his subalterns, before sending a detailed report to headquarters in Dublin.[18] The general impression that emerged from these reports was that Sinn Féin was relatively popular between September 1916 and the beginning of the second half of 1917. This was correct. Firstly, Sinn Féin won four by-elections during this period, in North Roscommon, South Longford, East Clare and Kilkenny City.[19] Secondly, the term Sinn Féin was above all synonymous with opposition, something not associated with the Nationalist party.[20] It may be reasonably assumed, therefore, that in moments of intense nationalist feeling or disgust with the British Government, many Irish people felt the urge to vote for Sinn Féin without really knowing what the party stood for. From the second half of 1917 until the conscription crisis of April 1918, Sinn Féin's popularity was declining. Military intelligence explained that this was due to the lack of organisation and leadership within the party and also to the Catholic Church's opposition. Finally, after April 1918, Sinn Féin was rapidly becoming the country's new political force, after its role in the conscription crisis.[21] In November 1916, the officer in charge of the Midlands and Connaught District sent his monthly report to Dublin. This officer paid more attention to the political evolution of the Catholic Church than his Northern and Southern District colleagues. He had discerned the beginning of a division between younger and older clergy, in fact a conflict of generations concerning the national question, the war and Sinn Féin:

> Taking it broadly the Clergy are opposed to Sinn Féin as they think it is socialistic and is a secret society. The senior Clergy and Bishops are generally opposed to it as they believe Ireland's cause is only to be gained by constitutional means. Some of the younger Clergy espouse its views, as they prefer to believe and teach that Ireland should be an independent State free from the hated English rule.
>
> (PRO, London, CO904/157, Midlands and Connaught District Report, November 1916, p. 204)

The association of the Irish Volunteers and the IRB with James Connolly's ICA was now somewhat detrimental to Sinn Féin if this party wanted to represent true Irish nationalism. Socialism was felt to be a foreign influence in Ireland and the Church feared it. This development had already been analysed by Paul Cambon, the French Ambassador, in May 1916.[22] The officer also noted that the clergy were losing their moral grip on the population and that they dreaded losing control completely if any supported recruitment and conscription. He added: 'The clergy live by the people, come from the people, and in many cases seem to guide where really they are led.'[23] The military intelligence officer confirmed that there were definite limits to the power of the clergy in Ireland, which was already apparent before the Easter Rising. There was not much hope for the authorities seeing the Church actively collaborating with the war effort if the people had lost any interest in the conflict. In December 1916, the same officer wrote that in his district Sinn Féin was 'negligible' as far as opposition to law and order was concerned but that it could successfully influence the people if it had leaders and a better organisation, seeing that there was still a strong nationalist feeling.[24] Regarding manpower for the Army, he believed that only conscription would round up those farmers fit for service. Prosperous economic conditions had been one of the British Army's main handicaps in Ireland. It is under these uncertain circumstances that the year 1917 began.

David Lloyd George had many worries about Ireland but mostly in relation to the war in Europe. Military reports estimated that only about 4,000 men had joined the colours between October 1916 and January 1917.[25] This figure was far from satisfactory. In October 1916, Henry Duke, the new Irish Secretary, told Herbert Asquith that there were 160,000 men fit for service in the country.[26] In 1917, Lloyd George asked Duke for his opinions on conscription: 'Military authorities are worrying me on the subject, and it is clear we shall have to discuss the best methods of utilising the man power of Ireland.'[27] Duke answered that Ireland would oppose it but if it had to be implemented, Home Rule would have to be granted simultaneously. The Prime Minister followed Duke's advice and conscription was deferred for the time being.

Nevertheless, British public opinion was growing impatient. *The English Review* published a vitriolic article against the Irish Catholic Church, accusing it of allowing itself to be manipulated by foreign powers to the detriment of Britain. The author stated that the Church encouraged rebellions in the country and as an example he quoted Bishop O'Dwyer who had appealed for support for Sinn Féin.[28] In the meantime Mgr Curran informed Mgr O'Riordan in Rome that 'politics here [have] calmed down very much since the danger of conscription [has] passed'. But, he also referred to the Irish rebel prisoners, still detained in England, and treated as 'ordinary convicts'.[29] This question greatly preoccupied O'Dwyer. In April 1917, a letter signed by Niam ni Pluingcead and Maire ni Rian was published by the press, describing how badly those prisoners were treated. The Bishop was furious, took up his pen and wrote a savage attack on the British Government. The authorities tried to suppress the letter but Sinn Féin got hold of it and turned it into a pamphlet which was rapidly distributed throughout the country.[30] O'Dwyer vented his spleen and believed that '[General] Maxwell's summary method of dealing with Irish rebels was less cruel than the slow torture and degradation of Penal Servitude'. But after this display of strong feelings, O'Dwyer's tactical sense got the upper hand. Very cleverly, he evoked international public opinion in this matter, especially in the United States where there was a powerful Irish-American lobby. To the Allies' relief, the Americans had just entered the war and the Bishop knew that the Irish question could be a thorn in

Anglo-American relations, and that perhaps the powerful United States could hasten the solution to the Home Rule crisis:

> Then it occurred to me to consider whether the people of the United States will be allowed to know the facts of this case, and collate them with the suggestions, sincere or hollow, as the case may be, that are being offered for the political emancipation of Ireland. Is it all humbug? Is there any intention to give us Home Rule in any shape or form, or are all the discussions that are being carried on about it merely the latest shape which British perfidy assumes for its own purposes? I rather think they are. But whether they are or not we are a mean nation if we take the benefit of the sacrifices of our fellow-countrymen, and allow themselves to linger and rot in English jails without at least a protest which the world will hear.
>
> (DDA, Curran papers, 'Important pronouncement by the Most Rev. Dr O'Dwyer, Bishop of Limerick', 30 April 1917)

The sole fact that Sinn Féin had used O'Dwyer's letter proved that the Bishop had become the 'moral leader' of the opposition. He was that charismatic leader Redmond's opponents had been looking for. Even the Irish Volunteers appealed to him regarding the prisoners in Britain. In May 1917, an organiser of the Irish National Aid and Volunteers' Dependents' Fund invited him to come to one of their meetings and make a speech, and asked him to support the demand that the prisoners be treated like prisoners of war. O'Dwyer refused to go but assured the INAVDF that it had his fullest sympathy. Nonetheless, he did not endorse the idea of a prisoner of war status, he went further than that: 'I say liberate them. A secret court martial pronounced them criminals. Their country repudiates that verdict, and regards them as true soldiers and noble patriots.'[31] Two distinct nationalist opposition movements had now asked for his help, as Count Plunkett had also consulted O'Dwyer in April 1917 a few days before his nationalist convention in Dublin.[32]

It is difficult to establish whether O'Dwyer's intervention played a part in the liberation of the last prisoners in Britain, but, on 15 June, Andrew Bonar Law announced in the House of Commons that they would be liberated and sent back to Ireland so that the Irish Convention could work in a better political climate.[33] Among the first prisoners to return were Eamon de Valera and Countess Markievicz. These two republicans were quite amazed by the welcome of the Dubliners since they had been jeered in Dublin immediately after their surrender during the Easter Rising. The sudden change in public opinion had been remarkable but not everybody was a Sinn Féin supporter. On 9 July

1917, for instance, Markievicz was attacked by a hostile mob in Ennis in Co. Clare, even though Sinn Féin was relatively popular in this particular county, and was backed by Dr Fogarty.[34]

At the beginning of 1917, Lloyd George was notified that voluntary enlistment only produced about eighty recruits a week in Ireland. He told T.P. O'Connor, who had orchestrated the first French mission, that if recruitment did not improve, he could lose the House of Commons' confidence and lose his job as Prime Minister, which would lead to a Conservative cabinet.[35] The Conservatives had always made it clear that they were opposed to Home Rule in any shape or form. In this way Lloyd George hoped to put pressure on the Nationalist party to boost the war effort. John Redmond was in a difficult situation since the Prime Minister did not put forward any concrete plan to help him out, and the Irish people had absolutely no reason whatsoever to enlist en masse. In fact, Lloyd George was at a loss when it came to Irish affairs. He did not understand Irish nationalism and the Irish psyche, and completely underestimated Sinn Féin's increasing popularity in the country.[36] Irishmen understood that this war was about great powers, not small nations. Mgr Curran had no illusions about the Prime Minister's sincerity. On 18 January, he wrote to Mgr O'Riordan: 'He was so sorry to see the state of the Irish question, but he had no time to deal with Ireland. He was so engrossed championing the causes of small nationalities and putting down militarism that he could not attend to his own small nationality and the martial law under which the country is governed.'[37]

The hierarchy was still very much divided on the issue of recruitment whereas its younger clergy were definitely opposed to it. The visit of a Canadian regiment of Irish origin to Ireland was a case in point. On 27 January 1917, the regiment had been invited by the Lord Mayor of Dublin to attend a reception at Mansion House. A letter from Redmond was read out and it was obvious that the soldiers were being used for recruitment propaganda. Archbishop Walsh had naturally declined the invitation and a mass for the regiment was to take place in Armagh rather than Dublin. According to Curran, the recruitment authorities foresaw 'the answer they would receive for a mass in the Pro-Cathedral [in Dublin]'.[38] Cardinal Logue, however, was willing to welcome the Canadians in his archdiocese. For once, Lord Wimborne and the DRI had done their homework. The Cardinal was still in favour of the British Empire and the Canadians' visit could not fail to catch his attention. Curran had become aware of Logue's opinions and of the real meaning of the regiment's visit: 'The whole incident is another illustration of the wily procedure of the Government and its desperate efforts to try and persuade us and persuade the world that we are identical with the Empire and the Colonies and, incidentally, to gather recruits.'[39] Bishop Cohalan of Cork had also guessed the real nature of the visit and refused to meet the regiment in Cork. Back in Armagh, Logue gave a very imperial sermon in his cathedral. The Cardinal was completely at loggerheads with Walsh and O'Dwyer. He declared that the Irish were grateful that the Canadians had come over to Europe to defend the 'centre of the Empire' and the cause of civilisation and freedom. The *Tablet* published large extracts of his pronouncement:

> They in Ireland had preserved the faith in spite of persecution and even death itself, and they had carried it to distant Canada, Australia, and America, and wherever the British flag flew. The Irish Catholic was a missioner, and contributed to the grand old, unfailing Irish faith in all these countries ... What he would like to suggest to them [the Canadians] was that they were not only soldiers, but Christian soldiers ... He had seen splendid instances of where English, Irish, and French soldiers have shown that spirit of humanity to the enemy that had fallen into their hands.
>
> (*The Tablet*, 3 February 1917)

Although Logue had unquestionable sympathy for the Allies, it is difficult to know why he made such a speech at that particular time, just after Lloyd George's nomination as Prime Minister and his well known plans to partition the country. A likely explanation could be related to the North Roscommon by-election, which was due to take place on 5 February 1917. Count Plunkett had decided to be a candidate. Plunkett was of course connected to the Easter Rising through his son, Joseph Mary, who had been executed and through his secret mission to the Vatican. To the Cardinal, the Count embodied this revolutionary spirit which he deeply despised. His speech for the Canadians could have been a veiled threat to those Irish who were willing to vote for Plunkett. Logue sensed that the Irish Catholic Church, of which he was the highest dignitary, was still able to make a difference in the country's political evolution. It seemed that this had been his real intention, for in 1918 he did all he could to defeat Sinn Féin in a series of by-elections and operated like a grey eminence.[40] The North Roscommon election had been precipitated by the death of the Nationalist MP, James O'Kelly on 22 December 1916. Shortly afterwards, Fr Michael Flanagan and J.J. O'Kelly, the editor of the *Catholic Bulletin*, asked Plunkett to stand for the election. The Count accepted and stated that he wanted to represent Ireland at the future peace conference.[41]

Only a few days before the election, the Nationalist party was severely criticised by Dr Morrisroe, the Bishop of Achonry, who had sent a letter to a public meeting held at Swinford where John Dillon was to make a speech. The Bishop's words must have disappointed Dillon for they were an attack on the alliance between the Nationalists and the English Liberals. Morrisroe argued that one could simply not trust the Liberals and said that partition symbolised the corruption of statesmen. He added, however, that 'the betrayal of the Party by its English friends [had] restored to Irishmen unfettered independence'. He concluded his letter on the financial issue of the Home Rule crisis with a hint of irony: 'Home Government for all Ireland with complete fiscal autonomy... is the least that the gallant defenders of small peoples ought to grant to long-suffering Ireland.'[42] Morrisroe fully agreed with O'Dwyer and O'Donnell on this issue. His suggestion was surely the only way forward to increase recruitment figures but Lloyd George decided not to pay heed. Morrisroe's letter was published by the *Irish Nation* under the title 'Up Roscommon!' It was obvious that the first election between an opposition and a Nationalist candidate would be a great test. True to form, the opposition used as many Catholic clergy as possible. Fourteen curates and two parish priests campaigned in favour of Plunkett.[43] Fr Flanagan spoke of the liberty of small nations and demanded 'that the freedom to be accorded to Ireland... be the same as that of Belgium, Serbia, Bohemia, Romania, France and Germany'.[44] On 3 February 1917, the first opposition nationalist was elected Member of Parliament with 3,022 votes against 1,700 for the Nationalist candidate. The press spoke about Plunkett as an independent candidate, which was correct. J.J. O'Kelly admitted that Plunkett had indeed been elected to represent Ireland at the peace conference.[45] North Roscommon had been an opportunity for the people to express their dissatisfaction with John Redmond's policy. The *Freeman's Journal* conceded defeat and stated that it was a big blow to the satisfactory settlement of the Home Rule crisis.[46] But, what was Count Plunkett to do with his victory?

In February 1917, the bishops made known their Lenten pastorals, which provided clues to the hierarchy's frame of mind. The *Irish Catholic Directory* gave a summary of the pastorals each year and indicated that most of them concerned directly or indirectly the war. It emphasised that the bishops had asked the farmers to increase their tillage[47] as the German Admiralty had just ordered unrestricted submarine warfare.[48] Bishops Mangan of Kerry and Browne of Cloyne had publicly asked the farmers to make even more efforts. Mangan expressed his satisfaction that priests were involved in local committees that looked after food supplies.[49] This was another incentive for farmers to stay at home rather than face a deluge of shells on the front. Archbishop Harty, still in favour of the Allies, and Bishop Morrisroe broached the subject of the Easter Rising again and reminded their diocesans that they should refrain from all attempt to rebel against the Government to seek justice for their country. Dr Browne and, curiously Bishop Fogarty, from whom a strong denunciation of the war might have been expected, spoke about the purifying effect of the conflict.

Dr Kelly believed the war had been caused by materialism. Bishop Hoare of Ardagh vehemently denounced the Turks and asked the faithful to pray 'that the authors of the Armenian massacres, who [have] never learned the arts of civilisation, [will] be expelled from Europe and the Holy Land'.[50] Archbishop Walsh observed his usual prudent approach and did not made any significant comments. He simply asked the Dubliners to pray for peace and the soldiers and civilians at the front. Walsh also defended the priests of his archdiocese who had volunteered to serve as chaplains and paid tribute to their courage.[51] The Archbishop was answering a critique regarding the lack of Irish chaplains in the Army.

Nevertheless, it seemed that there was a genuine problem. On 15 February 1917, Bishop Kelly wrote to Mgr O'Riordan in Rome that the bishops had asked seminarians in Maynooth to volunteer, but that he had noticed that the younger clergy were not particularly enthusiastic. He admitted that he did not know why.[52] It appeared that Kelly had not correctly analysed the evolution of the younger priests. They were more inspired by the ideals of the Easter Rising than by the war in Europe. Cardinal Logue's Lenten pastoral was eagerly awaited as it was just after the North Roscommon by-election. He devoted a large section to the war and stated that it had produced great poverty among wage earners but that it had enriched the farmers whose prosperity was all too obvious. He spoke about the sad fate of Belgium and Poland, and of the Syrian Christians who were harassed by the Turks as soon as the French left their protectorate. He deplored Germany's new unrestricted submarine warfare, which could provoke a serious food shortage, and asked the farmers to produce even more. Logue also called for the clergy to encourage farmers to do so. Finally, he asked his diocesans 'to avoid all superfluities and practice rigid economy'.[53] On the whole, his pastoral was largely in favour of the Allies. Bishop O'Donnell developed an interesting theme and argued that a league of nations would have to be set up and that religion had to be the 'cement' between all the different peoples. Like Logue, he appealed directly to the farmers: 'In these awful times men, permitted to stay at home far away from the bloodshed of the trenches, are earnestly required to work long hours on their own soil to raise super-abundant crops.'[54] O'Donnell had not mentioned recruitment, which was out of favour with the public, but there was still a global war effort in which they should fully participate.

But, the Lenten pastoral that would grip the country and condemn the war was once again the Bishop of Limerick's. O'Dwyer had correctly guessed that it was now a war of attrition that could go on for several years. Before the publication of his pastoral, he sent a copy to his friend Dr Fogarty and wrote that the British authorities would accuse him of being pro-German. O'Dwyer did not care, however, since anybody who was openly against the war was generally so accused. He stated that he wanted to denounce Allied politicians who demanded an unconditional German surrender, and John Redmond was among those arch-apostles of war.[55] The Bishop criticised the press that had become the Government's propaganda tool, feeding the people with hatred for the Germans. The controversial passage that could be interpreted in favour of Germany concerned the Kaiser and his latest peace proposals:

> After two years and a half of bloodshed the Emperor of Germany proposes to his enemies to enter into a conference, and the proposal is summarily rejected. The present Prime Minister of England said that if England and her allies went into such a conference that would put a rope around their necks. But he has not been asked to explain how that figure of speech is justified.
>
> (DDA, Curran papers, Lenten pastoral Bishop O'Dwyer, February 1917, p. 7)

Being aware that his enemies might reproach him, O'Dwyer added that if Germany were too demanding at such a conference, she would have to endorse the moral blame for its failure. Concerning alleged German atrocities, he wrote that he did not doubt their veracity, but in characteristic provocative fashion compared them to British atrocities during the Easter Rising. O'Dwyer was of the opinion that Austria-Hungary's ultimatum to Serbia in 1914 had been severe but that Serbia was responsible since she was Russia's 'creature' in the Balkans. According to him, Russia's ambitions and England's fear of Germany had been at the origin of the war. The Bishop added that he was not justifying Germany but that he was trying to prove that not everything could be blamed on it. He also denounced the hypocrisy of the war for self-determination and freedom for small nations, and compared Russia's treatment of Poland to England's treatment of Ireland. What the Bishop did not add was that Germany and Austria-Hungary had a share of Poland. O'Dwyer eulogised Benedict XV's initiatives in favour of peace, thus showing once more his strong ultramontane tendencies. Finally, he inveighed against the war of attrition and made some cutting remarks on Irish farmers who had earned much because of the conflict. Contrary to Logue and O'Donnell, he wrote that those farmers were naïve because the money they got was only paper: 'Where is the gold? It is easy enough to print bank notes, but unless there is gold behind them they are worthless. When the war is over the crash will come.' He warned the people that Ireland's prosperity was 'fictitious' and told them 'to think and speak for themselves ... and press their representatives in Parliament to have some regard for the interests of their own country'.[56] The last remark was a gibe at the Nationalist party.

O'Dwyer's pastoral must have reflected most of the people's frame of mind as it had lost all interest in the war. In the last seven months, only

8,178 men had joined the Army.[57] O'Dwyer could be accused of scaremongering but his arguments carried weight and probably had more effect than Logue's, O'Donnell's, Redmond's and Dillon's. Nobody from the Nationalist party took it upon himself to publicly contradict the Bishop of Limerick. This was a serious mistake. On 19 February 1917, Dr Fogarty sent a congratulatory letter to O'Dwyer, saying that his pastoral was 'a treat to read' and that 'England [was] the real cause of this war'.[58] The Bishop of Killaloe's nationalism was not without its jingoistic moments. A few days later, he sent another letter in which he wrote how much O'Dwyer had become popular in the region:

> Your Pastoral has created a furore of delight [illegible] amongst the people. They are all scrambling, especially the young, to get a copy of it. It echoes their heart. They are sick of the falsehood, hypocrisy and cowardice with which the papers drench them – By the way the priests tell me that a favourite name in Baptism is now 'Edward Thomas'.
>
> (LDO, O'Dwyer papers, file O, Fogarty to O'Dwyer, 25 February 1917)

Edward and Thomas were O'Dwyer's two first names.

Like the military intelligence officer of the Connaught and Midlands District, Fogarty had noticed a new nationalist élan among the younger generation. The explanation was simple enough as Irish youth did not want to fight in the trenches. There were many young men fit for service in the country because the war had practically put and end to emigration. In 1914, 20,314 Irish people had left the county whereas in 1917, the figure was 2,111 and in 1918, a mere 980.[59] From August 1914, only O'Dwyer and the opposition had consistently opposed recruitment and defended young Irishmen. Their popularity among that age group was, therefore, hardly surprising.

In the meantime, the debate on Home Rule was utterly fruitless. In March 1917, a heated disagreement took place in the House of Commons in London. The *Tablet* reported that T.P. O'Connor, who wanted the immediate implementation of Home Rule, 'traced the growth of the revulsion of feeling in Ireland owing to the malignity and ineptitude of the War Office'. Major William Redmond asked Sir Edward Carson if 'the sentiments engendered at the Boyne [Battle of 1690 between Protestants and Catholics] were to go on for ever in the face of a war which was threatening civilisation and destroying all that mankind had built up in the Christian Era'. Sir John Lonsdale explained that it was impossible to implement Home Rule for the entire island of Ireland and 'that this was no time for dealing with so controversial a problem'.[60] David Lloyd George felt the urge to state the obvious and said: 'In the north-eastern portion of Ireland you have a population as hostile to Irish rule as the rest of Ireland is to British rule . . . as alien in blood, in religious faith, in traditions, in outlook as alien from the rest of Ireland in this respect as the inhabitants of Fife or Aberdeen.'[61] After these words, which may have been true but were not necessarily tactful, all the Irish Nationalist MPs left the House in protest. If the Prime Minister was anxious not to alienate the unionist population in Ulster, he had no hope whatever of reviving recruitment in the South. And he simply could not ignore those 160,000 young men fit for service at a time when the Tsar had abdicated in Russia. If Germany concluded peace on the eastern front, would she not be able to transfer all her divisions to France and make a decisive breakthrough there? Surely this probability must have been envisaged in London and Paris. The opposition press regularly reiterated its objection to conscription. The *Irish Opinion* wrote that there were many young unemployed people in Dublin. According to this newspaper, it was 'economic conscription' for the employers preferred they join the Army.[62] When the United States entered the war on the Triple Entente's side on 6 April 1917, this was a serious setback for Sinn Féin and the opposition as it put an end to their hopes of seeing the Americans intervene in nationalist Ireland's favour.[63]

A solution to the Home Rule crisis in Britain's favour was equally far from obvious.

On 17 March, Count Plunkett had put forward the idea of a convention of all opposition nationalists, which was due to begin on 19 April at the Mansion House in Dublin. Plunkett had understood that it was time for unity and concerted effort against the Nationalist party and the Government. One of his first moves was to ask Bishop O'Dwyer to send a letter of support to his convention and to allow his priests to participate.[64] Plunkett's action was hardly surprising. It is not known whether the Bishop sent a letter but he definitely allowed his priests to go to Dublin since Fr Wall and Fr Hayes, who had been involved in the Maxwell episode in 1916, went to the convention.[65] About 150 priests were present and Count Plunkett wrote that forty-nine of them were classified as 'seditious' and had been brought along by Fr Michael O'Flanagan.[66] However, not all the bishops allowed their clergy to go.[67] Plunkett suggested discussing certain topics, such as Ireland's representation at the future peace conference, the threat of conscription and the country's financial situation and fiscal contribution, a theme that O'Dwyer had been the first to broach in 1915. But it soon emerged that the opposition movement was indeed very much divided. The Irish Nation League was of the opinion that all opposition MPs should continue to go to the Westminster Parliament. Arthur Griffith and Sinn Féin seemed to be ruffled by the Count's initiative. The republican Cathal Brugha, though a member of Sinn Féin, categorically opposed Griffith's idea of a dual-monarchy for Ireland based on the Austro-Hungarian model.[68] For the intransigent Brugha, it was a republic and nothing else.

Eventually, and quite miraculously, a common declaration written by Fr O'Flanagan and Griffith, recognising the existence of the Irish nation and its wish to participate in the future peace conference, prevented the convention being a complete fiasco. A fragile unity had been established and a more orchestrated effort against the British authorities was now, perhaps, feasible. A test soon appeared in the South Longford by-election, scheduled to take place on 9 May 1917, during which the lack of unity within the Catholic Church was very palpable. On 30 April, Bishop O'Dwyer wrote a vehement letter against the Nationalist party. It was perhaps his most bitter attack on Redmond and his parliamentarians. The letter was distributed before the election in Longford under the heading 'Important Pronouncement of the Bishop of Limerick'. It read:

> What has brought Home Rule to the front and given it the chance which it has at present of becoming law? Is it the droning of the English 'friendlies' that they call the Irish Party? They are the 'patriots' that allowed the wretched measure which has been passed by Parliament to be hung up during the war, and having suspended the liberties of their country to recruiting in Ireland for the British Government. They were 'the one bright spot', and whether it was stupidity or knavery, the distinction of it will attach to them for ever... They are British Parliamentarians; and when they lost touch with their own country, and were absorbed in their dealings with the Liberal Whips, a new Ireland was growing up reviving the language of their fathers, reading the history of their country, and breathing a spirit of manhood and independence.
> (DDA, Curran papers, 'Important Pronouncement of the Bishop of Limerick', 30 April 1917)

The 'one bright spot' was an allusion to Sir Edward Grey's speech in the House of Commons in August 1914. Grey's remark had been a warning to Germany that Ireland, 'the one bright spot', would not be a consideration in Britain's dealings with various European powers. A few days later, on 5 May, *New Ireland* published an extract of O'Dwyer's Freedom of the City speech of September 1916, in which he had declared his support for Sinn Féin and his demand that Nationalist MPs leave the House of Commons to look after Irish affairs.[69]

The South Longford by-election would provide the newly 'unified' opposition with an opportunity to test its political credibility. On 25 April, John Redmond wrote to Dr Hoare that he was confident 'the election in South Longford [would] afford a vindication of the policy of the Irish Party, and secure safety of the Constitutional Movement'. The Bishop of Ardagh replied to Redmond that 'they would all obey [his] ruling' and he hoped that 'they would reverse the decision of Roscommon'. He also hoped that physical force was no longer a threat.[70] What the Nationalist leader and Hoare implied was that the opposition was committed to violent means to obtain liberty for Ireland. The Bishop was an ardent supporter of the Nationalist party and naturally favoured its candidate, Patrick McKenna, against the Sinn Féiner, Joseph McGuinness. On 5 May, Dr Fogarty wrote to Bishop O'Dwyer that he was pessimistic about the outcome of the election. He believed that the Nationalist party would win because 'the older folks, and especially the older clergy [were] not prepared for complete abstention'.[71] Abstention was the opposition's new policy, which consisted of not taking up seats in the British Parliament in case of electoral victory. Incidentally, Fogarty reported a sensational story that a '[German] submarine allowed a grain ship to pass when they heard it was for the Bishop of Limerick!' It seemed that O'Dwyer's popularity had stirred people's imagination. On 28 April, the *Roscommon Herald* wrote that nearly all the young priests were for Sinn Féin and the *Irish Times* expressed the view that many priests involved in Sinn Féin's campaign were republicans.[72]

Shortly before the election, however, Andrew Bonar Law, a staunch Conservative and Unionist, declared that the Government would soon try to find a solution to the Home Rule crisis. Many people interpreted this as the implementation of partition. Charles McHugh of Derry asked all Catholic and Anglican bishops to sign a petition against partition and eighteen Catholic and three Anglican prelates obliged.[73] The document was published just before the election and stressed the fact that 'there [had] been no organised effort to elicit the expression of Irish opinion regarding the dismemberment of [the] country', whether this dismemberment was 'temporary or permanent'.[74] The word 'temporary' clearly referred to Redmond's position during the Belfast meeting in the summer of 1916. The petition was a severe blow to the Nationalist party's chances of winning at South Longford. Mgr Curran made an interesting analysis of the situation: 'Apart from the invalid Archbishop of Tuam, Dr Healy, the bishops who did not sign were Dr O'Donnell of Raphoe, Dr Foley of Kildare, Dr Hoare of Ardagh, who had nominated the party candidate for South Longford, Dr Cohalan of Cork, Dr Mangan of Kerry, Dr O'Kelly of Ross and Dr O'Dea of Galway. The first three of these were strong supporters of the Irish Parliamentary Party.'[75] The only bishop who stood out was Cohalan, of whom an approval might have been expected. Very prudently, the *Freeman's Journal* approved the bishops' initiative.[76] It was crucial not to widen the gap between Redmond and the Church.

But, the main event of this election saga was Archbishop Walsh's return to the political scene. He interrupted his silence once again with a strong letter, published by the *Evening Telegraph* in which he explained why the bishops had signed the petition. He warned all nationalists that partition was still a real danger, and that those who did not believe it '[were] living in a fool's paradise'. Walsh ended with a very accusatory postscript, saying that 'the mischief [had] already been done, and that the country [was] practically sold'.[77] He implied that the Nationalist party was in league with those who approved of partition. His letter, like O'Dwyer's, was published as a pamphlet and distributed at the polling stations.[78] Later, in June 1918, Walsh wrote a revealing letter to Mgr O'Riordan and explained why he felt obliged to intervene in the South Longford election:

> As for myself, I have taken very little interest in Irish public affairs since the Irish Party went, as I considered, hopelessly wrong, twelve or thirteen years ago. The shameless abandonment of independent opposition policy, and alliance with Asquith and Co., could only have one ending and that ending it has in universal shipwreck. I could never understand how so many of the Bishops – practically all, indeed, who took part in public affairs – went on supporting such a set of renegades. Twice I broke silence. It was to warn the country of the 'partition' trap that was set for it, more especially in 1917, on the day of the Longford election. A victory they [the Nationalist Party] counted as a foregone conclusion... My letter, even at the last moment, turned the scale, and the leaders were balked... But thereupon they took to assailing me, up and down through the country, openly as 'a liar'! And no one thought of raising a voice in protest.
>
> (ICR, O'Riordan papers, no. 19, letter no. 41,
> Walsh to O'Riordan, 16 June 1918)

Walsh's disappointment with the Nationalist party and his disillusionment with Irish politics in general were all too obvious, but Sinn Féin did win the election at South Longford with a majority of only thirty-seven votes. There can be little doubt that O'Dwyer and Walsh's interventions had been determining. The *Freeman's Journal* commented that the party had been grossly insulted and that the younger clergy had campaigned for Sinn Féin despite the fact that Bishop Hoare had given his support to the Nationalist candidate. The newspaper demanded to know what Walsh meant when he wrote 'that the country [was] practically sold'. By whom and for what, asked an offended journalist.[79] The Archbishop was now openly accused of sowing discord within the Nationalist ranks. In Cork, for instance, James Greene, president of the

United Irish League openly asked Walsh for explanations.[80] Walsh, as might have been expected, never complied. John Dillon blamed David Lloyd George for having destroyed the Nationalist party and said that all Sinn Féin needed was a leader.[81] Support among the youth for Sinn Féin had been noticed by the military intelligence officer of the Northern District. The officer mentioned, in particular, some revolutionary zeal among the Christian Brothers who were mainly devoted to education throughout the country.[82] In May 1917, it seemed that the younger clergy were following O'Dwyer whereas Cardinal Logue, Bishops O'Donnell, Hoare and Kelly, and the parish priests remained faithful to the nationalist politicians whose grip on Ireland was loosening day after day. They had not much of an alternative. On 25 May, O'Dwyer was at long last severely criticised in a seemingly endless letter published by the *Freeman's Journal*. The author, who wisely preferred to remain anonymous, summed up the Bishop's political evolution, and reminded the readers that O'Dwyer had been opposed to the Plan of Campaign in the 1880s, which, according to him at least, had played right into the unionists' hands. Provocatively, he wrote that the Bishop had once admired John Redmond, implying that he was a hypocrite and an opportunist. Finally, the author stated that the Bishop supported Germany in the war.[83]

It was obvious that some Nationalist party members were showing increasing signs of frustration with O'Dwyer and now also Walsh. Their leaders simply did not know how to tackle this independent ecclesiastical opposition. O'Dwyer, true to form, lost no time in replying and the *Cork Examiner* published his caustic reply the next day. The Bishop wrote that he had indeed supported the Nationalist party and Isaac Butt in 1870. But, concerning Redmond, he admitted that he had made a mistake and gave the leader the rough side of his tongue: 'I thought at the time that he was an Irishman. I have learned since that he is not even a man. He is a mere figure-head, painted green ... But the war has shown what he is made of, and the partition of Ireland, which he attempted to smuggle through, is the best indication of his ability and patriotism.'[84] The opposition was gloating. As for the Nationalist leader, he did not make the slightest effort to defend himself from that terrible accusation. At the end of this eventful month of May 1917 the intelligence officer of the Southern District sent his monthly report to Dublin. He had become aware of this political divide between younger and older generations of Irishmen. Like his colleagues in the Northern and Connaught and Midlands Districts, he was of the opinion that the same could be said about the clergy:

> I consider that it may now be broadly stated that all the younger men of the Roman Catholic mercantile and lower classes in this

District are adherents of the Sinn Féin policy. The older men and professional element are still loyal to the 'constitutional' movement. This also applies to the Church, the Parish Priests as a rule being Redmondites and their curates Sinn Féin.

(PRO, London, CO904/157, Southern District intelligence report, 31 May 1917, p. 157)

The Catholic Church was undergoing an internal revolution. What would Lloyd George, the Welsh Wizard, do to find a key to the disastrous Irish problem without harming the war effort?

A SOLUTION IN SIGHT?

On 15 May 1917, the outline of a possible solution appeared. During a banquet in Dublin, John Redmond told Lord Crewe that a convention of all the different Irish political parties could resolve the Home Rule crisis. The same night, Crewe informed the Prime Minister about Redmond's idea.[85] The next day, Lloyd George sent a letter to the Nationalist leader, putting forward this convention or else the immediate implementation of the 1914 Home Rule bill with a five year exclusion of some Ulster counties.[86] Redmond accepted the first offer for he could not allow himself another confrontation with Irish public opinion or the Catholic Church.

To Lloyd George, such a convention was an advantageous solution to his present problems. It allowed him to defer conscription in Ireland and to avoid pressure from British public opinion and the generals. Firstly, compulsory military service could not be introduced while all Irish politicians were debating about the political future of their country. Secondly, if the convention was a success and an acceptable solution was found, the war effort could be boosted again. Thirdly, whatever the conclusions of the convention, the Prime Minister would have saved a lot of time during which the American divisions would have reached Europe. In the last case, it would no longer be necessary to recruit or conscript those tens of thousands of young Irishmen. The convention would also have the merit of demonstrating Britain's goodwill towards Ireland and silence Irish-American discontent. It was now crucial that this lobby did not hinder British–American relations. Lloyd George seemed to have succeeded on that point. The *New York Times* deemed that 'the Irish [had] a splendid opportunity to give the lie to history to turn over a new leaf, and to come to an agreement which [would] settle the Irish question'. The *Washington Times* was of the opinion that Ireland's future was now within Irishmen's hands.[87] It was clear that Ireland should not be an obstacle for the Allies to win the war.

France was equally concerned. From 16 April to 9 May 1917, the flamboyant General Nivelle launched a disastrous offensive on the *Chemin des Dames*, which resulted in 271,000 French casualties. The French Army's morale reached rock bottom. A weary General Philippe Pétain, who had taken over from Nivelle, declared: 'I am waiting for the Americans and the tanks'.[88] Pétain would have to wait, indeed. On 25 May, the *Figaro* hoped a solution would rapidly be found to the religious problem in Ireland. According to the French newspaper, England was able to interpret freedom and implement it in Ireland. It quoted South Africa as an example and it hoped that the Irish would become more actively involved in the war.[89]

The hierarchy showed a varied reaction to Lloyd George's announcement but generally it was seen favourably. Logue and Kelly approved of the idea. The Cardinal knew that not only the Nationalist party would represent Ireland, but also independent nationalists who would not be at all favourable to partition in whatever form. The Bishop of Ross had declared in London that he sincerely believed the cabinet's goodwill.[90] Walsh was far more cautious. Although he eventually agreed with it, he initially was sceptical. In a letter to Mgr O'Riordan on 22 May 1917, Curran wrote that 'many [had] no faith in the Conference, including the Archbishop'.[91] The secretary explained that Walsh had become the Nationalist party's *bête noire* and that Sinn Féin was opposed to this convention. The Archbishop changed his mind probably because he did not want the Church to be accused of rejecting this new idea out of hand and, therefore, being responsible for the failure of a peaceful and constitutional solution to the Irish question. On 6 June, the shrewd O'Dwyer shared his views with O'Riordan about Lloyd George's latest initiative:

> The Convention is all the talk now...But, they want the Irish in Ireland and America so badly, and the 'small nationality' cry is re-echoed on all sides that they may do something. But my idea is to let them hold their convention, and make their proposals, and let nationalist Ireland give its answer but to take no responsibility at this stage.
>
> (ICR, O'Riordan papers, no. 18, letter no. 73,
> Curran to O'Riordan, 22 May 1917)

The Bishop had correctly guessed that the convention came into being above all because of the war. On 10 June, Cardinal Logue circulated a letter that was to be read in all the churches in his archdiocese. He regretted that the end of the war was not yet in sight and warned the Irish that 'the slumbering forces of unrest...waking into activity, [threatened them] with even greater calamities than those which the war [had] entailed'.[92] After the elections of North Roscommon and South Longford, Logue was clearly alluding to the veiled threat of Sinn Féin and the republicans. He ended by saying that he prayed God 'to inspire those on whose deliberations [Ireland's] future destiny [might], to a great extent, depend'. Only a few days before, he had agreed to consult Walsh on the nomination of an ecclesiastical delegation that would go to the convention.[93] Logue saw in this idea the last chance to save Ireland from republicanism. On 19 June, the Cardinal presided over the annual meeting of the hierarchy in Maynooth and read out a letter from Lloyd George, asking the Church to send four bishops to the convention. The prelates agreed to do so and nominated Harty of Cashel, O'Donnell of Raphoe, MacRory of Down and Conor and Kelly of Ross.[94]

Why did the hierarchy decide to accept the Prime Minister's offer? A letter from O'Dwyer to O'Riordan sheds light on the bishops' meeting and decision. The Bishop of Limerick explained that Harty, O'Donnell, MacRory and Kelly were 'all staunch Party [underlined in original text] men' and remarked that 'if [the bishops] refused, the Government might drop the whole thing, and then say that the Catholic Bishops killed Home Rule'.[95] Prudence and distrust reigned supreme and one could hardly reproach the Catholic Church for such feelings after all the events since 1914. Shortly afterwards, on 3 July 1917, in one of his last letters to the rector of the Irish College in Rome, O'Dwyer gave more details about the meeting and divulged that it was he who had suggested sending a delegation to the convention in order to prevent Lloyd George from blaming the Church if no solution to the Home Rule crisis was found. Concerning partition, he told O'Riordan that the Church was to refuse it no matter what: 'We elected almost unanimously four stalwarts Cashel, Ross, Belfast and Raphoe, but (this is private) on the understanding that they are not to agree to partition in any shape or form.'[96] There appeared to be some solidarity between the northern and southern bishops. O'Dwyer also stated that many prelates, probably a majority according to him, were now looking 'to John Dillon as the Israelites did to Moses'. This remark was relevant for it proved that the hierarchy was in a political vacuum. John Redmond was no longer in favour, but Sinn Féin could not be trusted either because of its revolutionary image and its association with socialists during the Easter Rising.

Ironically, the hierarchy's hopes were now on Dillon, a man who had displayed anti-clerical feelings in the past. Dr MacRory confirmed O'Dwyer's statements in a letter which he sent to the rector of the Irish College in Rome. Like the Archbishop of Dublin and the Bishop of Limerick, MacRory was not optimistic about the convention but was still a Nationalist party supporter.[97] He would not, however, follow Redmond at any price since he told O'Riordan that 'he [intended] to be present and oppose partition with all [his] heart'.[98] The hierarchy's meeting also tried to give guidelines regarding clerical involvement in politics. The prelates had become aware of the activities of their younger priests. Some were frankly worried, including Logue, Harty, Kelly and O'Donnell. Bishop Coyne of Elphin had tried to discipline Fr O'Flanagan who was opposed to the war and openly in favour of Sinn Féin.[99] A number of bishops expressed their concern and wrote a statement for their clergy, asking them to remind the people of the Church's doctrines on peace and war. The hierarchy believed that 'the clergy should earnestly exhort their people to beware of all dangerous associations, and sedulously shun all movements that [were] not in accord with the principles of Catholic teaching and doctrine'.[100] It was, of course, an allusion to the IRB, the Irish Volunteers and Sinn Féin. The statement ended with a reminder of the National Synod, which reiterated that all curates had to ask permission from their parish priests to attend a political meeting and that all problems should be settled by the bishop if need be.

It is hard to see O'Dwyer, Walsh and Fogarty agreeing with this, but the statement only bore Logue, Kelly and Browne's signatures,[101] which allowed O'Dwyer, Walsh and Fogarty not to be identified with the document. Furthermore, the general rule was that if bishops did not agree between themselves, a statement representing the views of the majority was adopted on behalf of the entire hierarchy.[102] This corroborated O'Dwyer's remarks when had he stated that a majority of bishops still followed the Nationalist party in the summer of 1917. The whole incident was in fact an attempt to bring back young priests to the fold. Joseph Devlin, the northern Nationalist leader, jumped at the opportunity and used the hierarchy's statement as a pamphlet in Belfast in order to influence public opinion in Ulster. It was immediately denounced by Arthur Griffith in *Nationality*. Griffith reminded his leaders in a trenchant and ironic article that Devlin was a friend of René Viviani, the notorious French anti-cleric, whom he had met during the Irish delegation's visit to Paris in 1915:

> Mr Joseph Devlin, as a friend of Viviani's, is no doubt an authority on Catholic theology... At the Catholic church-doors in Belfast the other Sunday Mr. Devlin's pious lieutenants distributed copies of the document written by the Bishop of Ross and signed by that ecclesiastic and Cardinal Logue and the Bishop of Cloyne, in which it is written: 'All organisations that plot against the Church or lawfully constituted authority, whether openly or secretly, are condemned by the Church'. 'What', asks Mr Devlin, 'is lawfully constituted authority?' And the eminent theologian answers: 'It is the authority actually in possession'.
>
> (*Nationality*, 25 August 1917)

In 1917, various nationalist movements closely followed the political evolution of the Catholic Church. If the Cardinal had hoped to smash opposition trends within the younger clergy, he had been badly wrong. It seemed that young curates had no inclination to obey the hierarchy when it came down to the national question. Fr Michael O'Flanagan was a case in point. The military intelligence officer of the Midlands and Connaught District mentioned in his July report that the clergy no longer respected the bishops' decisions. He wrote that the number of Sinn Féin clubs was visibly increasing and that they were openly opposed to the Nationalist party. According to him, these clubs '[received] support from the Roman Catholic clergy, some secretly, as the bishops in this district [were] opposed to their supporting such clubs, but [did] not like to openly condemn them'.[103] This last remark was very significant as it meant that the hierarchy was not able to prevent the younger clergy from taking part in radical politics, and did not have the courage to speak out against Sinn Féin and discipline those young priests. The bishops' position, however, was very delicate, as a public denunciation would certainly have meant their isolation in the country.

EXIT O'DWYER, ENTER DE VALERA

In the summer of 1917, two important events took place in the course of Irish history, the arrival of Eamon de Valera in the political arena and the death of Bishop O'Dwyer. On 16 June, de Valera was liberated at a time when the East Clare by-election was about to begin. Rapidly, he was chosen as a candidate to represent the opposition. His campaign had militaristic overtones as he wore the uniform of the Irish Volunteers and was always accompanied by Volunteers who sang the 'Soldier's Song', the republican hymn. He regularly declared that he was faithful to the republic.[104] The young and relatively unknown politician caught O'Dwyer's attention, and the Bishop wrote to O'Riordan that he believed de Valera could win it, and that the candidate was 'a good Catholic and a clever fellow'.[105] The Bishop's remark illustrated the confusion and division within the opposition's ranks. In September 1916, O'Dwyer had said that he supported Sinn Féin.

But what did Sinn Féin or de Valera stand for? Count Plunkett's nationalist convention had mirrored all the divisions not only among nationalists but also within Sinn Féin. De Valera was a vulpine politician who immediately understood that his chance of winning the election would be considerably increased if he received the Bishop's public approval and set out for Limerick to meet O'Dwyer who warmly welcomed him. The day was not without emotion for de Valera as it was the Bishop who had confirmed him in 1894.[106] Now he came back as a prominent Sinn Féin politician, looking for O'Dwyer's advice and guidance. In typical straightforward fashion, O'Dwyer told him: 'If you want to have a real Irish nation, such as you desire, you, first of all, must clean out the rubbish and build from a decent foundation.'[107] Evidently, the rubbish was the Nationalist party, and de Valera grasped that it was not in his interest, nor in the opposition's, to bring down O'Dwyer's or the Church's wrath upon them. Logue, Browne and Kelly's recent statement had been a clear warning. De Valera must have known that the Church had been very effective in reducing the number of IRB members just before the war, and that the rebels during the Easter Rising had been genuinely concerned about the Church's attitude. That is why he wanted to reassure the voters in Co. Clare that despite his uniform, he was not a bloodthirsty revolutionary and that 'all his life he had been associated with priests, and [that] the priests knew him and were behind him in this election'.[108] It appeared that he was seeking respectability, a new image for Sinn Féin. On 10 July, de Valera, the republican, was elected, while Arthur Griffith, the party leader, wrote in *Nationality* that he still favoured the idea of a dual-monarchy.[109] The opposition was decidedly in a state of confusion despite all Count Plunkett's goodwill.

On 19 August 1917, Bishop O'Dwyer died at the age of seventy-five after a brief illness. His political evolution since the Plan of Campaign had been extraordinary. It was the Nationalist party that had encouraged recruitment in Ireland and had been discredited by the absurd decisions of the War Office and then the unimaginative and obscure Irish policy of the British Government, even if the cabinet's room for manoeuvre was considerably reduced by the international crisis. But it was O'Dwyer who had been one of the main influences behind John Redmond's demise in the country. Home Rule and partition had given the Bishop reasons to confront the Nationalist leader, but it was above all the war in Europe that enabled him to demolish Redmond's arguments. Amongst a completely disorganised opposition, especially after the Easter Rising, O'Dwyer had become the Nationalist party's main opponent. His popularity had made him the moral leader of the nationalist opposition. He contributed significantly to Sinn Féin's rise when he officially announced his support for Griffith's party, although Sinn Féin's battle was far from being won. The same Griffith honestly recognised this and wrote in *New Ireland* that the opposition's first successes were largely due to the Bishop's interventions.[110]

De Valera was told about O'Dwyer's death in Tipperary town where he was about to speak at a public meeting. On the platform, he paid a glowing tribute to O'Dwyer's contribution to the new nationalist revival:

When I came down to the East Clare election, when I first entered Limerick I asked to be taken to Dr O'Dwyer that I may pay my respects to him. When our countrymen were spat upon and kicked in the streets of Liverpool we know who it was – it was not a member of the Irish Party – who stood up for them. It was Bishop O' Dwyer who told the world that they were leaving their country because British law had made it impossible for them to gain a livelihood in it. If they were going at another time England would give them a free passage. All Ireland owed a debt of gratitude to Dr O'Dwyer and she will never forget that debt, and his name will live in the history and will be a model for Irish bishops who wish to win the hearts of their flocks. As long as there are bishops such as Dr O'Dwyer there will never be anti-clericalism in this land. In a down-trodden land such as this they are not merely our spiritual shepherds, but as citizens, as men of importance, they have a tremendous duty to this country. I say that a man like Dr O'Dwyer is a model for the Bishops of Ireland and to those who wish well to the Catholic Church in Ireland.

(*The Freeman's Journal*, 20 August 1917)

De Valera's words marked the final phase of the merger of Catholicism and nationalism, the consolidation of Irish identity and nationality. Protestants were not necessarily excluded but they had to be proven nationalists and anti-partitionists. The fact that Ireland's first president, Douglas Hyde, was an Anglican proves this point. De Valera's speech sounded like a warning to the hierarchy as it implied that a new nationalist Ireland was developing and that only bishops like O'Dwyer would be welcome.

John Redmond's most serious mistake was not to have countered O'Dwyer from the very beginning. This made sure that the Bishop became more and more popular as the Irish people grew more and more tired of the war. Once he had acquired this huge popularity, it became extremely difficult to dethrone him, as he had become the spearhead of the opposition. In September 1917 during his hunger strike in Mountjoy Prison in Dublin, the republican Thomas Ashe encouraged his fellow prisoners 'to pray to Bishop O'Dwyer and the dead who died for Ireland'.[111] All Ireland paid tribute to the Bishop of Limerick. Even the *Freeman's Journal* did not ignore the death of the Nationalist party's enemy, and wrote a long and detailed article about O'Dwyer's ecclesiastical and political career, but, ironically, it was published amongst articles reporting the latest Allied victories on the front![112] The journalists, almost euphemistically, described the Bishop's career as 'militant' and, not surprisingly, did not relate in great detail his confrontations with John Redmond. The newspaper also noted that the Catholic community of Derry, which could be excluded from Home Rule, deeply regretted the Bishop's passing away. The English Catholic newspaper, *The Tablet*, brushed away objectivity and published all of O'Dwyer's laudatory comments on Redmond, which he had made in 1913.[113] The opposition press was certainly more objective. *Nationality* was of the opinion that the Bishop had embodied the spirit of resistance to 'armed Tyranny' and wrote that 'his was the voice which spoke for the dead and the voiceless living'.[114] The newspaper published a poem with very strong militarist and clerical overtones:

> 'Edward' and 'Thomas', names well-met in you!
> Confessor kingly –
> Warrior-Bishop, battling for the true,
> Battling singly!
> Hatred of Powers and Principalities –
> You did not fear it:
> Flashed out against your dark adversaries
> The sword of the Spirit!
> . . .
> You were our Tower, and our Fiery Torch,
> Lofty and daring;
> Watchman and Shepherd: Angel of the Church
> Of Holy Eirinn!
>
> (*Nationality*, 25 August 1917)

New Ireland defended O'Dwyer's thundering personality and indulged in revisionism when it went as far as justifying the Bishop's position during the Plan of Campaign days.[115] The *Catholic Bulletin* stated that the Church had lost a great prelate and Ireland a true patriot and concluded: 'The heart of Ireland went out to him, because his children found in him a fearless and powerful defender in the time of their need...from his eloquent pen letters that will be treasured for ever in the history of the country.'[116] The '*Factionist*', which proudly claimed to be 'the smallest paper in the world', wrote that the people of Ireland had lost a 'national benefactor' and published poems about O'Dwyer that struck the people's imagination.[117] The *Limerick Leader* described the mood of the city under the title 'Illustrious Churchman passes away': 'When the news was received by the citizens it caused a shock of dismay and when the sad intelligence was flashed over the wires to different parts of the country it had an overpowering effect on the minds of the people who found the nation at once bereft of a distinguished churchman and a fearless son.'[118]

The Bishop's funeral was a grandiose affair, almost militaristic in style. About 500 Irish Volunteers 'made a soldierly and imposing display' during the burial ceremony.[119] Cardinal Logue was present among his *bêtes noires* such as Countess Markievicz, Count Plunkett's wife, and family members of the executed rebel leaders of 1916, and must have felt out of place. Archbishop Walsh did not come but the warlike Auxiliary Bishop of Dublin, Dr Donnelly, did attend the funeral. Some 300 priests and fourteen prelates were also in Limerick.[120] O'Dwyer had systematically, courageously and openly opposed the war effort between 1914 and 1917. Whether one approves of his actions or not, it cannot be denied that his impact on the course of Irish politics was of paramount importance. Paradoxically, just as the thousands of Irishmen who participated in the First World War, O'Dwyer's rightful place in history has been almost totally forgotten and ignored.

It remained to be seen how the hierarchy and the nationalist opposition would fare without the tumultuous Bishop.

FROM CONVENTION TO CONSCRIPTION

O'Dwyer's death was a serious blow to the opposition. Its leaders rapidly realised that they had to have an ally within the hierarchy and it was quite natural that they asked Bishop Fogarty to take over from the Bishop of Limerick, which he agreed to do.[121] Fogarty tried to emulate O'Dwyer and soon the people could read on a leaflet entitled 'The Sinn Féin Banner of Irish Independence – A letter from the Bishop of Killaloe' the following striking words: 'We had almost ceased to be Irish until Sinn Féin arose and struck the English rust from the soul of Ireland. Unfortunately, that rust had eaten deep and spoiled many a good Irish heart.'[122] No doubt, O'Dwyer would have approved of Fogarty's style. After the liberation of the last rebel prisoners, the opposition had devised a new strategy to make British rule almost impossible in Ireland by boycotting the Government's administration throughout the country. This plan could only work if it had the support of the numerous farmers.[123] This might prove difficult since most of them were enjoying economic prosperity and might, therefore, express very little interest in an Irish republic or anything that might have repercussions on their current prosperity. In May 1917, the military intelligence officer of the Southern District had noticed that 'public feeling generally [was] either apathetic or disloyal'.[124] Moreover, if the farmers remained indifferent to John Redmond's pro-recruitment policy they still remembered that it was his party that had diminished the power of landlords and had been responsible for the redistribution of land to the people. James Greene, a member of the Nationalist party, reminded the farmers of this fact during a meeting in Cork in May

1917.[125] De Valera and Griffith knew that it would not be an easy task to destroy the Nationalist party.

But rural and urban Ireland had some reasons for complaining, since food prices were increasing and farmers were forced to follow strict tillage regulations, which they did not like.[126] A few days before the beginning of the Irish Convention in Dublin, Daniel Cohalan, the Bishop of Cork, publicly declared: 'Our greatest difficulty is want of national unity... amongst those who call themselves Nationalists, though belonging to different political organisations.'[127] The Bishop's statement accurately reflected the difficulties of de Valera, Griffith, MacNeill and Count Plunkett. Concerning Sinn Féin, Cohalan made an indirect appeal:

> The Sinn Féin Party is henceforth on its trial. Hitherto its work has been the work of the opposition – of pulling down. If it is to justify its existence, it must have a practical constructive policy. Sinn Féin, it is said, is divided. So far, there has been no authoritative statement of constructive Sinn Féin policy. We are driven, therefore, to consider the various positions which are possible under the general head of Sinn Féinism. Sinn Féinism may recommend physical force, or it may organise abstention from Parliament, or it may claim to be heard before the Peace Conference on behalf of an Irish Republic. Now I hope that few, if any, will be found to introduce trouble amongst us by advocating physical force, and I appeal to the young men of the diocese to have nothing to do with any policy or organisation that would put them in a position of hostility to their Church.
>
> (*The Tablet*, 7 July 1917)

Cohalan's statement was simultaneously an appeal and a warning to the opposition in general and Sinn Féin in particular. The time had come for unity and the Bishop did not exclude out of hand any Sinn Féin participation in the running of the country provided this party rejected the use physical force. It had to become respectable so that the Church would not have to systematically oppose it.

Arthur Griffith, and later Eamon de Valera, paid heed to Cohalan's warning and began a new exercise of public relations which consisted of presenting Sinn Féin as a good Catholic party. On 25 August 1917, for instance, Griffith's *Nationality* published a rather long article on the bishops, John Dillon, Joseph Devlin and partition. It informed its readers that the Sinn Féin MP Joseph McGuinness from South Longford had been notified by the Westminster Parliament that the British Government was about to introduce a new law, making divorce easier in the United Kingdom. The newspaper was shocked by the

Government's initiative, called the new legislation 'divorce-while-you-wait' and commented ironically: 'It is never to be forgotten that England is waging war in defence of Christianity against the Hun.'[128] Griffith's opinions had suddenly changed, for in 1906, he had defended the French Government's anti-clerical measures![129] The Irish Volunteers, however, appeared not to take into account Cohalan's warning. They were convinced that sooner or later armed force would have to be used and had no time for Sinn Féiners who were not members of their organisation. De Valera did his best to prove to the people that Sinn Féin and the Volunteers were two distinct movements, although he had worn a Volunteer uniform during the East Clare by-election. The reality was that local Volunteers were not always controlled by their central committee in Dublin, and that they were quite simply preparing for war against the British authorities.[130] This posed a serious problem for de Valera when he became simultaneously president of Sinn Féin and the Irish Volunteers in October 1917 as it endangered his policy of respectability. In November 1917, the *Freeman's Journal* published the poignant appeal of Fr Bolger, a parish priest in Co. Wexford, begging the Irish to renounce violence and rebellion even if they were Sinn Féiners.[131] As for John Redmond, he was still in favour of the war and did not want to consider public opinion in the country. In the foreword of a book entitled *The Irish on the Somme*, he reiterated his ideas of 1914 concerning Ireland's new nationhood born during the conflict, the rights of small nations and the advantage of belonging to the British Empire.[132] It was in this political atmosphere that the Irish Convention began in Dublin on 25 July 1917.

Sir Horace Plunkett, a liberal Unionist, was presiding over the debates in the Convention. The Nationalist party was represented by John Redmond, Joseph Devlin and Stephen Gwynn. The Catholic Church had sent Archbishop Harty and Bishops O'Donnell, MacRory and Kelly, and Sinn Féin had refused to participate. The Convention would last until April 1918 and the hierarchy was largely pessimistic about the outcome. In September, Cardinal Logue wrote to Mgr O'Riordan in Rome that he was not 'sanguine' about the whole matter and that he feared 'a certain section of the Convention [was] only marking time till the Americans [were] thoroughly committed to the war'.[133] However, the fact that the Church had agreed to participate was dangerous for the opposition in the sense that a majority of bishops were still behind the Nationalist party. If the negotiations were successful, the Church could re-operate a rapprochement with Redmond, and public opinion could swing again to the advantage of the Nationalist party. Logue was fully aware of this and knew that if the Convention was able to negotiate some favourable settlement regarding Home Rule and partition, the young clergy would withdraw their support for the opposition. On 22 October, the *Freeman's Journal* published a short and alarmist message of the Cardinal, saying: 'Do not approve of revolutionary action. Have no control over Sinn Féiners. Success of Convention only remedy. If it fails – Chaos!'[134] Only a few days before, Redmond had been stoned and nearly thrown into the river by a hostile mob in Cork.[135]

And yet, despite Logue's criticisms and the fact that the more militant nationalists were an explicit threat to law and order in the country, the opposition was to benefit from two events. Firstly, the death of the Sinn Féiner Thomas Ashe who had been on hunger strike in a prison in Dublin. His funeral was the occasion of a huge opposition demonstration. Between 30,000 and 40,000 people attended the funeral and the *Daily Mail* was of the opinion that Ashe's death had made 100,000 Sinn Féin supporters out of 100,000 Nationalist party supporters.[136] Two members of the hierarchy had publicly expressed their views on this event. Bishop Fogarty had sent a letter to the *Freeman's Journal* in which he stated that Ashe had become a martyr of the Irish cause and that his death would increase the hatred of the people for Lloyd George's cabinet. He wrote: 'The world sees already in these hideous atrocities what the triumph of English culture means for small nationalities.'[137] Archbishop Walsh had also taken up his pen and informed the Lord Mayor of Dublin that he '[felt] it a duty to take part in the public protest that [would] find expression in the funeral'. He did not go personally but sent his car.[138] The military intelligence officer of the Midlands and Connaught District thought that 'the death of Thomas Ashe in Dublin [was] rather unfortunate, as it [would] fan the flames of Sinn Féin that were dying down in many places'.[139] He remarked that parish priests refused to allow their curates to go to Sinn Féin meetings, including in Co. Limerick, since Bishop O'Dwyer's recent death. Finally, he stated that an important number of young priests had volunteered to become chaplains in the Army. The officer's observations were relevant on several accounts. Firstly, the younger clergy seemed to be falling back into line and some plausible explanations can be put forward for this such as the opposition's lack of a clear political programme, the violence throughout the country, and the Convention to which the Church had sent an independent delegation. Secondly, it also appeared that the ageing Cardinal Logue still had some influence for it was he who had appealed for more chaplains in the *Irish Catholic* in September 1917.[140] He had succeeded at an unexpected moment.

The other main events that favoured the opposition were the Sinn Féin and Irish Volunteers conventions, held at the Mansion House in Dublin, on 25 and 27 October 1917 respectively. The debates were sometimes stormy but unity was eventually achieved, and the opposition became formally known as Sinn Féin with Eamon de Valera as president, and Arthur Griffith and Fr Michael O'Flanagan as vice-presidents. Two days later, de Valera also became president of the Irish Volunteers. The official aim of Sinn Féin was to obtain a republican constitution for Ireland.[141]

Irish political life, however, was decidedly fickle and, despite unity, Sinn Féin still had a lot of work to do to persuade the people of the validity of its nationalist and republican policy. On 31 October, only six days after the Sinn Féin convention, the intelligence officer of the Midlands and Connaught District sent his monthly report. According to his analysis, the people were opposed to physical force and favoured Sinn Féin only because they believed the party was the best guarantee against conscription. The officer stated: 'As long as Sinn Féin lacks some great personality as leader, and has not the support of the united clergy of the Roman Catholic Church, the people will only support it as a passing show and as their strongest shield against being forced into military service'.[142] And so it was that Sinn Féin received most of its support, not for ideological reasons, but for fear of conscription.

It was imperative that de Valera proved his leadership qualities rapidly. Above all, the Catholic Church had to be convinced of Sinn Féin's respectability as a party, and like Arthur Griffith, de Valera would play the Catholic card. During the conventions in October, he had denounced the 'theologians' of the *Irish Times* and the *Freeman's Journal* who had argued that the Easter Rising had not been morally justifiable. He had told his audience that he was speaking like a Catholic and had said: 'I say in theology... of all subjects a little learning is a dangerous thing.'[143] *Nationality* began a campaign to demonstrate that Sinn Féin and Ireland were morally irreproachable whereas England was morally corrupt. The newspaper stressed that England was completely divided by different religions and sects that hated each other and that divorce and bigamy had become commonplace in English society. It also regularly denounced Joseph Devlin's friendship with the anti-clerical René Viviani in France, who had recently declared that the Catholic Church in his country had no legal sanction to look after the orphans of fallen soldiers.[144] In April 1918, the so-called Sinn Féin Public Health Department denounced the plan to set up hospitals that would look after patients who had contracted venereal diseases. The department was of the opinion that those diseases were not Irish and stated that 'the imposition on Irish ratepayers of a tax for their upkeep [was] unfair and altogether unjust'. It urged 'that every soldier returning to Ireland at the end of the war should have his blood tested' and all soldiers found to be infected 'should be isolated in special institutions'.[145] For all the soldiers of Irish divisions and regiments, the end of the war could, then, be the beginning of another one.

The hierarchy had become aware of Sinn Féin's new approach and some prelates were far from impressed. In November 1917, de Valera was in Loughrea where a Sinn Féin meeting was to take place. The very morning before the meeting, Dr Gilmartin, the Bishop of Clonfert, addressed his parishioners in the town's cathedral and declared that Ireland was entitled to be free for she was 'an ancient nation'. But, he continued, freedom could not be achieved at all costs and 'the end, no matter how noble, [did] not justify the means'. This was of course an allusion to the Easter Rising. Then, he reminded his parishioners of the theological conditions, which made an uprising justifiable. Among them was the fact that a government had to be tyrannical and Gilmartin believed that it was not the case in Ireland. He ended his preaching with a pertinent remark: 'In saying this I do not mean to cast any aspersion on the motives of those who may have seemed to take a different view.'[146] This last sentence targeted the Sinn Féin meeting. Although it appeared at first sight relatively innocuous and neutral, Gilmartin's remark placed his parishioners in a tricky position: should they listen to the Bishop, a theologian and a man of peace, or to de Valera, a radical nationalist who might be their best guarantee against conscription? The *Irish Catholic* published Gilmartin's statement under the title 'Playing with Fire – Sinn Féin flirting with Force'. De Valera was travelling throughout the country and was asking the Irish to repudiate the Irish Convention. He hoped that the American President's war policy would bring freedom to Ireland and other small nations and declared that if Ireland was given a guarantee that it would be the case, then half a million Irishmen would give a hand to the Allies.[147] The Sinn Féin leader was probably right, for only immediate freedom without partition could hope to revive recruitment in Ireland.

In Claremorris in Co. Mayo, Sinn Féin decided to adopt a resolution, asking Pope Benedict XV to include Ireland in the future peace negotiations. The party sent a copy of the resolution to Cardinal Logue, Archbishop Walsh, Bishops Fogarty and Higgins and Fr O'Flanagan. The initiative was unsuccessful as only Higgins answered and said that he was not willing to support it.[148] On 24 November 1917, the *Irish Catholic*, which represented the views of the hierarchy and which was published with Logue's imprimatur, was seduced by Sinn Féin's latest propaganda offensive and commented on it favourably in an article called 'The Irish Republic', which must have incensed Logue. It was of the opinion that de Valera's party had become more reassuring in its speeches and that its political statements were no longer of a warlike nature.[149]

Unfortunately for Sinn Féin, the *Irish Catholic*'s comments coincided with a letter from Cardinal Logue, which had devastating effects. Like Gilmartin, Logue attacked de Valera's party but in a more incisive way.

The Cardinal was worried as law and order could not be maintained in the country. In the city of Cork, for instance, women going out with American sailors were molested by the Sinn Féin Vigilance Committee.[150] The Irish socialists, who had fought with the nationalists and republicans during the Easter Rising, must have thought that their old allies had become the new moral crusaders in the country. In 1915, James Connolly's *Worker* had denounced similar activities of the Women Patrols and had spoken of 'a new form of Inquisition'. On that occasion, *The Worker* had stated rather humorously: 'It will give a splendid opportunity to a lot of old maids whom a wise Providence has left on the shelf to go officially and officiously nosing around the dark corners of the city, interfering with the love-making of every young couple.'[151] Logue was certainly not impressed by Sinn Féin's efforts even if it was clear that it sought to imitate the activities of the Dublin Vigilance Committee. This committee kept an eye on 'corrupting literature' and 'debasing performances in theatres' and harmful 'practices and courses of conduct'. In 1915, the very conservative Bishops O'Dea, Gaughran, Finegan, Hoare, Robert Browne, James Browne and Healy had sent letters of support and approval to the committee's annual meeting.[152]

To Logue, Sinn Féin was a pernicious influence and the country had to get rid of it, vigilance committee or not. On 25 November 1917, the priests of his diocese had to read out his circular letter to their flocks. The Cardinal regretted that the war was not about to end and that the belligerents had not taken into account the Pope's peace appeal. He claimed that one of the worst effects the war had had on the country was that some people had begun to dream about a republic and were thus threatening Ireland's stability and peace:

> ... an agitation has sprung up and is spreading among our people which, ill-considered and Utopian, cannot fail, if persevered in, to entail present suffering, disorganisation, and danger, and is sure to end in future disaster, defeat and collapse. And all this in pursuit of a dream which no man in his sober senses can hope to see realised: the establishment of an Irish Republic, either by an appeal to the potentates of Europe seated at a Peace Conference or an appeal to force by hurling an unarmed people against an Empire ... The thing would be ludicrous if it were not so mischievous and fraught with such danger, when cleverly used as an incentive to fire the imagination of an ardent, generous, patriotic people.
>
> (*The Irish Catholic Directory*, 1918, pp. 538j–k)

The letter created a sensation throughout the country. The *Freeman's Journal* published it under the heading 'Cardinal Logue and Sinn Féin' and underlined the passages concerning the dream of a republic.[153] Mgr Curran felt that although Logue was very independent in his political initiatives between 1917 and 1918, he 'was undoubtedly influenced on particular occasions by Dr Morrisroe, Bishop of Achonry, an ardent follower of John Dillon and of very narrow views'.[154] This might explain why Logue suddenly abandoned his usual reserve and caution and attacked Sinn Féin directly, which was not his usual modus operandi. Eamon de Valera, Fr O'Flanagan and seven other priests were at that particular time in Roscommon where the leader was about to make a speech. A few moments before the Sinn Féin president went on the platform, a journalist of the *Freeman's Journal* asked him what he thought of Logue's letter. De Valera replied that he refused to comment on it since it was a matter that related to the Church and more precisely the archdiocese of Armagh. What he implied was that there were other bishops who had other views. He would not risk contradicting Logue openly, which would be against his new policy of respectability. However, de Valera knew now who his main ecclesiastical enemy was and it was important to neutralise him.

In his speech in Roscommon, de Valera maintained that a republic for Ireland was not at all utopian, but did not quote Logue. Instead, he quoted Pope Leo XIII on the rights of small nations: 'Neither does the Church condemn those who, if it can be done without violation of justice, wish to make their country independent of any foreign or despotic power.'[155] Very astutely, de Valera had used a higher ecclesiastical authority than Logue in order to justify Sinn Féin's position. Ironically, he might not have been aware how much Leo XIII had supported Protestant England against Catholic Ireland during the Plan of Campaign. Arthur Griffith was also touring the country. At a meeting in Dundalk, he tried to persuade his audience that Cardinal Logue was wrong about Sinn Féin and that he too had severely criticised the English Government in the past, which was unquestionably true. He reminded the crowd of speeches the Cardinal had made in 1891, 1906 and 1907, and concluded 'that when His Eminence was not a politician he had a clear conception of what English government [stood] for in Ireland'.[156] Despite Griffith and de Valera's best efforts, the Cardinal seems to have won this political duel. In November, the military intelligence officer of the Midlands and Connaught District mentioned in detail the political evolution within the clergy:

The Catholic Church, by its Bishops, has condemned all appeal to arms as immoral. Cardinal Logue has forbidden his priests, under pain of suspension, to have anything to do with Sinn Féin, or to appear on the same platform with Father [O']Flanagan of Crossna.

This goes to show that the great power of the Roman Catholic Church is really against Sinn Féin, and no matter what some of the younger clergy may say or do, they cannot bring the country with them... In dealing with the question of the younger Roman Catholic clergy, especially East of the Shannon, many who held strong Sinn Féin views have toned down considerably. An extreme policy will not receive their support... As well as Cardinal Logue, Archbishop of Armagh, the Archbishop of Tuam, the Bishops of Kildare, Longford, Athenry, Elphin, Clonfert, Meath and Killala, have declared against the morality of Sinn Féin, viz. rebellion against a constituted authority.

(PRO, London, CO904/157, Midlands and Connaught
intelligence report, 31 December 1917, p. 99)

The Sinn Féin leadership had not won the political battle yet and its declaration in favour of a republic for Ireland meant for many that the party did not exclude revolutionary struggle. De Valera could not afford to remain passive and decided to meet the people personally. In December 1917, he was in Co. Cork, together with J.J. Walsh, trying to persuade farmers of Sinn Féin's just cause. *Nationality* published a rather short statement, saying 'that the meetings on Sunday were most successful'.[157] The truth, however, was quite different. The military intelligence officer of the Southern District confirmed the November report of his colleague from Midlands and Connaught. He wrote that de Valera and Walsh had organised a meeting in Cork and that between 6,000 and 8,000 people had shown up. But according to the officer, two thirds of them 'were quite apathetic, and had merely attended out of curiosity'. He pointed out that:

The tour in the country towns was most disappointing, from the Sinn Féin point of view. The attendance at the meetings was poor, and the young men of Kanturk, Skibbereen, and other places listened to the orators out of windows, but declined to march with the Volunteers. Walsh made vitriolic comments on their absence at more than one meeting. It may be said that the Sinn Féin 'boom' has passed its zenith. The general prosperity of the farmers and disinclination for any further rebellion, and the gradual coming out into the open of individual Roman Catholic Bishops and Parish Priests in opposition to the absurd nonsense talked about an 'Irish Republic' and the appearance of Ireland at the 'Peace Conference' are having their effect. The 'heroes' and 'martyrs' released in June 1917 are losing their freshness and novelty, and while the leaders and extremists are and will remain as fanatical as ever, the movement is losing the support given it by the general public for the lack of any really material grievance to agitate about, such as the land question thirty years ago. The leaders contradict themselves and each other in every fresh speech they make, and there is no practicable policy advocated.

(PRO, London, CO904/157, Southern District intelligence report, 31 December 1917, p. 83)

Once again, what Bishop O'Dwyer had said in 1915 about poor peasants who preferred to till their potato gardens in peace and who were not interested in cosmopolitan considerations about the war put forward by the Nationalist party, was now going against Sinn Féin. De Valera and Griffith were aware of this political apathy and had begun a new campaign directly aimed at farmers. *Nationality* took advantage of the fact that some disorganisation had occurred in the country after Lord Rhondda's Cattle Prices Order had come into operation. This resulted in export and food crises. The newspaper blamed the English Government for not having solved the problem in time and spoke about a future famine in Ireland. It was pleased to inform its readers that Sinn Féin priests had successfully convinced and assisted farmers in the west in building up supplies of flour which would last until the coming summer.[158]

The beginning of 1918 was characterised by an increase of violence in the country. Some Volunteers were looking for arms and harassed local populations, and land was confiscated in the name of an Irish republic that had not yet evolved. Sinn Féin was simply not able to control them. The young Michael Collins declared that those Volunteers did not receive orders from the Sinn Féin leadership,[159] and it was clear that de Valera's policy of respectability was seriously endangered. In the meantime, the long-winded negotiations in the Irish Convention were continuing when a sudden turn of events took place. No progress had been made regarding reconciliation between nationalists and unionists and a debate was dragging on about Customs and Excise if Home Rule were to be immediately implemented. In an attempt to divide Ulster Unionists from southern Unionists, John Redmond accepted the latter's proposal that the future Home Rule Parliament would not have the right to claim excise duties. On 15 January 1918, Bishop O'Donnell, who had been the Nationalist party's staunchest supporter within the hierarchy, begged to differ on this point. O'Donnell was of the opinion that the people could not accept Redmond's idea. As long as Ulster refused to accept Home Rule, the Bishop thought that the rest of the country should ask for complete fiscal autonomy. Redmond's problem was that a fraction of his party, including Joseph Devlin, agreed with O'Donnell. Therefore, he was obliged to publicly renounce his plan. It was a terrible humiliation for Redmond and his reputation sank to a record low.[160] Dr Kelly, another member of the ecclesiastical delegation to the Convention, was quite pessimistic regarding the chances of finding a solution to Ireland's political problems. He wrote to Mgr O'Riordan that the Convention had been set up by the Government 'not through love of Ireland, but because it suited them'. According to him, a solution was practically impossible since the Unionists would not 'change their pre-historic attitude' and that a 'a section of Nationalists, instead of moving towards compromise, [had], through fear of Sinn Féin, been raising their demands'.[161] It seemed that the Convention was in a deadlock. Once more, the Nationalist party had proved that it was not able to solve the Home Rule crisis.

At the end of January 1918, Edward Lysaght, an independent nationalist who sided with William Martin Murphy, the owner of the *Irish Independent*, and the writer George Russell ('Æ'), announced that he was leaving the Convention. He had asked David Lloyd George's assurance that the Government would accept the decision of a majority of the Convention and had also demanded a clarification of the Prime Minister's notion of 'substantial agreement'. Lloyd George, the undisputed master of ambiguity, had answered that it was up to the Government to determine what 'substantial' meant.[162] Bishop Fogarty sent Lysaght a letter in which he expressed his fear that Home Rule would only be a sham. He believed 'that a country without control of its own trade would be like the Irish farmer in the past, who would not get his daughter married without the permission of his landlord', and concluded by saying that 'the country [was] sick of all this huxtering'.[163] The Bishop was openly in favour of Sinn Féin but it can be reasonably assumed, after Lloyd George's latest tactless remark that he had voiced the feelings of the entire hierarchy.

In February 1918, the bishops made public their Lenten pastorals. All agreed that the Convention was in a critical phase. Cardinal Logue believed that its success was of vital importance not only for Ireland but also for the Empire. His opinions had not changed much since 1900 despite the fruitless policy of the British Government and the War Office. He warned, however, 'that it would be lamentable if, after the long and patient labour of so many men of good will, a measure were produced which the people would reject with contempt, as they [had] so often rejected worthless projects'.[164] Chaos and revolution were looming on the horizon. Archbishop Walsh shared the Cardinal's opinion. Walsh had always been afraid that some wild elements among the Volunteers would put an end to the constitutional cause. The violence throughout the country only confirmed his fears. That is why he wrote that the Convention should reach an equitable and lasting settlement 'and not one which it [might], unhappily, be a duty of national honour, as well as of sound policy, for the country to reject'.[165] He also reiterated the fact that the Church was strictly opposed to secret societies, including Fenians. Bishop MacRory hoped that the Convention would unite all the Irish of all different religions. According to him, a solution would put an end to the anti-English campaign, and a failure would only intensify it.

His words were prophetic. Lysaght's resignation and Lloyd George's notion of 'substantial agreement' had provoked numerous warnings from the hierarchy. Bishop Hoare also asked the population and his priests to be on their guard against secret societies. Dr Morrisroe agreed with him.[166] As president of the IRB, Michael Collins must have been aware of the influence of the hierarchy on his organisation. The most awaited pastoral was Bishop O'Donnell's, just after his public disagreement with John Redmond. The Bishop wrote at length about the war and did not mention the Convention once, which was in itself very revealing of his frame of mind. Nevertheless, he alluded to it, saying that it was on behalf of liberty for small nations that the war had been declared and adding: 'The cry of liberty is on the lips of all. May the sentiment also be in the hearts of all, and in the end may true liberty for the nations, our own little one included, come as some compensation for so much sacrifice of life and property.'[167] The word 'true' suggested a warning to the British Government, especially in the aftermath of the debate on Customs and Excise. Furthermore, O'Donnell reminded the cabinet that the Irish had joined the Army to fight for Ireland and the Empire and that in return they expected Home Rule.

The Bishop's apprehensions were fully justified. Shortly afterwards, indeed, the Prime Minister informed Sir Horace Plunkett, the president of the Convention, that the customs question between Ireland and Britain would not be settled while the conflict in Europe lasted. Lloyd George felt 'that during the period of the war and for a period of two years after, the control of Customs and Excise should be reserved to the United Kingdom Parliament'.[168] It seemed that Ireland's freedom was becoming more and more nominal. Curiously, a copy of Lloyd George's letter to Plunkett is in the Irish College in Rome. It was clear that Mgr O'Riordan and Mgr Hagan were well informed about the progress of the Convention. Archbishop Walsh had been right when he had complained to Sir MacKenzie Chalmers in 1916, that the envisaged Home Rule law would not bring much freedom to Ireland. The hierarchy understood, as it had initially believed, that this Convention meant nothing for the country, and its politics had been radicalised.

Alfred Blanche, the French Consul at Dublin, had noticed the bishops' anger. On 11 February 1918, he sent a report to the Quai d'Orsay in Paris, in which he summed up the situation:

All the Irish bishops, in their Lenten pastorals that were read out yesterday, have mainly dealt with the Convention. Despite the moderating influence that many of them have had lately on their flocks and clergy members, they could not refrain from insisting on the necessity to grant the country a complete and unlimited autonomy if one wants to reach a solution worthy of the name.

(Quai d'Orsay, Paris, vol. 547 Grand-Bretagne/Irlande,
letter no. 10, Blanche to Ministre des Affaires
étrangères, 11 February 1918)

As an example, the Consul translated a passage from Logue's pastoral. France and her new Prime Minister, the energetic Georges Clemenceau, paid particular attention to the situation in Ireland for the war had had worrying developments for the Allies, (which will be dealt with in a later chapter). If Clemenceau had been able to read Bishop MacRory's letter to Mgr O'Riordan, he would have been instantly convinced of the veracity of Alfred Blanche's report on Ireland. MacRory, indeed, wrote a very angry letter in which he expressed his abhorrence of the Convention after Lloyd George's intervention on Customs and Excise:

The whole thing is disgusting...It is an outrage after all these months of anxious labour. We shall end the Convention in a week or two, and most probably there will be three reports – a result that might have been attained in a week or even a day. The Government, it is thought, will then attempt to impose some settlement, and God knows what may follow. The country is in no mood to accept such a settlement as is likely to be offered. There is even still, I learned to-day, a danger of an attempt being made, and very soon, to impose Conscription. If so, there is sure to be bloodshed.

(ICR, letter from the Bishop of Down and Connor,
dated 2 March 1918)

The Government did not take into account the political climate in Ireland, so well analysed by its military intelligence officers. This attitude not only led to the widening of the gap between Britain and nationalist Ireland, but also between the Catholic Church and the authorities. According to Mgr Curran, 'perhaps a third of the bishops in 1918 sympathised with Sinn Féin'.[169] Other bishops had certainly become independent nationalists at this stage. The dilemma they faced was either to support an ineffective Nationalist party or a Sinn Féin party with republican and, perhaps, revolutionary doctrines. Their only alternative for the time being was to wait and see. Soon, as MacRory had guessed, conscription would be introduced and a crisis would develop which might bring about a new political departure. On 4 April 1918, the Irish Convention closed all its debates and produced a report that was approved by forty-four votes, including twenty-six nationalists and nine unionists, against twenty-eight votes, including eighteen unionists and eleven nationalists. This report recommended Home Rule for Ireland but no fiscal autonomy, at least not immediately. Among the eleven nationalists who had voted against the report was the ecclesiastical delegation. Sir Horace Plunkett believed they were 'Bolshevik Bishops'.[170] Not having obtained definite guarantees on fiscal autonomy and partition, the delegation did not vote in favour as the hierarchy had instructed them to do in June 1917 at their Maynooth meeting. This vote signalled a clear radicalisation within the hierarchy.

On 9 April 1918, the 'Bolshevik Bishops' decision was vindicated as Lloyd George gave his own interpretation of democracy. He refused to take into account the majority opinion of the Convention, arguing that it did not represent this 'substantial agreement' he had spoken of. He also announced that conscription would be introduced and that the Government had the intention of introducing some measure of autonomy for Ireland.[171] Mgr Curran wrote in his memoirs that Lloyd George's notion of 'substantial agreement' was a 'dishonest device of ensuring disagreement and a breakdown in the Convention unless Carson's own terms were conceded'.[172] It was true that the Unionist delegation had used the war theme in the Convention and had stressed 'Ulster's whole-hearted provision of men and munitions during the war'.[173] As an ex-Minister for Munitions, Lloyd George knew that it was not in the United Kingdom's interest to hinder or upset those who were behind the war effort at home. Nationalist anger was understandably boiling. It is said that the ecclesiastical delegation's vote against the report provoked a fear of clericalism among the Unionists at a time when they were beginning to respect John Redmond during the negotiations.[174] But, if this was really the case, can the Catholic Church be seriously blamed for adopting a hostile and distrustful attitude to the Convention? The war had dictated the Government's Irish policy and it was one of duplicity, or one that lacked clarity and foresight, to say the least. Lloyd George's interventions as a negotiator during the partition crisis of 1916 were a prime example. The War Office's almost systematic mishandling of nationalist feelings was another one. Furthermore, it was unlikely that the Unionists had had to wait until April 1918 to be convinced of John Redmond's sincerity towards Britain and the Empire. Just like them, the Nationalist leader was an Irishman and a loyalist, and by no means a republican or a clerical politician, but, in sharp contrast to Unionists, he was persuaded that Ireland could look after herself within the framework of the British Empire.

However, what was the political climate in Ireland on the eve of the conscription crisis? In December 1917, Irish newspapers had reported that the Vatican had been excluded from the future peace conference in a secret treaty between Italy and Britain, signed in 1915.[175] This could not have failed to increase the ecclesiastical delegation's distrust towards the Government during the Convention negotiations. Some bishops denounced this anti-papal attitude in their Lenten pastorals of February 1918. The *Freeman's Journal* published various extracts of the pastorals in an article entitled 'Pope Defended'. Logue, indeed, defended Benedict XV's neutrality and initiatives in favour of peace. The Cardinal denounced the hostile attitude of some statesmen towards the Pope, probably influenced, he believed, by 'wretched Italian politicians', and also the vitriolic attacks of the British press. Walsh wrote that it was the duty of the Irish people to pray for the Pope 'and for the peace and happiness of the Church, especially in those countries in which its liberty or its rights [were] being interfered with by hostile legislation'. Bishop McKenna of Clogher declared that the British Government 'was guilty of the outrage of mocking him by sending an Ambassador to his Court, while all the time they were bound by secret treaty not to listen to his voice'.[176] *Nationality* published an article in which it vehemently criticised John Dillon and John Redmond's participation in the war effort. It was especially Dillon who incurred the newspaper's wrath. Arthur Griffith had felt that he was the new ascending force in the Nationalist party. For this reason, *Nationality* reminded its readers what Dillon's opinions on partition were and quoted speeches of Walsh and McHugh against partition.[177] During January and February 1918, some Irish Volunteers increased violence in the country.

If the military intelligence officer of the Midlands and Connaught District noticed in November 1917 that the young Catholic clergy had fallen back into line, it was only temporarily. In February 1918, the officer of the Southern District was of the opinion that the gap between bishops and parish priests on one hand, and young curates on the other was widening again.[178] There were several explanations for this. Firstly, the public disagreement between the bishops and Redmond in the Convention. Secondly, the disclosure of the secret Anglo-Italian treaty. Thirdly, the German-Russian peace negotiations that could mean the extension of conscription to Ireland, as extra men would be needed to face a new German onslaught on the western front. And fourthly, the Fourteen Points peace programme announced by President Woodrow Wilson on 8 January 1918, in which it was stated that small nations would have the right to self-determination. All these reasons incited young priests and some bishops to prefer Sinn Féin, a party that was more determined against war, conscription and the Government's Irish policy. The military intelligence officer wrote that bishops were no longer able to control the political evolution of their priests. Some of them even helped the Irish Volunteers:

> The Roman Catholic Church Authorities have been reduced to impotent silence save a few individual Bishops and Parish Priests who have had the courage to denounce the introduction of the methods of Russian Bolshevism into Ireland, and to these all honour is due. As for the junior Clergy the majority appear to approve of these methods, and sometimes take the lead in applying them.
>
> (PRO, London, CO904/157, Southern District intelligence report, 28 February 1918, p. 62)

The French Consul in Dublin confirmed the officer's report. According to Blanche, Cardinal Logue was openly 'held in contempt and held up to ridicule' by young seminarians in Maynooth.[179] How could it have been otherwise? Logue was the embodiment of this old conservative imperial mind that rejected the political aspirations of younger Irish generations. In April 1918, *New Ireland* published an article entitled 'Theologians and the young men of Ireland', which had been written by a priest on 24 February. The author warned the hierarchy that it could lose all grip on Catholic Ireland if it did not pay sufficient attention to younger people. He wrote: 'If Bishops undertake to pronounce a just verdict according to Catholic principles on the new developments of Irish politics, they ought to give full consideration to the views of this younger generation. If they only give consideration to the views of men who have entered "the dangerous age", or perhaps to their own political views, they are apt to pronounce a verdict which is founded on an inaccurate estimate or assumption of fact, and which therefore is of no real weight.'[180] Logue's problem was that he refused to admit that Ireland no longer had any interest in Home Rule, an idea that had been discredited by recent political events. Bishop Foley of Kildare and Leighlin, another imperial mind but more realistic than Logue, had eventually admitted that priests had the right to become Sinn Féin members provided they renounced violence. Foley's only consolation was that priests could be a moderating force within the republican movement.[181]

On 6 March 1918, John Redmond died suddenly in London. With him disappeared the idea of Home Rule for the Irish nation. Reactions within the hierarchy were rather diverse. Mgr Curran did not regret the Nationalist leader's passing away at all:

> John Redmond died today. Heart failure after operation on Friday last (1st of March). His death is no loss to the cause of nationality.

His weak, compromising policy, his repeated surrender of the national position – the latest at the Convention on the 15th of January – his attempt to commit Ireland to the war and his attitude on conscription were fatal weights on our necks.

(NLD, O'Kelly papers, MS 27728(2),
Curran's memoirs, 6 March 1918)

These were bitter comments but the likelihood was that they accurately reflected the general frame of mind in an Ireland that had become more nationalist than the Nationalist party itself. Sinn Féin literary activists felt the need for irony to mark this occasion and circulated a leaflet on which people were able to read: 'John Redmond is Dead; The flag of England droops in sorrow; the Union Jack, the symbol of English Imperialism, hangs at half mast in token of Britannia's regret at the loss of her dear friend.'[182] Not only Home Rule, but also the war had been responsible for the slow disintegration of the party and its leader. Curran noted in his memoirs that it had been advised that Redmond's funeral should take place in Wexford, his home town, and not in Dublin lest troubles broke out. According to him, Archbishop Walsh did not even send a message of sympathy to the family and even refused a requiem mass for Redmond. Bishop Hallinan of Limerick had also refused. *Nationality* believed 'that the voice of the new Bishop of Limerick [rang] out for Ireland as vigorously as that of his great predecessor'.[183] Timothy Healy, the independent nationalist, wrote 'that no clergyman of the Archdiocese of Dublin met the coffin – so intense was the bitterness against [Redmond's] policy'.[184] Bishop MacRory wrote: 'It is a pity poor Redmond didn't die a couple of months ago, before he consented in the Convention to give up the control of Customs. His attitude has emboldened the Government which now refuses, during the war, Customs, Excise, Police and Post Office.'[185] Bishops O'Donnell and Hackett, and Archbishop Harty sent a simple telegram of condolence. Bishop Coyne of Elphin, who had tried to discipline Fr O'Flanagan on several occasions, regretted the death of this 'most sterling patriot and one of [Ireland's] best and noblest sons'.[186] Cardinal Bourne, the Primate of the English Catholic Church, declared that the Catholics of the United Kingdom had lost a great defender of the faith.[187] Bourne understood that he had just lost a most precious ally in Westminster Parliament. As for Cardinal Logue, he sent a letter to the *Evening Telegraph* in Belfast in which he expressed his regrets, but above all passed a more objective and compassionate judgement on Redmond than Walsh, Curran and Hallinan. After all, Redmond's biggest mistake had been to trust almost blindly in the British Government:

Like many others, I may not have always been in perfect agreement with the details of his policy, but I have never even dreamt of questioning his patriotism and singleness of purpose and disinterested devotion to the welfare of his country or his commanding abilities...He may have sometimes made mistakes, but the statesman who has never made a mistake is a worthless statesman.

(The Evening Telegraph in *The Freeman's Journal*, 7 March 1918)

A few days later, John Dillon was appointed leader of the Nationalist party. Redmond's death was quite symbolic for it corresponded with a political upheaval that would change Ireland's destiny forever: the conscription crisis. The war was entering its final phase in Europe, so it seemed. On 3 March 1918, Germany had concluded peace with Russia and the nightmare scenario of Allied generals now became a reality, as German divisions on the eastern front were transferred to the western front. Perhaps the mightiest German offensive of the war began on 21 March on the Somme and on 9 April in Flanders. France's eyes were once again set on Ireland where there were so many potential recruits even though the Quai d'Orsay's latest report had estimated that all young Irishmen and priests were against the war.[188] France's anxiety was rather understandable, as American troops were not in a hurry to fight. What would David Lloyd George's Government do about this situation? In this grave moment, nationalist Ireland no longer had two of its main leaders, John Redmond and Bishop O'Dwyer. But, the stage was now set for four men, Cardinal Logue, Archbishop Walsh, Mgr Curran and Eamon de Valera. It was they who determined and masterminded the struggle against conscription.

6 The conscription crisis of 1918

April 1918
'I think this is the worst day's business the bishops ever did.'
Cardinal Logue to Archbishop Walsh after meeting
a delegation led by Eamon de Valera

April 1918
'The bill does not prescribe the implementation of the compulsory military service to Ireland.'
General de la Panouse, French military attaché London, to
Deuxième Bureau Paris, French military intelligence

'I hate a priest...whenever I see one'.
David Lloyd George, British Prime Minister,
to a close friend, undated

The conscription crisis of 1918 marked a new era in Irish politics as the crisis drew together the Catholic Church, the Nationalist party and above all Sinn Féin. Eamon de Valera's party and the Church emerged as the real victors in this crisis. Sinn Féin finally gained respectability as the hierarchy agreed to talk and negotiate with it, and subsequently claimed all credit in dissuading the British from enforcing conscription in Ireland. The crisis would pave the way to Sinn Féin's landslide victory in the general election of December 1918, less than two months after the end of the war in Europe. The Catholic Church was heartily welcomed in the political arena, as it had embraced, almost to a man, the radicalisation of nationalism during the crisis. In April 1918, the British Government had reached a nadir in its mismanagement of Irish affairs and there was little excuse for the cabinet, especially David Lloyd George, for not having anticipated the political cataclysm that conscription provoked in Ireland. Irish resistance to the Compulsory Military Service Bill sent shock waves throughout the Empire, the United States and some neutral countries. France, desperate for manpower in 1918, wondered if hundreds of thousands of Irishmen would ever come to its help.

Lenin's seizure of power in Russia in October 1917 had most serious repercussions on the political evolution in Ireland as the British Government now felt obliged to impose conscription on the country in order to face the new German offensive, reinforced by divisions that had been previously fighting on the Russian front. The United Kingdom was already facing a serious manpower crisis in 1917, after the disastrous battle of Passchendaele in Belgium where the Army had almost drowned in mud. The number of British casualties was as high as 760,000 that year and many of these soldiers had not been replaced. Consequently, certain divisions were reduced from twelve down to nine battalions. Morale was not good.[1] General Philippe Pétain of the French High Command was worried as American reinforcements were not forthcoming. On 21 March 1918, the Germans attacked en masse and the results were a catastrophe for the Allies. At 4.40 a.m., the German artillery obliterated the Allied defences. The bombardment went on for five hours and soldiers had to face an unprecedented deluge of high explosive and chemical shells. The British 5th Army was the worst hit.[2] In the resulting chaos, the 16th Irish Division and 36th Ulster Division, both part of the 5th Army, fought bravely and succeeded in delaying some of the German advance but by 23 March, they too were in retreat. As the offensive progressed, the two divisions suffered heavy casualties as the 16th Irish Division lost 6,435 men and the 36th Ulster Division 6,109.[3] On the same day well behind the German lines, the Kaiser's train pulled into a railway station where his staff were waiting for him on the platform. In a triumphant and jubilant mood, like a child not able to conceal its excitement, Wilhelm II pulled down a window and shouted: 'The battle is won, the English have been utterly defeated!'[4] The same night, champagne was served to the Imperial entourage while German soldiers were advancing through the inferno. The Kaiser had some reasons to be satisfied as the British and French armies suffered over 300,000 casualties at the end of April 1918.

Conscription was now like a sword of Damocles above Ireland but there were some problems along the way. Back in 1910, the Liberal, David Lloyd George, had told the Conservative, Arthur Balfour, who had once been Irish Secretary, that conscription would never be envisaged, and, in 1914, Winston Churchill had also forcefully argued in favour of compulsory service but in vain. Sir Edward Grey, the then Foreign Secretary, had been of the opinion that the United Kingdom could 'pursue a European policy without keeping up a great army'.[5] As late as 1917, Lloyd George was still maintaining that conscription could not be introduced in Ireland. It was true that his arguments were quite convincing: 'If you passed the act you would get only 160,000 men and you would get them at the point of the bayonet...These men are producing food which we badly need.'[6] By March 1918, farmers or not, all men were badly needed at the front before it was too late and the Prime Minister changed his mind. He was fully aware, of course, of the volatile political climate in Ireland where violence was increasing, and numerous young men, fit for service, had joined Sinn Féin either because they genuinely believed in the political aspirations of that party, or because they thought it was their best protection against conscription. De Valera's party was now better organised in the country and it could mount a serious challenge to the Nationalist party. There were about 1,200 Sinn Féin clubs, numbering more that 250.000 members.[7] As for the hierarchy, it had tremendous difficulties in controlling its younger priests. In fact, the Church was in no position to change the course of events. At best, it could only go with the tide.

Why, under these circumstances, did Lloyd George take the decision to go ahead with conscription in Ireland, assuredly a most slippery slope to embark upon. There were four main reasons. Firstly, he had to take into account British public opinion. The latter would simply not have accepted that Ireland would be exempted from compulsory military service at a time when the war was entering its final phase and its outcome was far from certain.[8] On 15 April, the Prime Minster was warned that a fraction of public opinion was against conscription being introduced in Ireland but that other regions in the country like Scotland, Lancashire, Yorkshire and Cornwall considered that the laws of Parliament should be applied to the entire United Kingdom.[9]

Secondly, Lloyd George had to placate and reassure some politicians and militaries. General Gough's 5th Army was retreating. Field Marshal Haig, the Commander-in-Chief of the British Army, announced that the situation was critical. Winston Churchill, Minister for Munitions, and Sir Henry Wilson, an Irish unionist general who was Commander of the Imperial General Staff (CIGS), wanted conscription at once.[10] On 6 April, Lloyd George travelled to Beauvais in northern France where he met several generals and Georges Clemenceau, the French Prime Minister, in order to discuss the situation. On his return to London, he told the cabinet: 'I cannot tell you what happened, nor can General Wilson tell me nor Field Marshal Haig. The Fifth Army has practically disappeared.'[11] Some MPs demanded that Ireland participate in the defence of the United Kingdom. Yet, Lord Wimborne, Sir Henry Duke, the Irish Secretary, Sir Edward Carson and Sir James Campbell advised the Government not to impose conscription on Ireland. Campell's view was that Sinn Féin was no longer only composed of extremists but was also supported by the clergy.[12] He was right.

Thirdly, there was French pressure. As the Americans were slow in coming to the front line, Clemenceau and General Ferdinand Foch, the

23. David Lloyd George, Britain's second war-time Prime Minister (courtesy of the National Library of Ireland)

24. Eamon de Valera cemented alliance of the nationalist opposition with the Catholic Church during the First World War

MARCHING TO BERLIN.

By "THE RAJAH OF FRONGOCH."

Air—" Marching to Georgia."

1914.

Loudly sound the trumpet, boys—by jingo, we will fight
For France and plucky Belgium in the sacred cause of right.
" Tipperary" we will whistle as the Germans feel our might,
    As we go marching to Berlin.

    Chorus ;

Hurrah ! Hurrah ! in three weeks we'll be back,
And from the Kaiser's Palace we'll fly the Union Jack ;
A hundred thousand million quids we'll take from Billy's sack,
    As we come marching from Berlin.

1915.

We hadn't got enough of shells when first we fought the Hun.
You'll want to send us thousands more to get him on the run.
Let " More Shells " be England's cry, then all that's to be done
    Is to proudly go marching to Berlin.

    Chorus :

Hurrah ! Hurrah ! We're only here a year,
And if we were set back a bit of that you have no fear.
More Shells ! More Shells ! More Shells ! We want to make Old England cheer,
    As we go marching to Berlin.

1916.

We had the Germans beaten till the Irish they did rise.

The " dogs " they stabbed us in the back and caused a big surprise.
But now we've shot their leaders, plainer still the road it lies
    On to our goal—that is Berlin.

    Chorus :

Hurrah ! Hurrah ! We've got the shot and shell,
Lloyd George he swears we're going to give 'em Hell,
The bells of old Cologne will ring the Kaiser's death-knell,
    As we come marching from Berlin.

1917.

You must conscript the Irish crowd if we are going to win.
Nine hundred miles it must be tramped before we strike Berlin,
The Hun will not be beaten if the Irish won't come in—
    There's no use talking of Berlin.

    Chorus :

Hurrah ! Hurrah ! was what we used to cheer,
But now the sound grows fainter every year.
Oh, back to dear old Blighty I wish we all could steer.
    There's no use talking of Berlin.

1918.

Final Chorus :

Hurrah ! Hurrah ! Old Ireland she is free,
John Bull at last no longer rules the sea,
The world in arms had no effect on good old Germany.
    The joy-bells are ringing in Berlin.

25. Pro-German song 'Marching to Berlin', composed by Irish republicans (PRO, London, CO 904/161)

IRELAND, ENGLAND

AND

THE WAR.

The accompanying leaflet was dropped from a German aeroplane into the English lines in France. As the matter is of very important and very general historic interest, it is hoped that its presentation in pamphlet form will be of use. No change has been made in the wording, though there are a few obvious misprints.

WHO IS THE REAL FOE OF THE IRISH ?

(By Hugh O'Neill).

The Easter Week Rebellion in Ireland was one of the most important events in the world's war. It showed the world the hollow pretence of England, and saved Ireland from the ignominy of surrender by her corrupt representatives at Westminster. It proved to the world that the Irish had not lost their spirit of nationality—that they had not become the willing participants in the crimes of England ; that the Irish would not, at the behest of Redmond, Dillon, Devlin, and other place-hunting politicians, surrender the ideals of the Irish race for a mess of pottage or a miserable pittance called Home Rule; that the Irish were no slave-minded West Britons, ready to participate in England's dark doings in the hope of sharing in her spoils; that the Irish did not wish their land to be an integral part of the British Empire but a separate and independent nation.

Men who did not know the Irish race and its loyalty to principles thought that the Irish would be satisfied

26. German propaganda leaflet for Irish soldiers dropped into British lines (PRO, London, CO 904/161)

newly promoted Commander-in-Chief of all the Allied Armies on the western front, closely followed the events in Ireland where, it was estimated, 150,000 men were fit to fight. On 17 April 1918, General de la Panouse, the military attaché at the French embassy in London, sent a report to Clemenceau. It was an estimate of the number of Irish recruits since 1914. De la Panouse wrote that 58,438 Ulstermen and 65,147 men of the other three provinces had joined up.[13] To the French, these numbers were not satisfactory. They had become obsessed by the question of Irish recruits and regularly inquired about it. General Sir Nevil Macready, who later commanded the British forces in Ireland during the War of Independence, wrote: 'Monsieur Clemenceau was not satisfied with the efforts of Great Britain to provide men, and no doubt was unable to understand why our Prime Minister could not tap the large reserve existing in Ireland, a state of affairs which would have been very soon put right by our friends the French had they faced a similar situation.'[14] A Colonel Roure was soon sent over to Britain by the French to examine the problem. Thus by introducing conscription, Lloyd George would also reassure France, Britain's main ally.

Fourthly, there was the manpower problem in Britain. There were too many skilled workers in the Army and the country was dependent on skilled labour. In April 1918, the Minister for National Service had pointed out this fact to Lloyd George. Furthermore, Britain had an exceptionally high number of strikes during the war,[15] and this was not the time to alienate the working classes. It is, therefore, reasonable to assume that Lloyd George thought he had very little choice but to tap the Irish reserve of men.

On 25 March, the Prime Minister made his decision to introduce compulsory military service in Ireland despite the warnings against it by Henry Duke who sarcastically remarked: 'We might as well recruit Germans.'[16] Nevertheless, Lloyd George decided to give Ireland some degree of autonomy, undoubtedly to sugar the pill for the nationalists. He asked Duke to think about this and on 5 April, the Irish Secretary put forward a solution: the Military Service Bill would be voted and approved by Westminster Parliament but its implementation would be delayed by an order in council until the House of Commons adopted a Home Rule Bill. This initiative became known as the 'dual policy'.[17] This approach was very profitable for Lloyd George as it enabled him to gain time, waiting for the international situation to become more favourable. He knew that 88,000 men were on leave in Britain and managed to send them back to the front within one week. Moreover, he had convinced President Wilson to send over 100,000 American soldiers each month to Europe.[18]

Lloyd George's new policy looked like a well-thought-out gamble. On 9 April, he announced his decision in the House of Commons in

London. John Dillon and the other Irish MPs were incensed and frightened for the future of their party as they were in no position to vote down the cabinet. The cabinet's announcement assured Sinn Féin's victory in Ireland and surely provided the last nails in the Nationalist party's coffin. The Bill stated that all men aged between eighteen and fifty-one had to do their military service and, astonishingly, even Catholic and Protestant priests were to be conscripted. This made sure that the Catholic Church would oppose conscription. It was a rather strange decision, if not a blunder of the highest magnitude, and one wonders why Lloyd George wanted to enlist priests like the French Government had done. It seems, in fact, that he had a prejudice against Catholicism. He reputedly once told a Welsh friend of his: 'I hate a priest, Daniel, whenever I see one.'[19] When the scale of the Catholic Church's opposition to conscription in Ireland became known, he lost his nerve. H.R. Fisher, who was present at the time, wrote Lloyd George's words in his diary: 'L.G. furious against the priests, thinks that English public opinion would applaud violent enforcement of conscription.'[20] In that, he was badly mistaken too, as will be seen. The Prime Minister did not even take into account the report of the Irish Convention, which had just finished, and said vaguely in the House of Commons that his cabinet '[intended] to invite Parliament to pass a measure of self-government in Ireland'.[21]

On hearing this, Henry Duke immediately resigned as he wished the Government to be more frank about Home Rule. Lord Wimborne followed the Irish Secretary's example shortly afterwards. They were replaced by Edward Shortt and Lord French respectively. Even General Mahon, then commanding the British forces in Ireland, had tried to dissuade the cabinet from introducing conscription. According to him, the cabinet believed that no less than 400,000 Irishmen were fit for compulsory military service, whereas it had been calculated that 'at the utmost there were only 180,000 men of military age available for conscription. But the then Coalition Government thought they knew better, and did not trust their officials in Ireland.' Instead, Mahon put forward that volunteers in Ireland should serve in the American and French Armies but the Government would not consider this. Mahon added bitterly: 'Thus we saw things going from bad to worse.'[22] The French authorities were not impressed by Lloyd George's latest political manoeuvres. On 22 April, General de la Panouse sent a report to the French High Command and the Deuxième Bureau, the military intelligence service:

> First of all, the bill does not prescribe the implementation of the compulsory military service to Ireland; it only authorises this implementation, if the case arises, in accordance with an order in

council. Then, there is no military census in Ireland, no list of men fit for military service, and the preparation of those lists would take some time even if the order in council was published tomorrow. But, the order in council will not be published tomorrow, nor after tomorrow for the Government, facing difficulties that emerged during the discussion of the bill in Parliament, has promised not to extend conscription to Ireland before the presentation to Parliament of a Home Rule project which it is presently preparing and which will be introduced in the House of Commons as soon as possible, as it has pledged to do.

(Quai d'Orsay, Paris, vol. 544 Grand-Bretagne/Irlande, report
no. 59, de la Panouse to état-major de
l'armée et au deuxième bureau)

Lloyd George's new dual policy was not new at all since it was the same approach as Herbert Asquith's in 1914. But instead of recruitment for Home Rule, it was conscription for Home Rule. The Prime Minister's approach had some merit, though, as it solved his own immediate problems. To many Irish nationalists, however, it looked like a political blackmail and even Sir Edward Carson himself denounced the Government's plan in Westminster:

You ought to have made up your mind: was conscription possible in Ireland under the present circumstances or was it not? If you made up your minds it was, and that it was right, then you ought to have passed it. If you made up your minds it was wrong, you ought not to have tried to pass it by a bribe, and by throwing over those who have been faithful to you in the past. You have tried, I suppose, to please everybody, and I believe in the long run you will please nobody.

(Ward, 'Lloyd George and the 1918 Irish Conscription Crisis',
Historical Journal, p. 114)

This was the opposite of what Carson had said in the House of Commons in the summer of 1916. At that time he had told those in favour of Home Rule, not without a hint of sarcasm, that it was their duty to accept conscription since matters of national defence were decided by the Imperial Parliament in Westminster. Carson's sudden volte-face was by no means due to a sudden urge of fair play. In April 1916, the Easter Rising had been a rather local event in the sense that it had been confined merely to Dublin. It had not been too serious from a military point of view. Immediately after the troubles in Dublin, and with hindsight, Carson could be very satisfied since the rising justified his Ulster separatism.. In April 1918, the international situation was completely different and he had no longer any reason to be satisfied. In fact, he was on tenterhooks. By then, Sinn Féin and the Volunteers had become rather noisy and above all better organised and more determined. If conscription went ahead, civil war would break out in the country and the unionist population was heavily outnumbered by the nationalists. Carson's army, the UVF, was in France where it had been badly mauled by German machine-gun fire during the Somme offensive in 1916, and was again during the new German offensive. Moreover, hundreds of thousands of American soldiers had reached the shores of Europe in order to fight for the freedom of small nations, according to their Democratic President, Woodrow Wilson. Ireland was such a small nation.

The Irish in America always voted largely in favour of the Democratic Party. In May 1916, the German Ambassador in Washington had informed Chancellor von Bethmann Hollweg that the Irish 'influenced' and 'dominated' this party.[23] Consequently, if civil war broke out in Ireland, Wilson, despite his Ulster Presbyterian origins, would have probably asked the British to implement Home Rule at once to the entire island so as not to hinder the global war effort and to satisfy the Irish-Americans. This scenario was partly confirmed by David Lloyd George himself two months later, on 25 June 1918, when he declared in the House of Commons: 'Not to settle [Home Rule] is not merely increasing our difficulties in conducting the war; it is increasing the difficulties of the USA in conducting the war.'[24] That was why Carson opposed conscription. The Nationalist party had to remain in place, it was the only party which had envisaged some form of partition, even if it was only on a temporary basis. Conscription would irrevocably mean the rise of Sinn Féin in the country. However, neither Dillon, nor Carson were able to change the Government's decision and Parliament approved the bill by 301 votes against 103. Even if British public opinion wanted the Irish question settled once and for all, not everybody in Britain approved of Lloyd George's initiatives. The *Daily Chronicle* and the *Saturday Review* were against the cabinet's decision. The Manchester Guardian went as far as to comment: 'The first and greatest military gain that we can look for in Ireland is the satisfaction of the Irish people, which will set free the troops that we are now obliged to keep in the country.'[25]

The Prime Minister had made a serious mistake in including the Catholic clergy in the Military Service Bill and would bitterly regret it in the months to come, as Ireland's opposition to conscription, largely orchestrated by the Catholic Church, would drastically change the nature of Anglo-Irish relations. And yet Lloyd George should have known what to expect from the clergy. In 1917, the Italian authorities had threatened to conscript the students of the Irish College in Rome. Mgr O'Riordan had written personally to the

Prime Minister and asked him to intervene.[26] The Italians did not insist. But it was easy to predict from that moment onwards how the Church would react if the Government attempted to conscript its priests. But, as far as Irish affairs were concerned, Lloyd George seemed to possess that kind of experience Frederick the Great of Prussia had once warned against: 'Experience is useless unless the right conclusions are drawn from it'. On 9 April, the Irish hierarchy officially announced its opposition to conscription. On 12 April, the cabinet met to discuss the situation and Arthur Bonar Law declared that Sir Auckland Geddes, the Minister for National Service, was against the inclusion of priests in the bill. Other ministers did not agree but according to Thomas Jones, the Prime Minister's personal secretary, the Prime Minister had changed his mind after the hierarchy's announcement. Cardinal Bourne of Westminster was also opposed to it. The cabinet cancelled its plans regarding the conscription of clergy,[27] but it was too late. The deed was done and the government was about to face the most formidable nationalist opposition ever seen in Ireland, unified for the first time since the onset of the war. Michael Collins wrote: 'I am very anxious to know what Lloyd George has done about conscription for this country. If he goes for – well he's ended.'[28] It was not the Prime Minister's end yet, but most certainly the beginning of the end of British rule in Ireland.

MGR CURRAN'S DECISIVE INTERVENTION

The standing committee of the hierarchy lost no time; they met on 9 April in Dublin and decided to oppose conscription. It was of crucial importance that all nationalists were united in this fight. The bishops' action would not only unify popular resistance to the Government's intentions, but also unify the clergy. Eight prelates wrote the hierarchy's official statement against compulsory military service in Ireland. They were Logue, Harty, O'Donnell, O'Dea, Foley, Kelly and Browne (all very conservative and opposed to any radical political movement), and Walsh. They wrote:

> Since the outbreak of hostilities four years ago the War Office has shown such utter lack of real touch with Irish conditions that it is quite possible something may now be proposed, which, if attempted, would only crown the disasters which want of knowledge and want of sympathy have already entailed. To enforce conscription here without the consent of the people would be perfectly unwarrantable and would soon inevitably end in

defeating its own purposes...With all the responsibility that attaches to our pastoral office, we feel bound to warn the Government against entering upon a policy so disastrous to the public interest and to all order, public and private.

(O'Faich, 'The Irish Bishops and the Conscription Issue 1918', *The Capuchin Annual*, p. 352)

The statement was remarkable simply because it had been drawn up and approved by utterly different men such as Logue and Walsh. It denounced in quite an objective way the Government's disastrous Irish policy since 1914, and implied that it had itself to blame for the lack of recruits in the country. The sentence 'to enforce conscription here without the consent of the people' almost implied that Ireland was independent and had, therefore, no obligation to obey Westminster Parliament's decisions. Lloyd George had just provoked a political cataclysm. It is believed that Logue was the main author of the statement.[29] Mgr Curran had more information about this meeting, notably on the bishops' frame of mind. On his return to the Archbishop's House, Walsh had told Curran that he had been taken aback by the 'almost revolutionary sentiment of some of the bishops who had spoken on that day'. The war had simply taken its toll. The Archbishop made a relevant remark about Logue: 'The Cardinal was entirely nonplussed at the strong attitude of some of his usually ultra-prudent colleagues but consoled himself by his own conviction that the clergy would be exempted even if the Conscription Bill were foolishly applied to Ireland. With the clergy exempted, the bishops would not be called to step into opposition leadership.'[30] Thus, Logue had been forced to adopt a strong attitude towards the Government lest he became completely isolated within the hierarchy. He was still hoping, however, that the Church would be able to avoid being dragged into the coming crisis. The bishops had also taken the secret decision to meet again if the Government persisted in conscripting priests.

The next day, the *Freeman's Journal* published the bishops' statement under the headline 'Irish Hierarchy warn the Cabinet'.[31] The people were shocked when conscription was officially announced but it was obvious that they would not accept it. The republican Cathal Brugha told Richard Mulcahy, the Chief of Staff of the Irish Volunteers, that he would go to London with a few men and attack the cabinet if it really meant to implement conscription. He left Ireland on 30 April.[32] On 10 April, Henry Duke relayed the full gravity of the situation to the cabinet and warned that Eamon de Valera had advised Sinn Féin to oppose conscription by organising strikes and, if need be, shooting on the RIC and the Army. According to the Prime Minister's secretary, the cabinet only devoted two minutes to this piece of information. Lloyd George was remarkably nonchalant, and said: 'That is a thing the Home Forces must see to. They have tried dock strikes here also, and we must make it clear to every dock labourer that if he isn't working at the docks, he will be in the Army.'[33]

On the same day Curran noted that there was a very strong determination throughout the country to resist compulsory military service. Some wanted to take up arms. Volunteer manoeuvres were taking place every night and Walsh's secretary feared a bloodbath.[34] The RIC had noticed a radicalisation among the clergy and reported a case in which a priest, sticking up anti-recruitment posters, had tried to hit a police officer.[35] John Dillon reiterated his opposition to conscription and was clearly far more aggressive in his dealing with the cabinet than John Redmond had ever been. Dillon had to give a better image of the Nationalist party which had been discredited by Lloyd George on 9 April, once more, when the Prime Minister had reminded the House of Commons that Redmond had been in favour of the war and had voted for it. The *Tablet* published the Prime Minister's remarks and seized the opportunity to state that Dillon himself had envisaged conscription in 1916 if the United Kingdom was about to lose the war. It was indeed correct that Dillon had stated: 'I would not hesitate to support conscription tomorrow if I thought it was necessary to maintain liberty, and if without conscription we ran the risk of losing the war.'[36] If the *Tablet*'s aim had been to turn supporters of the Nationalist party into Sinn Féiners, it had undoubtedly succeeded. As for Lloyd George, he did everything he could to win the war and lose Ireland. The *Freeman's Journal* felt obliged to publish an article entitled 'What the dead leader said', regarding Redmond's refusal to accept conscription.[37] The settling of scores between the Nationalist party and the English Liberals had begun.

It was at that time that Mgr Michael Curran intervened decisively in the unfolding crisis. It is unlikely that Curran was aware of the far-reaching consequences his intervention would have, but, in this case, there can be little doubt of the supreme importance of individuals shaping the course of history, whether intentionally or not. In his memoirs, Walsh's secretary credited himself with having linked up the lay opposition with the ecclesiastical opposition to conscription. The question remains as to what extent his memoirs are reliable. It has been said that his writings 'suffer at times...from a retrospective view of history from a republican stand point.'[38] However, Curran's behaviour on this particular occasion accurately reflected his liking for cloak-and-dagger work, as has been seen previously. Furthermore, what is stated in his memoirs largely corresponds with what is written in his private letters to Mgr Hagan and Mgr O'Riordan in Rome. There are no inconsistencies there at least, so it appears that one may reasonably rely on his description of those crucial days.

On Friday 12 April 1918, a worried Eamon de Valera arrived at the Archbishop's House in Dublin and told Curran that Sinn Féin intended to firmly oppose conscription. Curran could not remember whether de Valera personally met Walsh on this occasion. However, the two men had a long conversation and the secretary realised how much de Valera feared the hierarchy's intervention in the crisis. His visitor believed that indecisiveness or passive resistance could seriously hinder effective opposition to the Government's intentions. Curran described in his memoirs how he took a most crucial decision. It is worth quoting a large extract:

> I did not mention to [de Valera] that evening the proposed general meeting of the bishops, since I did not know at that time whether the summons was issued or on what day the meeting was fixed for; but, learning later that night or next morning that the meeting was summoned and the date fixed, I began to form a plan in my own mind of linking up the action of the bishops with that of the political leaders. In our private conversations the Archbishop talked much about the crisis that was already upon us. He invariably revealed that two points constantly occupied his mind, firstly, the strong attitude and outspoken views of some normally moderate bishops and, secondly, how disturbed he was over the Cardinal's misgivings and by the fact that, at the general meeting of the bishops, the Cardinal might secure support from the more conservative elements of that body. Seeing that de Valera's acute anxiety that the bishops should not bar or attenuate strong action coincided precisely with the Archbishop's anxiety over Cardinal Logue, I resolved to tell de Valera of the meeting and its purpose, of the strong attitude of the bishops of the Standing Committee and of the possible existence of a less courageous section among the general body who might be disposed to modify or tone down the strong action that would be undoubtedly advocated by the more stalwart. I, therefore, determined to propose to him that the political leaders should meet at once, formulate their strong policy, inform the bishops and ask them to give their adhesion. The bishops would thus be relieved, I thought, of the initiative and would find it easier to follow on in support of the laymen.
>
> (NLD, O'Kelly papers, MS 27728(1),
> Curran's memoirs, p. 254)

Thus, the shrewd Curran realised that the bishops did not want to be compromised politically. Logue was the best example of this, but Walsh also appeared not to know what to do or was quite hesitant in the whole matter. Curran decided not to inform the Archbishop for the time being. The two men agreed that Miss Gavan Duffy, the daughter of the lawyer who had defended Sir Roger Casement during his trial, would act as intermediary between Curran and de Valera. On 13 April, Cardinal Logue, knowing that priests would be included in the new Military Service Bill and that the country would soon be in an anarchical turmoil, decided to call all the bishops for an extraordinary meeting. He sent Walsh the following telegram: 'I find whole country expects general action by bishops. I am calling general meeting at Maynooth Thursday 18th at noon.'[39] Logue was right. Whether the Government still intended to conscript priests or not no longer mattered. He knew that the people were waiting for the hierarchy to undertake some action after its declaration of 9 April. The spirit of rebellion had taken hold of the country and Logue was morally obliged to intervene. The problem was how? On 14 April, Fr Joseph Brady from Armagh took the initiative to organise a series of meetings against conscription. He asked the people to formally reject the new manpower law by signing a petition which, ironically, resembled Sir Edward Carson's anti-Home Rule 'Solemn League and Covenant'.[40] However, contrary to Carson's initiative, Brady did not ask the Irish to take up arms because Logue had sent a message of support to the meeting, in which he stated: 'There is nothing for it but passive resistance to it in every shape and form.'[41]

Walsh and de Valera's fears were now justified as Logue had revealed his vague approach. On the same day, Bishop Foley of Kildare and Leighlin severely denounced the Government and considered that it had been largely responsible for Ireland's depopulation. According to him, conscription was useless as the end of the war was near and that it would take too long to train new soldiers. His argument was certainly logical. Foley insisted that all the Irish had to unite in this crisis. This was also stressed by Bishop Naughton of Killala. As for Fogarty and Hallinan, they did not seem to exclude violence. The Bishop of Killaloe referred to the Penal Laws and wrote: '...the people are, therefore, entitled to resist it. What form that resistance is to take in order to be effective is for the nation in its wisdom to decide.'[42] Bishop Cohalan was in a nationalist mood. In a letter published by the *Freeman's Journal*, he referred to the Penal Laws, the Famine of 1845–1849, the Land War of the 1880s, the Army's mutiny in the Curragh against Home Rule, Carson and Campbell's entry into the coalition cabinet, the hypocrisy of the war in favour of small nations and eventually the secret Anglo-Italian treaty that excluded the Pope from the future peace conference.[43] On 14 April, he sent a circular letter to all the churches in his diocese in which he expressed the idea that the Government had no right to impose conscription 'against the will of our nation'.[44] It is to be noted here that Cohalan and Fogarty had used the word 'nation', implying that Britain had no right to rule for Ireland. Archbishop Harty wrote to Mgr Hagan in Rome: 'I have never known the country to be in such a determined state of opposition. The Government is simply gone mad.'[45] If there was a real desire for unity between all nationalists and the Catholic Church, how could it be achieved?

Curran was fully aware of the complexity of the situation. On 14 April, he met the new Lord Mayor of Dublin, the very nationalist minded Larry O'Neill. O'Neill had announced on 8 April that a meeting of all nationalists should be convened rapidly in order to formulate a coherent opposition to conscription. Curran informed the Mayor about his discussion with de Valera and insisted that O'Neill go ahead immediately with his planned meeting. The Lord Mayor, however, feared that de Valera might be arrested and that John Dillon and Joseph Devlin, who were debating in the House of Commons in London, would not be able to reach Dublin in time. All Curran could do was to try and persuade him 'that no time must be lost and that the laymen should set the deadline for action'.[46] He was of the opinion that the hierarchy would follow a concerted and vigorous action undertaken by the political leaders, and that an isolated intervention of the bishops would probably not be appropriate. O'Neill's hesitations could have proved fatal for the situation was quickly deteriorating in the country. On 13 April, Irish Volunteers attacked a RIC barracks in Co. Kerry and two men were killed.[47] In Cork, things were going from bad to worse. Liam Deasy, a Volunteer leader, organised 'the collection of shotguns and ammunition from friendly neighbours, and led a party to seize them from those who were unwilling to offer them voluntarily.'[48] Deasy also noticed that 'political differences were temporarily submerged in face of the common danger' and that young and old, pro-Redmond and anti-Redmond nationalists 'flocked to the ranks of the Volunteers'. On 14 April, Bishop Brownrigg of Kilkenny sent a letter to an anti-conscription meeting in which he appealed to the people and the young clergy not to fight and remain calm.[49]

On 16 April, Westminster Parliament voted in favour of the Compulsory Military Service Bill for Ireland, but the clergy was exempted. It was a poor attempt to dissociate the Church from the people. It was at that time that Archbishop Walsh decided to intervene publicly. The widespread civil war which he had dreaded since the creation of the Irish Volunteers in 1913, was looming. Only the Church could prevent it, by siding with the people and trying to calm down its passions without, at the same time, discouraging its determination against conscription. Walsh knew that above all Logue's influence had to be neutralised. He wrote a letter to the people, published by the *Freeman's Journal*, in which he demonstrated his superb tactical skills. The Archbishop insisted on two points. Firstly, he wholeheartedly agreed with the people that conscription should be opposed but asked if they had been instructed what to do if the Government carried out its plans. This remark was meant to dismiss the Cardinal's vague idea of passive resistance. Secondly, he asked the Irish people to think very carefully about Lloyd George's new dual policy approach:

> I hope that I am not mistaken in taking for granted that when any Irish Nationalist seems to regard with favour this coupling of the Conscription Bill with Home Rule, he must have in contemplation, not a Home Rule Bill that may have been merely introduced into the Imperial Parliament, and that may never become law, but a Home Rule that has been actually passed into law and has moreover brought into existence an Irish Parliament, and that the only Conscription Bill he contemplates is one framed by that Parliament and passed by it into law.
>
> (*The Freeman's Journal*, 17 April 1918)

Walsh had openly expressed his radical views and was now closer to Fogarty, Hallinan and Cohalan. In doing so, he forced Logue and other conservative and cautious bishops to find a new definition of passive resistance lest they split the hierarchy in two opposite camps and render opposition to conscription less effective. British authorities in Ireland began to seriously worry about the latest political developments. General Mahon informed Lord French, the country's new Viceroy, that insurrection was unavoidable if the Government persisted in its plans. According to him, the Catholic Church could have a negative influence on the loyalty of the RIC and, consequently, he demanded 12,000 extra troops with artillery and even the Air Force. Lord French obliged but remarked that the Scottish command would be totally deprived of its mobile troops and that the defence of the northern coast would be seriously weakened.[50]

And so it was that for the sake of thousands of unwilling Irish conscripts, the Government decided to weaken its defence in the middle of a powerful German offensive in France. Apart from Lord French who adopted a diehard attitude in the conscription crisis, the cabinet must have known the extent of the disaster it had produced in Ireland by 17 April. Curran remarked that the country was being occupied militarily and that Dublin city centre and the railway stations were guarded by soldiers and, apparently, Ghurkas and Bengal Lancers had left for Mullingar or Tullamore. He stated that people talked about 'tanks, poison gas and other frightening eventualities'.[51] Curran wrote about rumours but could not have known that there was some truth in them. Indeed, on 18 April, Lord French sent a report to David Lloyd George regarding his plans to discipline the Irish and force them to accept conscription. The Viceroy believed that the Church was largely responsible for the present situation, and that the press had to be muzzled. As for the enforcement of conscription, French was quite optimistic. He assured the Prime Minister that 37,000 British soldiers based in Ireland could do a good job with the support of the Royal Air Force which could 'play about with either bombs or machine guns . . . and ought to put the fear of God into these playful young Sinn Féiners'![52] Lloyd George realised that shooting young men into conscription was self-defeating and never authorised Lord French to go ahead with his strategy. This was probably his most lucid intervention in the cauldron of Irish politics.

Larry O'Neill, at last persuaded by Curran's arguments, had officially invited all nationalists, and also unionists who declined the invitation, to come to Dublin on 18 April and formulate their policy against conscription. Their meeting would coincide with the hierarchy's, in Maynooth. The day before, however, the Lord Mayor had met Walsh in order to go over certain details. He did not tell the Archbishop that he already knew an exceptional meeting of the bishops was due to take place on the same day. The two men elaborated the following plan. O'Neill would phone Maynooth from the Mansion House and warn the hierarchy that a delegation of nationalist politicians intended to consult the bishops, and Walsh's role would be kept secret.[53] The Archbishop's House became a centre for plotters as, on Thursday morning 18 April, de Valera also called on Walsh to ask him if he had any questions for him and to beg, once more, the bishops not to say anything 'that would hinder those who were prepared to defend themselves with arms to the last'.[54] Walsh told Curran that it was 'safer not to see him' and the secretary alone spoke to the republican leader. By now, the Archbishop was fully aware of Sinn Féin's determination. Responsibility rested on him to avoid war against the British Army and between nationalists and unionists. Unity had to be achieved at all costs to prevent a certain bloodbath.

THE EPISCOPAL MEETING OF 18 APRIL 1918

On Thursday morning 18 April, all the main nationalist leaders met at the Mansion House in Dublin: Eamon de Valera and Arthur Griffith represented Sinn Féin; John Dillon and Joseph Devlin made it in time from London and represented the Nationalist party; William O'Brien and T.M. Healy were independent nationalists; E. Egan, Thomas Johnson from Belfast, and William O'Brien represented the Irish Labour party. Very rapidly, de Valera took control of the discussion. According to O'Brien, the independent nationalist, the Sinn Féin president was obstinate in his ideas to oppose conscription but managed to convince the others by his kindness and sincerity and kept repeating: 'You will bear with me, won't you? You know I am an old schoolmaster.'[55] The delegates were able to bear with him since they adopted a declaration that incorporated much Sinn Féin ideology although this must have been very difficult for Dillon to swallow. He had become 'the leader of a lost cause',[56] and the meeting had all the hallmarks of a handing over of power to Sinn Féin.

The declaration stated that Ireland and Britain were two distinct nations and that the British Government was 'an external authority', which had no right 'to impose compulsory military service in Ireland against the clearly expressed will of the Irish people'. It also said that the British House of Commons' decision '[had to] be regarded as a declaration of war on the Irish nation'. This was a clear violation of the rights and independence of small nations for which, according to the main belligerent powers, the present war was fought. The statement concluded: 'The attempt to enforce [conscription] will be an unwarrantable aggression, which we call upon all Irishmen to resist by the most effective means at their disposal.'[57] This last sentence had been cleverly phrased for it did not necessarily refer to armed resistance, which the bishops would have rejected out of hand, but it was still possible to interpret it in various ways. Both Sinn Féin and the Catholic Church could thus be satisfied. Now the moment had come to put Curran's plan into operation. Eamon de Valera surprised all the delegates at Mansion House when he suggested going to Maynooth and meeting the bishops. Apart from Larry O'Neill who had phoned Maynooth in the meantime to warn the bishops of their imminent arrival, the leaders were somewhat taken aback by this suggestion. T.M. Healy remembered this instant:

> To [de Valera] belongs the credit of proposing that the Conference should send a deputation to Maynooth, where the Irish bishops were sitting. When this was agreed to, the problem arose as to who should go. On my name being suggested, I demurred, saying I was unaccustomed to meeting bishops and archbishops. 'Oh', said de Valera, 'there's nothing in that. I have lived all my life among priests'. I asked, 'Have you lived all your life among bishops?'
>
> (Healy, *Letters and Leaders of My Day*, vol. II, p. 595)

The deputation, composed of Eamon de Valera, John Dillon, T.M. Healy, Larry O'Neill and the Labour leader, William O'Brien arrived at Maynooth at noon. Healy told one of the bishops: 'Here we are, my Lord, the lion and the lamb'. To which the bishop smartly replied: 'Oh yes, but which is which?'[58] The hierarchy received the deputation after lunch, at 2 p.m., and discussions began immediately. According to Curran, all participants were in complete agreement. Healy was especially impressed by Walsh, who was very confident, and also by Fogarty, in other words the radical bishops. The Archbishop of Dublin must have been very shrewd and diplomatic to convince the Cardinal and the hierarchy not to contradict popular will. The confrontation between Logue and de Valera was not long in coming. The Sinn Féin president was of the opinion that passive resistance would be of no use since the Irish Volunteers would fight if conscription were implemented. According to him, it was therefore necessary to avoid mentioning it in the hierarchy's future declaration. Logue, who must have made superhuman efforts to bear de Valera's presence, replied drily: 'Well now, Mr de Valera, when I talk about passive resistance, I don't mean we are to lie down and let people walk over us.'[59] Fogarty asked de Valera if the deputation would object to the hierarchy mentioning in its declaration 'according to the moral law'. De Valera answered that he understood this theological expression but believed the people could misinterpret it.[60]

The bishops left the politicians to deliberate. Not much is known about this deliberation since it took place behind closed doors. However, Curran's memoirs give some valuable information. Walsh did manage to convince Logue and other conservative bishops that the episcopal declaration had to correspond to the one of the Mansion House leaders:

> I remember vividly the elation of the Archbishop of Dublin that evening on his return. He related to me every incident of the day and took a certain amount of malicious pleasure in picturing the discomfiture of the Cardinal, how he was led from point to point before he realised it. He had first advocated 'passive resistance' but the Archbishop of Dublin and others made short work of his passive resistance, for nobody could define what passive resistance meant, and passive resistance was the only panacea of the Cardinal.
>
> (NLD, O'Kelly papers, MS 27728(1),
> Curran's memoirs, p. 263)

The confrontation between Logue and Walsh, two men who represented two distinct nationalist currents, had turned to the Archbishop of Dublin's advantage. Thus, the hierarchy accepted the moral-political leadership of nationalist Ireland and would follow or lead the people in their opposition to conscription.

Suddenly, the chances of a full scale conflict between the British Army and nationalists became more remote as the bishops and political leaders' decision to assume the defence of the country together, channelled the people and the Volunteers' will and determination. It would give them precise orders, coming from a central political-ecclesiastical command, just as Walsh had wished in his letter of 17 April. For the first time since August 1914, the war had united the Church. It became now practically impossible for David Lloyd George and Lord French to impose conscription on Ireland. Undeniably, if his memoirs are objective enough, Curran had played a most crucial role in this crisis. What worried Logue considerably, was that the hierarchy had been forced to recognise the emergence of a new political force, Sinn Féin. The sole fact that de Valera had been received in Maynooth showed the people that the Church had accepted that he and his party were 'respectable'. On 18 April 1918, Sinn Féin's policy of playing the Catholic card had been crowned with success. At 4.30 p.m., the hierarchy finished deliberating and presented its declaration, signed by twenty-seven bishops:

> An attempt is being made to force conscription upon Ireland against the will of the Irish nation and in defiance of the protest of its leaders. In view especially of the historic relations between the two countries from the very beginning up to the present moment, we consider that conscription forced in this way upon Ireland is an oppressive and inhuman law, which the Irish people have a right to resist by all the means that are consonant with the law of God.
>
> (ACA, O'Donnell papers, 'Ireland's Solemn League and Covenant', April 1918)

This extract of the episcopal declaration sums up Walsh's triumph and Logue's defeat. The term 'nation' implied that Ireland was no longer part of the United Kingdom, and 'historic relations' was a reminder of Ireland's tragic history since the two countries had become involved with one another. The Empire, Logue's favourite theme, was not even mentioned. The idea of passive resistance was replaced with 'to resist by all the means that are consonant with the law of God'. This did not exclude armed resistance since the bishops had declared that conscription was 'oppressive and inhuman', and that the Government that wanted to impose it was not Irish. Consequently, armed resistance could be envisaged if all peaceful and political means had failed to stop the British authorities. The hierarchy had also given instructions to the clergy. Firstly, a mass of intercession to avoid conscription would be celebrated on Sunday 21 April in every church in the country. Secondly, on the same day, the clergy were to collect funds outside the churches that would be used against conscription. Thirdly, still on 21 April, the clergy would organise the signing of a petition against compulsory military service, stating: 'Denying the right of the British Government to enforce compulsory service in this country, we pledge ourselves solemnly to one another to resist conscription by the most effective means at our disposal.'[61] De Valera could not have hoped for better.

After the episcopal meeting in Maynooth, Michael Logue and William Walsh were waiting for their respective cars. The Cardinal was bitterly disappointed and told the Archbishop: 'I think this is the worst day's business the bishops ever did.' A cheerful Walsh did not agree and thought the meetings had gone rather well. The Cardinal was adamant and simply repeated: 'I fear this is the worst day's business the bishops ever did.'[62] Logue knew he had lost the day. He felt powerless and had at long last accepted the fact that he was living in a changing Ireland whose destiny he could not alter. But, as will be seen, the shrewd Cardinal had not said his final word yet. However, on 18 April 1918, Walsh and de Valera were the great victors and had every reason to be pleased. But for how long?

OPPOSITION TO CONSCRIPTION

The alliance between the hierarchy and the nationalist leaders was sensational and the tense situation seemed to ease. Richard Mulcahy believed that the Maynooth meeting had given more precise objectives to the Volunteers and thought it had a function of authority.[63] The Inspector General of the RIC was of the opinion that the alliance between the political leaders and the bishops probably prevented large-scale violence.[64] On 19 April, the *Irish Independent* ran as a headline: 'Momentous Irish Conferences'. The newspaper gave a detailed account of the previous day. Apparently, de Valera and Griffith had been the most acclaimed leaders in Dublin. The seminarians had also given the lay deputation a warm welcome in Maynooth. Lord French, on the other hand, had not been so warmly welcomed in the Irish capital. He had just arrived from England to take over command from General Mahon and supervise the implementation of conscription. Six hundred young Dubliners went to the Shelbourne Hotel where the new Viceroy was staying and shouted vociferously: 'No conscription!'[65] No further trouble broke out. Mgr Curran wrote sarcastically that the unionist *Irish Times* must have been 'nonplussed' for it had not published any important article on conscription but had given a complete summary of the meetings in Dublin and Maynooth.[66] De Valera and Healy went to the Archbishop's House to discuss the functioning of the anti-conscription fund with Walsh. The three men agreed to appoint Larry

O'Neill and Walsh himself as trustees of the fund.[67] It became known as the Irish National Defence Fund of which a branch had to be established in every parish and managed by the local clergy.[68] On 1 May, the *Irish Independent* mentioned that already between £100,000 and £150,000 had been collected in Ireland and that this figure would probably increase. The newspaper was right since on 30 August, the amount of money was more than £250,000.[69] The clergy were also involved in the Parish Defence Committees. On 1 June, the national committee of the Irish Volunteers sent a circular letter to the bishops, informing them of the latest developments in defence against conscription. The Volunteer leadership had decided that the fight against compulsory military service should be centred 'round the church in every parish'. The Volunteers should collaborate with the Parish Defence Committees and the priests. The idea behind this, according to the Inspector General of the Volunteers, was to help the committees in collecting funds, stocking supplies of food and conveying instructions regarding defence.[70]

Sunday 21 April 1918 was an extraordinary day. There was a very palpable fevered atmosphere. In all the parishes, people were signing the petition against conscription and priests and bishops were involved in the operation. In Dublin, it was estimated that 150,000 Irishmen had signed. According to the *Freeman's Journal*, it had been impossible to organise public meetings in some parish halls for there was not enough space, and the petition was thus signed in several locations within the same parish.[71] Even some Protestants supported the anti-conscription campaign despite the fact that the Anglican Archbishops of Dublin and Armagh had agreed with the Compulsory Military Service Bill.[72] Curran expressed far less sympathy for the Protestants' point of view. He wrote: 'A few Protestants here and there also took the pledge but the vast majority held aloof while prepared gladly to avail of the protection of their Catholic fellow-countrymen.'[73] It is difficult to know to what extent Curran was right. However, this alliance of the Catholic Church and nationalist parties proved to Protestants that an independent Ireland could be achieved without them and that their ecclesiastical role was or would not be that important, in the south of the country at least.

According to Walsh's secretary, the day passed without any particular incident. There were no flags, no parades and no mob hysteria only an 'unmistakable deep tense determination to fight conscription and Britain to the end'.[74] People were handed leaflets against conscription which stressed the ghoulish fate of those Irish soldiers who had made the mistake of enlisting. On one of them, Irishmen could read de Valera's own words on the matter: 'Their bones bleach upon the soil of Flanders, or moulder beneath the waves of Sulva Bay.'[75] But, what Curran wrote about Dublin was not always valid for the rest of the country. In Co.

Donegal, the pupils of Saint Eunan's school in Letterkenny paraded together with 500 Sinn Féiners and the band of the Ancient Order of Hibernians.[76] Elsewhere, it seemed that miraculous apparitions were at work. In Aughrin in Co. Galway, the Holy Virgin appeared, while in Kiltrustan in Co. Roscommon, a black pig was sighted, generally considered a bad omen by the rural population. 'Sinn Féin patriots were being reinforced by voices from heaven.'[77] The bishops were particularly active on that day as some of them went for the first time to the meetings. Among them were Archbishop Harty and Bishop Kelly who had both been involved in the first French mission. Times had changed and Walsh had been right when he had said that some prelates had suddenly been overcome with revolutionary sentiments. They now believed that they had been duped by the Government after the Irish Convention, and that if the Church wanted to retain some power in the future, they would have to swim with the new nationalist tide. During mass, Harty criticised the hypocritical attitude of the main powers towards small nations. In the afternoon, he went to the anti-conscription meeting and made a warlike speech. He believed that nobody could force the Irish nation to accept compulsory military service and that it had the right to decide freely about its own taxation system. This was an allusion to the recent debates in the Convention. He concluded with an extremely patriotic appeal, containing definite revolutionary overtones:

> I proclaim here that the Act of Conscription is unjust, hypocritical, and I shall now proceed to the Confraternity Hall to sign the protest against it. Every man with a drop of Irish blood in his veins should do so. We shall march to victory and shall plant the flag of Ireland in an impregnable position, proudly floating over this free nation.
>
> (*The Freeman's Journal*, 22 April 1918)

Harty's words seemed to announce the end of the United Kingdom. Bishops Finegan, Fogarty, O'Donnell, Gilmartin, Foley and even O'Dea who had disagreed with O'Dwyer's anti-war crusade in 1915, also used the term 'nation' for Ireland.[78] David Lloyd George's conscription law had provoked strong separatist feelings among the Irish, and this mixture of radical and conservative bishops was a case in point. It was Fr Arthur Ryan from Tipperary, once a great supporter of John Redmond and his pro-war policy, who best defined the country's frame of mind: 'This pledge we take to-day in every parish in Ireland will ring like the tocsin of freedom through the coming centuries.'[79] Bishop Gilmartin, who in 1917 had tried to dissuade his parishioners from going to a Sinn Féin meeting in which de Valera was to speak, said: 'Ireland is a distinct nation from England geographically, economically, and socially distinct... But the Union, such as it was, was a political Union which the Catholic people of Ireland had no power to resist.'[80] The conscription threat had initiated an unheard of nationalist opposition and *raison d'être*, but also a smooth revolution within the hierarchy. If at first the bishops had mainly wanted to avoid a bloodbath, they had now become the people's main allies in the crisis, either because they were genuinely convinced that conscription was wrong, or because they could not run the risk of losing all control over their young clergy and the people. In fact, the crisis allowed them to draw closer to the priests and the Catholic people.

However, the rejection of conscription also meant the rejection of Westminster Parliament's authority. The whole Church was suddenly on a path that seemed to take it further than Home Rule. The nationalist press in favour of Sinn Féin, had perfectly understood this turn of events. On 27 April, *New Ireland* stated: 'There was never a time when the hierarchy and the people were so closely united upon any question of Irish statesmanship.' *Nationality* went even further and played the Catholic card once more: 'The Catholic hierarchy of Ireland has been true to its great mission... and its action in ranging itself in the van of the nation ensures that between religion and patriotism no conflict will ever occur in Ireland.'[81] In fact, *Nationality* confirmed that Eamon de Valera's words, pronounced in Tipperary town on the occasion on Bishop O'Dwyer's death in August 1917, had been vindicated. The alliance of the Catholic Church with the people had produced a new nationalism, no longer constitutional, but popular, religious and almost revolutionary. This nationalism seemed to leave little room for Protestants. But most of the Protestant Churches, like the Presbyterians in Ulster, favoured conscription. The war had opposed Catholicism and Protestantism and opened up an unbridgeable chasm between them.

During the months of April and May 1918, all the bishops made declarations that stressed the importance of unity. All agreed that the Irish, especially the younger generation, had to remain calm. Bishop Hoare hoped that 'young men would be led by the old men'.[82] They had to follow the united leaders in their opposition to conscription. The best example was given by Eamon de Valera and John Dillon when they stood together on a platform at a meeting in Ballaghadereen to denounce the British Government. Bishop Morrisroe, previously described as being ultra-conservative by Curran, paid tribute to Cardinal Logue and the Lord Mayor of Dublin's initiatives on 18 April. Obviously, Morrisroe was not au fait with Walsh's role. The Bishop of Achonry seized the opportunity to criticise seven hundred years of British rule in Ireland and called the unionists 'the pampered minority' who had trampled upon democracy and Home Rule, and described them as being 'the foreign garrison in our midst'.[83] His statement was harsh but had the merit of accurately reflecting nationalist Ireland's frame of mind. The conscription crisis had engendered a certain degree of sectarianism, and it was also clear that it had been building up since August 1914. The military intelligence officer of the Southern District had noticed the intransigent behaviour of those opposed to conscription not only towards the police but also towards everybody who did not share their views:

> Some very strong speeches have already been made, and threats made by priests, especially against the Police ... Nobody publicly supports the conscription proposal, as the scattered loyalists, whilst ready to submit to it themselves, can hardly be expected to make themselves unpopular by advocating it publicly. Father Maguire, P.P. of Flagmount near Lough Graney, Co. Clare, was rash enough to denounce the signing of the Anti-Conscription Covenant, on 21st April, so an attempt, fortunately unsuccessful, was made to burn his church three days later.
>
> (PRO, London, CO904/157, Southern District intelligence report, 30 April 1918, p. 41)

His colleague from the Northern District also wrote about religious intolerance caused by the conscription crisis:

> The appearance of the Roman Catholic Church in the question has given the matter a sectarian aspect, in Belfast, at least, there are symptoms of a revival of the old religious animosities. Some Roman Catholics are in favour of conscription but they are chiefly women or old men whose sons are serving or have served; they are swamped by those opposed to it, but in the main at present the question is being discussed on religious lines.
>
> (PRO, London, CO904/157, Northern District intelligence report, 4 May 1918, p. 34)

The Home Rule and partition crises and the War Office's Irish policy had succeeded in instilling a revanchist spirit in Irish nationalists that found expression in sectarianism and intolerance. Fr Hore, member of a Parish Defence Committee in Wexford, reminded his parishioners of all the blunders of the War Office.[84] David Lloyd George knew he had lost his battle to impose the Military Service Bill by 23 April, the day a general strike took place against conscription. Only Ulster, not surprisingly, did not participate. The Irish showed their determination to go to the bitter end if necessary. The Prime Minister admitted that only the immediate implementation of Home Rule might allow conscription to happen. Arthur Balfour, once Irish Secretary, agreed and was of the opinion that it would be 'a greater weakness to do something in Ireland than to do nothing'.[85] Lord Wimborne, who was about to resign, wrote to Lloyd George that to turn 'the British Army under one of its most distinguished Commanders into a coercive press gang [would] be, at best, a sorry spectacle for our allies'.[86] He was undeniably right.

On 9 May, the war cabinet gathered in London to discuss the Irish situation. All the ministers present had different opinions but all agreed that if one wanted to implement conscription or Home Rule in Ireland, the authority of Westminster Parliament had to be restored. Lloyd George no longer wanted to conscript the Irish but Sir Walter Long believed that all Sinn Féin members who were plotting with the Germans had to be arrested at once. According to him, the arrests would separate the Catholic Church and the Nationalist party from Sinn Féin. It was a classic divide and rule policy, thought up by somebody who had no notion of Ireland's long history of martyrs for the cause of liberty. Long put forward the idea that Lord French should issue a proclamation, justifying the arrests and announcing the end of conscription provided that recruitment figures improved.[87] At first, it seemed a clever manoeuvre of the Government for it ended conscription by giving a last chance to the Irish to participate voluntarily in the war effort. In fact, it looked more like a face-saving operation as Lloyd George was informed that, at long last, the first American soldiers had begun fighting on 1 May 1918. If the front stabilised and the Germans were repulsed, conscription in Ireland could be quietly shelved.

On 17 May, more than eighty Sinn Féin members were arrested. Eamon de Valera, Arthur Griffith and Countess Markievicz were among them.[88] The next day, the *Freeman's Journal* published Lord French's proclamation under the headline 'Government strikes'.[89] The Government, however, was seriously wrong if it had hoped to destroy Sinn Féin and create a division among the nationalist camp. The arrests were utterly counterproductive as the nationalist population was not persuaded of the Sinn Féiners' culpability. Many Irish believed that it was an attempt to muzzle a party that was telling the truth. As could have been expected, it made de Valera and others martyrs. This rather farcical episode became known as 'the German plot'. Diverse personalities like de Valera, Lord Wimborne and even General Mahon believed that the arrests were absolutely unjustified.[90]

As expected the Church reacted in favour of the prisoners. Mgr Curran wrote to Mgr O'Riordan in Rome 'that there [was] not a little of evidence against De V., Griffith, Darrell Figgis and such people...and the proclamation [was] primarily intended for foreign assumption'.[91] Bishop Fogarty believed 'the German plot' to be 'an insult to human intelligence' and, not unreasonably, feared that young people would now be very difficult to control since their leaders were in prison.[92] Bishop Hallinan said that it was rather a 'British plot'.[93] Such reactions from radical bishops were hardly surprising, but even someone like Archbishop Harty did not mince his words. Harty had received Eoin MacNeill in Thurles, and took the opportunity to compliment the professor on his work on the Irish language and said that he was one of the leaders who represented united Ireland in her fight against 'tyranny and inhumanity'. Concerning de Valera and Griffith who were now in English jails, he affirmed that 'those men had been deported because of a supposed German plot, which plot Lord Wimborne said he was unaware of until the British Government discovered it'. Lloyd George's divisive policy had failed. As for Lord French, he had made it his objective to recruit no less than 50,000 Irishmen before 1 October. The Viceroy was evidently suffering from a bout of excessive optimism, although 9,845 men joined up between August and November 1918.[94] It was an unsuccessful attempt but it did not matter since the German Army was retreating at that stage of the war. Conscription had been a real disaster for the British. Mgr Curran gave a rather objective and humorous account of the crisis in his memoirs:

> Our *resorgimento* was indeed already well ablaze but conscription fanned the torch into an all-consuming conflagration that instantaneously swept all over the country...It would be a platitude to say that conscription was not merely a crime but a blunder...The climax of British folly and blindness was the attempt to conscript the Irish clergy. One thousand Irish clerics would count mighty little against even one cohort of the Kaiser's legions. But this most stupid of all steps inevitably drove the most conservative of conservative Irish bishops to share the leadership of opposition with Sinn Féin...In those ten days Lloyd George brought down the so-called 'constitutional' movement represented by the Irish Party which Tories, Unionists and Orangemen had failed to do in ten decades.
>
> (NLD, O'Kelly papers, MS 27728(1),
> Curran's memoirs, pp. 272–5)

Curran had written the truth. There was no longer any moderate nationalist force in Ireland. Westminster Parliament's authority had been questioned and the Catholic Church had played a central role in this questioning. As David George Boyce succinctly writes about the situation in 1918: 'It is, perhaps, both ironic and appropriate that the Union should have been the creation of one great and desperate conflict [the Napoleonic wars], and the casualty of another.'[95] It remained to be seen whether the nationalist alliance between the Church, Sinn Féin and the Nationalist party was as solid as it appeared.

THE HIERARCHY UNDER ATTACK

The hierarchy's position in the conscription crisis had put the Church in the limelight, and the British and unionist press, including certain politicians, were at daggers drawn with the clergy. Some English and Scottish dailies accused the Irish bishops of sapping the war effort at a very critical time. Others believed that the intrigue-ridden world of the Vatican had orchestrated the whole anti-conscription campaign. *The Times* spoke about 'the Roman hierarchy', implying that the Irish bishops took their orders from the Holy See and were, therefore, not really representing the interests of their own nation but rather of a foreign power. The conservative newspaper went as far to accuse the bishops of having 'shaken to its foundations the whole edifice of religious tolerance in these islands'.[96] If it was true that there had been an outburst of sectarianism in Ireland, it was, however, quite exaggerated to speak of 'religious tolerance' when the 36th Ulster Division, for instance, continued to operate a sectarian recruitment policy with impunity. It would have been more accurate to speak about a fragile truce between Catholics and Protestants during the continuation of the war. The nationalist press defended the bishops. The *Irish Independent* immediately replied that *The Times* had approved the Ulster Covenant against Home Rule in 1912, signed by unionists and Protestants. But, *The Times* pursued its journalistic offensive against the hierarchy and, on 24 April, it published a vehement letter of a Bart Kennedy, entitled in French 'Voilà l'ennemi' (there is the enemy). The author, himself a Catholic, claimed that the mass celebrated on Sunday 21 April was not valid and resented the signing of the petition against conscription. Kennedy stated: 'Berlin was behind this mass. It was celebrated for the purpose of helping the Hun and to crush and enslave mankind...The Vatican was behind the defeat of Italy. The Vatican is working with the Hun...It is betraying Irishmen to eternal shame and dishonour so as to help Germany.'[97]

The *Morning Post* was of the opinion that the bishops and priests were giving Germany a great opportunity to win the war and wondered whether the Irish hierarchy was instructed by the Vatican in the present crisis. The *Daily Express* wrote: 'The priest is always out of place in politics.'[98] The *Observer* spoke about the 'intolerable pretensions' and the 'secret anti-ally bias' of the bishops, and declared that it had to be faced 'by the whole power of the State and [had to] be beaten'.[99] In brief, the Church was described as a seditious force and Mgr Curran wrote in his memoirs 'that a rabid anti-Catholic (No-Popery) campaign

231

began in the English press'.[100] The problem for the *Observer* though was that there was no unity of opinion in Britain concerning conscription in Ireland. Herbert Asquith, for instance, had wisely voted against the Military Service Bill. The *Star* awarded *The Times* 'the palm for hypocrisy' and reminded its readers of the position the conservative newspaper had adopted during the Ulster Covenant signing in 1912.[101] The *Daily Chronicle* deplored the delay in implementing Home Rule and paid tribute to the Irish hierarchy's intervention as it had avoided an armed struggle. It also believed that Cardinal Logue and the bishops had been unjustly criticised in Britain.[102] The *Catholic Herald* denounced 'the blood tax which Orange Freemasons and Unionist Huns [were] about to impose'.[103] The *Glasgow Herald* criticised the Vatican's attitude towards the Allies since the beginning of the hostilities in Europe.[104] But, the *Glasgow Observer* defended the Pope and attacked the anti-papal campaign in the country.[105] It appeared that a fraction of British public opinion supported the Irish in their opposition to the Government's plan, and also in their quest for Home Rule. On 29 April, Logue told the *Manchester Guardian* that the bishops had received no orders from the Vatican.[106]

Dr MacRory was struck by a nationalist élan and said that those same newspapers that had acclaimed the Belgian Cardinal Mercier in his heroic stand against the Germans, were now criticising Cardinal Logue's stand against a tyranny that was ten times worse. He believed that the press should bear in mind that Britain's Allies were mainly Catholic countries and that many American soldiers were of Irish descent. The Bishop of Down and Connor felt 'that the best service the Censor could do to the Empire would be to suppress all such senseless effusions of religious bigotry'.[107] MacRory implied that the no-popery campaign could have bad repercussions on the Allied war effort and, as will be seen, it was not an empty threat. It was extremely unlikely that the Irish hierarchy's intervention would have had some impact on the soldiers of republican France but, nonetheless, the Irish crisis preoccupied the French press as it could destabilise Britain. *L'Opinion* affirmed that the Allied nations were genuinely concerned by nationalist Ireland's fight and believed that an Irish parliament should decide on conscription. *La Vérité* agreed. *Le Figaro*, *Le Temps* and *Le Journal des Débats*, however, did not understand the nationalists' position.[108]

On 30 April 1918, a meeting of the Catholic Union of Great Britain took place in which Lord Denbigh and Admiral Walter Kerr of the Royal Navy participated. This Union claimed to represent the aspirations and the interests of British Catholics and was outraged by the Irish bishops' intervention. The Union deemed that all peoples of the Empire should participate in its defence and that the clergy should not intervene in politics. It desired to 'dissociate itself from a movement which [could not] fail to hamper the full development of the military forces of the Allies, and thereby endanger the causes of humanity'.[109] But the Union went further and announced its intention to send a copy of its resolution against the hierarchy to Cardinal Pietro Gasparri, the Secretary of State of the Vatican, in order to inform the Pope. By doing so, the Union provoked a political crisis that would seriously backfire. Cardinal Logue immediately wrote a letter to Archbishop Walsh in which he vented his spleen. He accused the 'insolent attempt of the Council of the Catholic Union to use the Pope as an instrument for the coercion of the Irish Bishops' and denounced the fact that the Vatican had been excluded from the future peace conference, which the Union had failed to denounce.[110] According to the Cardinal, it was all hypocrisy. Like Walsh, Logue resented the fact that the Vatican had been approached to discipline the Irish hierarchy with 'spiritual arms'. Dr Fogarty said that the Union was composed of aristocrats who had never done anything for the Catholic religion.[111] Archbishop Harty sent a letter to a public meeting in Tipperary in which he stated that the Irish could not care less about all these attacks on the hierarchy and believed that everybody approved its intervention. He added: 'We are confident that history will see in our united efforts the true interpretation of the rights of nations, small and great, to determine their own destinies.'[112] But, above all, the Irish bishops received much support from the British hierarchy. On 3 May, Dr Amigo, the Bishop of Southwark in London, informed Walsh that he had sent a letter to Lord Denbigh in which he had stated that if thirty bishops supported the people against conscription, they must have had a valid reason. He wrote: 'We can do no good by irritating, but if we soothe down the discontent it will help us with neutrals; it will strengthen us with the United States, with Canada and Australia; it will prevent our enemies taunting us with insincerity in regard to small nationalities... Ulster has been allowed to do what Catholic Ireland claims to do now.'[113] Amigo told Walsh he '[felt] very much for Ireland in this crisis'. The English Bishop was sincere and warned David Lloyd George on 28 May: 'You are going to have disaster and we shall lose the war unless the Irish question is settled once and for all... The Irish character is altogether different from the English. Why not try to rule Ireland accordingly.'[114] Amigo was not guilty of scaremongering as the Irish conscription crisis had had some serious repercussions on the Empire, the United States and some Catholic countries (which will be discussed later). In May, eleven English and Scottish bishops openly declared their support for the Irish hierarchy.[115] The Prime Minister had succeeded in dividing British public opinion on the subject. Finally, the Vatican was obliged to intervene and settled the difference in the Irish bishops' favour. Gasparri informed the president of the Catholic Union that the Holy See would not be involved in the matter.[116] The Cardinal's decision was not surprising in the light of the secret Anglo-Italian treaty.

However, the British Government stubbornly persisted in its efforts to incite the Vatican to condemn the role of the clergy in the conscription crisis. Some priests had been noticed by the authorities for their harsh words against compulsory military service. In May 1918, the military intelligence officer of the Midlands and Connaught District had pointed out that the Catholic Church had become frankly anti-British and that it would have difficulty in dissociating itself from radical anti-conscription movements. He quoted the example of a priest who had allegedly declared that if the RIC helped the Government, they would be traitors to the Irish cause. He also mentioned that Bishop Gilmartin and other prelates believed that their clergy were going too far in their stand against conscription.[117] Arthur Balfour, the Foreign Secretary, passed on this information to Count de Salis, the new head of the British mission to the Vatican. In his report, Balfour included a list of twenty-six particularly seditious priests who were accused of instilling hatred against Protestants and RIC men, and also of advocating physical force against the authorities. De Salis sent the list to Gasparri and demanded that the Vatican take disciplinary action against them.[118]

The British were trying to devise a new divide and rule policy involving the Vatican, just as they had persuaded Leo XIII to intervene against the Plan of Campaign. Logue received a letter from Gasparri, informing him of de Salis' request, and was obliged to start an inquiry. If some priests were indeed guilty, others seemed to be completely innocent. In Co. Limerick, Fr Thomas Wall, who had been defended by Bishop O'Dwyer against General Maxwell in 1916, wrote to Mgr O'Riordan that his words had been taken out of context.[119] Bishop Fogarty was more precise. He told the rector of the Irish College that one of his priests was alleged to have said: 'Let every man, woman, boy and girl be ready to do something. Even a clasp knife can be used. They were used by Germany and other countries in the war when fighting at close quarters.' The priest in question had denied this statement and spoken of a 'grotesque travesty and misrepresentation of [his] remarks on that occasion'.[120] As for Logue, he informed O'Riordan that the priest was not even in his church the day he was supposed to have made heinous comments. The Cardinal concluded by saying: 'As you rightly conjectured, the reports are mere representations, from memory, of policemen. This proves the arrival of a practice against which I protested energetically to Mr. Balfour in Land League days, that of degrading Catholic policemen by sending them to churches in districts where there are no police to act as spies under the pretext of hearing mass.'[121]

O'Riordan prepared the defence of these twenty-six seditious priests and had frank discussions with two members of the Roman Curia. Cardinal Vanutelli told him that he was worried about the situation in

Ireland to which the rector replied that the Vatican should stay out of it for the Irish people had lost its trust in the Vatican since Leo XIII's intervention against the Plan of Campaign. O'Riordan told Archbishop Bonaventura Cerretti, the Under-Secretary of Extraordinary Ecclesiastical Affairs, that England and its press would use the Curia as a simple instrument and then discard it. He relayed the details of his meetings with Cerretti to Archbishop Walsh.[122] A few weeks later, in July 1918, he had an audience with Benedict XV who told him that he was very satisfied with the letter that the Irish hierarchy had sent him about the current difficulties and the infamous secret Anglo-Italian treaty. Afterwards, O'Riordan sent a letter to Bishop O'Donnell, saying that the hierarchy should no longer be worried about the whole matter.[123] The rector had once again successfully used his talents as a diplomat. On 9 July, Cardinal Gasparri simply informed Count de Salis that unfortunately some priests were not always cautious but that some of the accusations against them were probably unfounded as the words they were reported to have said, were directly against Catholic doctrine.[124] British diplomatic initiatives had met with a rebuff at the papal court. David Lloyd George had felt the weight of the Church during the crisis, and Protestants and unionists must have felt even more threatened by their possible inclusion in an independent state in which the Catholic Church would be prominent. However, the Primate of All Ireland began to wonder if the Church had not gone too far in its opposition to conscription.

The Cardinal knew that some of his clergy were now in favour of Sinn Féin, including some bishops. This list of twenty-six seditious priests had upset him as he was still supporting the Allies and the Empire, although his support was anything but active. Regularly and characteristically, he would advise the people to be on their guard against secret societies, which were infiltrated, according to him, by spies of the Government.[125] On 30 April, he felt compelled to declare to the *Manchester Guardian* that he continued to be opposed to Sinn Féin.[126] Perhaps even more revealing of his frame of mind was his letter to Bishop Amigo in which he expressed resentment at being accused of betraying the Empire. He wrote that the hierarchy did everything it could to avert violence but that he still feared 'a massacre'.[127] Bishop Foley was satisfied that Lord French was prepared to try voluntary recruitment and hoped that he would get 50,000 men, which would prevent conscription.[128] Bishop Gaughran, like Logue, also warned the people against secret societies.[129] Dr Gilmartin had circulated a letter among the priests of his diocese, forbidding them to mention conscription in churches. He definitely believed that the clergy had gone too far.[130] Their worries were understandable as Eamon de Valera had recently declared that 'if they had to actively oppose conscription, [it] would be the truest fight that would be fought on the globe at present', and even Bishop Fogarty had advised Irishmen that 'their duty was to prepare for the worst'.[131]

Logue was fully aware that the Church's involvement had stirred up anti-Catholic feelings in Ulster and that partition was now a very likely possibility. The Protestant Primate of All Ireland rebuked the 'No Popery Cry' in the country and expressed his support for Logue: 'My interests – like those of the venerable Cardinal Logue, whose friendship I greatly value – are wrapped up in 'all Ireland' from Cape Clear to the Giant's Causeway.'[132] The unionist *Evening Telegraph* regretted the Primate's words and his desire to see the Nationalist party succeeding in avoiding partition and finding a political solution acceptable to all.[133] It appeared that the Protestant Archbishop feared a division between southern and northern unionists and that partition would become ineluctable if Sinn Féin took power in the South where the Anglicans would be in a minority. But, the Primate did not speak for all the Protestants. In Belfast, the General Assembly of Presbyterians demanded that conscription be implemented immediately and reiterated its claims that Home Rule would be disastrous for the country and the Empire.[134]

On 30 April, the military intelligence officer of the Midlands and Connaught District claimed to have been reliably informed that the Catholic hierarchy, during its crucial meeting on 18 April, had taken the decision to bring pressure to bear on the RIC and the Dublin police if they attempted to implement conscription.[135] Unfortunately, the officer did not mention his source. This contrasts with the monthly report of the Inspector General of the RIC for April in which he wrote that 'the Clergy as a body, [had] not openly engaged in this conspiracy to corrupt the Constabulary, but [that] certain priests [had] addressed very strong appeals to them on spiritual grounds'.[136] However, bearing in mind Logue's imperial opinions, it seemed very unlikely that he would have agreed to let the hierarchy make such a decision. In June in the House of Commons, Sir Edward Carson used this information to denounce the hierarchy's activities:

> The police of Ireland, who are 95 per cent to 98 per cent Catholics, have been told that they would commit a sin against their Church if they carried out the decrees of the Imperial Parliament, and that those who resisted them, or were told to resist them, have been told they would be committing meritorious acts if they did so...Is it any wonder that we did not feel our liberties safe when the bishops were capable of pushing religion in a manner which would not be allowed in any other country in the world?
>
> (Harris, *The Catholic Church and the Foundation of the Northern State*, pp. 68–9)

Logue was outraged by Carson's remarks but knew in his heart of hearts that the Church's intervention in the conscription crisis had widened the gap between nationalists and unionists. It is thought that Walsh and other bishops were ill at ease faced with the political situation at that time. Walsh did not understand how the Irish National Defence Fund functioned and threatened to resign. When the Nationalist party and Sinn Féin argued about the nomination of one nationalist candidate for the East Cavan by-election, Walsh wrote to Larry O'Neill that if they did not agree, the sooner the Mansion House Convention was dissolved, the better it would be.[137] While it was unquestionably true that some bishops had reservations, Walsh had no reason at all to be ill at ease since Irish nationalism had returned back to the days of independent policy. His above-mentioned statements rather show a lack of patience with the anti-conscription movement than anything else. On 9 May 1918, Curran had a conversation with Walsh and wrote in his memoirs that the Archbishop 'spoke with amused raillery of the idea some people had of republicanism, associating it with the excesses of the French Revolution and forgetting all about the United States of America'.[138] The secretary was of the opinion that Walsh was referring to Logue and other bishops who still feared Sinn Féin and its republican agenda. On 27 June, Walsh refused to celebrate a requiem mass for fallen soldiers, which had been requested by Edward Shortt. He deemed that the moment was not at all appropriate and that the Dublin population might interpret this mass as a provocation.[139] It was one of the very last times that the Archbishop had been approached for reasons relating to the war and, until the very end, he had been consistent with his anti-war policy.

The alliance between the Church, the Nationalist party and Sinn Féin seemed to dissolve slowly and a real test lay ahead in the East Cavan by-election where two candidates were facing each other: Arthur Griffith, still imprisoned in England, and the Nationalist John O'Hanlon. In the Mansion House Convention's spirit of unity between nationalists, the parties tried to nominate one candidate only. Dr Finegan, the Bishop of Kilmore, intervened and asked John Dillon and Eamon de Valera to find a compromise and ordered the local clergy to help in the matter.[140] Since the ward had previously elected a Nationalist candidate, Dillon believed that Sinn Féin should withdraw its candidate and fully approved of Finegan's intervention. The clergy, however, did not follow the Bishop's instructions and openly supported Sinn Féin by asking the electorate to vote for Griffith.[141] Fr Michael O'Flanagan and Fr Paddy Browne, who was a professor in Maynooth, were involved in the Sinn Féin campaign despite the fact that they did not belong to the diocese of Kilmore. O'Flanagan affirmed that the Irish had every right to resist conscription as Ireland wanted to be recognised as an independent nation. He added: 'Those royal cousins who rule England and Germany will come together and clink their champagne glasses over the graves of millions of the flower of the manhood of Germany and England.'[142] (O'Flanagan could not have known that the Kaiser had indeed tasted champagne the day thousands of his soldiers fell during the last German spring offensive.)

Both parties were unwilling to compromise and eventually Griffith was elected. Dillon was livid with rage and denounced the priests and their 'most violent spiritual intimidation'.[143] Curran noted that Mrs Griffith had been intimidated by soldiers and that the Army had forbidden the Irish Volunteers to parade.[144] Tension between the Nationalist party and Sinn Féin, and also between the Nationalist party and the clergy was very palpable and it had not escaped the Northern District military intelligence officer's attention just before the election:

> The Church and the Parliamentary Party are using their influence to keep the resistance of a passive kind, but it remains to be seen whether they will succeed in restraining the Sinn Féin Party. The alliance is not a happy one and there are signs that it will not last, e.g. the election in East Cavan; at various meetings too, it was easy to see that each member of the alliance was inclined to claim all the credit to his party.
>
> (PRO, London, CO904/157, Northern District intelligence report, 4 May 1918, p. 34)

The officer was correct in his analysis. In the 1918 first post-war general election, Sinn Féin asserted that it had been mainly responsible for defeating the Government in its plan to conscript Irishmen.[145] This was a distortion of the facts, probably the fruit of republican bombast, since it was the Church's intervention, and in particular Archbishop Walsh's and Mgr Curran's, which had eventually brought about the peaceful defeat of conscription.

The events of East Cavan would once again divide the hierarchy. Fr O'Flanagan was immediately suspended by Bishop Coyne who had supported the war effort.[146] On 25 June, the bishops assembled in Maynooth to discuss the situation in the country. Dr Finegan denounced Fr Paddy Browne's activities and demanded disciplinary sanctions, which indicated that he had supported the Nationalist candidate in the by-election. It was suggested that from now on in order to travel, priests had to obtain not only their bishop's permission but also the permission of the bishop of the diocese they wanted to go to and where they wished to speak publicly at meetings. Logue, Finegan and Hoare favoured these travel restrictions but to their surprise it was rejected by Walsh, Harty and a majority of bishops and, therefore, the motion was not adopted.[147] It was clear that politically conservative bishops were now in a minority within the hierarchy.

The British authorities realised that the nationalist alliance was weakening and tried to use the usual divide and rule policy. As has been seen, Edward Shortt had asked Archbishop Walsh to celebrate mass for fallen soldiers. Then, some Catholics were appointed to important positions such as James MacMahon who became Irish Under-Secretary despite the Unionist James Campbell's protests. MacMahon had been appointed because he had useful contacts with the hierarchy.[148] The Government was engaged in a new public relations approach and was trying, as in the aftermath of the Easter Rising, to improve its image in Ireland. In July, Shortt wrote personally to Cardinal Logue and asked him if he knew Catholics, lay or ecclesiastical, who would be willing to look after education matters, an area in which the Church had always been heavily involved. But Logue was not duped. He wrote to Bishop O'Donnell: 'As I think I told the Chief Secretary pretty straightly, Sir E. Carson is bossing the show here in Ireland; and I would be inclined to let Sir E. Carson and them to work it out to see what they can make of it. I have little confidence in the deliberation of commissions, judging by the past.'[149] Logue's last remark was an allusion to the failure of the Irish Convention. Lord French was also involved in a public relations offensive. He had abandoned his plans to bombard the Irish into submission with the Royal Air Force and had now opted for a more materialistic approach since he promised land to all the Irish who would join the Army.[150]

However, Sinn Féin had little to fear in the summer of 1918. Although Lord French's new recruitment campaign managed to get nearly 10,000 men in the last three months of the conflict, which was quite a remarkable figure, the war effort was as good as ended in Ireland. De Valera's party had succeeded in its policy of respectability and Sinn Féin could now rely on bishops like Walsh, Fogarty, Hallinan, Harty, McKenna, McHugh and Cohalan, and also on the younger clergy. It was inevitable that the nationalist alliance would weaken at some stage for the interests of the involved parties were so different. The alliance between the Church, the Nationalist party and Sinn Féin had only been a marriage of convenience, the Church acting like a buffer between the two other parties. The hierarchy's intervention in the conscription crisis had probably put Ulster Protestants and unionists off Home Rule for the foreseeable future. But, it would be only fair to attenuate the responsibility of the bishops here. When they intervened, the gap between nationalists and unionists was already unbridgeable because of the Irish policy of the Government, dictated by the war and, on occasion, by a complete lack of insight. Amidst the hierarchy the great loser was Cardinal Logue. He had been unable to stop Sinn Féin's rise. The Cardinal's imperial ideas were simply outdated compared to de Valera's. The Sinn Féin president knew that Logue had been beaten and yet he could not have anticipated that the Cardinal would be involved in an obscure plot to revive recruitment and destroy Sinn Féin, the second French mission in August 1918.

But, the conscription crisis had had far reaching effects as its ripples had reached American and Australian shores. Indeed, how did the Catholic clergy of Irish descent react in the United States and throughout the Empire? The question is important as that clergy reinforced the Protestant and unionist community's sense of isolation and siege mentality in a large Irish Catholic world. The cases of the United States and Australia will now be briefly examined.

THE IRISH CLERGY IN THE UNITED STATES

After the Famine years between 1845 and 1849, hundreds of thousands of Irish people, mostly Catholic, emigrated to the United States and countries of the British Empire, and, not surprisingly, quite a few members of the American and Australian hierarchies were of Irish descent.[151] Most of these emigrants firmly believed that England had been responsible for the dire economic situation in Ireland and closely followed the political evolution in their old country. Some of them had developed a hatred of Britain and had sworn to liberate their country or to upset English interests whenever possible. One of these nationalist-republican groups in the United States was Clan na Gael. The Nationalist party knew it was vital to counter the ideas of Clan na Gael and newspapers such as the *Gaelic American* and the *Irish Press* which represented a more radical form of Irish nationalism. The war in Europe had given the opportunity for Irish radicals in the United States to denounce Redmond's pro-empire policy. Soon, the British Ambassador to the United States, Sir Cecil Spring Rice, wrote that 'a most active propaganda is going on and all the enemies of England have been marshalled against us'.[152] John Redmond and his party were also targeted by this radical propaganda. At the beginning of the war, negotiations between Count von Bernstorff and Sir Roger Casement in New York about the setting up of a brigade composed of Irish prisoners of war detained in Germany, had persuaded John Redmond that the Clan na Gael and other Irish expatriates would take advantage of the international situation to destabilise England. This could have some serious repercussions on the Nationalist party's Home Rule policy. As the conflict in Europe went on, it became clear that sooner or later the United States would enter the war on the Triple Entente's side. President Woodrow Wilson wanted the British to find a solution to the Irish question so as to unite all emigrants. The British Government knew that the American Congress was favourably disposed towards nationalist Ireland and that it also had the power to support England in the war.[153] As long as Redmond supported the war effort and a majority of Irish nationalists followed him, the British cabinet had little worry about the situation in the United States. However, Irish enthusiasm for the war soon waned and the Easter Rising of 1916 showed Irish discontent with British rule to the rest of the world. Initially, the Irish population living in the United States was taken aback by the rising in Dublin, reacting with a mixture of approval and disapproval. When the execution of the rebel leaders became known, Irish-American opinion largely condemned the British Government and turned away from the Nationalist party. Redmond warned Prime Minister Asquith that his position in the United States was seriously threatened.[154]

That was why the Government approved of John Redmond and Shane Leslie's initiatives across the Atlantic. Leslie was an Irish journalist in favour of the Nationalist party, and who lived in the United States. The correspondence between the two men reveals their preoccupation with Irish America. Leslie assured Redmond that he had the support of the Irish-American clergy, notably of Cardinals Farley and Gibbons and Archbishop Ireland. He had become aware that nationalist opposition and German propaganda were very active and that it was a priority to neutralise their influence. The journalist put forward a proposal to launch a new newspaper that would reflect the policy of the Nationalist party in Ireland. Redmond had already sent somebody over to the United States to examine this possibility, but accepted Leslie's offer and shortly afterwards the pro-Nationalist newspaper *Ireland* commenced publication. On 16 May 1916, just after the Easter Rising, Leslie wrote to Redmond that Irish-American outrage was due to the executions and most definitely not by the Nationalist leader's politics,[155] and thought that ecclesiastical help on both sides of the Atlantic could be a determining factor in helping Redmond. He had useful contacts with Cardinal Farley, Cardinal Gibbons and Archbishop Ireland in the United States, and with Bishop O'Donnell in Ireland. Leslie would regularly transmit O'Donnell's letters to Farley, the Cardinal of New York. In August 1916, he wrote to O'Donnell that the United States' participation in the war would be essential for the implementation of Home Rule as 'Ireland [was] the key to American feeling'.[156] Soon, Leslie asked O'Donnell to write for *Ireland* and the Bishop's articles would, of course, be largely in Redmond's favour. But Leslie's political convictions appeared to be somewhat confused. The journalist also exchanged letters with Mgr O'Riordan in Rome. In that correspondence, it is rather obvious that Leslie was far more nationalistic than the party whose views he was meant to represent in the United States![157] And yet he continued to support Redmond as a letter of his, published by the *Freeman's Journal* in February 1917, proves.[158] On 10 November 1916, Leslie warned Redmond that Irish opinion in the United States believed that 'without Home Rule the Irish troops [were] in the trenches under false pretences'.[159] The Easter Rising and the partition and Home Rule crises of the summer of 1916 had convinced the Irish-Americans that the British Government did not include Ireland in its fight for the independence of small nations. Leslie received a long letter from O'Donnell, which he published immediately. The Bishop of Raphoe knew that unity was important and that nationalist Ireland had to keep supporting Redmond. According to O'Donnell, Redmond was human and could sometimes make mistakes, but only he and his party could lead the country to autonomy. The Bishop wrote that he was against conscription but that he fully endorsed voluntary enlistment in the country. He deplored, however, the tactless attitude of the British Government and the War Office towards Irish war effort. Finally, he declared that he was worried about the Nationalist party's image in the United States and tried to persuade Americans that Irish parliamentarians in the House of Commons in London would always remain Irish whatever happened.[160] Leslie informed O'Donnell that Cardinal Farley had read his latest article in *Ireland*.[161] It remained to be seen whether Leslie and O'Donnell's orchestrated efforts had managed to convince Irish-American opinion of Redmond's able leadership. According to the journalist they had been successful. In December 1916, he wrote a letter to the Bishop of Raphoe in which he gave a résumé of the state of affairs in the United States:

> You have no idea how much you are helping us to hold Irish America together for Redmond...The Clan na Gael used the enormous influence the executions gave them to try to affect the election here. Hughes [presidential candidate] was weak enough to negotiate with them, whereas the Redmondite strength went chiefly to Wilson. I am now editor of the <u>Dublin</u>, I believe. The owners of the review have given me a free hand to make it fair to Redmond. I wish you would encourage the Irish Bishops to become subscribers and sometimes contributors. We want to make it international and the link between English and Irish Catholics, especially as the Germans here are sowing discord that way.
>
> (ACA, O'Donnell papers, Leslie to O'Donnell, 13 December 1916)

It was true that diplomatic relations between the United States and Germany were rapidly deteriorating, which played right into the

Nationalist party's hands as it supported war against Germany. In sharp contrast to the Nationalists, Clan na Gael favoured the Germans. But, Leslie had been too optimistic. Opposition nationalists had equally understood that the United States was worth fighting for as its support could determine the course of events in Ireland. The *Irish Opinion* denounced O'Donnell's American initiatives and deemed that the Bishop's main worry was 'the strengthening of England's international relations'.[162] Bishop O'Dwyer, as has been seen, wrote an article published by the *American Ecclesiastical Review* in which he denounced Redmond's servile attitude towards 'his English allies or masters'.[163] A few months later, in 1917, Leslie made the incredible mistake of defending O'Dwyer against General Maxwell in his newspaper *Ireland*! The journalist was obviously far removed from the Irish political scene. Quite naturally, some members of the Nationalist party criticised Leslie for this article and the journalist felt obliged to write a letter of support to Redmond, guaranteeing his loyalty.[164] As for Mgr O'Riordan, he sent letters to Cardinal Farley in New York in which it was crystal clear that he sought to separate the Irish Catholic Church from the English Church, something Leslie was particularly trying to avoid. On 21 and 22 December 1916, O'Riordan informed Farley that some English ecclesiastics were interfering in Irish affairs at the Vatican, and criticised the intervention of Cardinal Bourne of Westminster in Sir Roger Casement's execution.[165] The American Cardinal was able to appreciate how much nationalist Ireland was divided.

On 1 February 1917, Germany began her unrestricted submarine warfare and two days later the United States broke off all its diplomatic relations with Berlin. The same month, Bishop O'Donnell wrote that the Irish in the USA were 'a permanent menace to the good relations of America with Great Britain ... [and that] in war or peace the friendly attitude of America [was] of priceless value to Great Britain'.[166] O'Donnell's opinions were confirmed by Ambassador Spring Rice in 1917 when he wrote in his report for London: 'The fact that the Irish question is still unsettled is continually quoted against us, as a proof that it is not wholly true that the fight is one for the sanctity of engagements or the independence of small nations.'[167] When the Americans entered the war two months later, Mgr Curran was of the opinion that 'from 1917 onwards, public opinion in America, and even in Australia, in favour of Irish claims became a great source of anxiety to the British'.[168] O'Donnell and Curran were both right. On 25 April, David Lloyd George told Sir Edward Carson that the Irish question was an obstacle for the war effort and that the Americans were putting pressure on him.[169] The British Government had to find a solution rapidly. In the United States, the Secretary of State, Robert Lansing, also believed that Ireland was like a thorn in Anglo-American relations.[170] It remained to be seen whether the

United States' entry into the war would benefit the Nationalist party or Sinn Féin. Lloyd George's clever answer to American pressure was the creation of the Irish Convention, in the summer of 1917. In this way, President Wilson and the American people could no longer accuse the British authorities of doing nothing for Ireland. Archbishop Ireland thought that Home Rule had to be implemented immediately and Cardinal Gibbons was of the opinion that the Convention would settle nothing at all.[171] Gibbons was not particularly confident in the abilities of the British to solve the Irish crisis. In May, he had replied to a letter from Cardinal Bourne, saying that he was pleased that the United States were participating in the defence of the freedom of nations. But Gibbons could not refrain from reminding Bourne that small nations had the right of self-determination, as President Wilson had stated in his Fourteen Points declaration.[172] It would seem that the United States' entry in the war had temporarily favoured the Nationalist party, until April 1918 at least, when the conscription crisis broke out. The intervention of American soldiers had excited the United States' patriotism. To Americans, it was John Redmond who was associated with the war effort and Britain, not Eamon de Valera and Sinn Féin. Senator William King declared that the time of 'hyphenated Americans' was over.[173] By this King meant that one was American first, then Irish, Polish, German etc. This remark reflected the political climate in the USA and made life harder for Clan na Gael and the *Gaelic American*. On 20 December 1917, the Irish Fellowship Club of Chicago stated that it was fully in favour of John Redmond's policy and to be against anybody who tried to weaken the Allies. The club sent a statement of its resolutions to all Irish organisations in the country.[174] William McKinley, former speaker of the Illinois House declared: 'England may have blundered but England's cause now is our cause.'[175]

However, if the United States' declaration of war on Germany had initially favoured John Redmond, Bishop O'Donnell, Shane Leslie and David Lloyd George, the conscription crisis of April 1918 would squander some of their advantage as it divided American opinion and the American Catholic Church. Before introducing the Compulsory Military Service Bill, the Prime Minister had asked Arthur Balfour to consult the American Government on the issue. Lloyd George was convinced that the Irish-Americans would be no major problem since conscription had been introduced in the United States. But Woodrow Wilson begged to differ for he believed that it would 'accentuate the whole Irish and Catholic intrigue which [had] gone hand in hand in some quarters in the country with German intrigue' in the United States.[176] The President's apprehensions were justified for on 11 May 1918, 15,000 Irish-Americans applauded speeches of a Fr Berle and some members of the Congress, who were against conscription in

Ireland. The President of the Chicago Irish Fellowship Club sent a telegram to Wilson, asking him to act in the Irish conscription crisis and reminding him that 'Irishmen everywhere [looked] with hope to President Wilson as the champion of the rights of small nations'.[177] On the other hand, newspapers such as the *Buffalo Express*, the *Ohio State Journal*, the *Kansas City Times*, the *St. Louis Post-Dispatch*, the *New York Herald* and the *New York World* denounced Irish opposition to conscription. The *Christian Science Monitor* believed that there was a worldwide Catholic plot against conscription and named Cardinal Logue in Ireland, Archbishop Mannix in Australia and Cardinal Begin in Quebec as the main orchestrators.[178] The *Christian Science Monitor's* comments seemed rather far-fetched but the French diplomatic services had grounds to share this perception. In March 1918, the French Foreign Office Secretary in the Quai d'Orsay in Paris was informed that Canadian bishops of Irish descent were hostile to the war effort.[179]

The American Catholic Church was divided on the Irish hierarchy's intervention in the conscription crisis. Cardinal Logue received a letter of support from Irish-American priests who had once been seminarians in Maynooth.[180] During a meeting in Philadelphia, Mgr Gerald Coghlan declared his support for Logue and believed that conscription in Ireland was meant 'to annihilate or wipe out the remnant of the manhood of [their] race in the old land'.[181] But some Irish-American bishops could not afford to oppose conscription publicly, even if it was a long way away in Ireland, as it was tantamount to opposing the war in which American soldiers were now fighting. A letter from Bishop Kiely of the diocese of Savanah in the State of Georgia to Archbishop Walsh was an example. Kiely asked Walsh to explain why the Irish and their Church were so opposed to the Compulsory Military Service Bill. The American Bishop added that the 19,000 Catholics of the State were harassed by the other two and a half million Georgians who believed that the Catholic Church was helping Germany.[182] Kiely, Farley and Cardinal O'Connell of Boston had no other choice but to openly support the war against Germany lest their Church became the focus of unwanted political attention. Later, in September 1918, the *Irish Soldier*, a new propaganda newspaper in favour of the Allies, published extracts from these three American prelates.[183] On 11 November 1918, the day the armistice was declared in Europe, O'Connell sent a telegram to the British Government in which he urged the cabinet to find a solution to the Irish question, as Irish-Americans were vehemently against England.[184] Mgr Curran had noticed this somewhat forced change in the attitude of American bishops of Irish descent. On 18 September 1918, Cardinal Farley of New York died and Curran wrote the following passage in his memoirs:

He had been in the past a staunch Nationalist but, from the time of the United States' entry into the war, he incurred considerable odium in Irish circles by his opposition to Sinn Féin organisations and particularly his action in listening to the protests of Anglophiles the previous May against the participation of priests at Irish meetings organised by Sinn Féin...It must be said, however, that Cardinal Farley gave his support to the beginnings of the Irish National Fund Aid in USA.

(NLD, O'Kelly papers, MS 27728(1),
Curran's memoirs, p. 298)

Conscription in Ireland had had repercussions in the United States. Like its counterpart in Ireland, the American Catholic clergy was faced with military and political questions which put it in the limelight, much against its will. After the Easter Rising of 1916, the Irish nationalist opposition and Sinn Féin were quite popular in the United States but when the Americans entered the war, things changed. The Irish-American clergy supported the Irish Catholic Church in its fight against David Lloyd George and his cabinet, but the Irish-American hierarchy, prudently and wisely from its point of view, decided to fully support its own country first and Ireland after. The British Government could be fairly satisfied with the situation across the Atlantic even if initially it had had genuine reasons for concern. But in Australia, the situation the British authorities had to face was not reassuring as the formidable Archbishop of Melbourne, Daniel Mannix, caused William Hughes persistent problems.

CRISIS DOWN UNDER

There was a large Irish presence in Australia. In 1911, about 200,000 inhabitants were Irish-born, out of a population of five million.[185] The feeling among Australians was that they were proud to belong to the British Empire and, since 1905, they had celebrated Empire Day on 24 May. In 1910, however, the Catholics of Sydney rebaptised this event Australia Day.[186] According to them, Australia was their fatherland, not England. The majority of these Catholics were of Irish origin and the Australian Catholic clergy also numbered ecclesiastics who had Irish roots. Among them was Dr Daniel Mannix, born in Charleville in Co. Cork. Mannix had been professor of philosophy at Maynooth and became Coadjutor Archbishop of Melbourne in 1912. Although he was in favour of Ireland's cultural revival, he had never been a staunch nationalist before his departure to Australia. In fact, on one occasion in Maynooth he lambasted some members of the Gaelic League for their

246

extremism.[187] In 1911, he displayed loyalty to the Empire when he welcomed the King in Saint Patrick's College and yet, by 1921, he had become a republican.[188] He disliked the Army intensely and later, in 1945, he strongly condemned the use of the atomic bombs on Japan.[189] His arrival in Australia was to provoke political unrest as he would confront the militarist Prime Minister William Hughes during the war.

Like Ireland in 1914, Australia believed the war to be a means of affirming its existence as a nation and many men enthusiastically joined the Army. Conscription did not exist but recruitment figures were excellent, especially after the landing of the ANZAC force at Gallipoli, in Turkey, in April 1915: in June, 12,500 men joined; in July, 36,000 men enlisted; and in August 1915, the number was 25,700.[190] Clergy of all denominations visited families whose relatives were fighting in France and Turkey. The Australian Catholic Church exhorted men to participate in the defence of the country. The Archbishop of Sydney, Michael Kelly originally from Co. Waterford, even went as far to declare that the war 'would be blessed by God'.[191] By and large Irish Australia heartily welcomed John Redmond's decision to commit Ireland to the war and the defence of the British Empire.[192] But, the war had had bad repercussions on the Australian economy as prices rocketed, British imports were no longer arriving and salaries did not increase.

In April 1916, the Easter Rising took place in Dublin and many Irish-Australians were outraged by the executions of the rebel leaders. Some of them asked themselves why their sons were fighting for the British Empire.[193] The Catholic Church and Catholic newspapers initially denounced the rising. Archbishop Kelly of Sydney described it as 'misconceived patriotism' while others stated that 'German intrigue' was behind it.[194] On 20 May 1916, Archbishop Mannix chose to comment on the Easter Rising and said that the event was 'deplorable' and that Catholics had to think the same. Nevertheless, he explained why some Irish nationalists had decided to fight. According to him, Sir Edward Carson was partly responsible because he had shown how to resist the Government by setting up the UVF. But in spite of his views on this paramilitary force, Mannix continued, the Irish Volunteers did not have any choice but to confront 'the forces of the Crown'. He added: ' The Carsonites... got a free hand, though some of them boasted that they were intriguing with the German enemy. They were assured, on the authority of Mr Asquith, that the British Army would never point a gun at them; their leader, instead of being sent into prison, was taken into the British Cabinet.'[195] On this point, Mannix's position was identical to that of Logue, Walsh, O'Dwyer and Fogarty. Thus, the Archbishop of Melbourne believed that the political centre of the Empire, the British Government, had been at least partly responsible for the recent rising in

Ireland. Mannix took great care not use the words Empire and Protestant lest he upset Australian public opinion. What Mannix did not approve of and did not hesitate to make known, however, was that he did not agree with Herbert Asquith and David Lloyd George's Irish policy. In May 1917, Dr Fogarty wrote to Bishop O'Dwyer: 'Dr Mannix is making a fight in Australia, [illegible] like your own.'[196] To many Irish-Australian Catholics the Easter Rising had estranged their adoptive country from Britain. This was obviously not the case for Protestant Australians of English and Scottish descent. *The Times* correspondent noticed that the Australians closely followed the Irish Convention put forward by Lloyd George, but he was of the opinion that they did not believe it would succeed. The journalist concluded that Irish-Australian discontent might have 'a disruptive influence throughout the Dominions'.[197] His predictions proved to be true. Unfortunately, Mannix's intervention and comments on the Easter Rising marked the beginning of a sharp rise in sectarianism in the country. In August 1916, Oswald Snowball, a staunch Orangeman and member of the Parliament of Victoria, openly accused the Archbishop of having a 'pro-German attitude'.[198] Moreover, Prime Minister Hughes's personality would only fuel this rising sectarianism in Australian society.

In October 1915, William Hughes, of the Australian Labour party, had replaced Andrew Fisher as head of Government. Hughes was an energetic, very outspoken man who had a liking for militarism. He loved his country and the Empire and had denounced members of his own party for not supporting recruitment. As for trade unions, the Labour politician believed they had no nationality, no religion and no principles.[199] The political climate that the war had generated in Australia was tense, to say the least. People whose patriotic feelings were not immediately noticeable became suspects and were even threatened with internment. Australians with German names had a rough time. Hughes accused Mannix of being sectarian, which was the fruit of his extreme patriotism. In fact, it was Hughes who was blatantly sectarian as he wanted to close down all Lutheran churches in the country for the sole reason that they were of German origin although German-Australians had been loyal to the war effort. The Archbishop defended the Lutherans on this occasion and some jingoistic Australian newspapers vehemently denounced his intervention. This upset Mannix and as a result he became the country's most 'notorious disloyalist'.[200] When recruitment figures began to decrease, Hughes organised a referendum on conscription at a time when Australia seemed to have had enough of the war.[201]

The Prime Minister's sense of timing was not the best. The country was very much divided on the issue of compulsory military service. The pro-conscription Universal Service League in New South Wales, for instance, had Archbishop Kelly of Sydney as a vice-president.[202] Hughes's main opponent was Mannix and the Archbishop won since the Australians voted against compulsory military service. Clearly not satisfied and hurt in his national pride, Hughes went on to organise a second referendum in December 1917 and, once more, Mannix and the anti-conscription movements carried the day. Hughes was frustrated and appealed to Arthur Balfour in London. He explained to the Foreign Office Secretary that Mannix had used his ecclesiastical influence to oppose not only conscription but also voluntary enlistment. Hughes had included in his letter a report on Mannix's activities in which it was stated that of all the Australians, Catholics were the ones who had joined the army in the least numbers. The Archbishop was obviously au fait with the Catholics' poor record and said that this did not surprise him. What did surprise him, however, was 'that [Catholics] had been so self-sacrificing as to what they had done in face of the treatment they had received'.[203] Hughes accused a section of the Australian population of being less loyal than others and, consequently, a sectarian division between Catholics and Protestants was slowly emerging. It was undeniably true that during these two referenda on conscription, wealthy classes, the press and the Protestant clergy had voted in favour of compulsory military service whereas the working class and the Catholic Church had voted against it.[204] These referenda were fraught with racism for some people had been exhorted to vote for compulsory military service and for a 'free and white' Australia.

It appeared that two conceptions of Australian identity were confronting each other, one that wished to break off with the Empire and that was backed by Mannix and Catholics, and another one that wanted to remain closely involved with Britain and that was supported by Hughes and Protestants. In November 1917, Dr Blattaney, the Apostolic Delegate of the Vatican in Sydney, decided to inform Rome about the Australian situation. Blattaney was obviously aware of the Catholics' hostility to conscription and Mannix's role in their opposition. This could have undesirable diplomatic repercussions on the Holy See as many Allied statesmen were convinced that it was discreetly favouring Germany and Austria-Hungary. Mannix's anti-militaristic activities could only add weight to their arguments. Blattaney pointed out that the press accused the Archbishop of Melbourne of being disloyal and being a mouthpiece for Sinn Féin, which was not entirely incorrect. According to this press, Mannix's slogan was 'Australia first, the Empire next'. Obviously, Mannix's loyalty to the Empire was largely conditioned by the British Government's Irish policy. The Apostolic Delegate concluded his letter to the Vatican by saying 'that the Orangemen [were] breathing fire and fury in trying to implicate the Catholic dignitary, as usual'.[205]

Mannix understood that certain politicians were trying to accuse him of dividing the country between Catholics and Protestants at the expense of the war effort. He decided to defend himself publicly at a meeting of some 50,000 Australians, which took place in Victoria. The Archbishop did not mince his words and blamed sectarianism on Hughes and his Government:

> The first lesson of the Campaign . . . is that sectarianism has got a severe blow – I hope its death blow – in Australia. Mr Hughes and those associated with him openly pinned their faith in the most shameless way to sectarianism and racial hatred. They thought by stirring up religious bigotry and the jealousy and animosity which they supposed to exist against Irish Catholics and their descendants, they would succeed in carrying conscription. They are wiser men now. I hope that those who have been associated in this campaign against conscription – Catholics and Protestants – having felt the value of mutual assistance, and having grasped the hand of friendship, one with another, will never again be imposed upon by those who, for their own political or sectarian purposes, would attempt to drive a wedge between those who do not worship at the same altar.
>
> (*The Freeman's Journal*, 29 April 1918)

It was unlikely that Mannix wanted to stir up sectarianism to oppose conscription, especially after his own experience of religious discord in Ireland. A sectarian policy would not have helped Australia and would lead to nothing but hatred. It was undeniable, however, that the archbishop's anti-conscription crusade became political for he remained an ardent Irish nationalist. As expected, many Irish-Australian Catholics followed him and questioned their country's role within the British Empire. In return, they were opposed by Australian Protestants and the backlash was sectarianism. The whole situation was not helped either by the personality of Australia's Prime Minister. Hughes was discredited by those he was supposed to represent, the Labour party, the trade unions and the working classes.[206] Even so, Mannix was definitely guilty of provoking his opponents on occasion. On Saint Patrick's Day 1918, he refused to take his mitre off as 'God save the King' was played but did take it off when a float representing the 1916 Easter Rising passed in front of him during the parade.[207] In Ireland, Mannix's struggle had not gone unnoticed. On 1 December 1917, Arthur Griffith's *Nationality* played the Catholic card once again by stating that the Archbishop of Melbourne had endorsed Sinn Féin's policy and described Hughes as 'the ludicrous Premier of Australia'.[208] In the Vatican, Cardinal Pietro Gasparri, the Secretary of State, must have realised that Ireland was more than a small island in the Atlantic.

But it was the conscription crisis in Ireland that would rally all the Irish-Australian Catholic clergy against David Lloyd George. In December 1916, Hughes had already warned his British counterpart that if the war effort in Australia was to be revived, a solution in Ireland was urgently required for the Home Rule crisis made imperial unity impossible.[209] At first, Lloyd George agreed with this opinion for in February 1917, he declared that conscription could provoke discontent in Canada, South Africa and Australia.[210] Yet, despite his awareness of this possible problem, the Prime Minister decided to go ahead with conscription in Ireland and brought about a general outcry, just as he had predicted. On 15 April 1918, Morgan Jaguers, the president of the Australian United Irish League, declared his support for John Dillon.[211] On 19 April, Archbishop Kelly, on behalf of the Australian hierarchy, sent a telegram of support to Dillon and also to Eamon de Valera, undoubtedly bearing in mind the unity of the nationalist camp. The Australian bishops believed that the British Government had no right whatsoever to impose conscription upon Ireland and demanded that Home Rule be implemented immediately. They emphasised that only a free people would be able to contribute effectively to the war effort.[212] The *Irishman* reported that the Mansion House Convention had asked Larry O'Neill to send a message of thanks to the Australian hierarchy.[213]

The nationalist alliance in Ireland could rely on international support, organised by Catholic clergy of Irish descent. On 15 May 1918, the new Apostolic Delegate of the Vatican to Australia, Mgr Cattaneo, decided to call a meeting of all the archbishops to discuss the tense political climate. Mannix was willing to do his best to appease the people and put forward a motion that was unanimously adopted. He believed that the Catholic clergy had to be extremely cautious and prudent in its public declarations on conscription, recruitment and the Irish question. Everything that could incite people to think of sedition and disloyalty had to be avoided. Clearly, Mannix would no longer make stunts in the style of Saint Patrick's Day. All the archbishops agreed that a public declaration concerning their resolution was not necessary but that they would give precise instructions to their clergy instead.[214] The goodwill of the prelates, especially of Mannix since he proposed the motion, seemed quite evident. Yet, the Australian authorities were not satisfied and decided to appeal, once again, to the British Government. On 22 May, the Foreign Office in London received a report from the Governor of the State of New South Wales. The Governor wrote that the city of Melbourne had been outraged by Sinn Féin flags and portraits of the executed rebel leaders, which had been used during Saint Patrick's Day. He stressed that Mannix had been the cause of all those troubles and that the Australian Government would perhaps be forced to expatriate him. He also mentioned Mgr Cattaneo and was of the opinion that the apostolic delegate had not publicly kept his distance from Mannix and had even accompanied him to meetings in Sydney.[215] And so it appeared that William Hughes and the authorities had envisaged using force against the Archbishop of Melbourne. The Australian Government was suddenly very eager and impatient to get rid of Mannix, for Saint Patrick's Day occurred on 17 March, almost two months before Mannix's motion of 15 May. The Governor did not seem to have more recent information on the Archbishop. Those remarks on Mannix and Cattaneo led to a diplomatic duel between Britain and the Vatican. Count de Salis, head of the British mission to the Vatican, was ordered to ask the Holy See for explanations regarding Cattaneo's conduct. On 10 July, Cardinal Gasparri informed the British Envoy that the Apostolic Delegate had sent Mannix a letter in which he stated that he had noticed his attitude on 'the burning question of military recruitment'. On that occasion, Cattaneo had advised the Archbishop to be very cautious in the interest of the Church, but that he was entitled to have personal opinions. In his reply to de Salis, Gasparri included a copy of Cattaneo's letter to Mannix. Finally, the Italian Cardinal added very diplomatically that he had seen evidence that some politicians had been wrong about Cattaneo, in other words members of the Australian Government.[216]

But the end of the affair was not in sight yet. On 26 July 1918, Arthur Balfour sent a very detailed report on Mannix's activities to de Salis. The Foreign Office Secretary wrote that he had had a frank conversation with Hughes about the whole situation: 'The Prime Minister of Australia has talked to me very earnestly about the case of Archbishop Mannix. He is most anxious that the Vatican shall recall him – nothing less, in his opinion, is sufficient, and he tells me privately that, if the Archbishop remains, a rebellion may result from his activities.'[217] Therefore, Balfour asked de Salis to do his best to persuade the Vatican to comply with Hughes's demand. The report the Australian authorities had sent concerning Mannix was rather biased. All the Archbishop's activities were mentioned, including his so-called plan to separate Catholics from Protestants. Mannix was in fact far from being a bigot, but he had anti-imperial opinions that understandably worried the Government. His resolution of 15 May was not quoted in this report, which could be justified as the archbishops' meeting had been private, but far worse was the omission of Mannix's public speech in Victoria in which he had openly denied being anti-Protestant and sectarian. The vicious attacks of the Australian press had also been conveniently forgotten.

On 15 August, Balfour again sent a cable to de Salis, reminding him that Hughes would not be satisfied with a strong reprimand from the Vatican. If the Holy See refused to recall him, Balfour warned, the Australians would banish him themselves which would 'lead to an outburst of public opinion against the authorities of the Roman Catholic Church throughout the Empire and possibly in the United States'.[218] If Balfour, de Salis and Hughes had hoped to impress the Vatican that way, they were badly wrong. Cardinal Gasparri knew that the British diplomats were bluffing. In August, the German armies were retreating and it seemed that the war was entering in its final phase. The Irish conscription crisis and Mannix's opposition to the war effort were no longer that important. Banishing the Archbishop would have made another Irish nationalist martyr of him. The Vatican supported the Irish and not the British who had excluded the Pope from the future peace conference. On 22 August 1918, Gasparri wrote the last letter of this long saga. Firstly, he informed de Salis about the episcopal meeting of 15 May and Mannix's role. Secondly, he denounced the Australian press for having bitterly criticised the Archbishop's refusal to participate in a recruitment meeting. The Italian Cardinal indicated that on that occasion the Mayor of Melbourne had been present on the platform whereas only a short time before, the Mayor had refused to officially welcome Mgr Cattaneo in Australia. Finally, Gasparri shrewdly pointed out that Mannix was extremely popular among the working classes and that his arrest or deportation 'would undoubtedly aggravate the situation and create grave difficulties for the Government itself'.[219] In the end, Daniel Mannix was neither reprimanded, nor recalled by the Vatican. He died as Archbishop of Melbourne in 1963, at the age of ninety-nine.

Daniel Mannix's fight against conscription in Australia and also in Ireland proved that the Irish question was able to influence the course of diplomacy in the war. The interventions of the Irish-Australian and American Catholic Churches had demonstrated to Irish nationalists at home that they were not alone in their struggle against the British Government. It seemed that David Lloyd George's decision to impose conscription could have cost Britain's war effort and strategy dearly. A tempting question to ask is: if the Catholic Church had not intervened and armed resistance against the British authorities had become widespread and fanatical, could it have affected the outcome of the war? The answer will, of course, never be known since this is pure conjecture. However, one can hazard a few guesses. In April 1918, the Germans launched their last large-scale offensive and nearly reached Paris. If news had reached the retreating 16th Irish and 36th Ulster Divisions, and also British, Australian, Canadian and American regiments with a high number of Irishmen or men of Irish descent, that Lord French was bombing Ireland with the Royal Air Force, trying to enforce conscription, the impact on those soldiers' morale would have been devastating. American soldiers, who were slowly but surely arriving in France, might have wondered whether their President had been serious and sincere when he had stated that this war was in defence of democracy, self-determination and freedom of small nations, and against German militarism. Would a collapse in morale and possible mutinies in the British and Imperial armies have enabled Germany to win? Perhaps not, but it would have had serious international repercussions on the front and on Britain. Undoubtedly, the British Government would have been forced to give in to Irish nationalists' aspirations, and, at the same time, would have upset Ulster unionists. It seemed that Lloyd George had lived by the sword and had nearly died by the sword. After all, one can make a similar apocalyptic scenario about the French Army. What if the Germans had found out about the widespread mutinies that occurred in French divisions after the lamentable offensive of the *Chemin des Dames* in April 1917[220] and had immediately counter-attacked? As for the Ulster Protestants and unionists, they had realised that they were surrounded by a worldwide and powerful Catholic Church, able to disrupt conscription plans in Ireland and the Empire. To them, it was one big step further towards partition.

SUMMARY

The events that took place in Ireland between the end of 1916 and 1918 determined the course of Irish history. The failure of the Irish Convention and the attempt to impose conscription confirmed in the minds of the Catholic Church and the Nationalists that their country could expect nothing from the British Government. Many now believed that Home Rule was only a nominal freedom and that this law would divide the country into two parts. The Church could not accept this, especially the clergy in the north of the country. The nationalist population perceived the Compulsory Military Service Bill to be another cynical political manipulation. Contrary to John Redmond in 1914, the Irish in 1918 did not believe that the war would eventually elevate Ireland to the status of an independent nation. The War Office and the cabinet were much to blame for this. The ensuing radicalisation of public opinion could only play right into Sinn Féin's hands in the long run, and, to many, the Nationalist party had failed politically and was above all associated with the war effort. The decay of the Nationalist party between 1914 and 1918 was largely due to the personality of its leader. Although unquestionably sincere in his motives, Redmond had showed a fatal lack of political independence in his relations with the war cabinet, and maybe an even greater cause of his downfall was his refusal to publicly oppose Bishop Edward O'Dwyer. Eamon de Valera, a devout Catholic and much impressed by

O'Dwyer, decided to play the Catholic card and had cut the ground from under Cardinal Logue's feet. The less radically inclined bishops had been deeply suspicious of Sinn Féin's aims but were no longer able to effectively oppose this party after it had entered negotiations with the hierarchy on 18 April 1918 at Maynooth. The war, and the conscription crisis in particular, had definitely changed the face of Irish nationalism as constitutional politics were replaced by a new and widely supported militant separatism. Moreover, the war had also brought about the final touches to the merger of Catholicism and nationalism. As for the unionists and Protestants, they now feared even more for their civil and religious liberties in a future autonomous or independent Ireland.

The war had proved how much importance British and allied statesmen attached to the situation in Ireland. In Rome, one man was equally concerned. In an Italian capital that had become a hotbed of political intrigue, Mgr Michael O'Riordan, rector of the Irish College, patiently engineered the rapprochement between nationalist Ireland and the Vatican. In doing so, he received invaluable help from Limerick.

7 The Irish College in Rome, 1914–1918

January 1915
'Sir Henry Howard is here to counteract German falsehood by
English truth ... As I am not a Britisher, I did not go.'
Mgr O'Riordan's refusal to attend a reception in honour of the
new British mission, in a letter to Bishop O'Dwyer

March 1917
'Quell'uomo ha una testa' (The man has brains).
Pope Benedict XV on Bishop O'Dwyer during
Mgr O'Riordan's audience

The Catholic Church's spiritual and administrative centre is situated at
the Vatican in Rome. The Church itself is divided into a complex and
strict hierarchical structure at whose head are the Pope and the Roman
Curia. The influence and authority of the Church can be determining
factors for the conscience and decision-making of the faithful. When the
war broke out, Protestant Britain and anti-clerical France hastily
decided to send diplomatic representations to the Vatican, something
their enemies had already done. Rapidly, the Vatican became a
propaganda battleground for the belligerent countries. Britain had
declared war, officially at least, for freedom and the rights of small
nations. But would she respect the political aspirations of Ireland, her
own small nation where an important majority of Catholics lived?
Would Ireland not become a useful tool for enemy propaganda? It was
crucial for the British to convince the Pope and the Curia of their
country's good will towards Ireland and try to use the Vatican to
control and moderate Irish nationalism. Soon, a British diplomatic
mission left for Rome in December 1914. This mission rekindled old
fears among Irish ecclesiastics who could still remember Leo XIII's
controversial intervention in the Plan of Campaign. The question was
not simply how nationalists could effectively counter this latest British
diplomatic initiative, but more especially, who would be in the best
position to do so. John Redmond and the Nationalist party sided with
Britain and the Empire, and Ireland had no diplomatic legation in Rome
as she was not independent yet. The answer to the question was the
Irish College and its rector, Mgr Michael O'Riordan. He had strong

nationalist opinions and would adopt a separatist policy towards Britain. He was opposed to the war effort in Ireland as Home Rule had been shelved, and set out to convince the Vatican that his country had every right to become independent. The international situation would help O'Riordan to bring about new relations between nationalist Ireland and the Vatican despite repeated interventions of British diplomats and ecclesiastics in Rome. The scene was set for political machinations and heated arguments.

A TRADITION OF ROMAN INTRIGUES

In 1697, after William of Orange's victory over James II, Penal Laws were introduced in Ireland in order to curtail the liberty of Catholics and assure the security of Protestants in the country. The aim of the laws was to eliminate Catholicism eventually. If these laws had been strictly enforced, the Catholic religion would have disappeared in Ireland during the eighteenth century but fortunately for Catholics the Penal Laws were not consistently and systematically applied.[1] However, Catholic colleges and seminaries were closed down and those who wished to enter the priesthood were obliged to go abroad. This led to the creation of Irish colleges on the Continent, whose task was to educate young seminarians. It was in Spain, in Salamanca, where the first college started and soon others were created in Louvain, Douai, Antwerp, Lille, Bordeaux and Paris.[2] But it was the college in Rome that would play a most important role simply because of its proximity to the Vatican (of which Aristide Briand once said that it was 'the most vital listening-post in all the world's diplomacy').[3] What the French politician had stated was true, particularly regarding Anglo-Irish relations in which the Holy See intervened from time to time. The conditions for Irish Catholics improved as the Penal Laws were gradually abolished but the colleges abroad were maintained. During the nineteenth century, Irish nationalism quickly developed into a massive political force supported by the Catholic Church, notably by Archbishops Walsh and Croke.[4] The British Government looked on this unfavourably and decided to use its international influence to persuade the Vatican to control and restrain, if need be, Irish nationalism. In 1870, Pius IX had condemned the Fenians.

However, it was Leo XIII who was the originator of many troubles for the Irish hierarchy. This Pope condemned the nationalist Plan of Campaign in the 1880s in return for British support against the Italian Government which had the intention of confiscating papal property.[5] Nevertheless, the British Government did not send an official delegation to the Holy See but used individuals residing in Rome to interfere in the

27. Mgr Michael O'Riordan, rector of the Irish College in Rome, originated diplomatic relations between nationalist Ireland and the Vatican (with kind permission of the Irish College, Rome)

28. Mgr John Hagan, vice-rector of the Irish College in Rome and anonymous correspondent of the *Catholic Bulletin* (with kind permission of the Irish College, Rome)

29. Cardinal Francis Bourne, Archbishop of Westminster, and Major General Hickie inspect a battalion of the Royal Dublin Fusilliers at Ervillers, October 1917 (taken from Terence Denman's *Ireland's Unknown Soldiers*)

appointment of Irish bishops, the most notable being George Errington. Errington, a landlord in Ireland but who spent the winter months in the Italian capital, was a Liberal supporter of Home Rule who did not approve of Charles Stewart Parnell's tactics in the British Parliament, and who also believed that Archbishop Croke was a most imprudent man.[6] On this occasion, John Dillon commented bitterly that 'the voice of Catholics in England – a miserable crew – [prevailed] at Rome over the voice of our bishops'.[7] And so it was that Leo XIII supported Protestant England against Catholic Ireland. One of his reasons was that he ardently wished Britain to reconvert to Catholicism. Furthermore, the Vatican did not consider Ireland to be important from an ecclesiastical point of view.[8] Germany had closely followed this episode, for her Chancellor, Otto von Bismarck, was interested in the English approach to the Irish question as he had to deal with Polish nationalists, nearly all Catholics.[9] It seems that Bismarck used a similar diplomatic approach.

The consequences for Ireland were predictable. Archbishop Walsh wanted to minimise the Vatican's intervention at all costs before it caused an upsurge of anti-clericalism in the country. The Irish College in Rome would be at the forefront to counter British diplomatic moves at the Holy See, and to try to defend Irish nationalism. In Leo XIII's days, the rector was Mgr Tobias Kirby. When Kirby learnt that Archbishop McCabe was about to be created a cardinal in Ireland and was backed by Errington, he intervened and asked the Pope to consider Bishop Moran instead, a prelate in favour of Charles Stewart Parnell. Kirby was very frank with the Pope and spoke in violent terms against McCabe. Leo XIII was upset and deferred his decision although in the end McCabe received the red hat.[10] This affair was a foretaste of intrigues to come. At the beginning of the twentieth century, Britain still had no official representation at the papal court and British ecclesiastics residing in the Italian capital were generally entrusted with the mission to explain their country's policy towards Ireland. One of them was Cardinal Aidan Gasquet who had lived in Rome in the magnificent palace of San Calisto since 1907.[11] Gasquet did not approve of Home Rule and deliberately tried to damage the nationalist cause.

Mgr Michael O'Riordan came from the diocese of Limerick and had a good relationship with Bishop O'Dwyer. At the beginning of the century, he wrote a book entitled *Catholicity and Progress* in which he explained that Catholicism was not a hindrance to economic growth and prosperity, contrary to what some unionists and Protestants claimed.[12] Indeed, at the end of the nineteenth century, many in Victorian Britain, such as Arthur Balfour the Irish Secretary, believed that Roman Catholicism was an obscurantist religion.[13] O'Riordan's point was that Ireland would be perfectly able to take care of itself once Home Rule had become a reality. He became rector of the Irish College in Rome in 1905. Although he was a convinced nationalist, he regularly declared to Irish bishops that he did not deal with politics. Once, O'Riordan wrote to Dr MacRory, the Bishop of Down and Connor: 'I have never been a politician in the usual sense; never a reader of newspapers. Hence my political convictions are few, the fundamental being to trust neither Liberal or Tory and the former even less than the latter.'[14] O'Riordan believed that the Nationalist party should always remain independent. Mgr Hagan, the vice-rector, confirmed O'Riordan's declarations but was of the opinion that the English colony residing in Rome had forced him to change his mind and to become embroiled in politics.[15] For an apolitical man, O'Riordan's diplomatic skills proved remarkable. In 1910, the rector was persuaded that the Roman Curia had to be convinced at all costs of the difference between Ireland and Britain in order to avoid all unnecessary and harmful intervention of the Vatican. A few years before the war, he made a powerful speech at the Roman Academy entitled 'The Fight for Catholic Liberty in Ireland and in England' in which he explained in great detail the difference between the two countries. According to Hagan, it had been a real revelation for many cardinals present that day.[16] Nevertheless, O'Riordan was perceived as a radical nationalist by Cardinals Bourne and Gasquet simply because he wanted the Irish Church to be represented by Irish prelates. Like Hagan, he devoted himself to defending Ireland's distinct nationality between 1914 and 1918 against his English 'neighbours', as he used to call them. The rector liked to say: 'An Englishman, be he labelled Conservative or Liberal or Labour, is always an Englishman as far as Ireland is concerned and will always find a way of going back on his undertaking the moment it serves his purpose.'[17] Those were strong nationalistic feelings but perhaps not entirely unjustified bearing in mind Errington's mission to Rome, Leo XIII's intervention and the War Office's Irish policy during the war. This latent distrust was the rector's driving force.

Mgr John Hagan was O'Riordan's second in command in the college. He had come to Rome in 1904, was from the diocese of Dublin and was a close friend of Mgr Curran. Like the latter, Hagan was quite radical in his nationalism, flirting with republicanism. He regularly corresponded with Archbishop Walsh's secretary and kept him informed of all the latest political gossip in Rome and in the Vatican. Curran kept Hagan posted of the political climate in Ireland and particularly of Walsh's confrontations with the recruitment authorities. But, it was above all as the Rome correspondent of the *Catholic Bulletin* of J.J. O'Kelly that Hagan would be known. Every month, he wrote an article entitled 'Notes from Rome', which informed the Irish about events in the Italian capital. His nom de plume was 'Scottus'.[18] The vice-rector often denounced the Italian press for it based its information on Ireland on news from British Conservative newspapers. In January 1913, Hagan criticised the *Corriere d'Italia* for being openly anti-Irish: 'It is no excuse to say that this was done in ignorance, and was due either to the influence of one of the directors who has many family ties among the great conservative houses of England, or was actually dictated by certain English members, resident in Rome.'[19] It was an allusion to Cardinal Gasquet who was a friend of the editor of the *Corriere d'Italia*, a Mgr Pucci.[20] Hagan, like O'Riordan, was to follow a separatist policy and prove that Ireland was not a mere region belonging to Britain, and he also wished Ireland to be represented by Irishmen and not by Sir Henry Howard's British mission which had just arrived in Rome.[21] The German authorities had become aware of the fact that the college was a hotbed of Irish nationalism in Rome and had managed to turn one of its members into an informer. In January 1915, the Auswärtiges Amt (Foreign Office) in Berlin instructed John Devoy, the Irish republican in America, to 'send all possible literature to *Collegio Irlandese* Rome', but the British, however, had intercepted the German message and decoded it.[22] They were therefore au fait with the connection between the college and the German authorities. Although there is no evidence to suggest that Hagan was the man for whom this literature was intended, his political opinions would tend to indicate that he was at least a likely suspect. Indeed, in 1920 he was involved in a scheme to buy Italian guns for the Irish Republican Army during the War of Independence. The nationalist poet Gabriele D'Annunzio and the fascist leader Benito Mussolini promised assistance to the IRA. The negotiations proved to be difficult and eventually came to nothing.[23] As for O'Riordan, he was a nationalist but not a republican and it is unlikely that the Germans had contacts with one of the students, simply because they did not have much influence.

The two men could not have known that nationalist Ireland was to benefit from the international diplomatic situation. The Vatican, although officially neutral, was favourably disposed towards the Triple Alliance. From 1914 until at least the autumn of 1917, Germany backed the Vatican financially, for it was on the brink of bankruptcy. The financial transactions took place through Swiss banks. This was the work of Matthias Erzberger, a Catholic MP and also head of German propaganda in neutral countries. Benedict XV and Cardinal Gasparri fully appreciated this German generosity, and the grateful Pope went as far as to offer Erzberger his old cardinal's hat. In May 1915, Cardinal von Hartmann, the Primate of the German Catholic Church, had said at the Kaiser's headquarters that 'the Pope [was] frankly Germanophile'.[24] Under those circumstances, it was to be expected that the Vatican would not be favourably disposed to Britain and her aims in the war. Even if nationalist Ireland had no official legation at the Holy See, she could rely on the services of O'Riordan and Hagan. In 1914, their first task was to neutralise Sir Henry Howard's mission in Rome.

THE COLLEGE, THE MISSION AND THE VATICAN, 1914–APRIL 1916

When the war broke out in August 1914, Britain and France rapidly realised that they were not in a strong position at the Vatican as they had refused to open formal diplomatic relations with the Holy See. Russia had a representative, Dimitri Nelidov, but he was not particularly effective and it was much the same for Maximilien d'Erp, the Belgian Minister. On the other hand, Germany and Austria-Hungary did have legations with very able diplomats like Otto Mühlberg, Otto Ritter and Prince Johann Schönburg.[25] The Triple Entente was rightly convinced that the Vatican might be influenced and used by its enemies, and soon the British decided to send an extraordinary envoy to the papal court. Herbert Asquith's cabinet did not try to conceal the reasons behind Sir Henry Howard's mission to Rome. In January 1915, the English Catholic newspaper, the

Tablet, was allowed to publish a letter from Sir Edward Grey, the Foreign Office Secretary, containing instructions for Howard. The Extraordinary Envoy's task was to justify Britain's position in the war and persuade neutral countries of Britain's just cause and good will.[26] The conception of this British mission to the Vatican was important as it appeared that Cardinal Gasquet was largely involved. The English Cardinal was corresponding with John Redmond and on 7 November 1914, Gasquet summed up the political climate in Rome for the Nationalist leader:

> The attitude of the general ecclesiastic out here towards England and Belgium is very strange. I do not – of course – mean the authorities but the ordinary monsignori and I do not suppose it matters what they think, but it isn't pleasant. Most of them are very pro-German, without having studied the question and they get their ideas from the activity of the ministers of Prussia, Austria and Bavaria to the Vatican. We have no look in it at all.
>
> (NLD, Redmond papers, MS 15188, Gasquet to Redmond, 7 November 1914)

It is not surprising that Gasquet and Redmond were exchanging letters. In the past, the English hierarchy had often asked the Nationalist party to help it in religious affairs for there was no English Catholic party in the British Parliament. Shane Leslie, who wrote a biography of Gasquet, was of the opinion that 'it was at [the Cardinal's] desperate suggestion [that] the Foreign Office though divided against itself despatched a British Mission to the Holy See'.[27] According to Abbot Butler who resided in Rome, Redmond took the hint 'and privately aided the sending of the British Mission'.[28] The idea of Ireland having a diplomatic representation in the Italian capital was in the air. In January 1915, Archbishop Harty informed Bishop O'Dwyer that rumour had it that the Holy See had asked Redmond to send a Nationalist MP to represent the country in Rome. The Archbishop remarked that Redmond had refused lest he increased unionist opposition to Home Rule.[29] If this was indeed the case, the Nationalist leader had acted wisely and consistently with his policy of bringing Protestants and Catholics together in the war. Around 20 November 1914, Italian newspapers announced the opening of diplomatic relations between Britain and the Vatican. The *Giornale d'Italia* believed that this new attempt would be crowned with success and that Sir Henry Howard's mission would remain in Rome at least until the end of the war.[30] O'Riordan and Hagan immediately thought that Howard was a threat to nationalist Ireland, exactly like George Errington had been. The British initiative was viewed with deep suspicion in Irish ecclesiastical circles. Mgr Curran humorously wrote to Hagan: 'So you have got a Minister Plenipotentiary.

What Leo [XIII] spent a life time trying to achieve ... It looks very like as if the year that was to have seen Home Rule for Ireland will see Rome Rule with sauce *à l'Anglaise*'.[31] Although there was understandable reason for concern, O'Riordan, Hagan and Curran obviously did not know about the secret financial transactions between the Vatican and Germany that would play into their hands rather than Britain's. O'Riordan thought about a way to neutralise Howard's influence and to persuade Roman society, lay and ecclesiastical, that the British Extraordinary Envoy was Britain's representative, not Ireland's, and that the Irish College would have nothing to do with him. Ostracism was the rector's main battle plan. He outlined his approach to Bishop O'Dwyer:

> The new English Special Envoy has arrived. He has not called here yet, when he comes, I will return the visit *quo forma*. But this college shall not be identified with him on any public occasion. I think some move is being made for a reception at which all the British are to be invited. Gasquet is at it, and Fr David Fleming with his character in the versatility is engaged also. I don't know what the other Irish in Rome will do: but this college shall not be represented! To any who asked me what was said about the Special Envoy in Ireland, I replied that nothing was said – he does not concern them: he represents England, but not Ireland.
>
> (LDO, O'Dwyer papers file 'O'Riordan to O'Dwyer 1887–1917', 'O'Riordan to O'Dwyer, 28 December 1914)

O'Riordan would strictly follow this plan for the duration of the war. His letter also divulged a delicate problem, as not all the Irish in the city shared the rector's nationalism and separatism. Abbot Butler wrote that 'the intense feelings in Rome tended to bring out Nationalism and under their Catholicism, the Irish were more Irish than their leader John Redmond'.[32] There were many Irish religious orders in the Italian capital like the Dominicans, the Franciscans, the Carmelites, the Augustinians and the Christian Brothers. Hagan believed, for instance, that the latter were anglophiles.[33] The vice-rector took up his pen and wrote an article about Howard's arrival in the *Catholic Bulletin*. According to him, the Vatican was already infested with pro-British cardinals like Merry del Val, the old Secretary of State, Gasquet, Prior, Stanley and MacIntyre, the rector of the English College. He stated: 'We can only hope that [Howard] will carefully eschew the tactics of the heads of the Howard family whose interests in the welfare of Ireland has been known to manifest itself recently at home and abroad in ventilating the prophesy that Catholicity stands to lose in Ireland by the setting up of a Home Rule regime in that country.'[34] Hagan was alluding to the Duke of Norfolk, a relative of Howard, who had declared himself to be against Home Rule in 1912.[35] In the meantime, Gasquet took the initiative and lost no time in introducing Howard to ecclesiastical dignitaries and politicians in Rome. O'Riordan was invited to a lavish reception in honour of the new Extraordinary Envoy but refused to go. He wrote to O'Dwyer: 'Sir Henry Howard is here to counteract German falsehood by English truth ... As I am not a Britisher, I did not go.'[36] He regretted that the Irish Dominicans had accepted the invitation. Hagan informed his readers about the Dominicans' decision, and added that most of the Irish in Rome did not accept the invitation as they wished to show Howard that he had nothing to do with them and that he should mind his own business.[37] In Ireland, the nationalist opposition also published Hagan's latest article in *Scissors and Paste* under the heading 'The British Mission to the Vatican'.[38]

In Rome, the Pope and the Curia had not been deceived by Britain's diplomatic efforts and Cardinal Falconio sarcastically remarked on Howard: 'One spy the more in our house.'[39] On his arrival the Extraordinary Envoy Howard did not want to upset O'Riordan in any way. As a diplomat he was most certainly aware of Irish nationalist sensitivities. Nevertheless, he could not have known that his mission was doomed right from the moment he set foot in the Italian capital. In March 1915, Cardinal Gasparri was very active behind the scenes as he feared that Italy might enter the war on the Triple Entente's side. This was not in the Holy See's interest since it was not officially independent yet and this would have isolated it from an international point of view.[40] Gasparri got wind of the secret negotiations between the British and the Italians and this must have considerably influenced the Pope in his decisions vis-à-vis Britain and Howard. O'Riordan had regular audiences with Benedict XV during which he discussed not only religious affairs but also the political situation in Ireland. On 22 April 1915, the rector was at the papal court where the Pope told him that he had had a conversation with a 'diplomat' the day before. O'Riordan related his audience to Bishop O'Dwyer but refused to name the diplomat, fearing the censor, although it was plain that it was Howard. He wrote: '[The diplomat] asked the Pope if he had any subject in particular to speak about, as he had acquaintances over Europe, in all the belligerent nations. The Pope said he had not; but looking towards the window discussed on the promising improvement in the state of the weather'.[41] Benedict XV's rather detached attitude summed up his feelings for British diplomacy and the French fared no better. On 12 May 1915, only a few days before Italy's entry in the war, Victor Bucaille of the Quai d'Orsay reported that German diplomacy was very active at the Vatican. According to him, Archbishop Eugenio Pacelli, the Under Secretary of State and future

Pius XII, had much time for the Germans but very little for him.[42]

But Howard's mission was completely discredited when Italy and Britain eventually signed their secret treaty including the famous clause XV, which excluded the Pope from any future peace negotiations. The Holy See found out in December 1915, if not before. This could not have failed to affect Benedict XV and Gasparri and lead them to adopt a favourable attitude to the Central Powers and nationalist Ireland. Shane Leslie described the humiliation of Howard's mission, since the Extraordinary Envoy himself had been left completely in the dark:

> The British Legation were left by the Foreign Office to fight their battles blindfolded. They were not informed of the secret clause by which the Allies, in their anxiety to bring Italy into the war, had excluded the Holy See from the peace. Three months later Cardinal Gasparri, Secretary of State, had found out and asked the British Legation frankly. They looked very foolish but they had not played the knave. This was the only manner in which the Foreign Office misused the Papal confidence.
>
> (NLD, Leslie papers, MS 22892, 'Biographical study of Card. Gasquet')

It was perhaps 'the only manner' as Leslie euphemistically wrote, but the Foreign Office had shown considerable duplicity on this occasion. Sir Henry Howard had no chance whatsoever of being successful as George Errington in influencing the Vatican on Irish affairs. In February 1916, the vice-rector wrote in the *Catholic Bulletin* that he had heard about clause XV but did not believe in it. He added: 'Should it turn out to be true, it would be a curious illustration of the advantages the Catholic Church is deriving from the existence of a British Catholic Envoy to the Holy See.'[43] His remark was logical but the truth was indeed astonishing. Given the choice between a small Catholic country that wanted independence and its deceitful master, it was easy to guess whom the Pope and his Secretary of State would support. Without knowing it, the Irish College had obtained an easy victory over the British mission in the early months of the war. The international situation had prevented Howard from becoming another Errington, if that had been his initial intention. However, O'Riordan and Hagan would need all their political cunning to put Cardinal Gasquet on the sidelines.

DUEL BETWEEN THE IRISH COLLEGE AND CARDINAL GASQUET

Aidan Gasquet had been prior of the Benedictine abbey of Downside in England. He was an ardent British patriot who had defended the behaviour of British soldiers during the Boer War in South Africa and was subsequently described as a 'most thorough-going John Bull'.[44] In 1908, Pius X appointed him head of the Pontifical Commission for the Revision of the Vulgate in Rome and in 1914, he received the red hat in Italy.[45] On this last occasion, the Irish College had been invited to the ceremony but had refused to go. O'Riordan explained to O'Dwyer that Gasquet had had the arrogance to include the Irish in the term 'British'. The rector went further and told the Bishop of Limerick that he had denounced Gasquet and his anti-Irish activities to Pius X.[46] He believed that the English Cardinal's intentions were to sow discord at the Vatican concerning Irish nationalism. Relations between the two men did not get off to a good start and Gasquet had noticed the coolness of the college towards him. In 1916, he complained to Archbishop Walsh about this and also about rumours, saying that he was anti-Irish:

> Perhaps I feel strongly on the matter, because ever since I have been Cardinal, our friends at the Irish College here have boycotted me and the reasons assigned in a letter written to me by the vice-rector [Hagan], are one and all absolutely false. I am supposed to be anti-Irish and to have acted as such on many occasions. Never in my life have I done anything in regard to Ireland, either with the Pope or otherwise.
>
> (DDA, Walsh papers, 388I/1916, Gasquet to Walsh,
> 6 January 1916)

Walsh was Hagan's ecclesiastical superior and perhaps Gasquet was hoping that Walsh would discipline the vice-rector, but nothing of the kind happened. In fact, Gasquet was a complex man when it came down to Irish affairs. It is stated that he liked jokes with racist undertones, showing the stupidity of the Irish people. When the Cardinal heard that Hagan had said that he was working against Home Rule for £900 a year, he replied: 'For £900!!! I would work against Home Rule for half that amount.'[47] Shane Leslie, in a letter to O'Riordan in April 1915, assured the rector that the Cardinal was harmless: 'I look upon Gasquet as an old bear with the smallest capacity or desire to intrigue.'[48] In this instance, Leslie proved to be a poor judge of character.

The British mission, as has been seen, was Gasquet's brainchild. According to Abbot Butler, the palace of San Calisto, the Cardinal's residence, became 'a second centre of allied propaganda' in Rome.[49] When Gasquet learnt that the Irish College would not go to the reception in honour of Sir Henry Howard, he believed that O'Riordan and Hagan wanted to show their objection to the presence of the British Extraordinary Envoy at the Vatican. However, he did not think the two men had anything against the presence of an English cardinal in the Curia.[50] His assessment was correct but what the college vehemently objected to was Britain's interference in Irish-Papal relations. A confrontation between Gasquet and Hagan eventually took place in October 1914 during a dinner in Rome. Hagan related the incident in detail to O'Riordan who was then on a holiday in Ireland. At the dinner table, the two men were sitting next to each other and Gasquet, knowing that Hagan had recently been in Ireland, asked him 'how did [you] leave the most distressful country?' The vice-rector boldly retorted: 'Which country? [Do you] mean England?' Thereupon, a frank discussion began:

> I [Hagan] informed him that I had passed very severe strictures on his attempt to influence the Holy See and the Cardinal Secretary of State against Home Rule on the ground that it would be inimical to the interests of the Church in Ireland. You can imagine the sensation at the table and you can also imagine the surprise of all present when he stated point blank that this was not true, that he never did anything of the kind – and not only this but that he was altogether opposed to the Holy See mixed in the matter, that it was not a question for the Holy See, that his only objection against Home Rule lay in the possibility of disruption of the Empire, that this danger was now shown to be non-existent.
>
> (ICR, O'Riordan papers no. 15, letter no. 215,
> Hagan to O'Riordan, 25 October 1914)

According to Hagan, nobody present that night believed that Gasquet was telling the truth. Nevertheless, the Cardinal's fear of Home Rule being a threat to the Empire in time of war was not surprising, bearing in mind his ardent patriotism. It would seem that John Redmond's ideas regarding Ireland's participation in the war had changed Gasquet's mind. Hagan decided to keep duelling with the Cardinal and on 29 October 1914, he sent him a long and outspoken letter. The quarrel between the two men dated back to 1910, when Gasquet had explained to the Vatican why Home Rule might be against the interests of Catholicism in Ireland. Unfortunately, the vice-rector did not give more details on Gasquet's arguments but it was very likely that he said that Home Rule would bring about secularism in the country. Hagan told the Cardinal that he had an informer in San Calisto who had reported this to him, but that he had also personally heard Gasquet saying this. Then he claimed that the very pro-British Secretary of State at the time, Cardinal Merry Del Val, had expressed his concern on the matter to five Irish bishops who were in Rome. The whole matter was a perfect illustration of political table talk in the ecclesiastical world of Rome. The vice-rector concluded his letter by evoking the absence of the college at Gasquet's consecration. He wrote that Gasquet's speech on that occasion suggested that he would be 'a cardinal in Curia not only for England but also for Ireland', and added that their absence 'was almost the only means [the college] had of refusing to lend colour to the assumption contained in the address'.[51] Hagan had clearly shown his separatism and had little time for Imperial unity in the war. The next day, he received a reply from Gasquet who denied that Home Rule was a threat to Catholicism and that he had ever tried to influence the Holy See in Irish affairs: 'I do not think there is any need to go into the details for my general denial that I have used any influence I may have had against the policy of Home Rule for Ireland with the Vatican authorities.'[52] O'Riordan, who was in Dublin at the time, complimented Hagan on his witty reply on England to the Cardinal and wrote that he had been right: 'It was terrible in the truth it implied; for they are in dread terror of William [the Kaiser] at present.'[53] The rector related a similar story about Gasquet's opinions on Ireland, which seemed to be contradictory. O'Riordan's source was also an informer and he commented ironically: 'Which Gasquet is correct? That is the whole question.'[54] The Cardinal's attitude was indeed ambivalent and O'Riordan and Hagan had every reason to be on their guard.

If Gasquet and Merry Del Val hoped to influence in one way or another the highest authorities in the Vatican, their chances of success were, however, rather slim. Del Val's power had considerably diminished when Pius X died. Pietro Gasparri, his successor, was one of his greatest rivals and the new Cardinal Secretary of State's Under Secretary was Bonaventura Cerretti who firmly believed in the rights of small nations to self-determination.[55] Cerretti and Hagan met regularly and exchanged ideas about Ireland. In November 1914, Cerretti had come back from England where he had spoken with several personalities. He gave a full account of his meetings to Hagan:

> Cerretti told me while in London Bourne and Norfolk tried to impress him with the danger that Home Rule was certain to bring to the Church: it would deprive the English Catholics of the support of the Irish MPs; it would lead to the formation of anti-clericalism; and several of the bishops (Irish) and many priests were afraid of it but were afraid to speak out.
>
> (ICR, O'Riordan papers no. 15 letter no. 221, Hagan to O'Riordan, 21 November 1914)

This letter was very relevant on several accounts. Firstly, it showed that Cardinal Bourne and the Duke of Norfolk, one of the rare British aristocrats to be Catholic, had analysed the situation in Ireland in-correctly, or else they had the firm intention to mislead Cerretti and hope for the Vatican's intervention against Irish nationalism. As has been seen, the overwhelming majority of the clergy in Ireland supported John Redmond, Britain and the war effort in 1914, and only a handful of bishops and priests did not approve of Redmond's political initiatives. Secondly, it unveiled a potential threat to the English Catholic Church. If Home Rule was implemented, Irish MPs would leave Westminster Parliament and English Catholics would become voiceless. Gasquet, too, must have had this problem on his mind. It was quite likely that Bourne, Norfolk and Gasquet knew about the Irish Catholic Church's favourable attitude to Home Rule at the beginning of the war. Norfolk himself was a unionist and his judgement might have been biased, to say the least. Finally, the sole fact that Cerretti freely informed Hagan in great detail about his meetings in London, tended to prove that the Vatican was slowly but surely putting an end towards its pro-British attitude.

Gasquet's task, if he really had one, to persuade the Holy See that Irish nationalism was contrary to Catholic interests was an arduous one. The Cardinal was not helped either by J. Gregory, Sir Henry Howard's secretary. Gregory's diplomatic skills lacked subtlety and tact, and it was quite a wonder that he had been able to pursue a career in diplomacy. The secretary was not particularly discreet and had strong opinions on many people in Rome, including Benedict XV, which he did not hesitate to share. Hagan wrote to Bishop O'Donnell 'that he [was] making himself remarkable for the imprudent use of his tongue'.[56] The vice-rector had written the truth for at the end of 1915, Gregory was eventually called back to Britain. O'Riordan commented sarcastically 'that he had a bitter tongue, even against the Vatican, which he evidently looked on as a powerful machine to be waked during the war in the cause of civilisation'.[57] In January 1916, O'Riordan wrote to O'Dwyer and informed him on the latest developments and rumours in Rome. He said that Cardinal Bourne had visited certain Irish regiments and that he had explained to them that there was now a union between Britain and Ireland. The Cardinal had taken upon himself to persuade these soldiers of the noble cause of the British Empire. On 14 November 1915, Bourne had addressed the men of the 16th Irish Division, who represented Redmond's ideals, and congratulated them on participating voluntarily in the war and answering the Nationalist leader's call.[58] A few weeks later, the Cardinal went to Rome where he granted an interview to the *Corriere d'Italia* in which he claimed 'that England and Ireland had acted like two sisters who quarrelled together, but when they were threatened by an outsider at once turned against the latter'.[59] This kind of familial image grated on O'Riordan's ears. On 5 January 1916, he shared his feelings with O'Dwyer:

Card. Bourne made it known through the <u>Corriere d'Italia</u> [*sic*] also about this unity of spirit, then he addressed the Irish soldiers at the front – he was referred to in the <u>Corriere</u> [*sic*] which reported the interview as the <u>Primate d'Inghilterra</u> [*sic*, Primate of England]; and I suppose by inference of Ireland also. Card. Gasquet and others here would give their eyes to have it appear that we are all one now. He paid me two visits in hospital. Some of the Irish residents here have fallen into the trap: but they are beginning to feel the foolishness of it. <u>Unity</u> [*sic*] means <u>absorption</u> [*sic*] for our good neighbours [the English].

(LDO, O'Dwyer papers, file I, O'Riordan to O'Dwyer,
5 January 1916)

O'Riordan and Hagan were not to be easy victims of Gasquet's and Bourne's guile and their best defence was to openly display their separatism. They knew well that nationalist Ireland was split into two camps, those who followed Redmond and his pro-war and pro-Empire policy, and those who were against the war as long as Ireland was not officially independent or autonomous. Unfortunately for Gasquet, the two Irishmen belonged to the latter camp. A member of the British Foreign Office said quite rightly: 'Gasquet fought a brave battle with few supporters and not much ammunition in face of a highly organised offensive.'[60] It was true. The combination of the Vatican and Germany on the one hand, and the management of Irish affairs by O'Riordan and Hagan on the other, made Gasquet's victory at the Holy See very improbable. The rector was closely monitoring the situation in Ireland because of the Bishop of Limerick's letters. Soon, it appeared that O'Dwyer and O'Riordan would work together and be the originators of a rapprochement between nationalist Ireland and the Vatican.

CORRESPONDENCE BETWEEN MGR O'RIORDAN AND BISHOP O'DWYER

Mgr Michael O'Riordan was on very good terms with Bishop O'Dwyer. Before becoming rector of the Irish College in Rome, he had been a history teacher in Saint Munchin's College in Limerick. Like many of his compatriots, he had embraced Home Rule and John Redmond's Nationalist party. Most of his ideas were in tune with the Bishop's and he did not always agree with the party's tactics in the Westminster Parliament. Like O'Dwyer, he wished it to be more independent in its dealings with the English Liberal party as he felt that the Liberals could not always be fully trusted in Irish affairs. His opinion of Redmond as a leader varied from time to time. In 1910, he completely agreed with

Redmond when he defended the position of Catholic schools in Britain as the Liberals had plans of secularisation. On this occasion, the rector had written a memorandum on the issue for the Roman Curia.[61] This political debate illustrated how much English Catholics depended on the Nationalist party. The United Kingdom's entry into the war changed O'Riordan's opinion on the party and from then on the gap between him and Redmond gradually widened. At the beginning of the hostilities in Europe, O'Riordan was on holiday in Ireland and his opinion on the political climate in the country was negative. He did not agree with Redmond's decision to follow Britain against Germany and his appeal to Irishmen to join the colours.

When O'Riordan returned in Rome in December 1914, Hagan noticed that he had changed his mind concerning the Nationalist leader. He believed that the British Government's assurances regarding Home Rule were too vague and that the cabinet could not be fully trusted. Therefore, he was of the opinion 'that it was nothing short of a crime for any public man . . . to use his influence to induce young Irishmen to offer the sacrifice of their lives for ideals that were of questionable sincerity'.[62] On 28 December 1914, the rector sent his first wartime letter to O'Dwyer in which he commented on his recent holiday in the country:

> Two things struck me during my stay in Ireland: one was the actual prosperity of the country; the other was a lowered sense of national dignity which had, I thought, fallen more since the war began, than in thirty years before. It was in evidence everywhere. Nations, like persons, are most respected by others when they respect themselves.
>
> (LDO, O'Dwyer papers, file 'O'Riordan to O'Dwyer, 1887–1917', O'Riordan to O'Dwyer, 28 December 1914)

The rector shared the Bishop's views, namely that Ireland was the victim of a political blackmail, Home Rule in return for recruits, and that economic prosperity had blunted the edge of Irish nationalism. Concerning the war, O'Riordan did not specifically blame Germany and in January 1915, he wrote to O'Dwyer that he had initially thought Germany would be beaten because of a lack of food supplies, but he had revised his opinion and believed that it would not be the case. O'Riordan feared instead that the war could drag on and said that he had found '[his] friends in England too boastful'.[63] According to him, it was rather 'a sign of fear' and he had found 'many similarly painted in Ireland – with a thicker coat on'. He also informed the Bishop of Limerick about Sir Henry Howard's arrival in Rome. The rector's letter showed how the two men would operate: O'Riordan would inform

O'Dwyer about the latest Roman machinations, and O'Dwyer would enlighten O'Riordan about the situation in Ireland, from his point of view obviously. This collaboration would last until the Bishop's death in August 1917.

In November 1914, as has been noted, O'Dwyer publicly denounced the war for the first time, notably the diehard attitude of some politicians like Redmond. On 6 January 1915, O'Riordan wrote to O'Dwyer: 'I am surprised you are still alive; that the military authorities have not shot you for having dared to say that William of Germany is not at all a devil and that you dared to hint that John Bull is not quite a saint.' The rector mocked the press and its daily reports of sensational Allied victories. Then he heaped derision on Redmond's policy by saying: 'How are "our troops" doing? And are the hopes of the "Hiberno-English Empire" high?'[64] Clearly, O'Riordan did not share Redmond's enthusiasm for the creation of the 16th Irish Division. On 7 February 1915 a highly effective collaboration between the two men was set in motion. Benedict XV had ordered it to be a day of prayer and expiation for peace in the world.[65] The Pope had made clear that he would be neutral in the war, even though he appreciated the fact that some of the Vatican's money was coming from Germany. It was on this policy of neutrality that O'Riordan and O'Dwyer would base their political activities.

A week later, the Bishop published his Lenten pastoral in which he explained that all the nations were responsible for the present dreadful war.[66] The rector received a copy and was very much impressed by O'Dwyer's forceful arguments and his eloquence. He voluntarily undertook the translation of the pastoral into Italian to distribute it in Rome. According to Hagan, O'Riordan saw there an opportunity to improve O'Dwyer's public image, which had suffered because of the Bishop's attitude towards the Plan of Campaign.[67] But, above all, the rector understood that he could draw together the Vatican and the Bishop of Limerick by proving to the Pope and the Curia that O'Dwyer was following Benedict XV's peace initiatives. An anti-militarist bishop from a belligerent country could be used by the Vatican for propaganda reasons. Furthermore, and most importantly, O'Riordan grasped that this could benefit nationalist Ireland and neutralise all British interference in Irish-Papal relations. Once the translation was completed, he gave two copies to Cardinal Gasparri, the Secretary of State, and Cardinal De Lai from the Holy Office and also one to Benedict XV. Shortly afterwards, he told O'Dwyer what the Pope had thought of his pastoral:

> The Pope read some of it in my presence, and seemed pleased. I was moved to translate it because I knew that its neutral tenor

would please him. However, I dare say it will not draw an autograph from him as in the last case. The rival belligerents are watching like cats for every look or word of his – or words which are not his at all.

(LDO, O'Dwyer papers, file, O'riordan to O'Dwyer, 1887–1917, O'Riordan to O'Dwyer, 20 March 1915)

O'Riordan had succeeded in bringing O'Dwyer to the attention of Benedict XV. The rector wrote that De Lai intended to have the pastoral published in the *Bulletino Diocesano di Sabina*. This contrasted starkly with Mgr Hogan, the President of Maynooth, who had criticised Benedict XV for not having spoken out for the Allies. O'Riordan had little time for Hogan's pro-allied stance and had ironically suggested to him that 'they should excommunicate the Pope for neglecting his duty'.[68] On 8 April 1915, O'Riordan replied to a letter from O'Dwyer and said that he was not surprised his 'pastoral disappeared as a pebble in the lake, in the actual Ireland'. However, this was far from being the case in Italy. Cardinal Ferrari of Milan and Archbishop Sbarretti, the old Apostolic Delegate in Canada, had expressed their greatest satisfaction with O'Dwyer's pastoral while Cardinal De Lai had asked for even more copies.[69] The reaction of these ecclesiastical dignitaries was hardly surprising since at that particular time the Curia did everything it could to keep Italy out of the war.[70] It appeared that the international diplomatic situation had helped O'Riordan to make O'Dwyer's name known in Italy. On 6 June, two weeks after Italy's declaration of war on Austria-Hungary, the rector wrote that De Lai still wanted more copies, that the Archbishop of Florence had congratulated O'Dwyer and that the Cardinal of Naples had used it for his seminary.[71] O'Riordan also took the opportunity to comment on the current situation in Ireland. He regretted the formation of the coalition cabinet, including Sir Edward Carson, as he thought it left 'Hibernian trustfulness in an awkward state'. Concerning conscription, he remarked lucidly: 'I doubt very much that any Government will have the hardihood to attempt to raise forces by conscription in Ireland or in England. It is against the spirit and the traditions of both peoples. It is possible that more men fit for fighting should be occupied in enforcing it than its enforcement would gain recruits.'[72] Little could the rector have known how he had been simultaneously wrong and right.

O'Riordan was fully aware of the real intentions of the different foreign legations at the Vatican, and must have guessed that the Triple Entente's diplomats were thinking they had an easier task since Italy was now siding with them in the war. His regular audiences with Benedict XV revealed to him the Pope's frame of mind. The latter was not interested in knowing what the belligerent countries thought of him. According to one of the rector's informants in the Vatican, Benedict XV refused to give tacit support to either side.[73] Obviously Cardinal Gasquet and Sir Henry Howard's role was to persuade the Pope to support Britain and it was this Achilles' heel of their policy which played right into O'Riordan's hands. The rector and the Bishop of Limerick realised that the best way to neutralise British influence on the Holy See was to show allegiance to the Pope. In the summer of 1915, a serious crisis broke out between Cardinal Bourne and the Irish hierarchy on the issues of correspondence between the Vatican and the Irish hierarchy, and authority over the chaplains in the British Army. It would take too long to discuss these crises in detail here. But briefly Bourne took the initiative to settle the problem of correspondence between the Irish hierarchy and the Vatican without consulting Cardinal Logue.[74] Then, he took the liberty to remedy the lack of chaplains for the Army by appointing Irish priests over whom he had no ecclesiastical authority and whose nationality he refused to recognise. The Irish hierarchy strongly resented Bourne's intrusion and soon O'Riordan had to intervene in the crisis and display his talents as a diplomat. During an audience, the Pope reassured the rector that the Irish bishops had nothing to fear from him and that their complaints about Bourne were justified. In fact, even Gasquet wrote that Benedict XV was very vexed by Bourne's attitude.[75] O'Riordan decided to be frank with the Pope and expose the true nature of ecclesiastical power in Britain and Ireland. His message was that the Irish Catholic Church was more powerful and important than the English Catholic Church, a fact Leo XIII had refused to admit. He wrote to O'Dwyer:

> In fact, I added, Card. Bourne or the English Bishops have no influence whatever on the Government: the Irish Bishops have much influence, not because they are Catholic Bishops or Irish, but because they have the Irish Parliamentary Party to enforce their views in Parliament; that Government never has [sic], and never will [sic], grant any favour to Catholics, for the sake of Catholicism, but for the sake of the voting power of Irish Catholics in Ireland and in England, and of the power of the Irish political party in Parliament. That is the secret of the only Catholic influence there can be in the Government. He [the Pope] asked me if the Irish political party are all Catholics. I said they nearly all are Catholics; but that the non-Catholic members vote with them on all questions of importance.
>
> (LDO, O'Dwyer papers, file 'O'Riordan to O'Dwyer, 1887–1917', O'Riordan to O'Dwyer, 13 July 1915)

Herbert Asquith could not have disagreed with this explanation. As for O'Dwyer, he could only appreciate this denunciation of English realpolitik of which the Pope was now informed. But, O'Riordan went further and described a conversation he had with Benedict XV on the Irish situation. His description sheds light on some of the Pope's opinion on the matter:

> Some time ago the Holy Father said to me 'Well, Home Rule is passed at last'. I said 'Yes, it is law, but not effectively'; he said 'but Fr David Fleming told me it is finally concluded, and all that was sought for has been granted'. I said that Fr Fleming is not quite accurate: that the Bill passed through Parliament; that the King refused to sign it, till the war broke out, and he feared his refusal to sign it would prevent recruits in Ireland; that then he signed it but provisionally, in as much as it shall not take effect till the war is over, and that then certain amendments (the nature of which nobody knows) are to be engrafted into it. He said 'But those amendments may spoil it'. I said 'And very many think that they will spoil it in favour of the Orangemen'. He said 'I was much surprised that a question so long agitated and fiercely disputed was settled so suddenly. I now see the reason'.
>
> (LDO, O'Dwyer papers, file 'O'Riordan to O'Dwyer, 1887–1917', O'Riordan to O'Dwyer, 13 July 1915)

It appeared that O'Riordan had gained the ear of the Pope.

On 28 July 1915, Benedict XV wrote a letter for peace in the world. In Limerick, Bishop O'Dwyer, full of confidence after his first Italian success, decided to voice the Pope's initiative and publicly asked John Redmond to use his influence on the British Government to enter peace negotiations, which the Nationalist leader flatly refused to do. O'Dwyer was bitterly disappointed but not surprised, and informed O'Riordan that he had received numerous letters of support.[76] The rector decided, once again, to translate the Bishop's letter into Italian and distribute it to the Curia. It had the desired effect. On 18 September, O'Riordan told O'Dwyer about his latest initiative:

> Did you get the copies of the Italian translation of your letter which I sent you? If not, I can send you more. The under-secretary of State [Eugenio Pacelli, the future Pius XII] told me the Pope was very pleased with it, and was having some of it printed in the Osservatore Romano [sic]. I have not seen it appear yet however. Perhaps it should have appeared in one of these bald spots which the censor keeps immaculate in the Osservatore [sic] as in other papers.
>
> (LDO, O'Dwyer papers, file 'O'Riordan to O'Dwyer, 1887–1917', O'Riordan to O'Dwyer, 18 September 1915)

O'Dwyer thanked the rector profusely and said that he was honoured that the Pope had approved of his letter to Redmond.[77] This did much to increase the Bishop's ultramontane tendencies. Ironically, his very ultramontanism had led him to oppose Irish nationalism during the Plan of Campaign days. Some thirty years later, it was the reverse. In December 1915, O'Dwyer wrote a long letter in which he resumed his confrontations with Redmond, his refusal to believe in German barbarism and the war in favour of small nations. It was published in the United States by the *American Ecclesiastical Review*. O'Riordan, as usual, promptly translated it and edited it in a pamphlet entitled *L'Appello del Santo Padre per la Pace* (the Holy Father's appeal for peace). It came to fruition in January 1916 and was given to the Pope and Italian cardinals.[78] In a footnote for the Italian readers, O'Riordan explained that it was the Irish Bishop's desire to prove how much Redmond was wrong and that Home Rule had been granted to Ireland but suspended for the entire duration of the war and that the law could be modified. The rector's latest initiative, with O'Dwyer's indirect help, was directed against Cardinals Bourne and Gasquet. The two men had been trying for some time to convince the Pope that there was a 'unity of spirit' between Ireland and Britain due to the war, and that Redmond represented the true feelings of Irish opinion. This had indeed been the case in the first months of the conflict but by January 1916 this claim was totally exaggerated. O'Riordan explained to O'Dwyer how he was moved to make this new pamphlet:

> I add my note, both to explain clearly to the Romans what I think to be your mind; and also to disabuse those here of an idea which English residents here, such as Card. Gasquet, and lately Card. Bourne, have been trying to put into the thoughts of those in authority: namely, that as between Ireland and England the past is past, that the war has unified them in the 'cause of civilisation' and 'common interests'. The Pope asked me lately 'Isn't it a fact that there is a <u>perfetta unità di spirito</u> [*sic*] in Ireland and England now', and he quoted his authority. I replied <u>'ne dubito assai'</u> [I quite doubt that]. And I gave him an explanantion which I had already given to him on another occasion and which you will find in my note. Card. Vanutelli asked me the same question when I went to invite him to a conference on Sant Colombano; to which I replied more strongly than I replied to the Pope. The Pope is very quick to take in an idea, and he keeps it once he gets it.
>
> (LDO, O'Dwyer papers, file 'letters from Rome',
> O'Riordan to O'Dwyer, 5 June 1916)

Mgr Hagan also denounced Bourne's new approach of 'the union of hearts in the United Kingdom' in the *Catholic Bulletin* of January 1916.[79] The same month, the vice-rector wrote about his impressions of Redmond to Bishop O'Donnell: 'The more recent news from Ireland would seem to indicate that Mr. Redmond has not the country with him in some of his movements; and personally I wish he had a better acquaintance with Irish History.'[80] O'Donnell could now see that his Redmondite ideas were not shared in the Irish College in Rome. Unquestionably, the relations between O'Dwyer, O'Riordan, Benedict XV and other Italian cardinals were real and solid, and favoured Irish nationalism although not Redmond's version. The British stood little chance of winning diplomatically at the Holy See. The combination of secret clause XV of the Anglo-Italian treaty and O'Dwyer's forceful denunciations of the war was far too strong for Howard, Gasquet and Bourne. Not even the Easter Rising of April 1916 would change this state of affairs. O'Riordan would again prove his diplomatic skills.

THE RED BOOK

The Easter Rising in Dublin did not catch O'Riordan and Hagan off guard since they had been informed of it by Count Plunkett during his mission to the Vatican. This was further proof that the two men were trusted by the nationalist opposition. They both knew that the rising would provoke a political storm in Rome and that Sir Henry Howard would grasp this unique opportunity to regain the diplomatic initiative. His likely argument would be a strong condemnation of the rebels in particular, and of Irish nationalism in general. Some two hundred Irish residents in Rome had sent a telegram of support to John Redmond, assuring him of their loyalty and wishing him and his party 'complete success', presumably in the difficult political times that lay ahead after the rising.[81] O'Riordan did not need more convincing and decided to anticipate British moves in the Vatican by writing a forty-three page book, describing in detail the negative effects of English policy in Ireland, the relation between Home Rule and the war and the War Office's disastrous approach to Irish recruitment. O'Riordan's initiative deeply upset not only the British mission but also the French embassy in Rome.

Shortly after the execution of the rebel leaders in Dublin, O'Riordan sent a letter to O'Dwyer in which he deplored General Maxwell's actions. He believed that the summary execution of the pacifist Francis Sheehy-Skeffington would incite the population to think that the rebel leaders had been shot in the same way and that they would become martyrs of the Irish cause. He added that as far as wisdom was concerned 'there [was] not a pin to choose between the executive and the insurgents'.[82] The rising had had some noticeable effects abroad which were damaging to Britain. In Spain, the British embassy was successful in persuading the Spanish Government to forbid a mass for the fallen rebels.[83] Only a few days before the Irish rebellion, Consul de Longchamps in Dublin informed the Quai d'Orsay in Paris that Irish Catholic opinion had some bad repercussions on neutral countries, notably Spain and the United States.[84] In Dublin, Mgr Curran noticed that many Irish ecclesiastics returning from Rome were of the opinion 'that for the first time in many quarters, the difference of the two countries was realised'.[85] On 27 May 1916, O'Riordan congratulated O'Dwyer for his letter to General Maxwell and wrote: 'I hope he has brains enough to learn the lesson'. He informed the Bishop that he hoped to meet the Pope soon in order to give him a detailed explanation of the events in Dublin. He had in mind to use documents such as speeches from Herbert Asquith and Augustine Birrell, and quote extracts from the Royal Commission, which had investigated the causes of the Easter Rising. He outlined his plan: 'I want others to have time enough to exhaust their lying froth. Then I will come, with cold facts, based on official testimony. If it will do no good, it will prevent possible evil.'[86] The rector knew that the British Prime Minister had recently had an audience with Benedict XV and that it was very likely that the two men had discussed the situation in Ireland. As usual, rumours were rife in Rome and people were saying that Asquith had asked the Pope to silence the Bishop of Limerick. The rector wanted to reassure O'Dwyer immediately and dismissed these rumours as mere gossip:

> It is pretty clear that the wish has been further to the thought with some persons, who have been trying to make persons believe that Mr Asquith has spoken to the Pope; that the inference should be that the Pope is displeased with you, and so on etc etc. And those people are so distracted that they are not left sense enough to see that to be displeased with your pastorals would be to feel displeased with himself: since you have simply followed the line he traced for peace.
>
> (LDO, O'Dwyer papers, file 'letters from Rome',
> O'Riordan to O'Dwyer, 27 May 1916)

His explanation was convincing. Asquith had not much hope of influencing the Pope unless, perhaps, he renounced clause XV of the secret Anglo-Italian treaty and began financing the Holy See too. On 28 April 1916, Cardinal Gasquet tried to minimise the importance of the rising during his audience with the Pope and suggested that Archbishop Walsh be created cardinal, but Benedict XV refused. It is not clear why Gasquet made this suggestion but an educated guess would be that he hoped that Walsh, as a cardinal, would be a moderating influence on the nationalist opposition. More interesting was the fact that he had noticed that the Pope was very well informed on Anglo-Irish relations and that he was familiar with the opinions of the Irish College.[87] This was proof of O'Riordan's influence. Straight after the rising, worrying rumours about the rector spread in Rome. Hagan told O'Riordan that the French-Canadian Bishop Dontonville had said: 'What can you think when the rector of the Irish College is a fenian!'[88] This incident was not surprising since there was a fierce ecclesiastical rivalry between French and Irish-Canadian bishops. It appeared that some French-speaking members of the Canadian hierarchy wanted to have spiritual authority over Irish Catholics living in Canada.[89] All these rumours prompted O'Riordan to write a book, which would give rise to much controversy. On 16 June, he decided to inform Cardinal Gasparri about his intentions. He wrote in his letter that the British Government had not been entirely sincere about the rising and that the Irish in Ireland, America and England were very unsatisfied. This was a clever geopolitical statement since he showed Gasparri how widespread the Irish nationalist and Catholic world was. Then, he made the following offer to the Secretary of State of the Vatican:

> Being the rector of an ecclesiastical college I have habitually absented myself from all political questions and other matters of this type. It is rumoured however that some representations may be made to the Holy See by the British Government in regard to the recent revolt in Ireland and with regard to the conduct of some ecclesiastics in it. I do not know if this is true however. I dare to turn to Your Eminence to make you aware that I am in a position to furnish you with [illegible] information whether it be official documents or private letters sent to me by authoritative persons in Ireland.
>
> (Archivio degli Affari Ecclesiastici Straordinari, Vatican, file 'Guerra anno 1914–1918, rubrica 244, tax. 92, rubrica 244D3', O'Riordan to Gaspari, 16 June 1916)

Gasparri and Benedict XV listened to O'Riordan since both men received a copy of the Red Book a few months later. The rector began his work immediately. In 1919, Mgr Hagan remembered that O'Riordan's aims had been to silence those Irish who represented Sinn Féiners as thugs, who had no time for their country and God, and those English who wanted the Pope to intervene against O'Dwyer. During the elaboration of the book, Hagan became critically ill and it was left to O'Riordan to write the whole document. The vice-rector added that he had based the book entirely on accounts of Augustine Birrell before the Royal Commission, newspaper articles on the rising, official speeches by Asquith, letters from militaries, O'Dwyer's letters and press comments on the Home Rule and partition crises of the summer of 1916.[90] O'Riordan explained to the Bishop of Limerick how he had conceived the book and that he alone took full responsibility for it and that the Irish hierarchy had never asked him to take up his pen in defence of Ireland.[91] In September 1916, the Pope and the Curia were able to read on a red cover *La Recente Insurrezione in Irlanda* (the recent insurrection in Ireland) with the subtitle *Esposizione delle sue Cause e delle sue Consequenze* (account of its causes and consequences). The author's name was not mentioned, nor was the publishing company's. The book was a sensation in Rome and rapidly became known as the Red Book. Later, in December 1916, O'Riordan explained to Cardinal Farley from New York that the colour of the cover was 'for the sake of etiquette . . . [and that] wisely foolish people saw some deep diplomatic mystery in the colour of the cover'.[92] He also indicated that the Pope had received a white-covered copy of the Red Book.

The Red Book was divided into seven long paragraphs and the quoted sources were nearly all English except the following ones: the *New York World*, the *New York Post*, the *Freeman's Journal*, the *Irish Independent*, three letters from Patrick Pearse, Con Colbert and Thomas Kent to their respective families, the correspondence between Bishop O'Dwyer and General Maxwell, O'Dwyer's letter regarding the Irish emigrants at Liverpool and finally a letter from Mgr Curran to the College. What struck the reader was precisely all those references to English sources which left a clear impression of objectivity and impartiality. It became a criticism of British policy in Ireland by the British themselves. O'Riordan had, of course, included personal remarks but largely backed by British documents.

The first paragraph was entitled 'L'Inglese segretario in capo per l'Irlanda spiega il movimento "Sinn Féin", e indaga le cause della insurrezione' (The Irish Secretary explains the Sinn Féin movement and investigates the causes of the insurrection). The rector used mainly two sources here: Augustine Birrell's report and the Royal Commission's report published by *The Times*. The reader could appreciate that Catholic Ireland resented the Act of Union of 1801 and that the Church of Ireland (Anglican) was in a privileged position despite the fact that a great majority of Catholics lived in the country. These were Birrell's own words. The Irish Secretary did not believe a rebellion would ever take place to which O'Riordan added that indeed only a few Irish had participated.[93] The rector then quoted the Royal Commission's conclusion that the UVF had illegally imported arms from Germany. Regarding John Redmond, the rector wrote that the Commission had stated that he had acted in a most patriotic manner but that many Irish people believed that the Government had later turned him into a recruitment sergeant. To highlight this fact, O'Riordan wrote this passage in italics. This paragraph introduced the reader to Ireland's long list of grievances.

The second paragraph was headed 'Una serie di fatti che provocò l'insurrezione' (A series of facts provokes the insurrection). O'Riordan used *The Times*, a conservative and unionist newspaper, the *Daily Chronicle* and extracts of the Royal Commission to explain that some members of the Conservative party like Andrew Bonar Law and Arthur Balfour had supported Sir Edward Carson and the UVF. He pointed out that Carson was about to resist Home Rule, which had been democratically decided by the British Parliament. His paramilitary organisation would use physical force if necessary. On the formation of various Volunteer movements in the country, he remarked: 'There is no intention of the nationalist Volunteers to rebel. On the contrary, their organisation was perfectly constitutional and never broke the law, whereas the Orangemen were getting ready for rebellion'.[94] To demonstrate how differently the Government had treated the Irish Volunteers and the UVF during their respective gun-running operations, he quoted the Bachelor's Walk Massacre in Dublin, where nationalists had been fired upon by the British Army, while the British Navy had been conspicuously absent when arms were disembarked at Larne in Ulster. The aim of this paragraph was to persuade the readers that the Irish Volunteers were those who had acted legally and that they never had had the intention to rebel, simply to protect Home Rule. They were, therefore, not a seditious and revolutionary force, which could be condemned out of hand by Catholic theology.

The third paragraph was devoted to the war and entitled 'Inducendo il re a firmare il progetto di legge di "Home Rule", il governo tende semplicemente un tranello onde fare arruolare irlandesi' (Having persuaded the King to sign the Home Rule Bill, the Government simply set a trap in order to enlist Irishmen). O'Riordan's aim was to persuade the readers of the duplicity and sheer incompetence of the cabinet and the War Office. He explained why Home Rule had been suspended until after the war and that the Irish people had resented the fact that Sir Edward Carson and James Campbell had been appointed in the coalition Government. Like James Connolly, he denounced the practice of economic conscription, which consisted in laying off employees and forcing them into the Army as a last resort and means of survival. The rector quoted O'Dwyer's letter on the Irish emigrants at Liverpool in full, showing that some Irish bishops openly disagreed with the British authorities. But, in this paragraph, O'Riordan especially lambasted the War Office for all its blunders and incompetence and suggested that it was a deliberate ploy:

> In 1915, various events showed to the Irish how the Government had decided to implement Home Rule and how all its promises and assurances were made in order to get recruits in Ireland. Moreover, it appeared that Irish recruits were sent to bloody fights in a few offensives, like Mons where thousands of them were slaughtered; that they were the main body of troops sent to this crazy expedition at Gallipoli where they were almost totally annihilated by the Turks; that in the end, whereas military reports from Gallipoli mentioned their courage to the War Office, the War Office ordered that only Australians would be mentioned in the reports.
>
> (*La Recente Insurrezione in Irlanda*, pp. 12–13)

What the rector wrote was a serious accusation namely that the Government was trying to suppress the renaissance of Irish nationality through the war, which had been John Redmond's idea. But was he right? Lord Kitchener was not particularly fond of things Irish. A recent biography of Kitchener unfortunately says almost nothing about his handling of Irish recruitment apart from the fact that he believed Irishmen would not be very enthusiastic about joining the Army.[95] In another book about Irish soldiers in the Great War, however, it is quite clear that Kitchener did not want the Irish to have a separate army or division, and Augustine Birrell himself admitted: 'Everything the War Office did was wrong in handling recruitment...all the arrangements were made on the assumption of Ireland being an English county'.[96] It seemed that O'Riordan's accusations were well-founded.

Now, the rector had the delicate task to describe and comment on the Easter Rising and this required a tour de force. He carefully thought over his arguments and decided to contrast the rebels' behaviour during the fighting, in the fourth paragraph entitled 'Carattere personale degli insorti: comme essi mantennero la insurrezione' (Personal character features of the rebels: how they behaved during the insurrection), with the behaviour of British soldiers evoked in the fifth paragraph called 'Come invece si sono diportate le autorità militari' (How, as opposed to the rebels, the military authorities behaved). O'Riordan wrote that the Dublin population had initially been against the rising and that the Government had presented the rebels as 'out-and-out revolutionaries'. The rector said, however, that some of them were professors, lawyers etc. and that they were all good Catholics. In order to emphasise the last point, he showed that some of the rebel leaders were pious believers and quoted letters of condemned men, written to their relatives and wives, just before their execution. These letters had a strong Catholic flavour and the aim was to identify nationalism with Catholicism. At the same time in Ireland, the *Catholic Bulletin* had also begun a similar campaign by publishing pictures of those rebels who had died during the rising.[97] This was in sharp contrast to newspapers which supported the Nationalist party, like the *Cork Examiner*, and which published pictures of fallen Irish soldiers in France.[98] The press seemed to be engaged in a war to depict the real Irish heroes, those who fell in the fields of France against those who fell in the streets of Dublin. Then, O'Riordan went on to quote Herbert Asquith who had declared that the insurgents 'had fought with dignity' and that most of them had committed no crimes. His source was *The Times* of 12 May 1916. To conclude this paragraph, he cited a Captain Brereton who had stated that the rebels 'had fought like gentlemen'.[99] O'Riordan's main aim was undoubtedly to do the rebels justice but also to put an end to certain rumours in Rome. In March 1917, Mgr Hagan wrote in the *Catholic Bulletin* that shortly after the Easter Rising, an alleged diary of a Dubliner that described the Irish Volunteers and Sinn Féiners as barbarians was circulating in the Italian capital. As Hagan believed this diary was full of 'intense human interest', he quoted some bloodthirsty passages: 'They have just shot five soldiers, and when they fell wounded, the wild beasts killed them out... They killed a poor wounded man home on leave – the beasts.'[100] The vice-rector could not refrain from adding that Protestants were behind this. Nationalist frustration had reached boiling point. The diary probably explained why O'Riordan wrote this passage and why he contrasted it starkly to some actions of British soldiers. He quoted the summary execution of Francis Sheehy Skeffington and quoted *The Times* of 12 May 1916. But that was not all. He stressed that he possessed a whole range of documents that established beyond any doubt the culpability of British soldiers. To illustrate this point, he used extracts from the *Irish Independent* of 6 May 1916 and a letter from Mgr Curran.[101]

In the sixth paragraph, entitled 'Il clero e il movimento insurrezionale' (The clergy and the insurrectionist movement), O'Riordan depicted the noble attitude of the clergy during the Easter Rising. This was an important passage since the Catholic Church had very strict rules concerning the right to rebel and take up arms. The rector tried to persuade Italian ecclesiastics that the Irish clergy had not supported the rebels at all, but had intervened in the rising for purely humanitarian reasons. He quoted O'Dwyer's letters to Maxwell and pointed out that the Bishop of Limerick was not seeking popularity and reminded his readers that he had opposed the Plan of Campaign. By now, the Curia must have been convinced that O'Dwyer was indeed playing a most singular role in Ireland. Bishop Cohalan's intervention during the rising in Cork was also evoked as was Cardinal Logue's speech at the Maynooth Union in which he refuted the fact that the young clergy were in favour of Sinn Féin. The rector made a point of clarifying why the British Government had never liked the Irish Catholic Church. Firstly, because it had succeeded in maintaining the Catholic faith in Ireland despite injustice and oppression. Secondly, because the Church enjoyed the people's trust, which frustrated the Government. Thirdly, because the Church acted independently and did not systematically help the Government and the Civil Service.[102] This could not really displease the Vatican which was trying to achieve its own independence from the Italian Government.

Finally, O'Riordan concluded the Red Book with a last paragraph called 'Il governo propone una convenzione per l'Home Rule. Il partito irlandese l'accetta. Il governo viola il patto' (The Government proposes an assembly for Home Rule. The Nationalist party accepts it. The Government violates the pact). The rector gave details about the Home Rule and partition negotiations of the summer of 1916 between David Lloyd George, John Redmond and Sir Edward Carson, and related how Redmond was stabbed in the back by Herbert Asquith's cabinet. O'Riordan wrote that this had even been denounced by some of the British press, like the *Manchester Guardian*, the *Daily Chronicle*, the *Daily News* and the *Daily Mail*. All condemned Lloyd George's insincerity as a negotiator. To an Italian cardinal, there could now be little doubt that the British authorities had acted badly towards Ireland and that they had not only provoked a spirit of resistance among the Irish people but also split British public opinion on the Irish question. In the last three pages of the Red Book, O'Riordan wrote that it was the British Government's insincerity that had led to the Easter Rising of April 1916 in Dublin. This was the conclusion he hoped his readers would reach. His arguments carried weight and he had conceived the Red Book cleverly. His final words were an ironic comparison between Ireland and Belgium, two small nations in the war:

Since the beginning of the war in Europe, English politicians and editors have shouted from the rooftops that by invading Belgium, Germany had violated a treaty, 'a scrap of paper': the sentence has become common in England. I have not sufficiently studied this delicate international question to allow myself to reach a personal conviction. However that may be, it is not up to me to make a statement on this debate. But in this case [Home Rule], it is an agreement that concerns Ireland, defined and put forward by the English State, and which the Government has openly violated. So, there is 'a scrap of paper' that England had torn without excuse or regret.

(La Recente Insurrezione in Irlanda)

He thus implied that the war in defence of small nations was a hypocritical argument of the great powers, be it Germany or Britain. To Benedict XV, Cardinal Gasparri and other members of the Curia this must have made sense.

It remained to be seen how the Red Book would be received in Rome. On 23 October 1916, O'Riordan told O'Dwyer that 'he [had] some strong letters from some cardinals'. The tenor of the rector's letter tends to indicate that they had largely approved of nationalist Ireland's case. Cardinal Maffi was asking for more copies. As for the Bishop, he was very satisfied with O'Riordan's work.[103] It is more difficult to know with certainty how the Pope had reacted. Nevertheless, if one bears in mind the international diplomatic situation, it is quite unlikely that he had any objections to it. However, Cardinal Gasquet's activities provided an extra clue. Gasquet had contacts with André Géraud, the organiser of the first French mission in Ireland. The world of international intrigue was a small one. In October 1916, just after the publication of the Red Book, Géraud quoted the Cardinal in a report for the Quai d'Orsay in Paris: 'Real acts of treason can be attributed to [O'Riordan and Hagan]...They have direct and clandestine access to the Pope...According to Cardinal Gasquet, they have a real influence over him.'[104] This was the irrefutable proof that Gasquet did interfere in Irish affairs despite his claiming the contrary, and that O'Riordan and Hagan had been right to be on their guard all along. Gasquet was showing obvious signs of frustration. The Red Book had been another diplomatic success for the Irish College. On 18 November 1916, the English Cardinal learned that O'Riordan could be made an archbishop. He furiously complained to Archbishop Eugenio Pacelli who told him that this rumour had no foundation.[105] In January 1917, Cardinal Bourne was back in Rome and had told a member of the Curia that he had been surprised by the fact that 'Dr O'Riordan who [had] always been so prudent and courteous should write such a document'. The Italian Cardinal personally reported this to the rector who, in turn, asked the prelate to tell Bourne 'that His Eminence [had] his friends here to blame', and that if they persisted in circulating rumours he would translate Sir John Simon's report.[106] This report was an investigation into the alleged brutalities of the British Army during the Easter Rising.

As could have been expected, English diplomatic circles were outraged by the Red Book. Sir Henry Howard, shortly before his resignation, got hold of a copy and promptly sent it to the Foreign Office in London. He suspected that its anonymous author was O'Riordan and wrote that his ideas played right into the Germans' hands. Howard suggested to Grey that he counter the Red Book by a similar action, representing the British view.[107] His suggestion was refused and on 7 December 1916 Grey was replaced by Arthur Balfour. Balfour had been Irish Secretary during the Land War and was not favourably disposed towards Irish nationalism. He believed in the superiority of the Anglo-Saxon race and that the Irish could benefit from this superiority. In fact, he did not particularly like the Irish as a people and thought they were lazy and good for nothing.[108] In the 1880s, he had instructed the RIC to use force, if necessary, against nationalists. In Mitchelstown in Co. Cork in September 1887, the RIC shot dead several nationalist protesters during a trial. As a result he had earned himself the nickname 'Bloody Balfour'. Thirty years later, he wanted to use force against the direction of the Irish College. Four days after his appointment as Foreign Secretary, Balfour allowed his heart to rule his head and sent a telegram to Count de Salis in Rome, who had just replaced Howard: 'I should be glad of your views as to the use you think you may be able to make of proposed prosecution of author and printer in inducing Vatican to remove Rector and Vice-Rector or to take drastic steps as will prevent Irish College from being used in the future as a centre of political intrigue against us'.[109] This telegram was frankly naïve. It was simply inconceivable that Arthur Balfour, even though only recently appointed as Foreign Secretary, was not au fait with the secret Anglo-Italian treaty and the Vatican's frame of mind. Some anti-Irish and anti-clerical sentiments must have incited Balfour to send this. De Salis realised that the demands of the head of British diplomacy would be rejected and on 21 December 1916, he sent back a tactful answer:

> I cannot advise you to continue prosecution. At best you could now obtain little or no good by it while the Vatican will appreciate a conciliatory attitude on your part. I would propose to do what I can [to] ensure this result without pressing for changes in the rectorship. The view about the college expressed in your telegram no 35 seems to me here somewhat exaggerated. As far as I know the college merely acts in these matters as the mouthpiece of the Irish bishops. A solution of the difficulty is to be sought in Ireland rather than in Rome but I should propose to do all I think properly can to diminish the tension hitherto existing here which creates a bad impression.
>
> (PRO, London, FO 380/8, de Salis to Balfour
> 21 December 1916)

The Irish College was never prosecuted for the publication of the Red Book. But the British Government was not alone in worrying

288

about O'Riordan and Hagan's activities. The French had also followed the whole affair. On 25 November 1916, their embassy in Rome sent a copy of the Red Book to the French Prime Minister. According to the embassy, the document 'was only an apology of the insurrection in Ireland and an indictment against British policy in this part of the United Kingdom'.[110] This sentence demonstrated how much the traditional Franco-Irish relations had been damaged due to the war. France now needed England against Germany and as a result her attitude towards Ireland had considerably changed. The embassy wrote that it had a reliable ecclesiastical informant in Rome who had told them that O'Riordan was the author and that the Vatican had printed the Red Book.[111] Unfortunately, this last remark cannot be substantiated. One or two centuries before, O'Riordan would have been a precious ally for the French. The First World War had made the rector an enemy of France's interests.

Michael O'Riordan's initiative was crowned with success. A striking fact about the Red Book was that all nationalist trends in Ireland would have approved of it, from Arthur Griffith to John Redmond. The Nationalist leader could hardly have disagreed with it after his disastrous negotiations with David Lloyd George in the summer of 1916. This was O'Riordan's major feat for the Red Book had not become a political pamphlet in favour of Sinn Féin, which would have been rebuked by the Vatican. It had been primarily conceived to neutralise British diplomatic initiatives at the Holy See after the Easter Rising. Nevertheless, the British threat had not been totally eliminated and Sir Roger Casement's execution would give the College the opportunity to get rid of another foe, Cardinal Francis Bourne.

CARDINAL BOURNE AND SIR ROGER CASEMENT'S EXECUTION

O'Riordan could be very satisfied with his initiatives so far. The British mission and Cardinal Gasquet were no longer much of a menace to Irish nationalism. However, the arrival of Cardinal Francis Bourne of Westminster in Rome brought some danger. Bourne was a devout British patriot and fully backed the Empire against Germany. On several occasions, he had interfered in Anglo-Irish relations much to Cardinal Logue's and Archbishop Walsh's annoyance. Bourne would continue interfering until the very end of the war, since in May 1918, the Cardinal was exchanging ideas with Walter Long, a member of David Lloyd George's cabinet, on a possible federalist scheme to solve the Home Rule crisis. Bourne acted as an adviser on this issue. More interesting was the letter he sent to Long on 17 May 1918, in which he suggested that the British authorities should immediately make Logue aware of the fact that some priests had used very strong and shocking language during the conscription crisis in April 1918.[112] So it appeared that it was Bourne who had been behind this list of twenty-six 'seditious priests' sent to Logue by the Vatican. O'Riordan, as has been seen, played a crucial role in this matter but did not know about Bourne's involvement. The rector was, nonetheless, well aware of the Cardinal of Westminster's involvement in Irish affairs. Two years before, when Sir Roger Casement was executed in London, he got wind of Bourne's very controversial intervention in the execution and had seized the opportunity to discredit him in Rome.

Casement's religious background was somewhat confusing. It seems that he was baptised a Catholic but brought up as a Protestant.[113] Casement was not really preoccupied by religious matters.[114] However, awaiting his execution for his role in the Easter Rising, he suddenly expressed his desire to be reconciled with the Catholic Church to Fr Carey, the chaplain of Pentonville jail in London, and wanted to be confirmed. One hypothesis concerning Casement's train of thought would be that he wanted to get closer to nationalist Ireland. Carey informed Bourne about the prisoner's wish. The Cardinal had no objections provided Casement signed a document in which he regretted his public and private behaviour in the past.[115] Sir Roger refused to sign the document in question but was eventually reconciled with the Church because he had been baptised, and also because Catholic theology stipulated that priests were obliged to give Holy Communion to everybody facing immediate death. This is called *in articulo mortis*, and was what happened to Casement since the chaplain gave him Holy Communion just before his execution despite the fact that he had refused to sign this document.[116] He was never confirmed, however. Naturally Bourne's interference had provoked great outrage in Catholic and nationalist Ireland especially since Cardinal Logue had appealed for Casement's pardon. George Gavan Duffy, who had been the prisoner's solicitor, was considerably offended and demanded explanations from Bourne. He wrote to one of the Cardinal's secretaries, Fr Daly, and asked for clarification regarding this strange document. Gavan Duffy pointed out that his client could have been confirmed twelve days before his execution if Bourne had not interfered, and that only the *in articulo mortis* rule had reconciled him with the Church.[117] It was Fr Bidwell who replied rather drily on behalf of the Cardinal. Bidwell wrote: 'I am directed by the Cardinal to say that certain statements in that [Duffy's] letter are in essential particulars not in accordance with the facts. The Cardinal is precluded from saying more than this owing to the confidential nature of the communications which passed between him and the Chaplain with who alone he had communication in the matter.'[118] The solicitor alerted certain ecclesiastics to these facts and sent copies of his correspondence with Daly and Bidwell to Archbishop Walsh, Bishop O'Dwyer and Mgr O'Riordan.[119] Gavan Duffy knew which prelates to warn in particular. Years later, Denis Gwynn, son of the Nationalist MP Stephen Gwynn, who had worked for the Ministry of Information during the war,[120] believed 'that the story was completely without foundation'.[121]

The archives of the Archdiocese of Westminster reveal the definitive explanation about the document. Gwynn was wrong. On 17 July 1916, Fr Carey informed Bourne that he had given Casement 'a copy of the formula which Your Eminence required him to sign'.[122] This is the document in question:

> I, n.n., hereby publicly express my sincere repentance for all actions in my public or private life opposed to the Law of God, and condemned as such by the Church and my sincere regret for the scandal they may have caused, and I further declare that I fully and unreservedly accept the authority and teaching of the Catholic Church in such matters.
>
> (Westminster Diocesan Archives, London, Bourne papers, AAW BO 3/5–11, undated)

Casement categorically refused to sign this document. On 20 July 1916, Carey explained to Bourne why the prisoner did not want to consent:

> His reason is, not that he is proud...he is convinced that, if and when the declaration was published, it would be interpreted as a confession that he was guilty of anything and everything that might be put into circulation about his public or private life, whether he was really guilty or not, and in circumstances, when, as a convict or a dead man, he would be unable to defend himself...He, therefore, asks Your Eminence not to insist on the declaration which for the reason given, he cannot sign. As far as I can judge Your Eminence may regard this as final on the part of the prisoner.
>
> (Westminster Diocesan Archives, London, Bourne papers, AAW BO 3/5–11, Carey to Bourne, 20 July 1916)

On 22 July 1916, Bourne replied to Carey: 'If and when the eventuality of which you write is certain to take place, any confessor may deal with the matter privately [sic] "in foro interno" on his own responsibility'.[123] It must be emphasised that Bourne did not prevent Casement from being reconciled with the Catholic Church as his letter to Carey proves.

However, matters were seriously delayed and the *in articulo mortis* rule had to be applied at the last moment. Gavan Duffy had every reason to be upset as the Cardinal's intervention was rather intriguing and bore all the hallmarks of sinister political motives.

This story seriously damaged Bourne's reputation. At the end of 1916 and the beginning of 1917, the Cardinal was in Rome when rumours about his attitude towards Casement began to circulate. Although it cannot be substantiated, it is possible that O'Riordan and Hagan were involved in this mud-slinging operation in order to eliminate the threat the Cardinal posed to Irish opposition nationalism. On 22 December 1916, the rector wrote a long letter to Cardinal Farley of New York to make Bourne's intervention known in the American hierarchy. O'Riordan was objective in the sense that he strictly used Gavan Duffy's arguments and facts, but he gave more information:

> I have read a typed copy of a correspondence which passed between Mr Gavan Duffy (Casement's solicitor) and the Archbishop's House, in which all I have said above appears [Bourne's intervention]. Mr Duffy sent it to a prelate who has lately visited Rome – is here actually now. He is an old army chaplain. He tells me that the affair has caused a good deal of suppressed anger in London especially too – because about the same time, and in the same prison, a convicted murderer was received into the Church and <u>was confirmed</u> [*sic*] in prison without any difficulty. Thus they say that Mr Casement's case, politics was the trouble. Those facts are without doubt. I give them; it may be useful for Your Eminence to know them.
>
> (Saint Joseph's Seminary, New York, Archdiocesan Archives,
> Farley papers, AANY 1–23, O'Riordan to Farley,
> 22 December 1916)

Months later, Farley replied to O'Riordan: 'The Card. B. episode bewildered me, and no wonder there was, as you say, much angry feeling aroused – thank God, the chaplain knew his duty'.[124] The rector had succeeded in tarnishing the Cardinal's reputation across the Atlantic. In Rome, Bourne began to feel ill at ease. On 30 December, Cardinal De Lai of the Holy Office asked him for an explanation. On 4 January 1917, Bourne answered De Lai's letter in French, by quoting an extract of the *Catholic Times* in which it was stated that Casement had to sign a document and that he had been reconciled with the Church only because of the *in articulo mortis* rule. Bourne told De Lai that this was 'defamation, carefully spread by its authors, here [in Rome], in Ireland, and in England'. He demanded to know who the people were that were accusing him and what evidence they had. Only then would he give 'a complete and detailed answer'. He went on to say that he had allowed two priests to deal with Casement and that 'His Holiness had been informed of his real character at the time of his condemnation'.[125] Even Benedict XV knew about the Casement affair. Although Bourne's statement was right concerning the priests, he had decided to conveniently forget about the existence of the document.

Bourne's Italian campaign was lost. He had come to Rome to settle the problem regarding chaplains for the Army and ask the Pope for a new division of certain dioceses, including the one of Southwark in London that had a boundary with Westminster. Peter Amigo, the Bishop of Southwark, was also on his way to the Vatican to oppose Bourne's moves.[126] On 30 December 1916, the same day De Lai wrote his letter to Bourne, Cardinal Gasquet had an audience with the Pope. Benedict XV was irritated by Bourne's behaviour. Gasquet wrote in his diary: 'The Holy Father spoke at length about Cardinal Bourne and the difficulty he was in from his insistence and remaining here . . . It is clear that the Holy Father is very discontented with the situation but whether he will give way before the opposition I don't guess.'[127] Benedict XV did not give way since Bourne never obtained the new division of English dioceses. He did not win regarding the chaplains either. Since January 1916, the Pope had been helping the Irish hierarchy in this long and complicated bureaucratic struggle about the spiritual authority over army chaplains. In January 1916, O'Riordan had written to Bishop Foley of Kildare and Leighlin that the Pope was doing everything he could to delay his final decision so as to permit the Irish bishops to prepare and put forward their arguments.[128] At the end of 1917, Mgr Keatinge was eventually appointed *episcopus castrensis*, Army Bishop. In March 1918, Mgr James Kennedy, an old Army chaplain residing in Rome, wrote to Archbishop Walsh that Bourne had done everything possible to oppose and change this decision.[129] This fact is confirmed in a biography of Bourne.[130] The Cardinal eventually left Rome but could not refrain from giving a flattering résumé of his activities in the Italian capital to the press. Mgr Hagan seized this opportunity for the readers of the *Catholic Bulletin* and commented ironically:

The *Independent* recently printed the following paragraph on the authority of the *World*: 'It appears that when in Rome Cardinal Bourne exerted all his authority to get the Pope to do all in his power to neutralise the revolutionary and irreconcilable elements amongst Irish Catholics so as to bring about a closer union between England and Ireland. Before leaving, the Cardinal believed his mission had been successful, and that the advice and persuasion of the Holy See will have excellent effect on the Irish situation'. 'Bosh', I think, was the comment with which one of the characters in the Vicar of Wakefield used to greet tall stories like the above.

(*The Catholic Bulletin*, 'Notes from Rome',
May 1917, p. 289)

If this was really what Bourne had said, Hagan's irony would be totally justified. O'Riordan expressed his pleasure at the Cardinal's departure in a letter to Bishop O'Dwyer. According to the rector, Bourne had personally told him that he was doing everything he could to make sure the Irish hierarchy would have control over Irish chaplains, which clearly O'Riordan did not believe. He wrote that Bourne had explained to people in Rome that it was because of the Irish bishops that Home Rule had not been implemented by the Government. He finished by saying that 'an indirect hint came from [Gasquet] that the Irish College should join him in opposing Card. Bourne in the chaplain question'.[131] But the rector refused to do so as he felt that it was up to the English to 'settle their own quarrels across the Channel. The college should not be drawn into them'. O'Riordan relentlessly pursued his separatist policy. The Casement affair had shown a darker side to politics and diplomatic relations in Rome. But after the Easter Rising and Casement's execution, O'Riordan made every effort to widen the gap between Ireland and Britain. This gap was made unbridgeable by the orchestrated efforts of O'Riordan and O'Dwyer.

RAPPROCHEMENT BETWEEN NATIONALIST IRELAND AND THE VATICAN

O'Riordan knew that the Bishop of Limerick had made a new political departure when he openly declared his support for Sinn Féin during the Freedom the City speech in September 1916. He had received a non-censored copy in Rome.[132] Nevertheless, he would not follow O'Dwyer. His reasons were practical rather than political. Two letters sent to bishops in Ulster reveal the rector's reasons. The first was sent to the very Redmondite Bishop O'Donnell of Raphoe. On 26 October 1916, O'Riordan inquired if he had received a copy of the Red Book and wrote a few lines on John Redmond and the Nationalist party:

> I hope that Mr. Redmond will take the actual difficulty to regain prestige in Ireland for himself and for the Party – and it seems they need it much. It seems plain that they missed some golden opportunities of striking a good bargain. Yet, they form the only Party Ireland has. They are already formed, and need only to be reformed. But to dethrone the chairman now would mean practically to dissolve the Party: and that would leave the country

in chaos. It is easy to destroy a party: but it takes more than a generation to build one up anew.

(ACA O'Donnell papers, O'Riordan to O'Donnell,
26 October 1916)

At that particular time, Sinn Féin was not able to rival the Nationalist party in organisation throughout the country. Therefore, to O'Riordan, the destruction of Redmond's party would be a fatal blow to Irish nationalism, in the constitutional arena at least, whereas O'Dwyer had lost all patience with the Nationalist Members of Parliament. A few days later, he sent another letter to Bishop MacRory of Down and Connor, whose diocese might be included in the suggested exclusion zone. The rector began by saying that he trusted neither Liberals, nor Conservatives. He briefly evoked the partition scheme and warned MacRory that it would probably be definitive. 'What power will make it transitory?' he asked. 'The Government will not [sic]; and the Irish Party cannot [sic]' was his answer to his own question. O'Riordan was alluding here to the disastrous negotiations of the summer of 1916, and explained what the 'great blunders' of the Nationalist party were. He believed that 'the successive outpouring of gratitude' shown to Herbert Asquith was one, called the Nationalist politicians 'slaves' and stated that Home Rule was 'the port payment of a right [sic] which [had] been wrenched away by fraud and force' and not 'a gift [sic]'. The second mistake was that the Nationalist party should have refused to negotiate the moment the Unionists spoke of partition. O'Riordan thought that the war would have put Redmond in a very strong position for 'the Government would [have paid] any price to allay' feelings of resentment among the Nationalists.[133] Perhaps the rector was right on this last point. If Redmond had not guaranteed nationalist Ireland's support for Britain and the war unless Home Rule without partition was granted immediately, the country's history might well have been completely different. Asquith and his generals would most definitely not have wanted an Ireland with Irish Volunteers, ready to fight against the British Army if Home Rule was not implemented.

On 6 December 1916, the rector announced to O'Dwyer the arrival of Count de Salis in Rome, incidentally another Limerick man. De Salis had told O'Riordan that he would soon pay a visit to the college and O'Riordan explained to the Bishop that he expected him and would meet the Count at the headquarters of the British mission. O'Riordan continued his policy of not associating the college with the British. He said that he would have done the same with Sir Henry Howard 'if some folk here had not arranged to "run" him and take us all under their and his wing'. The rector was referring to Gregory, Howard's secretary, and Cardinal Gasquet. He wrote: 'Our individuality has to be recognised now. Merely as a <u>Church</u> [*sic*] Ireland should have an individuality.'[134] O'Riordan remarked that he had received a letter from the Italian Bishop of Carrera, who regretted that the college was isolated. He immediately replied to this prelate that 'union with [the British] meant absorption'.[135] On 21 December, a M. Degrand of the French corps diplomatique in Rome informed the Quai d'Orsay that French seminarians had celebrated a requiem mass for old seminarians who had fallen at the front. He pointed out that the rectors of the English, Scottish and Belgian colleges had come but that O'Riordan had refused.[136] And yet, O'Riordan could have been on good terms with de Salis. The rector wrote to O'Dwyer that the diplomat was a friendly and affable man but that he himself would still not go to official receptions.[137] In fact, the rector mentioned on several occasions that he was favourably impressed with de Salis. It was true that he seemed to be a diplomat with a solid sense of realism as his letter to Arthur Balfour had proved. It was quite unnecessary for Hagan to write in the *Catholic Bulletin* that de Salis should not meddle in Irish affairs.[138]

In March 1917, an event took place that would bring about the definitive rapprochement between nationalist Ireland and the Vatican. In the previous month, Bishop O'Dwyer had written a very able and eloquent pastoral against the war and in favour of the Pope's peace initiatives. O'Riordan, true to form, translated it into Italian and gave copies to Benedict XV and to nine Italian cardinals: Gasparri, De Lai, Giustini, Ranuzzi dei Bianchi, Vannutelli, Bisleti, Serafini, Maffi and Ferrari, and also to the new Under Secretary of State, Mgr Tedeschini. Eugenio Pacelli, whom O'Riordan had met on several occasions, did not figure on this list since he was on his way to Munich to take up his new position as nuncio.[139] All the cardinals approved of O'Dwyer's pastoral and O'Riordan quoted laudatory comments. But, most importantly, the rector related in detail his latest meeting with Benedict XV:

I had an audience with His Holiness on Saturday. Whilst I approached him, after my genuflection, he stood up, and with a joyful smile told me at once that he thanked me for sending him the letter. He then began to launch out in its praise as he sat down, and spoke of it for quite four or five minutes. He commissioned me to thank you for it, and to tell you what he thought of it. He said Card. Gasparri came to him a few days ago bringing his copy and asked the Pope if he had seen it. 'I told him' said the Pope, 'that I had one myself'. 'It is really grand' said the Cardinal, 'it contains everything; the very things we have been saying for the last three years: it is a pity it cannot be published'. His Holiness also said that Card. De Lai at his audience on Friday began by telling him of the new Pastoral of the Bishop of Limerick. The Pope said what the pastoral says is all true: and the truth said with great accuracy and power. 'Quell'uomo ha una testa' [*sic*, the man has brains].

At dinner on St Patrick's day, Card. Giustini thanked me for his copy: and said that it is even better than the others you have written on the question. The Pope asked me if it was widely published in Ireland and in England. He desired me to give copies to Bisleti and Serafini ... I am very glad I have translated all these, they help to raise the prestige of the Irish Church.

(LDO, O'Dwyer papers, file I 'letters from Rome', O'Riordan to O'Dwyer, 25 March 1917)

There is no reason to believe that O'Riordan had embellished this account. After all, it was perfectly consistent with the Pope's attitude since the beginning of the hostilities in Europe, and, furthermore, his favourable attitude to nationalist Ireland had also been noticed by others like Cardinal Gasquet, the British mission and the French embassy. Since August 1914 , the rector had tried to prove that Ireland and Britian were two distinct nations. In March 1917, he had succeeded in doing so and O'Dwyer's writings had been an invaluable source of inspiration.

On 7 March 1917 in the House of Commons, David Lloyd George declared that the Irish did not get along between themselves because of racial, religious and political differences. On hearing this, the Nationalist party MPs walked out.[140] O'Riordan must have been pleased to learn this for he expressed his opinion to Bishop MacRory shortly afterwards. He believed that if the Government had been 'fair and straight' and granted Home Rule, Ireland would now be crippled 'with enormous war taxes'. He was alluding to the fact that Ireland would have had to make financial contributions to the Empire, a theme that O'Dwyer had regularly used. But, he pointed his finger at MacRory and stated: 'What with your imperialised Party, and their readiness to rely on the word of the Saxon (proverbially false). You would now find yourselves with an unmanageable Home Rule regime.'[141] This was the second time he addressed the Bishop of Down and Connor in a rather accusing tone. It is difficult to know why the rector had written so vehemently. Maybe he wished MacRory to bring pressure to bear on the Nationalist party and put an end to its political lethargy? One cannot be certain but O'Riordan had not changed his views concerning the party. According to him, it needed to radically transform its policy and continue to work in Parliament in order to avoid political chaos in Ireland. After the election of Count Plunkett in Roscommon and Joseph McGuinness in Longford, O'Riordian told O'Dwyer frankly about his concerns: 'I shudder at the thought of the disruption of that Party.' He explained that it had taken a long time to build up a constitutional movement and wrote prophetically: 'If it falls, only some great crisis, and extreme national need can form another.' That great crisis would be the conscription crisis of April 1918 and that party would be Sinn Féin. However, O'Riordan was willing to admit that the Nationalist party had made monumental blunders, but he still hoped it would revive:

> Do the Party think, then, that they have not blundered? If they think so, they are stone blind, and hopeless – or is it that they can see it and will not? That shows them more hopeless. If they see that they have blundered, then let them set themselves right by getting off the pedestal of political infallibility, begin to work with courage and independence, and win back the national prestige they have unquestionably lost. <u>They</u> [*sic*] are to blame in any case for the present state of things. Let them mend themselves, and things will be right.
>
> (LDO, O'Dwyer papers, file 'O'Riordan to O'Dwyer, 1887–1917', O'Riordan to O'Dwyer, 4 July 1917)

O'Riordan did not share O'Dwyer's trust in Sinn Féin. The two men agreed to differ but their difference of opinion did not terminate their collaboration. Like the Bishop, O'Riordan thought that the Irish Convention would settle nothing and that it had been conceived to show the Allies Britain's good will towards her own small nation. If it failed, he wrote in his letter, Lloyd George could point out that Irish politicians were to blame as they could not agree between themselves.[142] On 5 August 1917, O'Riordan sent his last letter to O'Dwyer. It was mainly about the Convention.[143] He put many questions to the Bishop but they remained unanswered as O'Dwyer died on 19 August. It was rapidly rumoured that O'Riordan would be appointed in Limerick. The *Tablet* raised this possibility and said that it would be like 'going to a strange place to knock at the door of the old house in the Via Mazzarino and find no Mgr O'Riordan'.[144] Undoubtedly Cardinal Gasquet and the British authorities did not share this point of view and would have welcomed his departure. Cardinal Logue thought about this matter and wrote a revealing letter to Archbishop Walsh:

> I think the vice-rector, Dr Hagan, would be a good and efficient rector...The only drawback is that I have observed that he is a good deal infected with the habit of chit-chat and gossip which goes on in Rome...He certainly would not get on very cordially with the English colony in Rome. In this, however, he differs very little from the present rector. Indeed, I have sometimes suspected the rector was a good deal led by Dr Hagan in this matter.
>
> (DDA Walsh papers, 389 I 385/8 1917, Logue to Walsh, 30 October 1917)

However that may be, the rector remained in Rome because Logue and Walsh were fully convinced that it was in nationalist Ireland's interest that he remained at the helm of the Irish College. On 22 August 1917, O'Riordan wrote a letter probably addressed to O'Dwyer's successor, Fr Hallinan, in which he paid tribute to the deceased Bishop:

> He has, after many strifes, gone out in the end in a blaze of glory. He has been beyond question the first bishop in Ireland these last years; and I have good reason for saying that in the mind of the highest ecclesiastics here he is one of the first bishops in Europe. His pastorals on peace made a real impression.
>
> (LDO, O'Dwyer papers, file 'O'Riordan to O'Dwyer, 1887–1917', O'Riordan to [probably] Hallinan, 22 August 1917)

This was an objective reflection on O'Dwyer's last years in the political scene. But, justice must be done to O'Riordan for it was he who had translated all the pastorals and was eventually responsible for the rapprochement between nationalist Ireland, her Church and the Vatican. The rector had nothing to fear after the Bishop's death. The Holy See would not change its attitude and the arrival of Archbishop Bonaventura Cerretti at the department of Extraordinary Ecclesiastical Affairs was a good omen for the Irish.

THE END OF THE WAR IN ROME

In June 1917, Hagan announced Cerretti's appointment in the *Catholic Bulletin*. The vice-rector gave a résumé of the Italian ecclesiastic's career. Cerretti had spent some time as secretary to the Apostolic Delegation in Washington, and was subsequently sent to Australia where, according to Hagan, his work had been much appreciated. Hagan was very pleased by this appointment as he wrote that Cerretti had learnt to know the Irish in Australia and in the United States, and hinted that he could be favourable to Irish autonomy.[145] It appeared, indeed, that Cerretti was in favour of self-determination for small nations and that he knew many Irish prelates all over the world.[146] It was true that he had been able to follow closely Archbishop Mannix's fight against the war effort in Australia, and certainly his knowledge of Irish ecclesiastical affairs must have influenced the Vatican. In the second half of 1917, diplomatic relations between the Vatican and Britain deteriorated considerably. On 28 November the Soviet newspaper *Izvestia* published the secret Anglo-Italian treaty and its clause XV, which embarrassed the British Government.[147] Shortly afterwards, the British press launched what can be best described as a classic anti-popery campaign. The *Morning Post* accused the Holy See of being responsible for propaganda that had caused recent Italian military defeats.[148] This was a clever way to deflect public opinion from clause XV. As for the *Globe*, it got its facts completely wrong when it made accusations about the very pro-British Cardinal Merry Del Val. The newspaper claimed that he was involved in a dark diplomatic machination against David Lloyd George's cabinet.[149] Cardinal Gasparri wrote to Cardinal Bourne and informed him that of all the lies about the Pope, the worst ones were fabricated in Britain.[150] But in some neutral Catholic countries, Britain was bearing the brunt of its ambivalent Irish policy, and in at least two countries, Spain and Argentina, she was in a rather uncomfortable diplomatic position.

In Spain, public opinion was decidedly very much against the British. As has been seen, some Spanish Catholics in Barcelona had tried to celebrate a requiem mass for the fallen rebels of the Easter Rising. In fact, even by 1914, Herbert Asquith's cabinet had asked Cardinal Bourne to help give a better image of Britain in Spain and Italy. Bourne had accepted and said that many Spanish and Italian Catholics were prejudiced against England.[151] In 1918, the situation was worrying enough for the Ministry of Information to approach Peter Amigo, the Bishop of Southwark, and ask him to go to Spain in order to explain exactly what the real nature of the relationship between Ireland and Britain was. Undoubtedly the public revelation of clause XV must have prompted the Government to make this decision. Amigo, however, had much sympathy for the Irish and was willing to go to Spain but not if this meant a greater estrangement between Britain and Ireland. He told the Ministry unequivocally: 'The Irish were altogether with us at the beginning of the war, but 'the stupidities or malignities' of the War Office, as Mr Lloyd George called them in October 1916, and other mistakes of our Government have chilled Irish enthusiasm and alienated Irish sympathy.'[152] Amigo also emphasised that the Irish were not pro-German and that they had many good friends in religious circles in Spain. He warned the Ministry that he would not defend Britain 'at the expense of [his] Irish friends' and that Britain had 'to show neutrals that [she] really [befriended] small nationalities'.[153] The English Bishop sent a copy of his letter to Archbishop Walsh, displaying his genuine pro-Irish feelings.

In Argentina, Britain was also facing some problems. On 7 April 1918, only a few days before the conscription crisis, Reginald Tower, a British diplomat in Buenos Aires, informed Arthur Balfour that the Irish were stirring up trouble in the country. In his letter, he included a pamphlet of the Irish Catholic Association in Argentina:

The Irish Catholic Association, echoing the wishes of his Holiness the Pope, calls upon all adherents to join in the pilgrimage [to the town of Lujan] and to pray for oppressed peoples and for inspiration in the negotiations for a universal and just peace which shall establish the definite independence of Ireland; which shall return to the Argentine Republic the Falklands Islands; Gibraltar to Spain, and shall ensure the liberty of all peoples oppressed and exploited by the British Empire.

(PRO, London, FO 380/17, Tower to Balfour, 7 April 1918, p. 207)

It is important not to underestimate this discontent in Argentina. According to the country's most recent census at that time, 18,617 people were Irish-Argentines out of four million inhabitants. There were wealthy Irish landowners around Buenos Aires and the country produced much food, which the Allies bought. Later in 1919, the first Irish Dáil decided to send a diplomatic mission to Argentina before the United States and France.[154] If Irish nationalism could form an alliance with irredentist Argentine claims, it could prove to be a serious threat to British interests in the region, especially bearing in mind that the conscription crisis was about to begin in Ireland with all its consequences on the United States and Australia. The Foreign Secretary must by now have realised that the world of Irish Catholicism and nationalism was tentacular. If Balfour was still hoping to use spiritual arms against Irish nationalists, he was badly mistaken. The British Government had to revise its approach, for in 1918 the balance of power at the Holy See had definitely swung in favour of the Irish nationalist agenda. On 17 March, Mgr James Kennedy informed Archbishop Walsh that Cerretti was totally in favour of Catholic Ireland. He wrote that the Italian ecclesiastic had personally told him that it was the Irish clergy that had set up the Australian Catholic Church. Kennedy concluded: 'The British Empire is at a discount at the Vatican. The Holy Father knows what it is, and gets good information about its doings when wanted. Mgr Cerretti is quite convinced from the London *Tablet*, that the English Catholics, both cleric and lay, are English first and Catholics after'.[155]

Kennedy's last remark hit the nail on the head. It was all a question of allegiance. O'Riordan and Hagan had played the Vatican card all along whereas Gasquet, Bourne and the British mission had not. The crowning glory came on Saint Patrick's Day in 1918 with the beatification of Oliver Plunkett who was an Irish Archbishop, executed in England in 1681. During the ceremony, Benedict XV seized the opportunity to declare: 'The heroic Irish nation has always been a strenuous defender of the Catholic Faith.'[156] The Pope had spoken of Ireland as a nation and this did not go unnoticed in Ireland. The

Freeman's Journal published this papal declaration in an article entitled 'An Irish Martyr, The beatification of Oliver Plunkett, the Pope and Ireland'.[157] The British residents in Rome did not approve of the Pope's words. O'Riordan wrote to Archbishop Walsh that it was Benedict XV himself who had chosen the symbolic date of 17 March and that his 'imperial neighbours here severely [criticised] what the Pope said about Ireland on the occasion'.[158] And yet, despite this event and all the information he must have had on the activities of the Irish College in Rome and the Pope's feelings on Ireland, Arthur Balfour ordered Count de Salis to ask the Vatican to intervene in the conscription crisis of April 1918. O'Riordan had a relatively easy task in defending the Irish hierarchy's stand against compulsory military service in their country. He wrote two letters to Cerretti, in which he explained that the bishops had the situation well under control, and asked him if the Vatican could really trust RIC reports on the activities of seditious priests. He also warned him that if the Curia did intervene in favour of Britain, the Irish people might despise and negate their intervention: 'Hence I respectfully submit that it is best to let the English and the Irish fight out their national quarrels by themselves.'[159] Cerretti did not need much convincing at this stage. As has been seen, Cardinal Gasparri informed Count de Salis that he would not interfere in the crisis. It was very likely that Gasparri had taken this decision in consultation with Cerretti as the two men worked closely together.[160]

Michael O'Riordan and John Hagan had no more worries. They had not only successfully countered all the British diplomatic initiatives against nationalist Ireland at the Vatican, but also persuaded the Pope and the Curia of the legitimacy of Ireland's rights as a nation. Never again would the Holy See amalgamate Britain and Ireland and their respective clergies. In May 1918, the French embassy in Rome sent a report on the two men to the Quai d'Orsay in Paris. It had an informant who was in touch with one of the members of the Irish College. The report gave a fair account of O'Riordan and Hagan's activities:

> Benedict XV is totally won over by the Irish and will do nothing against Cardinal Logue and the bishops, who know that they have nothing to fear from him. They will be able to lead their campaign against conscription with impunity, and make propaganda through priests and seminarians. The intermediary between the Pope and the bishops is Mgr Michael O'Riordan who, since 1905, has been the rector of the Irish College in Rome but who has been in close contact with the Pope whom he knew as an ordinary prelate. He has easy access to Benedict XV and has seen him a lot recently. The Irish bishops and Cardinal Logue do not need to give the Pope a memorandum, justifying their conduct since Mgr

O'Riordan has become their lawyer and defender. Mgr O'Riordan is supported in his task by the vice-rector of the Irish College, a young and intelligent priest, very active, and very fanatical for the Irish cause, who makes a lot of propaganda in Rome and in ecclesiastical circles.

(Quai d'Orsay, Paris, vol. 547 Grande-Bretagne/Irlande, note no. 171, French embassy Rome to Ministre des Affaires étrangères, 6 May 1918)

At the end of the First World War, the Irish College had obtained an important diplomatic victory. In his handling of Irish affairs, O'Riordan proved himself to be the representative of an emerging strong nationality, that of Irish Catholic nationalism. The Vatican's intervention in the Plan of Campaign had led to a serious risk of anti-clericalism in Ireland. Some thirty years later, the First World War provoked a strengthening of the ties between Irish Catholicism and the Vatican. Both O'Riordan in Rome and O'Dwyer in Limerick had been the architects of this rapprochement.

The war in Europe appeared to be entering its final phase in the Marne and Somme regions near Paris. It was not yet clear whether the Allies or the Triple Alliance would be victorious. Ireland was heading towards a political upheaval as Sinn Féin had taken all credit for the opposition to conscription and the Nationalist party was on its way out. So it seemed. However, one last act was to take place when, in August 1918, a captain called Stuart Hay met Cardinal Logue in his country cottage at Carlingford.

8 The second French mission, the 'Hay plan'

August 1918
'Voulez-vous aller à la bataille?!' (Do you want to go to the battle?!)

General Foch, supreme commander of all allied forces to General Pershing, American High Command

August 1918
'Logue expressed the view that this scheme was the salvation of Ireland, as it brought [Ireland] into line with the Allies and would get rid of the disloyal element.'

Captain Stuart Hay on Cardinal Logue, after their secret meeting

December 1918
'No one, I think, could suspect me of favouring Sinn Féin policy. ... I have never concealed my views of its futility.'

Cardinal Michael Logue in the Independent, *after Sinn Féin's victory in the general election*

Rome was not the only place where one could find ecclesiastical intrigue. At the very end of the war, a final and rather obscure political plot took place in the archdiocese of Armagh. A second French mission appeared completely unannounced on Cardinal Logue's doorstep. Its aim was to boost recruitment in Ireland and to dissipate the worries of some leading French politicians and militaries who had expressed serious concern about the strength of the British Army. Their worries seemed to be justified as France and Britain's new allies, the Americans, were slow in taking part in the fighting. Furthermore, the Germans had concluded a separate peace with Bolshevik Russia, which enabled them to transfer all their divisions on the eastern front to the western front. In April 1918, the British failed in their efforts to impose conscription in Ireland and Lord French, the new Lord Lieutenant or Viceroy, as he liked to be called, was equally unsuccessful in his new recruitment campaign. It was thus that some British civil servants reflected on the old historical and military links between France and Ireland and that the idea of an Irish brigade fighting for the French was once more raised. The question was whether France was still able to influence Irish public opinion at this stage of the war. Was she not England's ally instead of her enemy in this war in which the Irish had lost all interest? Moreover, if the British and the French agreed to set up a mission, who would be willing to help them in Ireland?

After the conscription crisis, Sinn Féin seemed to be the new dominant political force in the country and was opposed to Irish participation in the conflict whereas the pro-war Nationalist party, even under John Dillon's leadership, continued to decline. Therefore, only one option remained, the Irish Catholic Church. The latter had just proven how effective its influence and organisation was against the Government's plan to conscript Irishmen. It had led and directed the unlikely alliance between Sinn Féin and the Nationalist party over the issue of conscription. The problem for British civil servants was to find a powerful ally within the Catholic hierarchy which had just rejected the war effort. The choice was in fact very obvious: Cardinal Michael Logue. First of all, Logue was the highest ecclesiastical dignitary in the country. He was Primate of All Ireland and might have enough influence over other bishops to make them agree to back this new recruitment operation. Secondly, and most importantly, Logue was definitely in favour of the Allies, especially France where he had studied as a seminarian in the Irish College in Paris. As has been seen, the Cardinal had been very reluctant to actively support the war effort, as he believed that Home Rule and partition had not been solved in a satisfactory way. However, would he consent to help the Allies in the summer of 1918, at a moment when the war was entering a crucial phase? Had he not told Fr Patrice Flynn in 1917, after the first French mission, that the French Government was anti-clerical? If he consented to help, what would be his motives, his price? Very rapidly, it transpired that this second French mission was a complex political manipulation engineered, among others, by the British Prime Minister himself, David Lloyd George.

IRELAND'S IMPORTANCE IN THE WAR IN 1918

When it became clear that conscription would not be put into operation in Ireland by the British Government, Paul Cambon, the French Ambassador to the United Kingdom, exclaimed that it was madness not to raise troops in that country when the French reserve was nearly fully used.[1] In order to understand Cambon's reaction, which at first sight might have seemed quite exaggerated, it is necessary to return briefly to the situation on the front. In 1918, the Allies' main concern was manpower. The French High Command, especially, was deeply worried

30. Alfred Blanche, French Consul in Dublin, reported to French Government on
political crises in Ireland (with kind permission of Fr Mark Tierney, Glenstal
Abbey)

31. The Great War monument in Limerick

32. The Easter Rising monument in Limerick

about the number of men facing perhaps the mightiest offensive the Germans had ever launched since the beginning of the war.[2] The French Army numbered 2,500,000 men, of whom 800,000 were at the rear. The aim of the generals had been to enlist about one million men between October 1917 and October 1918 for it was thought that future casualties would be as high as 920,000 men.[3] The British Army also had its own problems. In 1917, it had lost about 800,000 men and the required number of recruits for 1918 was 900,000 but, apparently, it could only muster 750,000 men.

France and Britain's new allies, the Americans, had entered the war in April 1917. The French generals were relieved for this would mean a significant number of extra soldiers. Their optimism was, however, short-lived. American help was rather slow in coming for its military organisation was very demanding concerning the training of soldiers. By the end of 1917, only a few units were fighting in the north of France in relatively quiet sectors. In March 1918, there were six American divisions in France, a total of 225,000 men, but the majority of them were at the rear and only one division was on the front, in the eastern region of Lorraine.[4] By May 1918, there were 600,000 Americans in France and in July this number rose to 750,000.[5] Despite these important American reinforcements, the French and British showed signs of frustration with the United States as most American soldiers were being trained and were not fighting. The British wanted the Americans to get into action as soon as possible with either French or British units. President Wilson had no objections but the American commander, General John Pershing, feared 'political repercussions in America'.[6] It seemed that the American High Command wished to remain independent.[7] In January 1918, General Philippe Pétain had met Pershing to discuss this matter and Pershing took the decision to send four Black regiments to the front under French command immediately. The American General said that they were not fully trained yet but that the regiments had a distinguished history during the Mexican War. Pétain was grateful.[8]

There was no doubt that in the spring of 1918, France's main allies were the British. That was why the French Government and its Prime Minister, Georges Clemenceau, paid particular attention to the internal situation in Britain and in Ireland. Clemenceau was aware of the American problem in France and the difficulties that the British had in Ireland where thousands of men could be enlisted into the Army if only conscription was put into operation. When he heard about David Lloyd George's new Military Service Bill, Clemenceau sent a brief message to the General in Chief of all the Armies in the North and North-East, General Philippe Pétain, on 29 March 1918:

The English demand even more energetically than we do the entry of the Americans into the present battle. Their main reason is that they are going to introduce recruitment [i.e. conscription] in Ireland and the day that American blood will have flowed, Irish opposition in America will become absolutely impossible.
So, act accordingly.

> (ASHA, fonds Clemenceau, file 6N53, Clemenceau to
> Commandant en chef des Armées du Nord,
> 29 March 1918)

The message showed Clemenceau's cold calculations for it was clear that American soldiers would no longer operate in a quiet sector. It also shows how important not only Ireland was at that particular stage of the conflict, but also the Irish Catholic world in general, as Ambassador Cambon had already stated as soon as 1915 during the first French mission to Ireland.

The Irish conscription crisis, which erupted in early April 1918, sent shock waves throughout the British Empire and its dominions. This situation naturally preoccupied the French High Command, especially when it soon became obvious that the British had been badly defeated in their attempts to enforce conscription in Ireland. General Ferdinand Foch paid much attention to the crisis. On 31 May 1918, General de la Panouse, the military attaché of the French embassy in London, informed Foch that only the immediate enforcement of Home Rule could make the Irish accept compulsory military service. He added that 'Mr Lloyd George is deferring day after day the operational date of home rule, obviously because he wants to please both Ulstermen and Nationalists.' He also wrote that Clemenceau was 'the only man who had a real influence on Mr Lloyd George' and suggested that the French Prime Minister could perhaps ask his British counterpart to 'hasten the discussion' on Irish autonomy. The French believed that the stakes were very high. De la Panouse concluded his report for Foch with the following observations:

> Undoubtedly, under the present serious circumstances, it is out of the question to put conscription into force immediately, but nothing should hinder solving as early as possible the question of autonomous government of the island, ... which is the first measure to take if one wants to have the 200,000 or 300,000 Irishmen who will constitute a substantial and solid extra help of men in the British armies in France.

> (ASHA, fonds Clemenceau, file 6N155,
> de la Panouse to Foch, 31 May 1918)

Two or three hundred thousand men were significant, particularly if one takes into account the fact that the British and French High Commands foresaw a continuation of the fighting until 1919 and also the American problem on the western front. These Irishmen could make a huge difference. Ambassador Paul Cambon's reaction to the abandonment of conscription in Ireland is now more understandable.

Conscription in Ireland, however, was finally quietly shelved and Lord French set himself the task to recruit 50,000 men before 1 October 1918. His task seemed enormous. He knew that the Catholic Church had been the main organiser of all the forces against conscription and the hierarchy had certainly not been persuaded by Lloyd George's vague promise that a solution concerning Home Rule and Ulster had to be elaborated on by the Imperial Parliament. Paradoxically, the Viceroy was convinced that the Church was the only force able to help him in his recruitment drive and in finding a definitive settlement of the Home Rule question. The very anti-republican minded Cardinal Logue was the obvious man to approach. In May 1918, James O'Connor, the Catholic solicitor working for the British Crown who had asked Archbishop Walsh to put an end to the rising in 1916, had informed A.W. Samuels, the Attorney-General, that the 'Cardinal [was] a moderate'.[9] James MacMahon, the Under Secretary for Ireland, was a personal friend of Logue.[10] On 27 June 1918, he set up a secret meeting between Lord French and the Cardinal at the residence of Lady Granard. The secret was so well kept that Mgr Curran was only informed of it by Sinn Féin twenty-four hours before it took place. Curran told Archbishop Walsh about this meeting, and he was much impressed by the Sinn Féin Intelligence.[11] It is difficult to know what the two men talked about but if one takes into account the political situation in Ireland and the situation on the western front at that moment, two hypotheses can be put forward. The first one concerns the urgent need for more men in the British Imperial Army. In April, David Lloyd George had asked Walter Long to liaise between the war cabinet in London and the British authorities in Dublin.[12] Long was a member of the Conservative party and a unionist. He had been briefly Chief Secretary for Ireland before the Conservatives lost the general election in 1906.[13] Long and French were both in favour of conscription in Ireland and believed in a policy of strength in order to put it into operation. Long had contacts with Cardinal Bourne of Westminster and asked him for his advice on Irish matters and the Irish Catholic Church. Bourne proved to be very willing to help Long. On 17 May, a few hours before Eamon de Valera and other nationalists were arrested for their involvement in the bogus 'German plot', the Cardinal wrote to him that the best option to settle the Irish question once and for all was the implementation of a federalist political structure. Interestingly, Bourne also told Long his opinion about conscription and enlistment: 'Give a <u>long</u> [*sic*] opportunity for voluntary enlistment before applying conscription, and then a <u>big</u> [*sic*] loophole on the plea of the need of agricultural labour. The tranquillizing of Ireland is of more importance than even men for the Army.'[14] The date of Bourne's letter tends to indicate that he was au fait with the Government's intention to arrest some Sinn Féin leaders and opt for recruitment once again. Long changed his mind completely about the practicability of conscription after a visit to Ireland between 23 and 28 May 1918 during which he recognised the importance and influence of the Catholic Church.[15] On 27 May, the German General Erich Ludendorff launched his last great offensive on the Marne near Paris and appeared to be successful. It is therefore reasonable to assume that Logue and French had met to discuss voluntary enlistment in Ireland and how the powerful Catholic Church could contribute to reviving recruitment.

The second hypothesis involves the federal project that Long had elaborated in order to solve the Irish crisis. This project consisted of establishing regional parliaments throughout the United Kingdom, which would have the power to decide on regional and local affairs whereas matters such as defence would be left to Westminster Parliament.[16] Long did not believe in Home Rule as he thought it would never satisfy the Unionists. At the beginning of June he had declared that the British Government should 'be prepared with all the machinery for the enforcing of conscription and to advocate the Federal system of Government all round'.[17] Lord French totally agreed with Long's point of view. It was very likely that he met Logue at Lady Granard's residence to ask for his cooperation in this new political project. The meeting, however, was not a success. In July, Mgr Curran wrote to Mgr Michael O'Riordan and told him what had happened:

> There was an interesting meeting on Thursday 27 June at Scullistown [*sic*] House, the residence of the dowager Lady Granard. Scullistown [*sic*] House is in a deserted countryside near Dunsink observatory. Some unknown statesman inspired a meeting between Cardinal Logue and Lord French. It was arranged through James MacMahon. Absolute secrecy was observed but I got news of it 24 hours before the meeting from a Sinn Féin source! The thing was delightfully ridiculous. Here was Sinn Féin watching the whole 'conspiracy', observing the Cardinal and James MacMahon arriving in closed cars at 3.45 followed by Lord French and two of his staff into the deserted district. The next day they learnt that the two principals were closeted together for one half hour and that Cardinal Logue

drove off in a hurry, in a great huff and to the chagrin of the dowager he would not wait for a cup of tea. I wonder what the Cardinal would have thought had he known that he was watched all the time!

(ICR, O'Riordan papers 19, letter no. 64,
Curran to O'Riordan, 8 July 1918)

Logue was obviously weary of British propositions concerning Ireland and no longer trusted solutions proposed by David Lloyd George or Herbert Asquith. In February 1918, he had been very clear on this subject: 'Half measures which have been the bane of this country in the past, so far from proving a remedy, would only aggravate the disease.'[18] In March, he had been even more explicit and had written to James O'Connor, an Irish lawyer, in no uncertain terms about Lloyd George's proposals and attitude towards the Irish Convention and Home Rule: 'I find it hard to resist the conviction that this whole business, Convention, and all, is a piece of clever play – it would be disrespectful to call jockeying – to keep the Irish question floating till the war is over, and then leave Sinn Féin, Carsonism and Socialism to fight each other over the fate of unfortunate Ireland.'[19] O'Connor, in turn, had sent a copy of Logue's letter to A. Samuels, the Attorney General, and had commented: 'Now the Cardinal is a moderate; so you may imagine what the more extreme Nationalists will say.'[20]

Lord French did not obtain Logue's help and the number of recruits was far from impressive. In the early days of August 1918 in Paris, Prime Minster Georges Clemenceau read a report sent by General de la Panouse from London. The General explained that between 1 January and 31 July 1918, the number of Irishmen who had joined the colours was about 8,000, and that the Viceroy's objective to recruit 50,000 men before 1 October would not be reached. He concluded by saying 'that the problem of Irish recruitment seems to be insolvable'.[21]

Would the French abandon all hope?

FRENCH HESITATIONS

If Britain was not able to raise the necessary troops in Ireland, could France help her or do it herself? After the failure of the first French mission in October 1916, the French cabinet continued to closely follow the situation in Ireland, and opinions diverged as to how to boost the war effort efficiently. The main question was whether to approach the Irish Catholic Church or not. In January 1917, a report for the French Army stated that France had a major role to play in the recruitment of Irishmen. The military officer was of the opinion that a rapprochement between France and Ireland had to take place on a political, commercial and lay level and not on an ecclesiastical level since the first French mission had shown that France's pre-war anti-clerical policy had upset the Irish Church. He believed that a corps of Irish volunteers in Ireland or in the United States could be organised and fight for France and not for England, 'their old enemy'. British public opinion would raise no objection since it would diminish the risks of insurrection in Ireland.[22] However, the report remained rather vague as to how the French would be able to operate a successful policy in Ireland. In fact, in 1917, only the immediate implementation of Home Rule without partition could have boosted the war effort in Ireland but this was a matter for the British Government to decide, not for the French.

The Home Rule question and American involvement were of crucial importance for the French in the first months of 1917. The battle of Verdun had ended in November 1916 and France had suffered about 377,000 casualties. The battle had had a huge impact on the United States and had gripped the American imagination as some American pilots had volunteered to fight with the French.[23] France was well aware that the Irish community in the United States was powerful and could possibly influence the Wilson government in their foreign policy. Therefore, Home Rule in Ireland could be the key point for the good continuation of the war. After the battle of Verdun in 1916, it was not surprising that the idea of an Irish-American corps was in the air across the Atlantic. In November 1916, Shane Leslie, the nationalist journalist, had suggested this to John Redmond. He had also mentioned that Irish-American opinion 'here is that without Home Rule the Irish troops are in the trenches under false pretences'.[24] A complex pattern between Home Rule, war effort, Britain and the USA was developing and worrying the French.

On 8 February 1918, Stephen Pichon, the French Foreign Secretary, notified the French Consul in New York that he personally believed in sending another ecclesiastical mission to Ireland and that 'the action of the French clergy on the Irish clergy should be elaborated'.[25] In Dublin, Consul Alfred Blanche did not agree with Pichon. On 11 February, he reported to the Quai d'Orsay that Cardinal Logue's popularity had diminished in Ireland because he was opposing Sinn Féin. Blanche also sent an extract of Logue's Lenten pastoral in which he expressed his hopes that the Irish Convention, which was trying to find a solution to the Home Rule and partition crises, would be successful so that it would bring peace to Ireland and the Empire.[26] This was good news for the French as it showed that the Cardinal had no republican ideals and that he was not a radical like Bishop Fogarty of Killaloe or Archbishop Walsh of Dublin. Logue's reference to the Empire implied that he was still in favour of the Allies. It would seem that if Pichon sent a mission over to

Ireland to foster recruitment, Logue would be the ecclesiastic to work with. On 19 February 1918, however, Blanche advised against any rapprochement between the French and the Irish clergy. He wrote to the Foreign Secretary that the Irish Catholic Church generally tended to establish a 'united opinion' in their country concerning matters such as the national question or foreign policy. But since 1916, the hierarchy had been worried about Sinn Féin's progress, notably about the influence of this party's republican ideas on the younger clergy.[27] Blanche was right. As has been seen, the British Military Intelligence had also noticed this state of affairs within the Church. Different agents throughout Ireland reported back to their superiors in Dublin that a generation conflict between older priests, supporting the Nationalist party, and younger ones, in favour of Sinn Féin, was taking place and that some bishops had serious difficulties in controlling the situation.[28] The French Consul went on to explain to Stephen Pichon why this was happening:

> All this proves that the most powerful feeling in Ireland at this very moment is not the Catholic feeling, but the national feeling; for a long time, and maybe still nowadays, these two feelings have totally complemented and mutually reinforced each other. But should they oppose each other, the national feeling would take precedence over the Catholic one, and neither the Vatican bulls, nor episcopal exhortations could counterbalance the hope of liberty.
>
> (Quai d'Orsay, Paris, vol. 547 Grande-Bretagne/Irlande,
> Blanche to French Foreign Office Secretary,
> 19 February 1918)

Alfred Blanche had correctly assessed the political mood in nationalist Ireland. In the first half of 1918, numerous priests were openly supporting Sinn Féin, notably during by-elections, and were rarely reprimanded by their bishops. The latter simply could not risk the chance of destroying the fragile unity of their Church. At this stage, Pichon must have had serious doubts about the usefulness of an ecclesiastical mission to Ireland. Would the help of the Catholic Church be that effective after all? Furthermore, in March 1918, André Géraud, who had masterminded the first French mission in 1916, signalled to the Quai d'Orsay that Mgr Hogan, President of Maynooth and staunch supporter of the Allies, had died and that one could take it for granted that 'all the Irishmen under the age of thirty-five had embraced Sinn Féin's cause'.[29] A new propaganda mission looked increasingly complicated and the French lost all hope regarding the situation in Ireland but not their worries concerning manpower. In June 1918, in the middle of the new German onslaught on the Allied positions, the French cabinet sent an officer over to London in order to examine the Irish problem.[30] The same month, Foch, the commander-in-chief of the allied armies in France had said that the British Army was in a bad state and that this might lead to defeat. His impressions were shared by an American general who believed British soldiers to be in poor physical condition. At that time, David Lloyd George's cabinet was conscripting men up to the age of fifty.[31] The Prime Minister was very much aware of this problem and had told his cabinet that he hoped to get 50,000 young Irishmen as the British Army was 'taking old men'.[32]

The Irish question provoked strains between the French and the British. Would those thousands of Irishmen idly watch the end of the war? Against all expectations, a recruitment mission directly involving Cardinal Logue and Cardinal Amette, Primate of the French hierarchy, saw the light at the end of July 1918. This mission came from England.

THE 'HAY PLAN'

On 20 July 1918, Stuart Hay, a British captain working for the Ministry of Information in the section Enemy Propaganda under the leadership of Lord Northcliffe, the English press baron, received an order from William Sutherland to set up a plan to persuade Irish nationalists to join the French Army on a large scale, first as labourers in specialised battalions.[33] Sutherland was one of Lloyd George's secretaries and was entrusted with very sensitive operations. It was he who liaised between the British Government and tsarist generals during the Allies' intervention in Russia in 1919. On 22 July, Hay met Sutherland and proposed the following plan. The Captain had the intention of appealing to Mgr Amette, the Cardinal Archbishop of Paris, in order to ask Cardinal Logue to encourage Irishmen to enlist voluntarily and help France against Germany. It would be Amette's task to persuade Logue to abandon his opposition to recruitment and to ask the Irish bishops' cooperation in sending 100,000 men to the French Army.[34] Obviously, the Cardinal would not know that the plan had been conceived by the highest authorities in London. According to Hay, the appeal of the French Catholics could only be heard by the Irish Catholic Church which had been too much compromised in the recent conscription crisis. By openly supporting the plan and the Allies, the hierarchy would show that its alliance with Sinn Féin had only been temporary. British public opinion, which had criticised the hierarchy's intervention in the crisis, would approve of the Church's action. Furthermore, the plan 'would, if successful, take away from Ireland many men who are now disturbing elements'. Hay concluded: 'The backbone of the Irish opposition to military service is the Church and if this backbone were definitely or even in a large measure converted and the support it has given to disloyal elements be not only taken away but thrown on to the other side in the controversy [the conscription crisis], much would be done for the future of the peace in Ireland.'[35] On 23 July, Hay met Edward Shortt who fully agreed with his plan and who told him that Lloyd George and Lord French were equally pleased and had decided to submit it to the War Office through the intermediary of Sir Frederick Shaw.

In the following days, Hay had several meetings with Shaw, Samuel Watt and General Nevil Macready in order to elaborate on his plan. Shaw was a unionist who had fought in France until 1916 and who often worked for Lord French. Watt came from Ulster and was a member of the Belfast Unionist Club. When he was appointed to the Irish Local Government Board, nationalists complained believing he was too 'orange'. On 27 July, under the approving eyes of Lloyd George, French and Shortt, Stuart Hay conceived the letter that Cardinal Amette had to write to Logue. On 29 July, the Captain met Mgr Jackman, Cardinal Bourne's secretary, and asked if Bourne could write a reference letter for Amette, introducing him and announcing that he had been entrusted with a most confidential mission. Bourne consented to do so. On 30 July, Sutherland gave Hay a reference letter for Georges Mandel, Georges Clemenceau's secretary and right-hand man (who would later be assassinated by the Vichy regime in 1944), stating what Hay's mission was and asking the French Government to think about the British proposal regarding Irish manpower. The same night, Hay left for Paris in the company of Prince Paul of Serbia. On arrival, he went immediately to the French War Office where Mandel welcomed him. The Frenchman thought it was rather strange that he had not been informed by the British Ambassador, Lord Derby, which was the usual procedure. Hay simply stated that his mission had to remain strictly confidential. A few moments later, Clemenceau himself told the English officer that he accepted and that he would ask the President of the Republic, Raymond Poincaré, to send Hay to Mgr Amette on his recommendation, Poincaré and Amette being on friendly terms.[36] That same afternoon, Hay met the Primate of the French Catholic Church who agreed to write the letter to Logue but who refused to send a French prelate to Armagh to hand it over personally to Logue. He said that he would send it through Clemenceau. On 1 August, William Sutherland sent a coded message to Hay, congratulating him and ordering him not to insist on the envoy of a French messenger.

Hay was back in London on 7 August and was informed by Sutherland that Edward Shortt had received Amette's letter, which the Archbishop of Paris had written on 2 August. Amette reminded Logue of the historic and traditional Franco-Irish friendship and asked the Irish people to come over to France as labourers so that Frenchmen could go to the front:

> Allow me to appeal to your well-known sympathy and, through Your Eminence, to Catholic Ireland's, in favour of France...Victim of an unjust and violent aggression of an enemy vastly superior in number, she has seen her territory invaded and devastated...We do not doubt that Ireland's heart, once more, will be inclined to help France in this critical hour. There is, it seems, a possible help that Ireland could easily give us: it would be to lend us workers [illegible]. France is obliged to keep, among the combatants, nearly all able-bodied men whom she has at her disposal. She has not enough men in the rear for work in services, supplies, transport of wounded and material, work on railroads, harbours etc. She needs a great number of auxiliary workers: could she not get them from your country? I understand that the French Government would be pleased to welcome them and incorporate them into regular battalions, to give them pay and look after the necessities of their wives and children. If Your Eminence believed that he could favourably receive this appeal and submit it to the Irish Catholics, it would be easy to get along with the public authorities in order to organise the enlistment of volunteers. In this way, Ireland would give invaluable help to our just and great cause, and would give herself a new right to the esteem and gratitude of France and the civilised world.
>
> (Maison diocésaine de Paris [Diocese of Paris], Amette papers, série 4B1, 6, Amette to Logue, draft letter)

The letter had been cleverly thought out. The last remark implied that Ireland had a unique opportunity to draw closer to the Allies and to be in a position of strength regarding her political future once the war had been won. This could not displease Logue, still favourable to the Allies and above all to a peaceful and constitutional settlement of the Home Rule crisis. Indeed, if Ireland participated generously in the war effort, she could be equally generously rewarded and Sinn Féin and its republican ideas would cease to exist. On 9 August, something rather curious happened. Shortt told Hay that he himself had to bring the letter to Cardinal Logue. An Englishman representing the French Catholic Church in a mission in Ireland was quite unusual, to say the least.

Hay immediately left for Dublin, arrived the next day and sent a telegram to Logue's secretary, announcing his intention to see the Cardinal. Fortune smiled on him since he met Mgr Michael Quinn in the train to Ulster, who informed him that Logue was at his country cottage at Carlingford and not in Armagh. The Cardinal warmly welcomed the Captain and on Saturday night, 10 August, Hay revealed the situation to Logue, emphasising France's urgent need for men. According to the British officer, Logue 'listened until a very late hour... but took no decision as to his reply to Cardinal Amette'. On Sunday afternoon, after mass, he told Hay that he had decided to support France with the help of the Irish Catholic Church. What plan did the Cardinal put forward? Logue said that he had thought in the first place to publish Amette's appeal 'in a circular letter both to the press and the Irish bishops'. Hay was very satisfied with this proposal for 'this course of immediate publicity had been recommended to [him] by Mr Sutherland just before [he] left Downing Street'.[37]

However, Logue changed his mind fearing that 'the British Government would consider this suggestion of Cardinal Amette's as a mere ecclesiastical trick to avoid national conscription'. The Cardinal, therefore, decided 'to defer action until assured by the French Government that the British Government would give the necessary permission to men wishing to enlist in the French Army to leave Ireland freely'. Hay understood Logue's cautious approach and was, of course, unable to tell him that it was the British cabinet who was behind the whole scheme and that everything had already been arranged. But Logue was at the same time so enthusiastic about the plan that he even put forward ideas as to how to embark all Irish volunteers for France. Why such an enthusiasm?

The Cardinal's political opinions had somehow changed in the summer of 1918. He did not believe in British promises and assurances concerning the Home Rule question anymore and was of the opinion that nationalist Ireland's salvation could only come from France and the USA. In December 1917 during the first French mission, he had declared to the French Fr Patrice Flynn 'that it was madness to think that [Ireland] could be represented at the peace conference'.[38] This idea had first been expressed by Bishop Fogarty of Killaloe who openly supported Sinn Féin. In August 1918, this idea was no longer considered as being mad. Hay reported Logue's remarks: '[Logue] expressed the view that this scheme was the salvation of Ireland, as it brought that country into line with the Allies and would get rid of the disloyal element. He pointed out that it solved ultimately the Home Rule problem, which could now be settled at the Peace Conference with the help of France and America.'[39]

The situation was ironic. Logue, although being anti-Sinn Féin, adopted Sinn Féin's idea to send Ireland to the peace conference in order to get rid of that same party. The letter conceived by David Lloyd George, Lord French and Stuart Hay, and written by Cardinal Amette had produced the desired effect. In Logue's mind, Ireland, by sending her men to the front, would affirm her existence as a nation and would be recognised as such by the French and American Governments. The latter could bring pressure to bear on Britain in order to settle once and for all the Home Rule problem. Sinn Féin would then lose its *raison d'être* and, moreover, the sending of thousands of young men would diminish the risks of a new rising in Ireland. Another explanation is Logue's frame of mind. He was a shrewd politician and knew he had been defeated by Archbishop Walsh during the episcopal meeting against conscription on 18 April. The whole debate had gone against his will. He might still have been resentful of this fact when he was approached by Hay, and might have seen the Captain's proposal as an opportunity to take revenge on Walsh and de Valera.

On Sunday night, 11 August 1918, Logue gave Hay the letter for Mgr Amette. The Cardinal evoked the traditional Franco-Irish friendship and assured Amette that Ireland wanted France's victory in the war. He outlined his plan to involve the hierarchy but stated that the French Goverment had to obtain Britain's formal promise to grant permission to the Irish volunteers to go freely to France. The Cardinal was of the opinion that the French would solve all the logistic problems inherent to the plan. Logue concluded: 'I am convinced that if British opposition could be avoided or suppressed, this undertaking could be very successful in Ireland.'[40] The Irish Primate could not have known that only the day before, on 10 August, hundreds of kilometres away, General Erich Ludendorff had tendered his resignation to the Kaiser. His Army had failed in its attempt to crush the Allies. The Emperor had refused but had admitted that Germany had no strength left and that the war had to stop.[41] Logue's letter was later forwarded to Georges Clemenceau on 16 August 1918.[42]

The next morning, Monday 12 August, before returning to London and Paris, Stuart Hay promised Cardinal Logue that he would come back on 17 August with the guarantees he wanted from the French and British Governments. The Captain could be very satisfied with the outcome of his mission to Armagh. In fact, it was the beginning of the end for him. The same afternoon, Hay met Samuel Watt, Edward Shortt's secretary, at the University Club in Dublin. Watt was extremely impressed by the officer's work and said that Logue's letter was the end of Sinn Féin. Later on that day, Shortt himself phoned Hay to congratulate him.[43] On 13 August, a satisfied Hay entered 10 Downing Street in London where he was met by J.T. Davies, the Prime Minister's personal secretary, and William Sutherland who, much to his surprise, not only expressed their own dissatisfaction but also that of Lord Derby, the British Ambassador in Paris, and General Henry Wilson. Hay wrote in his report:

Lord Derby was angry that the matter had not been passed through him, and 'that he objected to me personally'; that Sir Henry Wilson, C.I.G.S., was much annoyed and had threatened to have me arrested while carrying out the mission 'and was out for my blood'. That the policy was anti-Ulster and that I was a disgrace and must not return to Paris with my letter, but that I must get it over by other means.

(ACA, Logue papers, report of J.S. Hay)

It would seem that due to political considerations and rivalries, the 'Hay plan' had to be abandoned. Derby was attached to the Foreign Office which David Lloyd George mistrusted. On 2 August, Derby, who in the meantime had got wind of Hay's mission, had already complained about the plan to the Foreign Secretary, Arthur Balfour, who personally knew nothing about the whole scheme. Derby wrote: 'To employ the Roman Catholic Hierarchy to get Irishmen to show their loyalty to England by fighting under a French flag seems to me to be the height of folly and one which will be bitterly resented by a great number of people in England.'[44] To the Ambassador, it was a matter of national honour and pride. Hay, on the other hand, wrote: 'It seemed to me that the Government were now afraid of their own action because of the Ulster opposition, and I gathered at the time that I had to be sacrificed.'[45] Apparently, the first move to stop the officer carrying out his mission was made on 10 August when the Ministry of Information received the order to send him to a medical centre to be examined. Hay's superior, S.A. Guest, answered then that he would only do so on Lloyd George's personal order. The Captain, however, was obliged to go to this medical centre on 15 August after which he was declared unfit for active service.

Hay, who had promised Logue that he would be back in Armagh on 17 August, could no longer go. Samuel Watt simply informed him that Logue's letter was now in Clemenceau's hands and that the British Government was studying the plan. This surprised Hay since everything had been arranged before his departure for Paris and Ireland on 30 July.[46] He told William Sutherland that Logue might fear a 'plot against him' and that he had to send a letter to the Cardinal in order to reassure him. Sutherland said that the letter had to be approved by Samuel Watt first. Watt wrote a very short note for Hay, saying that he understood him, and that the letter had to be posted in Paris. Obviously, Logue had to believe that Hay was engaged in talks with the French Government. The Captain, pretending to be at the Conseil Supérieur de Guerre, the Supreme War Council, in Versailles near Paris, wrote two letters to the Cardinal and one of them, at least, reached Armagh. It reassured Logue that 'the matter... is being discussed in detail by the competent authorities which argue that there is every chance of success'.[47] Hay never received any news from Logue. Watt warned him that the authorities in Ireland were ready to carry out the plan if David Lloyd George could guarantee that there would be no objection in London. Nothing happened and Watt never obtained the Prime Minister's guarantees. Finally, on 5 September 1918, Hay made a last suggestion to Edward Shortt. He would send a letter to Logue informing him that the opposition of certain individuals 'was so bitter that the only way to carry the scheme through was to publish the letters he had written and received to and from Cardinal Amette'.[48] This would force the British Government 'to give the guarantees to France, or tell France boldly that they had changed their policy'. The next day, Hay received a very dry letter from Watt:

> I have your letter of the 5th instant, I think on further reflection you will see that it would be quite impossible to ask the Chief Secretary [Shortt] to countenance the step you suggest, and that it would be better to leave him to decide himself the course of action which he may consider it best to adopt.
>
> (ACA, Logue papers, report of J.S. Hay)

It was the end of the 'Hay plan' and the disavowal of the Captain by his superiors. The project dragged on and was simply shelved. Some time later, William Sutherland showed the officer a letter from a Mr Dormer of the Foreign Office to the Prime Minister including an enquiry from Clemenceau about the Irish who were to go to France. The Président du Conseil wanted to know what had happened to this recruitment plan. His old anti-clerical feelings had resurfaced despite France's *Union sacrée* as he had told Lord Derby in Paris that 'he did not like these sort of things with clerics'.[49]

The question is why did the British Government suddenly change its mind?

THE 'HAY PLAN': RECRUITMENT EFFORT OR PLOT?

It is difficult to state the real purpose of the 'Hay plan' without speculating. However, if one takes into account the reaction of General Henry Wilson concerning Ulster and Cardinal Logue's ideas about Ireland participating in the future peace conference, backed by France and the United States, the following explanations can be put forward.

On 17 July 1918, the German offensive stopped and General Ludendorff's armies began to retreat towards Flanders. It can, therefore, be reasonably assumed that from 20 July onwards, the day Captain Stuart Hay was approached to set up the plan, David Lloyd George began to think about an Allied victory. What would be the Irish nationalists' reaction then? Would they take advantage of the victory and appeal to the Americans to guarantee their rights as a small nation like their President, Woodrow Wilson, had stated in his Fourteen Points? Would Ireland fall into the hands of the Sinn Féiners, become a republic and be a threat to Great Britain? Could it all be stopped? The 'Hay plan' more or less helped the British Prime Minister to answer some of these questions.

In the summer of 1918, there were three main nationalist forces in Ireland. Firstly, the Nationalist party under the leadership of John Dillon. Successive British cabinets had always negotiated with this party but it was in a very difficult position at the end of the war and was likely to be beaten by Sinn Féin during the next general election. Secondly, Eamon de Valera's Sinn Féin was a threat to British interests. The Sinn Féin members favoured the idea of a republic for Ireland and had no interest in remaining within the Empire. Its leaders were determined to put their country's case to the peace conference. Thirdly, there was the Catholic Church. It was, of course, not a political party but its importance in Irish society simply could not be ignored. A fraction of the clergy and a few bishops supported Sinn Féin, whereas other members of the hierarchy, like Cardinal Logue, were vehemently opposed to de Valera and his followers.

After the Sinn Féin leaders were arrested during the 'German Plot', were the Church and its Primate in a position to restore order in the country, eliminate the republican threat and, consequently, help the Nationalist party to regain power? What were the intentions of the Church? The 'Hay plan' was a very appropriate answer to all these questions and whether the plan succeeded or not, in both cases Logue would have to reveal his intentions.

If the plan failed, it would mean that the Church had no plan whatsoever to support the war effort. It would also show that the Church had adopted a far more radical attitude towards Britain than ever before. If Logue did not accept this opportunity to destroy Sinn Féin, it would prove that the Church was simply not able or not willing to prevent Sinn Féin from taking over Ireland.

On the other hand, if the 'Hay plan' succeeded, 100,000 or 200,000 Irishmen would go over to France and reassure the French Government and High Command. Even if the plan was not immediately carried out and dragged on for a while, it would relieve Lloyd George's cabinet from the pressure of certain politicians in favour of conscription, like Winston Churchill and Georges Clemenceau. However, if Logue accepted Hay's proposal, it would surely not be for the love of anti-clerical France. So, what would be his motives? Once more, Cardinal Amette's letter to Logue, conceived in Downing Street, brought the answer: '...in this way, Ireland would give invaluable help to our just and great cause, and would give herself a new right to the esteem and gratitude of France and the civilised world'.[50] In other words, this meant that nationalist Ireland would be backed by France and the United States and this is how Logue interpreted the sentence. Lloyd George now knew that even the highest dignitary of the Irish Catholic Church had the same idea as Sinn Féin, which was to seek help from the most powerful nations to rest Ireland's case. British politicians could no longer rely on the Church to prevent Ireland from evolving towards a more radical nationalism. It would seem that the Prime Minister had cleverly sounded out Logue's opinions. It is said about Lloyd George that 'no other politician equalled him at fostering a situation where all options seemed to advantage him'.[51]

The whole 'Hay plan' was politically motivated. It was inconceivable, indeed, that Lloyd George seriously believed that young Irishmen would go over to work in France at a time when Ireland was enjoying important economic prosperity, and also so shortly after the conscription crisis. When Hay met Samuel Watt at the University Club in Dublin on his return from Carlingford, Watt said that Logue's approval of the plan meant the end for Sinn Féin. This is a relevant remark and indicates that the plan had darker motives.

Another, and more simple explanation, would be that Lloyd George was on tenterhooks and that he had panicked. He had badly miscalculated when he tried to impose conscription upon Ireland, and could not have foreseen the international protest and disapproval his decision would provoke in the Empire, the United States and other countries like Spain and Argentina. All this could have very serious consequences on the global British war effort. It is said that he knew some 88,000 British soldiers were on leave and would be rapidly sent back to the front.[52] This was not particularly reassuring news as the British Army had about 70,000 casualties a month.[53] Moreover, whatever guarantees he had received from President Wilson regarding the United States' participation in the war, the Prime Minister was fully aware of the American problem. As a matter of fact, as late as August 1918 when the Allies were about to counter-attack, the American High Command made the rather peculiar decision to withdraw nearly all their divisions from the front. This led to a heated exchange between General Foch and his American counterpart, General Pershing.[54] Perhaps the 'Hay plan' had been a desperate plan to get more men at the front. A few years later, in a speech delivered in London, Lloyd George went out of his way to praise the troops from the British Empire, carefully ignoring the names Ireland and Ulster, and spoke about 'the anxious time ... when France was thoroughly exhausted and her Army forced to rest. Britain almost at the end of her manpower; and America without a regiment in the trenches. What would we have done without [the troops from the Empire]?'[55] This declaration sounded like admitting that the manpower crisis had nearly provoked defeat.

Lloyd George never sanctioned the 'Hay plan'. It was very unlikely that the British Government wished to see an independent and united Ireland as Sinn Féin and the Catholic Church were demanding. Ireland was too important from a geopolitical and strategic point of view and the First World War had clearly demonstrated this. If for military reasons the British wanted to keep a pied-à-terre in Ireland, they had to avoid alienating the unionists or placing them in a delicate position. General Henry Wilson's reaction to the 'Hay plan' and to Cardinal Logue's acceptance would tend to show that this was indeed the case. Wilson hated everything in Ireland which was not orange.[56] David Lloyd George wrote about him that 'he hated Papists and Irish patriots'.[57] The General seemed to be in an offensive mood against Irish nationalism in the summer of 1918 for he refused to replace certain battalions of the 16th Irish Division with surviving battalions of the 10th Irish Division which had just returned from the Balkans to the western front. This led to the disappearance of the division that John Redmond had so cherished.[58] But, he was certainly not against conscription or recruitment in that country. On 1 May 1918, he had had a discussion with the Prime Minister on this matter and wrote the following in his diary: 'Lloyd George still out for conscripting Ireland using the men as labourers in France first of all. If we can discipline them this might do.'[59] And yet, he rejected the 'Hay plan' in August saying that it was 'anti-Ulster'. Indeed, if 100,000 or 200,000 men disembarked *voluntarily* in France, the General must have realised that nationalist Ireland would have been in a very strong position after the war, especially if it had the support of France and above all the United States where there was an important Irish-American community. It was, therefore, not surprising that he demanded the cancellation of the whole operation. In September 1918, Wilson promised Clemenceau that conscription would be introduced in Ireland.[60] But this was quite another thing. Conscription would not have had the same effect on the international community as voluntary enlistment. David Lloyd George never authorised the enforcement of the Military Service Act in Ireland, for by September 1918 the war was won and the British Prime Minister would not risk the chance of beginning another one against Irish nationalists.

As for Cardinal Logue, he must have bitterly regretted this unique opportunity to destroy Sinn Féin, as he believed. On 2 December 1918, he declared to the *Independent*: 'No one, I think, could suspect me of favouring the Sinn Féin policy... I have never concealed my views of its futility'.[61]

At the time, nobody could have known how sincere the Cardinal had been.

Aftermath

The reverberations of the shots fired at Archduke Ferdinand in Sarajevo on 28 June 1914 were not heard in Ireland but the political earthquake did reach Irish shores despite Ireland's somewhat remote position in Europe. If, at the beginning, the Irish nationalist people genuinely supported the war and embraced John Redmond's ideas, they rapidly withdrew their active support when it became clear that the British Government and the War Office were not sanguine in promoting Irish nationalism and bravery at the front. This was chiefly Herbert Asquith, David Lloyd George and Lord Kitchener's responsibility. Their handling of Irish affairs may seem at first sight clumsy and thoughtless, but it bears all the hallmarks of a deliberate policy. Once again, a continental war had shown how important Ireland's geographical and strategic location was for Britain, its allies and its enemies. Independence or autonomy for the whole of Ireland was too great a risk for British strategists. If the British wanted to have a permanent pied-à-terre in Ireland, Ulster would be an ideal solution. The so-called 'treaty ports' for the Royal Navy in the Irish Free State, established in the Treaty of December 1921, equally validate this argument. As Napoleon once said: 'The politics of a nation lie in its geography.' Irish nationalism and patriotism was, therefore, deliberately ignored in order to avoid all publicity for Ireland's claim to autonomy and independence.

The country would have been in a strong position at the Peace Conference if it had fully participated in the war effort. The War Office could have easily and judiciously exploited Irish nationalism and enthusiasm. After all, Britain was a democratic country and if Kitchener and his civil servants had been ordered by their Prime Minister to do so, they would have had to obey. This order, however, was never issued. Perhaps English Liberal politicians feared their own Army after the Curragh Mutiny in March 1914, when some high-ranking officers declared that they would not fight against the UVF to impose Home Rule in Ulster, as the freely elected House of Commons had decided. This raises fundamental questions about the British democratic system at the time. The Irish crisis and the European war proved too much for Asquith to handle and he found no better solution but to shelve Home

Rule until after the war, saying: 'The Irish on both sides are giving me a lot of trouble just at a difficult moment. I sometimes wish we could submerge the whole lot of them and their island for, say, ten years under the waves of the Atlantic,'[1]

In fact, the problem had been in the making well before the war broke out and successive Liberal and Conservative cabinets, and also some British generals, had contributed to rendering it even more opaque. John Redmond, a moderate nationalist, paid the price for his loyalty to the British Empire and his rather weak policy towards the war cabinet. This paved the way for a more radical nationalism, led by Eamon de Valera during the conscription crisis in April 1918. Sinn Féin won a landslide victory at the first post-war general election in December 1918 as the Nationalist party had been unable to solve political crises between 1914 and 1918 and had been largely associated with the much detested war effort. Appropriately, it was David Lloyd George who provided the last nail in the Nationalist party's coffin by declaring, a few weeks before the general election, that Home Rule would not be implemented 'until the condition of Ireland [made] it possible'.[2] In subjectivity, it largely equalled his notion of 'substantial agreement', a formula he had found for the deliberations of the Irish Convention. But in 1919, the Irish nationalist population would not wait and took up arms against the British Army, this time more effectively. As for the thousands of nationalist soldiers who had honestly believed that their country would best be served in the trenches of France and Belgium, they returned to a much changed Ireland and soon 'retired into historical oblivion',[3] a position they still occupy these days.

Not surprisingly, it was Lloyd George who was one of the first politicians to brush aside Ireland's contribution in the war, including Ulster's. In a most imperial speech entitled 'Citadel of Peace and Liberty' delivered at the Queen's Hall in London in 1924, the former Prime Minister paid tribute to the Empire's crucial war effort and mentioned countries as far afield as New Zealand and Newfoundland. Ireland and Ulster were conspicuously absent.[4] Maybe he was still resentful of the fact that it was this country, together with other diplomatic setbacks and internal feuds within the Liberal party, which had led to the fall of his Government in 1922.[5] 'Historical oblivion' was the fate of those soldiers who were lucky to have survived the onslaught of the Irish Republican Army (IRA) and the Black and Tans who fought for the British. Indeed, a number of ex-servicemen had to pay with their lives for the fact that they had joined the Army during the First World War. In the War of Independence and the Civil War in Ireland that immediately followed the Great War, war-veterans became a target for the IRA and the Black and Tans. It is estimated that between January and April 1921, almost one third of the civilians killed by the IRA were ex-soldiers,[6] who had survived Mons, Gallipoli, the Somme, Passchendaele and the last great German spring offensive of 1918. The reason for killing them was that they were deemed to be traitors of the nationalist and republican cause, but also because they were a potential threat. These men could use the experience they had obtained in the war, against the IRA or the British forces. The same was of course true for unionist soldiers. In 1914, General Richardson, one of the heads of the UVF, had warned that experienced war-veterans 'would return to the attack and relegate Home Rule to the devil'.[7] Major William Redmond, the Nationalist leader's brother, had a beautiful and idealistic vision of Catholics and Protestants forgetting their differences in the trenches and coming together. When he was mortally wounded, he was carried back to a field hospital of the 36th Ulster Division.[8] His death was very symbolic but the Redmond brothers' idea of healing the Irish through the experience of war was somewhat naïve. As early as September 1915, if not before, Sir Edward Carson had openly rejected John Redmond's idea and embarked on a separatist policy: 'No, we are all brothers. They [the soldiers of the 36th Ulster Division] are our own Volunteers; they are men of our own religion. They are men of our own way of thinking; they are men of the great Ulster tradition.'[9]

The Catholic Church closely observed the political scene in Ireland between 1914 and 1918 and little by little adapted itself to the changing circumstances. It could not afford to ignore the evolution of public opinion if it wanted to retain its power and prominence in the country, and carefully examined the triangular relations between the British Government, the Nationalist party and the population. In 1914 the Church largely approved of Ireland's participation in the war. By 1918, it was almost universally against it. Bishops and priests' support was dictated by the national question and by the popular will. Under no circumstances would the clergy have forced Irishmen to accept conscription lest it became completely isolated within the country. As they worked amidst their flocks, priests were the first to understand that the population had lost all interest in the war, and the hierarchy eventually followed suit.

The growing problem for the Church was its support for the Nationalist party which continued to back the war effort and paid little attention to public opinion. In the long run, this could only lead to an upset in the balance of power in Irish political life. The rupture between the Church and John Redmond's party was gradual as the clergy had, in the beginning at least, no other alternative to the Nationalist party since Arthur Griffith's and Eamon de Valera's Sinn Féin was first perceived as revolutionary. But Redmond's pro-war campaign caused his own demise, as Bishop O'Dwyer of Limerick took up his pen and began a virulent anti-war campaign which would deeply influence public opinion. The complacent Nationalist party did not bother to publicly oppose the Bishop and soon he became the champion of the nationalist opposition. Within the hierarchy, O'Dwyer was a lonely voice but in April 1918 during the conscription crisis, the overwhelming majority of the clergy spoke like him. The crisis is remembered essentially for Archbishop Walsh, Mgr Curran and Eamon de Valera's role, but with the benefit of hindsight one can safely say that it was O'Dwyer's posthumous victory.

After its decisive intervention in April 1918, it became clear that the Church would have to be taken into account in a future independent Ireland. This was soon confirmed as post-war governments in Ireland had various social programmes with a distinct Catholic flavour.[10] One of the very first politicians to realise this was de Valera. After his election as President of Sinn Féin, he began to play the Catholic card in order to achieve an alliance with the clergy that would definitely swing the balance of power in his party's favour. Naturally, an alliance with Bishop O'Dwyer had figured prominently in his plans. Notwithstanding his political motives, the rising Sinn Féin politician seems to have been genuinely inspired by O'Dwyer's writings. In 1922, after he had rejected the treaty that established the Irish Free State and implicitly recognised partition, de Valera set up his Republican Government and the Civil War broke out in Ireland. He justified his actions in a letter to Archbishop Mannix by quoting extracts of a speech made by O'Dwyer in 1916, in which he had warned that as long as Ireland was occupied by Britain, Irishmen would consider it a virtue rather than a sin to be engaged in fighting: 'God has made her a nation, and while grass grows and water runs there will be men in Ireland to dare and die for her.'[11] Bearing in mind the history of Northern Ireland, these were prophetic words. De Valera's policy of flattering the Catholic Church paid off. During the South Armagh by-election in 1918, Sinn Féin distributed leaflets entitled 'Irish Bishops recommend Sinn Féin'.[12] Soon, most of the hierarchy was convinced that de Valera was the man to back. Paradoxically, it was Bishop O'Dea of Galway in March 1919, who had opposed O'Dwyer in 1915, who confirmed that an alliance between the Church and Sinn Féin was on the cards, thus outlining the beginning of a new order: 'The Sinn Féiners in my diocese are the very reverse of anti-clerical or anti-religious.'[13] Bishop Foley, this most imperial mind and enthusiastic supporter of Ireland's participation in the war, also wrote the same month: Sinn Féiners 'are most exemplary in attending to their religious duties and living good Christian lives'.[14]

Various foreign observers, including French, German, American and Australian, had become aware of the importance of the Catholic Church in Ireland and throughout the Empire and the United States.

Some had correctly guessed that the British cabinet's disastrous Irish policy and the Unionist party's stubborn refusal to come to terms with the idea of Home Rule, despite John Redmond's rather obvious display of Empire loyalty, had made Irish nationalism more radical and more Catholic. After skilful diplomacy by Mgr O'Riordan in Rome, the Vatican had also been persuaded that nationalism and Catholicism were closely associated and that it would not be in the Curia's interest to intervene in Anglo-Irish relations. In fact, the war in Europe had brought about an unexpected rapprochement between the Holy See and nationalist Ireland, so much so that de Valera, in 1937, asked the Pope to approve Ireland's new constitution in which it was stipulated that the Catholic Church had a special position in the country.[15]

But above all, the First World War, unfortunately for Ireland, resulted in the complete separation of Catholic nationalists and Protestant unionists. Of course, there had been a long story of disagreement and distrust between the two sides, but the war turned the gap between them into an abyss, which would unavoidably lead to partition. The unionists must have been seriously worried when they saw what the Catholic Church was capable of during the conscription crisis, not only in Ireland but also in the Empire and the United States. The result was a reinforcement of their siege mentality. As nationalists were repeatedly frustrated in their political aspirations, the Church ran out of patience with unionists. Bishop Morrisroe's declaration that unionists were like a 'foreign garrison' in the country was not calculated to promote understanding between the two communities, but it reflected nationalist Ireland's feelings at that stage. It would be tempting for those who do not see the Irish Catholic Church in a favourable light to accuse it of being at the root of partition and the collapse of the moderate Nationalist party when the clergy began to support Sinn Féin. This shift of allegiance was a godsend to de Valera. However, can one seriously blame the Church after all the events between 1914 and 1918? Can one really blame bishops for adopting a more radical attitude towards Britain and the unionists and say that they paved the road to partition? Responsibility lay above all at the doorstep of 10 Downing Street and the War Office in London. The British Government's policy, totally subjugated by war considerations, caused a political climate in Ireland that sooner or later would erupt into violence. It became a reality when frustrated nationalists, socialists and republicans stormed the General Post Office in Dublin during Easter 1916. One has every reason to wonder what would have happened if the British Government had fully exploited Irish nationalism and patriotism into action at the front in France and if it had succeeded in making the war really popular in Ireland. As Bishop O'Dwyer said in September 1916: 'When war was being declared I would have said to the English Government: give us our national rights; set up a genuine parliament in Dublin, and we are with you; but if you will not, then fight your own battles.'[16] If the Government had listened, perhaps it would have forced the Unionist party to have a different outlook on Home Rule and come to an understanding with the Nationalist party. After all, unionists did not reject the measure of autonomy they received under the Government of Ireland Act of 1920.

The period between 1914 and 1918 opens up a historical debate which should take into consideration not only Ireland's military involvement in the war but also the consequences the war had on Irish political life. It seems that some national myths need to be seen in perspective, as the Easter Rising of 1916 has overshadowed for too long the more important political event which was the conscription crisis of April 1918. This book is an attempt to create a tapestry with new facts and characters whose importance has been hitherto largely unknown. It remains, however, an incomplete picture as the obscure 'Hay plan', for example, has not been completely explained. Some aspects of the story between 1914 and 1918 have been exposed to the dangerous science of speculation. It is to be hoped that research in the years to come will shed a clearer light on the Great War in Ireland.

Finally, what happened to some of the leading characters of this narrative? A year after the war, Mgr O'Riordan died in Rome. Perhaps one of the most influential clerics of the time, his name remains unknown. He was replaced by Mgr Hagan in 1919. Rome saw the arrival of Mgr Curran who found himself forced to leave Dublin. Asked by the press if Archbishop Walsh would condemn murders committed by the IRA, he replied that not all murders were the same. This was an embarrassment to Walsh.[17] Curran became vice-rector of the Irish College. Soon, Hagan and Curran were involved in cloak-and-dagger work as they tried to secure Italian support for the Irish Republican Army. Curran took over the direction of the college from Hagan but was, once again, removed from office in controversial circumstances. He died in Dublin in 1960. Archbishop Walsh passed away in 1921 at the age of eighty-one. Before his death, he had strongly opposed the Government of Ireland Act. Just as he had feared, partition became a reality. Today, Walsh has not been forgotten and has recently been the object of an outstanding biography.[18] The same cannot be said about Cardinal Logue, the great loser within the hierarchy in 1918. Imperial though he was, his nationalist feelings came to the fore when he denounced the British Government and its policy of reprisals during the War of Independence. Logue liked to operate in the shadows and not surprisingly he was approached to negotiate a truce between the British forces and the IRA. He died in 1924 at the age of eighty-five and was replaced as Archbishop of Armagh by Patrick O'Donnell, the Bishop of

Raphoe. Bishop O'Dwyer had died in 1917. Nowadays a small bridge in Limerick, built in 1931, bears his name. On it, an inconspicuous black plaque refers to the Bishop as 'an honorary Freeman of the City in recognition of his great services to Church and Country'. Like the Great War and its soldiers, O'Dwyer became a casualty of history.

Notes

NOTES TO PREFACE

1   David Fitzpatrick (ed.), *Ireland and the First World War* (Mullingar, 1988), p. viii.
2   Keith Jeffery, *Ireland and the Great War* (Cambridge, 2000), p. 1.
3   Kevin Myers in 'Sown in Tears and Blood', RTE, 1998.
4   Jeffery, *Ireland and the Great War*, p. 7.
5   *The Bandon Opinion*, December 1997, p. 28.
6   M.E. Collins, *New History in Context 2* (Dublin, 1996), p. 28.
7   For instance: Terence Denman, *Ireland's Unknown Soldiers, the 16th Irish Division in the Great War* (Blackrock, 1992); Tom Johnstone, *Orange, Green and Khaki, the Story of the Irish Regiments in the Great War, 1914–1918* (Dublin, 1992); and Jane Leonard, *The Culture of Commemoration: The Culture of War Commemoration* (Dublin, 1996).
8   For instance: Patrick Callan, 'Ambivalence towards the Saxon Shilling', *Archivium Hibernicum*, 41 (1986); Pauric Travers, 'The Priest in Politics: the Case of Conscription', in Oliver MacDonagh (ed.), *Irish Culture and Nationalism, 1750-1950* (London, 1983).
9   Wim Hornman, *Kinderen van het Geweld* (Haarlem: Gottmer, 1973), p. 13.
10 National Library of Ireland (NLI), MS 15439(6), *La Documentation Catholique*, no. 66, 8 May 1920, p. 633.
11 Ibid.
12 Ibid., p. 637.
13 Laurence Geary, *The Plan of Campaign 1886–1891* (Cork, 1986), p. 130.

NOTES TO CHAPTER 1

1   A.T.Q. Stewart, *Edward Carson* (Dublin, 1981), p. 78.
2   Calton Younger, *Arthur Griffith* (Dublin, 1981), p. 45.
3   George Dangerfield, *The Damnable Question* (London, 1977), p. 121.
4   David W. Miller, *Church, State and Nation in Ireland 1898–1921* (Dublin, 1973), p. 304.
5   Ibid., p. 306.
6   J.J. Lee, *Ireland 1912–1985: Politics and Society* (Cambridge, 1989), pp. 20–21.
7   Miller, *Church, State and Nation in Ireland, 1898–1921*, pp. 268–9.
8   Irish College Rome (ICR), O'Riordan papers, letter no. 170, Hagan to O'Riordan, 29 July 1914.
9   *The Cork Examiner*, 29 July 1914.
10 *The Freeman's Journal*, 3 August 1914.
11 Maurice Headlam, *Irish Reminiscences* (London, 1947).
12 *The Freeman's Journal*, 5 August 1914.
13 Charles Frederick D'Arcy, *The Adventures of a Bishop* (London, 1934).
14 Niall Ferguson, *The Pity of War* (London, 1999), p. 18, pp. 207–8.
15 *The Cork Examiner*, 6 August 1914.
16 Colonial Office, CO 904/94 microfilm, (Mary Immaculate College, Limerick), Inspector

General to Under Secretary, August 1914.
17   *The Belfast Newsletter*, 10 August 1914.
18   Ferguson, *The Pity of War*, p. 14.
19   *The Freeman's Journal*, 7 August 1914.
20   Ibid., 15 August 1914.
21   *The Irish Worker*, 22 August 1914, and the *Freeman's Journal*, 17 August 1914 and 18 August 1914.
22   *The Freeman's Journal*, 4 August 1914.
23   Terence Denman, *Ireland's Unknown Soldiers* (Blackrock, 1992), p. 28.
24   Stephen Gwynn, *John Redmond's Last Years* (London, 1919).
25   Denman, *Ireland's Unknown Soldiers*, p. 27.
26   Ian Colvin, *The Life of Lord Carson* (London, 1934).
27   *The Freeman's Journal*, 12 August 1914.
28   Ibid., 21 September 1914.
29   Younger, *Arthur Griffith*, p. 48.
30   Peter Beresford Ellis, *History of the Irish Working Class* (London, 1985).
31   Breandan Mac Giolla Choille (ed.), *Intelligence Notes 1914–1916* (Dublin, 1966), p. 105.
32   John S. Ellis, 'The degenerate and the martyr: nationalist propaganda and the contestation of Irishness, 1914–1918', in *Eire Ireland*, vol. XXXV: 3–4 (autumn/winter 2000–2001), p. 16.
33   Ibid., p. 14.
34   John Whyte, '1916; Revolution and Religion', in F.X. Martin (ed.), *Leaders and Men of the Easter Rising: Dublin 1916* (London, 1967), p. 215.
35   *The Irish Catholic Directory* (Dublin, 1915).
36   Sean Connolly, *Religion and Society in Nineteenth Century Ireland* (Studies in Irish Economic and Social History, 1985), p. 37.
37   Emmet Larkin, *The Roman Catholic Church and the Fall of Parnell 1888–1891* (North Carolina, 1979).
38   National Library of Ireland (NLI), Sean T. O'Kelly Papers, MS 27728(1), Mgr Curran's memoirs, p. 9.
39   See chapters 4 and 8 on the first French mission and the second French mission.
40   *The Irish Daily Independent*, 26 October 1901.
41   Pádraig Yeates, *Lockout, Dublin 1913* (Dublin, 2000), pp. 53–4.
42   Patrick Callan, in 'Ambivalence towards the Saxon Shilling', *Archivium Hibernicum*, p. 100.
43   ICR, Hagan Papers, letter no. 104, Curran to Hagan, 12 September 1914.
44   Keith Jeffery, *Ireland and the Great War* (Cambridge, 2000), p. 10.
45   *The Irish Catholic*, 15 August 1914.
46   *The Freeman's Journal*, 10 August 1914.
47   *The Irish Catholic Directory* (Dublin 1915), p. 538.
48   *The Freeman's Journal*, 22 September 1914.
49   *The National Volunteer* in *The Freeman's Journal*, 24 October 1914.
50   Figures based on different articles found in the Irish press and in Miller, *Church State and Nation*, and Patrick Callan 'Ambivalence to the Saxon Shilling', *Archivium Hibernicum*.
51   *The Irish Catholic*, letter of Cardinal Logue, 7 July 1917.
52   Ellis, 'The degenerate and the martyr: nationalist propaganda and the contestation of Irishness, 1914–1918', *Eire Ireland*, p. 12, n. 12.
53   Jeffery, *Ireland and the Great War*, p. 7.
54   George H. Kassar, *Kitchener: Architect of Victory* (London, 1977).
55   Denman, *Ireland's Unknown Soldiers*, p. 22.
56   General Sir Bryan Mahon, 'The Irish Welter as I found it', in William G. Fitzgerald (ed.), *The Voice of Ireland* (Dublin and London, Virtue and company Ltd. 1979), p. 126.
57   Denman, *Ireland's Unknown Soldiers*, pp. 34–5.
58   Dangerfield, *The Damnable Question*, p. 131.
59   *The Church of Ireland Gazette*, 13 November 1914.
60   Fitzpatrick, *Ireland and the First World War*, pp. 47–8.
61   Mahon, 'The Irish Welter as I found it', in Fitzgerald, *The Voice of Ireland*, pp. 125–6.

THE CATHOLIC CHURCH IN IRELAND, 1914–1918

62 *The Tablet*, 12 December 1914.
63 Mac Giolla Choille, *Intelligence Notes 1914–1916*, p. 119.
64 *The Irish Catholic Directory*, 1916, p. 502.
65 Nadine-Josette Chaline (ed.), *Chrétiens dans la Première Guerre Mondiale* (Paris, 1993), p. 154.
66 *The Freeman's Journal*, 15 February 1915.
67 Ibid., 16 February 1915.
68 *The Irish Catholic Directory*, 1916, p. 503.
69 *The Freeman's Journal*, 16 February 1915.
70 Ibid., 15 February 1915.
71 *The Irish Catholic Directory*, 1916, p. 503.
72 Pierre Miquel, *La Grande Guerre* (Saint-Amand, 1983), p. 339.
73 Denman, *Ireland's Unknown Soldiers*, p. 131.
74 Fitzpatrick, *Ireland and the First World War*, p. 53.
75 *The Tablet*, 3 April 1915.
76 *The Irish Times*, 17 April 1915.
77 Dangerfield, *The Damnable Question*, pp. 131–2.
78 Patrick Callan, 'Voluntary Recruiting for the British Army in Ireland during the First World War', Ph.D. thesis, UCD, 1984, p. 281.
79 *The Tablet*, 29 May 1915.
80 Miller, *Church, State and Nation in Ireland*, p. 314.
81 NLI, Redmond papers, MS 15188/5, Fogarty to Redmond, 3 June 1915.
82 *The Freeman's Journal*, 27 July 1915.
83 Denis Gwynn, *The Vatican and the War in Europe* (Dublin, 1940), p. 38.
84 *The Tablet*, 21 August 1915.
85 *The Freeman's Journal*, 24 August 1915.
86 *The Irish Times*, 4 October 1915.
87 Miller, *Church, State and Nation*, p. 312.
88 Denman, *Ireland's Unknown Soldiers*, pp. 132–3.
89 Ara Coeli Armagh (ACA), O'Donnell papers, O'Donnell to Brassil, 3 September 1915.
90 This figure is based on the bishops' Lenten pastorals in 1916, Miller's *Church, State and Nation*, and Callan's 'Ambivalence towards the Saxon Shilling'. Concerning Kelly of Ross and Harty of Cashel, the author has taken into account their subsequent participation in a French recruitment operation in Ireland in October 1916 (see chapter 4, The first French mission).
91 *The Freeman's Journal*, 6 March 1916.
92 Denman, *Ireland's Unknown Soldiers*, p. 131.
93 ACA, O'Donnell papers, anonymous letters file.
94 *The Freeman's Journal*, 6 March 1916.
95 *The Tablet*, 11 November 1916.
96 *The Irish Catholic Directory*, 1917, p. 508.
97 Mac Giolla Choille, *Intelligence Notes 1914–1916*, p. 119.
98 Quai d'Orsay, Paris, vol. 547, Grande-Bretagne/Irlande, p.19, Blanche to Ministry for Foreign Affairs, 19 February 1918.
99 Connolly, *Religion and Society in Nineteenth Century Ireland*, p. 38.
100 John Whyte, '1916: Revolution and Religion', in Martin *Leaders and Men of the Easter Rising: Dublin 1916*, pp. 216–17.
101 *The Freeman's Journal*, 1 August 1914.
102 Ibid., 21 September 1914.
103 Ibid., 11 October 1915.
104 Ibid., 6 October 1914.
105 ICR, Hagan papers, letter no. 104, Curran to Hagan, 12 September 1914.
106 ACA O'Donnell papers, anonymous letters file.
107 *The Hibernian*, 18 December 1915.
108 ICR, Hagan papers, letter no. 159, P.J. Walsh to Hagan, 20 December 1915.
109 *The Freeman's Journal*, 11 October 1915.

110 *Nationality*, 30 October 1915.
111 Ferguson, *The Pity of War*, pp. 187–9.
112 *The Church of Ireland Gazette*, 13 November 1914.
113 *The Irish Times*, 27 September 1915.
114 *The Freeman's Journal*, 24 December 1915.
115 Desmond Fitzgerald, *Memoirs of Desmond Fitzgerald 1913–1916* (London, 1969).
116 F.S.L. Lyons, *Culture and Anarchy in Ireland 1890–1939* (Oxford, 1982), p. 99.
117 Jeffery, *Ireland and the Great War*, p. 31.
118 David Fitzpatrick, *Politics and Irish Life 1913–1921* (Dublin, 1977), pp. 62 and 68.
119 Colonial Office, CO 904/99 microfilm (Mary Immaculate College, Limerick), Inspector-General to Under-Secretary, January 1916.
120 Yeates, *Lockout Dublin 1913*, pp. xxi–xxii.
121 Ferguson, *The Pity of War*, pp. 206–7.
122 *The Church of Ireland Gazette*, 30 April 1915.
123 Keith Jeffery, 'The Irish military tradition and the British Empire', in Keith Jeffery (ed.), *An Irish Empire? Aspects of Ireland and the British Empire* (Manchester, 1996), p. 97.
124 *The Freeman's Journal*, 11 February 1916.
125 Connolly, *Religion and Society in Nineteenth Century Ireland*, pp. 40–1.
126 Patrick Callan, in 'Voluntary Recruiting for the British Army in Ireland during the First World War' (doctorate, University College Dublin, 1984).
127 Whyte, '1916: Revolution and Religion', in Martin *Leaders and Men of the Easter Rising: Dublin 1916*, pp. 217–18.
128 Callan, 'Ambivalence towards the Saxon Shilling', *Archivium Hibernicum*, p. 108.
129 *The Irish Catholic*, 12 September 1914.
130 *The Irish Catholic Directory*, 1915, p. 536.
131 Ibid., p. 550.
132 Ibid, 1916, p. 504.
133 *The Tablet*, 5 December 1914.
134 *The Freeman's Journal*, 15 February 1915.
135 ICR, O'Riordan papers, letter no. 5, Kelly to O'Riordan, 1 January 1916.
136 Callan, in 'Ambivalence towards the Saxon Shilling', p. 105.
137 *The Irish Catholic Directory*, 1916, p. 499.
138 *The Tablet*, 31 October 1914.
139 Ibid., 23 January 1915.
140 *The Irish Catholic Directory*, 1917, pp. 505–6.
141 Miller, *Church, State and Nation*, p. 272, and Yeates, *Lockout Dublin 1913*.
142 *The Irish Catholic*, 15 August 1914.
143 Limerick Diocesan Office (LDO), O'Dwyer papers, O'Riordan to O'Dwyer, 28 December 1914.
144 ACA, O'Donnell papers, Lenten pastoral, 11 February 1915.
145 NLI, Joseph Brennan papers, MS 26166, circular letter to bishops, 16 July 1915.
146 Ibid., Cohalan to Harrington of the IWSC, 4 September 1915.
147 *The Tablet*, 7 July 1917.
148 Quai d'Orsay Paris, vol. 545 Grande-Bretagne/Irlande, mission en Irlande, 1 October 1916, p. 138.
149 Alan J. Ward, *Ireland and Anglo-American Relations, 1899–1921* (London, 1969), p. 156.
150 NLI, Brennan papers, MS 26166, Mathew Nathan to Augustine Birrell, 1 March 1916.
151 *The Freeman's Journal*, 27 July 1915.
152 Miquel, *La Grande Guerre*, pp. 246–7.
153 *The Irish Times*, 27 July 1915.
154 *The Tablet*, 21 August 1915.
155 *The Irish Volunteer*, 21 August 1915.
156 Ibid., 21 August 1915.
157 NLI, Brennan papers, MS 26166, pastoral letter of Bishop Gaughran, 24 December 1915.
158 Ibid., Mathew Nathan to Augustine Birrell on IWSC, 1 March 1916.

NOTES TO CHAPTER 2

1   *The Freeman's Journal*, 27 July 1915.
2   Oliver P. Rafferty, *Catholicism in Ulster 1603–1983* (Dublin, 1994), p. 170.
3   Emmet Larkin, *The Roman Catholic Church and the Plan of Campaign 1886–1888* (Cork, 1978), p. 145.
4   Thomas Morrissey, *William J. Walsh, Archbishop of Dublin, 1841–1921* (Dublin, 2000), p. 101.
5   Colonial Office, CO 904/99 microfilm (Mary Immaculate College, Limerick), Inspector General to Under Secretary, January 1916.
6   *The Irish Independent*, 29 September 1914.
7   *The Freeman's Journal*, 30 September 1914.
8   Ibid., 30 September 1914.
9   Callan, 'Voluntary Recruiting for the British Army in Ireland during the First World War', p. 280.
10 *The Irish Independent*, 15 October 1914.
11 *The Freeman's Journal*, 15 February 1915.
12 Ibid., 25 June 1915.
13 Miller, *Church, State and Nation*, p. 314.
14 *The Freeman's Journal*, 6 March 1916.
15 Ibid., 19 October 1914.
16 Ibid., 15 February 1915 and also 6 March 1916.
17 *The Church of Ireland Gazette*, 21 May 1915.
18 *The Freeman's Journal*, 19 October 1914.
19 Documents concerning the chaplaincy issue can be consulted in the Secret Archives of the Vatican, the Irish College Rome (O'Riordan and Hagan papers), Westminster (Bourne papers), Ara Coeli Armagh (Logue papers), Dublin (Walsh papers) and Carlow (Foley papers).
20 *The Freeman's Journal*, 15 February 1915.
21 Ibid., 25 June 1915.
22 Miller, *Church, State and Nation*, p. 312.
23 *The Freeman's Journal*, 25 June 1915.
24 *The Freeman's Journal*, 27 July 1915.
25 *The Daily Express*, 29 July 1915.
26 Lee, *Ireland 1912–1985: Politics and Society*, pp. 23–4.
27 Bodleian Library Oxford, Nathan papers, MS 468, p. 287, memorandum of a discussion between Wimborne, Friend and Nathan, courtesy of Dr Colman O Clabaigh (Glenstal Abbey).
28 Bodleian Library Oxford, Nathan papers, MS 469, p. 172, memorandum of Captain Kelly's interview, 4 January 1916.
29 Ibid., Nathan papers, MS 469, p. 377, memorandum of Captain Kelly's interview, 13 April 1916.
30 Larkin, *The Roman Catholic Church and the Plan of Campaign 1886–1888*, p. 145.
31 ICR, Hagan papers, 1915, letter no. 63, Curran to Hagan, 13 April 1915.
32 Morrissey, *William J. Walsh, Archbishop of Dublin*, pp. 5 and 11.
33 Emmet Larkin, *The Roman Catholic Church and the Creation of the Modern Irish State 1876–1886* (Dublin, 1975), pp. 253–301.
34 Morrissey, *William J. Walsh, Archbishop of Dublin*, p. 74.
35 Ibid., p. 101.
36 Miller, *Church, State and Nation in Ireland*, pp. 145 and 243–4.
37 NLI, Redmond papers, MS 18290, Walsh to Redmond, 20 March 1912.
38 Patrick J. Walsh, *William J. Walsh, Archbishop of Dublin* (Dublin, 1928), p. 571.
39 NLI, Seán T. O'Kelly papers, MS 27728(1), Mgr Curran's memoirs, p. 9.
40 Morrissey, *William J. Walsh, Archbishop of Dublin*, p. 245.
41 Brian Murphy, *John Chartres, Mystery Man of the Treaty* (Blackrock, 1995), pp. 27–8.
42 NLI, O'Kelly papers, MS 27728(1), Mgr Curran's memoirs, 'My opportunities, as secretary

to Archbishop Walsh, of frank discussion with him on public affairs'.

43   Dublin Diocesan Archives (DDA), Walsh papers, 386 II, Cunnigham to Walsh, 12 February 1914.
44   Ibid., Walsh papers, 386 I, Walsh to Aberdeen, 12 October 1914.
45   Ibid., Walsh papers, 386 II, Ward to Walsh, 24 November 1914.
46   NLI, O'Kelly papers, MS 27728(1), Curran's memoirs, p. 12.
47   ICR, Hagan papers, 1914, letter no. 110, Curran to Hagan, 30 September 1914.
48   NLI, O'Kelly papers, MS 27728(1), Curran's memoirs, p. 12.
49   ICR, Hagan papers, 1915, letter no. 72, Curran to Hagan, 17 May 1915.
50   NLI, O'Kelly papers, MS 27728(1), Curran's memoirs, 20 May 1915.
51   Callan, 'Ambivalence to the Saxon Shilling', *Archivium Hibernicum*, p. 102.
52   NLI, O'Kelly papers, MS 27728(1), Curran's memoirs, 25 May 1915.
53   Miller, *Church, State and Nation in Ireland*, p. 311.
54   Walsh, *William J. Walsh, Archbishop of Dublin*, pp. 556–70.
55   DDA, Walsh papers, 387 II, Basil Blackwood to Walsh, 7 August 1915.
56   *The Irish Catholic Directory*, 1914, p. 208.
57   ICR, Hagan papers, 1915, letter no. 159, Walsh to Hagan, 20 December 1915.
58   DDA, Walsh papers, 388 I–1916, Walsh to Kelly, 13 April 1916.
59   *Eire Ireland*, 23 November 1914.
60   DDA, Walsh papers, 388 II–385/7 1916, Kelly to Walsh, 15 April 1916.
61   *The Irish Times*, 15 February 1915 and 6 March 1916.
62   Morrissey, *William J. Walsh, Archbishop of Dublin*, p. 9.
63   *The Tablet*, 21 August 1915.
64   Edward O'Callaghan, 'Bishop Edward Thomas O'Dwyer and the course of Irish Politics, 1870–1917' (Thesis, UCG, Galway, 1976).
65   Geary, *The Plan of Campaign 1886–1891* (Cork, 1986), p. 36.
66   Morrissey, *William J. Walsh, Archbishop of Dublin*, p. 95.
67   F.S.L. Lyons, *John Dillon* (London, 1968), p. 91.
68   Geary, *The Plan of Campaign 1886–1891*, pp. 86–7, p. 130.
69   Larkin, *The Roman Catholic Church and the Plan of Campaign*, p. 46.
70   C.J. Woods, 'Ireland and Anglo-Papal Relations, 1880–1885', *Historical Studies* 69, (1972), pp. 29–30.
71   Geary, *The Plan of Campaign*, p. 88.
72   Ibid., p. 87.
73   Morrissey, *William J. Walsh, Archbishop Of Dublin*, p. 137.
74   ICR, O'Riordan papers, no. 15, letter no. 59, O'Dwyer to O'Riordan, 6 March 1914.
75   Moody, Martin, Byrne (ed.), *A New History of Ireland* (Oxford, 1976), vol. VIII, p. 385.
76   Larkin, *The Roman Catholic Church and the Plan of Campaign*, p. 47.
77   *The Tablet*, 21 November 1914.
78   *The Freeman's Journal*, 15 February 1915.
79   *The Tablet*, 13 March 1915.
80   Ibid., 1 May 1915.
81   LDO, O'Dwyer papers, O'Riordan to O'Dwyer, 20 March 1915.
82   Ibid., 8 April 1915.
83   Ibid., 6 June 1915.
84   Fitzpatrick, *Politics and Irish Life 1913–1921*, p. 105.
85   NLI, Redmond papers, MS 15188, Fogarty to Redmond, 3 June 1915.
86   Miller, *Church, State and Nation in Ireland*, p. 315.
87   *The Tablet*, 31 July 1915.
88   Ruth Dudley Edwards, *Patrick Pearse and the Triumph of Failure* (Swords, 1990), pp. 236–7.
89   *The Tablet*, 21 August 1915.
90   ICR, O'Riordan papers, letter no. 107, O'Dwyer to O'Riordan, 13 August 1915.
91   *The Irish Volunteer*, 21 August 1915.
92   ICR, O'Riordan papers no. 16, letter no. 122, O'Dwyer to O'Riordan, 8 September 1915.
93   Ibid., letter no. 120, O'Dwyer to O'Riordan, 13 September 1915.

94   LDO, O'Dwyer papers, O'Riordan to O'Dwyer, 18 September 1915.
95   *The Tablet*, 23 October 1915.
96   LDO, O'Dwyer papers, file O, O'Dea to O'Dwyer, 30 October 1915.
97   Ibid., Fogarty to O'Dwyer, 10 November 1915.
98   Denman, *Ireland's Unknown Soldiers*, p. 131.
99   *New Ireland*, 13 November 1915.
100 Ibid., 13 November 1915.
101 *The Tablet*, 27 November 1915.
102 *Nationality*, 20 and 27 November 1915; *The Irish Volunteer*, 20 November 1915; the *Hibernian*, 4 December 1915.
103 Mac Giolla Choille (ed.), *Intelligence Notes 1913–1916*, p. 119, pp. 164–74.
104 Colonial Office, CO 904/98 microfilm (Mary Immaculate College, Limerick), Inspector General to Under-Secretary, December 1915.
105 Miller, *Church, State and Nation in Ireland*, p. 317.
106 Colonial Office, CO 904/98 microfilm (Mary Immaculate College, Limerick), Inspector General to Under-Secretary, November 1915.
107 PRO, London, CO 904/207, 'printed copies of the Bishop of Limerick's letter', 25 November 1915.
108 Ibid., 'printed copies of the Bishop of Limerick's letter in Co. Donegal', 02 December 1915.
109 LDO, O'Dwyer papers, file O, Fogarty to O'Dwyer, 9 December 1915.
110 PRO, London CO 904199 Inspector General to Under Secretary, monthly report for February 1916.
111 NLI, Leslie papers, MS 22832, Leslie to Redmond, 11 November 1915.
112 Ibid., Redmond to Leslie, 27 November 1915.
113 LDO, O'Dwyer papers, file O, Fogarty to O'Dwyer, 9 December 1915.
114 Ibid., file I, O'Riordan to O'Dwyer, 5 January 1916.
115 Edward O'Callaghan, 'Bishop Edward O'Dwyer and the Course of Irish Politics, 1870–1970', *Collectanea Hibernia*, pp. 331–2.
116 Callan, 'Voluntary Recruiting for the British Army in Ireland during the First World War', p. 217.
117 ICR, O'Riordan papers no. 16, letter no. 17, O'Dwyer to O'Riordan, 12 January 1916.
118 *The Freeman's Journal*, 6 March 1916.
119 *The Spark*, 26 March 1916.
120 *The Catholic Bulletin*, vol. VI, March 1916, no. 3, pp. 122–3.

NOTES TO CHAPTER 3

1   Dangerfield, *The Damnable Question*, pp. 166–8.
2   David G. Boyce, 'British Opinion, Ireland and the War', *The Historical Journal*, VIII, 3 (1974), p. 576.
3   Moody, Martin and Byrne (eds), *A New History of Ireland*, p. 390.
4   Oliver P. Rafferty, *The Church, the State and the Fenians 1861–1875* (London, 1999), pp. 94–6, 147 and 151.
5   Miller, *Church, State and Nation in Ireland*, p. 298.
6   John Whyte, '1916: Revolution and Religion', in Martin, *Leaders and Men of the Easter Rising: Dublin 1916*, p. 216.
7   NLI, O'Kelly papers, MS 7728(1), Curran's memoirs, pp. 25, 33 and 41.
8   Brian Murphy, *Patrick Pearse and the Lost Republican Ideal* (Dublin, 1991), pp. 77–8.
9   Reinhard R. Doerries (ed.), *Prelude to the Easter Rising: Sir Roger Casement in Imperial Germany* (London, 2000), p. 206 (German Minister, Berne, to Foreign Office, Berlin, 5 April 1916), p. 208 (Plunkett to Casement).
10 Ibid., p. 206.
11 San Isidoro, Rome, church archives, Plunkett to Rope, 15 October 1938.
12 Ibid., the *Irish Press*, 2 June 1933, 3 June 1933, and correspondence between Plunkett and

Rope, 27 May 1933, 2 June 1933, 19 June 1933, 23 June 1933, 30 June 1933, 3 July 1933, 15 October 1938.

13   F.X. Martin, 'Select documents; XX. Eoin MacNeill on the 1916 Rising', *Irish Historical Studies*, XII (1961), p. 249 and footnote 42 p. 264.

14   Miller, *Church, State and Nation in Ireland*, pp. 319–20.

15   Archives of the Holy Congregation of Extraordinary Ecclesiastical Affairs, Vatican, Plunkett to Benedict XV, no 15543, Rubrica 244, fasc. 92, rubrica 244 D.3.; these documents were located in the Secret Archives until 3 July 1933, when Cardinal Tardini transferred them to the Holy Congregation; it is to be noted that Tardini took those documents, including Plunkett's letter, only one month after the public controversy between Plunkett and MacNeill.

16   San Isidoro, Rome, church archives, Plunkett's letter, 15 October 1938.

17   Murphy, *Patrick Pearse and the Lost Republican Ideal*, p. 78.

18   *The Irish Times*, 21 April 1949, 'The Easter Rising from the Inside-IV'.

19   William A. Renzi, 'The Entente and the Vatican during the period of Italian Neutrality, August 1914–May 1915', *The Historical Journal*, XIII, 3 (1970), pp. 491–508.

20   Maureen Wall, 'The Background to the Rising', in Kevin Nowlan (ed.), *The Making of 1916* (Dublin, 1969), pp. 179 and 182.

21   F.X. Martin, 'Selected documents; XX. Eoin MacNeill on the 1916 Rising', *Irish Historical Studies*, p. 246.

22   Charles Macksey, 'War', *Catholic Encyclopedia*, vol. XV.

23   San Isidoro, Rome, church archives, Plunkett to Rope, 23 June 1933.

24   Ibid., *The Irish Press*, 2 June 1933. In this article, Plunkett also wrote that, in 1920, Benedict XV had personally congratulated him on representing the Irish republican cabinet.

25   W. Alison Phillips, *The Revolution in Ireland 1906–1923* (Longmans, 1923), p. 97.

26   LDO, O'Dwyer papers, file M, MacNeill to O'Dwyer, 18 April 1916.

27   NLI, O'Kelly papers, MS 27728(1), Curran's memoirs, p. 27.

28   ICR, Hagan papers, 1916, letter no. 63, Curran to Hagan, 19 April 1916.

29   Alison Phillips, *The Revolution in Ireland 1906–1923*, p. 98, note 1.

30   Dangerfield, *The Damnable Question*, pp. 166–7.

31   NLI, O'Kelly papers, MS 27728(1), Curran's memoirs, pp. 32–3.

32   Ibid., p. 35.

33   Ibid., p. 37.

34   ICR, Hagan papers, 1916, letter no. 66, Curran to Hagan, 23 April 1916.

35   Alison Phillips, *The Revolution in Ireland 1906–1923*, p. 102.

36   San Isidoro, Rome, church archives, *The Irish Press*, 2 June 1933.

37   NLI, O'Kelly papers, MS 27728(1), Curran's memoirs, p. 40.

38   Ibid., p. 40.

39   *The Irish Catholic Directory*, 1917, pp. 509–14.

40   *The Freeman's Journal* in *The Tablet*, 13 May 1916.

41   Whyte, '1916: Revolution and Religion', in Martin, *Leaders and Men of the Easter Rising: Dublin 1916*, pp. 216 and 220.

42   NLI, O'Kelly papers, MS 27728(1), Curran's memoirs, p. 73.

43   ICR, O'Riordan papers, no. 17, letter no. 34, Cleary to O'Riordan, 25 June 1916.

44   Moody, Martin and Byrne, *A New History of Ireland*, p. 391.

45   DDA, Walsh papers, 338 I/1916, Walsh to Maxwell, 11 May 1916.

46   Morrissey, *William J. Walsh, Archbishop of Dublin 1841–1921*, p. 290.

47   NLI, O'Kelly papers, MS 27728(1), Curran's memoirs, p. 98.

48   P.J. Walsh, *William J. Walsh, Archbishop of Dublin*, pp. 592–3.

49   NLI, O'Kelly papers, MS 27728(1), Curran's memoirs, p. 99.

50   Moody, Martin and Byrne, *A New History of Ireland*, p. 391.

51   Murphy, *Patrick Pearse and the Lost Republican Ideal*, p. 71.

52   *The Irish Catholic Directory*, 1917, p. 519.

53   ICR, Hagan papers, 1916, letter no. 87, Curran to Hagan, 30 July 1916.

54   A.C. Hepburn, *The Conflict of Nationality in Modern Ireland* (London, 1980), p. 102.

55   Murphy, *Patrick Pearse and the Lost Republican Ideal*, p. 71.

56   Quai d'Orsay, Paris, vol. 545 Grande-Bretagne/Irlande, mission des évêques français en Irlande, p. 173.
57   Alison Phillips, *The Revolution in Ireland 1906–1923*, p. 105.
58   Ferguson, *The Pity of War*, p. 170.
59   Quai d'Orsay, Paris, vol. 545 Grande-Bretagne/Irlande, de la Panouse to the Ministre de la Guerre, 25 April 1916, p. 14.
60   Miller, *Church, State and Nation in Ireland*, p.323.
61   Secret Archives of the Vatican, file Segretario di Stato, Guerra anno 1914–1918, Rubrica 244, fasc. 92, Gasparri to Logue, 30 April 1916, and Logue to Gasparri, 2 May 1916.
62   Miller, *Church, State and Nation in Ireland*, pp. 323–4, p. 536 and endnotes nos. 55–8.
63   Quai d'Orsay, Paris, vol. 545, Grande-Bretagne/Irlande, letter no. 30, French embassy Rome to Président du Conseil, 4 May 1916.
64   Ibid., Paul Cambon to Aristide Briand, 3 May 1916, p. 22.
65   Whyte, '1916: Revolution and Religion', in Martin, *Leaders and Men of the Easter Rising: Dublin 1916*, p. 220.
66   Dangerfield, *The Damnable Question*, p. 204.
67   *The Tablet*, 6 May 1916.
68   *The Irish Catholic*, 20 May 1916.
69   *The Tablet*, 3 June 1916.
70   Colonial Office, CO 904/100 microfilm (Mary Immaculate College, Limerick), Inspector General to Under-Secretary, August 1916.
71   *The Freeman's Journal*, 9 May 1916.
72   Ibid., 9 May 1916.
73   *The Irish Catholic*, 13 May 1916.
74   Quai d'Orsay, Paris, vol. 545 Grande-Bretagne/Irlande, letter no. 178, Touchet to the Président du Conseil, 25 October 1916.
75   'Dilemma in Berlin, from Casement's diary', in Roger McHugh (ed.), *Dublin 1916* (London, 1966), p. 10.
76   *The Irish Catholic*, 13 May 1916.
77   Patrick Maume, *The Long Gestation* (Dublin, 1999), p. 174.
78   *The Tablet*, 3 June 1916.
79   Maume, *The Long Gestation*, p. 181.
80   Mac Giolla Choille (ed.), *Intelligence Notes 1913–1916*, pp. 199–220.
81   *The Freeman's Journal*, 22 June 1916.
82   Whyte, '1916: Revolution and Religion', in Martin, *Leaders and Men of the Easter Rising: Dublin 1916*, pp. 219–20.
83   ICR, O'Riordan papers, no. 19, Logue to O'Riordan, 8 July 1918.
84   Quai d'Orsay, Paris, vol. 546 Grande-Bretagne/Irlande, compte-rendu de la mission du Père Flynn en Irlande, discussion between Logue and Flynn, 2 September 1917.
85   Fitzpatrick, *Politics and Irish Life 1913–1921*, p. 66.
86   *The Freeman's Journal*, 22 June 1916.
87   Moody, Martin and Byrne, *A New History of Ireland*, p. 391.
88   Maryann Gialanella Valiulis, *General Richard Mulcahy, Portrait of a Revolutionary* (Blackrock, 1992), p. 18.
89   Jeffery, *Ireland and the Great War*, p. 7.
90   Alison Phillips, *The Revolution in Ireland 1906–1923*, p. 108.
91   *The Freeman's Journal*, 17 May 1916.
92   Leon O'Broin, 'Birrell, Nathan and the Men of Dublin Castle', in F.X. Martin (ed.) *Leaders and Men of the Easter Rising: Dublin 1916*, pp. 1–14.
93   Miller, *Church, State and Nation in Ireland*, pp. 314–15.
94   *The Catholic Bulletin*, August 1916, vol. VI, p. 412.
95   *The Freeman's Journal*, 12 May 1916.
96   *The Cork Examiner*, 17 May 1916.
97   ICR, O'Riordan papers, no. 17, letter no. 19, Macrory to O'Riordan, 4 May 1916.
98   Hepburn, *The Conflict of Nationality in Modern Ireland*, p. 97.
99   *The Sinn Féin Rebellion Handbook, Easter 1916*, p. 212.

100 Roy Foster, *Modern Ireland* (London, 1989), p. 484.
101 Dangerfield, *The Damnable Question*, p. 214.
102 John Begley, *The Diocese of Limerick from 1691 to the Present Time* (Dublin, 1938), p. 578.
103 LDO, O'Dwyer papers, Maxwell to O'Dwyer, 6 May 1916.
104 *The Capuchin Annual*, 1942, p. 334.
105 Mac Giolla Choille (ed.), *Intelligence Notes 1913–1916*, pp. 173–4.
106 LDO, O'Dwyer papers, Maxwell to O'Dwyer, 12 May 1916.
107 O'Callaghan, 'Bishop Edward Thomas O'Dwyer and the Course of Irish Politics 1870–1917', p. 348.
108 *The Tablet*, 13 May 1916.
109 Thomas Pakenham, *The Boer War* (London, 1998), pp. 1–5.
110 O'Callaghan, 'Bishop Edward Thomas O'Dwyer and the Course of Irish Politics 1870–1917', p. 448, note no. 45.
111 Pakenham, *The Boer War*, pp. 494 and 1–5.
112 NLI, O'Kelly papers, MS 27728(1), Curran's memoirs, 'Dr O'Dwyer's famous letter to General Maxwell', and ICR, O'Riordan papers, no. 17, letter no 37, Curran to O'Riordan, 29 May 1916.
113 Miller, *Church, State and Nation in Ireland*, pp. 331–2.
114 Alison Phillips, *The Revolution in Ireland 1906–1923*, p. 87.
115 Maume, *The Long Gestation*, p. 155.
116 ICR, Hagan papers, 1916, no. 100, Curran to Hagan, 15 October 1916.
117 Quai d'Orsay, Paris, vol. 545 Grande-Bretagne/Irlande, p. 141.
118 Ibid., p. 167.
119 ICR, O'Riordan papers, no. 17, letter no. 25, O'Dwyer to O'Riordan, 18 May 1916.
120 Lee, *Ireland 1912–1985: Politics and Society*, pp. 31–4.
121 Colonial Office, CO 904/100 microfilm (Mary Immaculate College, Limerick), Inspector General to Under Secretary, August 1916.
122 Murphy, *Patrick Pearse and the Lost Republican Ideal*, p. 67.
123 Miller, *Church, State and Nation in Ireland*, p. 339.
124 Quai d'Orsay, Paris, vol. 545 Grande-Bretagne/Irlande, rapport d'André Géraud, p. 175.
125 ICR, O'Riordan papers, no. 17, letter no. 34, Cleary to O'Riordan, 25 June 1916.
126 O'Callaghan, 'Bishop Edward Thomas O'Dwyer and the Course of Irish Politics 1870–1917', pp. 352–3.
127 Younger, *Arthur Griffith*, pp. 58–60.
128 T. Ryle Dwyer, *De Valera, the Man and the Myths* (Swords, 1992), p. 18.
129 ICR, O'Riordan papers, no. 17, letter no. 50, O'Dwyer to O'Riordan, 15 June 1916.
130 *The Irish Opinion*, 24 June 1916.
131 *The Irish Nation*, 15 July 1916.
132 Alison Phillips, *The Revolution in Ireland 1906–1923*, p. 107.
133 Johnstone, *Orange, Green and Khaki, The Story of the Irish Regiments in the Great War*, p. 235.
134 Younger, *Arthur Griffith*, p. 62.
135 Robert Kee, *The Green Flag* (London, 1969), pp. 60–1.
136 Alison Phillips, *The Revolution in Ireland 1906–1923*, p. 114.
137 ICR, Hagan papers, 1916, letter no. 87, Curran to Hagan, 30 July 1916.
138 Murphy, *Patrick Pearse and the Lost Republican Ideal*, p. 72.
139 ICR, O'Riordan papers, no. 17, letter no. 140, O'Dwyer to O'Riordan, 31 August 1916.
140 Murphy, *Patrick Pearse and the Lost Republican Ideal*, pp. 72–3.
141 O'Callaghan, 'Bishop Edward Thomas O'Dwyer and the Course of Irish Politics 1870–1917', pp. 337–41.
142 LDO, O'Dwyer papers, file O, Fogarty to O'Dwyer, 10 September 1916.
143 Dermot Keogh, *Jews in Twentieth Century Ireland* (Cork, 1998), p. 38, footnote 66 of chapter 2.
144 LDO, O'Dwyer Papers, file 'Irish Politics 1912–1922', Freedom of the City speech, 16 September 1916.
145 Miller, *Church, State and Nation in Ireland*, p. 346.

146 Walter McDonald, *Reminiscences of a Maynooth Professor* (London, 1925), p. 372.
147 LDO, O'Dwyer papers, file O, Fogarty to O'Dwyer, 17 September 1916.
148 *Irish Opinion*, 23 September 1916, and *New Ireland*, 23 September 1916.
149 ICR, O'Riordan papers, no. 17, letter no. 162, O'Dwyer to O'Riordan, 29 September 1916.
150 Edward O'Callaghan, 'Bishop O'Dwyer and Bishop Foley on the Rising', in *Collectanea Hibernica*, 18/19, 1976–7, pp. 184–212.
151 Leon O'Brion, *The Chief Secretary* (London, 1969), p. 189.
152 Quai d'Orsay, Paris, vol. 545 Grande-Bretagne/Irlande, rapport d'André Géraud, 3–20 June 1916, pp.130–1.
153 Mac Giolla Choille, *Intelligence Notes 1913–1916*, pp. 199–220.
154 Maume, *The Long Gestation*, p. 179.
155 Keith Jeffery, 'The Irish military tradition and the British Empire' in *An Irish Empire. Aspects of Ireland and the British Empire*, p. 98.
156 Maume, *The Long Gestation*, pp. 174–5.
157 Quai d'Orsay, Paris, vol. 545 Grande-Bretagne/Irlande, letter no. 31, de Longchamps to Ministre des Affaires étrangères, 6 May 1916.
158 Sir Basil Liddell Hart, *Liddell Hart's History of the First World War* (London 1992), pp. 154–5.
159 *The Tablet*, 13 May 1916.
160 Keogh, *Jews in Twentieth Century Ireland*, p. 32.
161 Quai d'Orsay, Paris, vol. 545 Grande-Bretagne/Irlande, de la Panouse to Ministre de la Guerre, 11 May 1916, p. 42.
162 *The Freeman's Journal* in *The Tablet*, 19 August 1916.
163 ICR, O'Riordan papers, no. 17, letter no. 155, Curran to O'Riordan, 24 September 1916.
164 Ibid., Hagan papers, 1916, letter no. 100, Curran to Hagan, 15 October 1916.
165 NLI, O'Kelly papers, MS 27728(1), Curran's memoirs, p. 171.
166 *The Irish Independent*, 19 October 1916.
167 David G. Boyce, 'The unknown Chief Secretary: H.E. Duke and Ireland, 1916–1918', *Irish Historical Studies*, 79, March 1977, p. 306.
168 Mac Giolla Choille (ed.), *Intelligence Notes 1913–1916*, p. 201.
169 Eamon Phoenix, *Northern Nationalism* (Belfast, 1994), p. 21.
170 Ibid., p. 21.
171 Ferguson, *The Pity of War*, p. 255.
172 Maume, *The Long Gestation*, p. 156.
173 Austen Morgan, *Labour and Partition, the Belfast Working Class 1905–1923* (London, 1991), pp. 190–1.
174 Phoenix, *Northern Nationalism*, pp. 22–3.
175 Mary Harris, *The Catholic Church and the Foundation of the Northern Irish State* (Cork, 1993), p. 51.
176 *The Tablet*, 17 June 1916.
177 Ibid., 17 June 1916.
178 Ibid., 17 June 1916.
179 Harris, *The Catholic Church and the Foundation of the Northern Irish State*, p. 48.
180 *The Tablet*, 17 June 1916.
181 Alison Phillips, *The Revolution in Ireland 1906–1923*, pp. 110–11.
182 ICR, O'Riordan papers, no. 17, letter no. 50, O'Dwyer to O'Riordan, 15 June 1916.
183 Miller, *Church, State and Nation in Ireland*, p. 337.
184 Phoenix, *Northern Nationalism*, p. 29.
185 Harris, *The Catholic Church and the Foundation of the Northern Irish State*, p. 53.
186 Phoenix, *Northern Nationalism*, p. 31.
187 *The Freeman's Journal* in *The Tablet*, 24 June 1916.
188 Harris, *The Catholic Church and the Foundation of the Northern Irish State*, p. 53.
189 ICR, O'Riordan papers, no. 17, letter no. 60, O'Dwyer to O'Riordan, 24 June 1916.
190 Quai d'Orsay, Paris, vol. 545 Grande-Bretagne/Irlande, de Longchamps to Aristide Briand, 24 June 1916, p. 80.
191 Begley, *The Diocese of Limerick, Ancient and Medieval* (Dublin, 1906), p. VIII.

192 ICR, O'Riordan papers, no. 17, letter no. 63, O'Dwyer to O'Riordan, 27 June 1916.
193 *The Irish Nation*, 23 September 1916.
194 Phoenix, *Northern Nationalism*, pp. 34–5.
195 *The Freeman's Journal* in *The Tablet*, 8 July 1916.
196 Hepburn, *The Conflict of Nationality in Modern Ireland*, p. 98.
197 LDO, O'Dwyer papers, O'Riordan to O'Dwyer, 12 June 1917.
198 *The Irish Catholic*, 29 July 1916.
199 *The Tablet*, 29 July 1916.
200 Miller, *Church, State and Nation in Ireland*, pp. 342–3.
201 DDA, Walsh papers, 388/I (385/3), Curran to Walsh, 26 July 1916.
202 Murphy, *Patrick Pearse and the Lost Republican Ideal*, p. 73.
203 *The Tablet*, 29 July 1916.
204 Miller, *Church, State and Nation in Ireland*, pp. 344–5.
205 LDO, O'Dwyer papers, Freedom of the City speech, 14 September 1916.
206 Phoenix, *Northern Nationalism*, pp. 34–5.
207 *The Tablet*, 12 August 1916.
208 *The Irish Catholic Directory*, 1917, pp. 528–9.
209 Quai d'Orsay, Paris, vol. 545 Grande-Bretagne/Irlande, p. 175.
210 *The Irish Catholic Directory*, 1917, pp. 528–9.
211 Quai d'Orsay, Paris, vol. 545 Grande-Bretagne/Irlande, p. 175.

NOTES TO CHAPTER 4

1 Boyce, 'British opinion, Ireland and the war', pp. 575–6.
2 Janick Julienne, 'La France et l'Irlande nationaliste de 1860 à 1890: évolution et mutation des liens multiséculaires', in Centre de Gestion de l'Edition Scientifique, *Etudes Irlandaises* (24–1 Lille, Spring 1999), pp. 124–7.
3 Ferguson, *The Pity of War*, p. 33.
4 Felician Prill, *Ireland, Britain and Germany 1870–1914* (Dublin, 1975), p. 67.
5 NLI, George Gavan Duffy papers, MS 15439(6), *La Documentation Catholique*, 8 May 1920, p. 632.
6 Tim Coates (ed.), *The Irish Uprising 1914–1921* (London, 2000), p. 35.
7 Ibid., pp. 38–9.
8 Doerries, *Prelude to the Easter Rising: Sir Roger Casement in Imperial Germany*, von Bernstorff to Auswärtiges Amt, 28 December 1914, pp. 70–1.
9 *The Freeman's Journal*, 9 May 1916.
10 Ibid., 8 May 1916.
11 Coates (ed.), *The Irish Uprising, 1914–1921*, pp. 40–1.
12 Doerries, *Prelude to the Easter Rising*, p. 11.
13 Ferguson, *The Pity of War*, p. 170.
14 Arthur Mitchell and Pádraig O'Snodaigh (eds), *Irish Political Documents 1869–1916* (Dublin, 1989), p. 179.
15 Ibid., pp. 180–2.
16 Mac Giolla Choille (ed.), *Intelligence Notes 1913–1916*, p. 119.
17 Ferguson, *The Pity of War*, pp. 80 and 156.
18 Quai d'Orsay, Paris, vol. 545 Grande-Bretagne/Irlande, Cambon to Président du Conseil, 3 May 1916.
19 Maison diocésaine de Paris, dossier Irlande 1914–1920, Cambon to Amette, 5 December 1914.
20 Ibid., Cambon to Amette, 5 December 1914.
21 Ibid., O'Connor to Cambon, 6 December 1914.
22 Nadine-Josette Chaline (ed.), *Chrétiens dans la Première Guerre mondiale* (Paris, 1993), p. 11.
23 *The Tablet*, July–December 1914.

24 Brigitte Waché, 'Un parlementaire catholique dans la guerre, Denys Cochin', in Nadine-Josette Chaline (ed.), *Chrétiens dans la Première Guerre mondiale*, pp. 51–2.
25 Auswärtiges Amt, Bonn, Den Krieg 1914, file R 21158, report of Oberleutnant Boehm, 2 March 1915, p. 83.
26 Doerries (ed.), *Prelude to the Easter Rising*, pp. 69 and 147.
27 Auswärtiges Amt, Bonn, Den Krieg 1914, file R 21158, report of Oberleutnant Boehm, 2 March 1915, p. 83.
28 *The Freeman's Journal*, 15 February 1915.
29 DDA, Walsh papers, 1915, 387 II, 'The reception in Paris'.
30 Ibid., 'The reception in Paris'.
31 Ibid., 'The reception in Paris'.
32 Quai d'Orsay, Paris, vol. 545 Grande-Bretagne/Irlande, Géraud to Ministère des Affaires étrangères, p. 143.
33 *The Daily Chronicle* in *The Tablet*, 15 May 1915.
34 Doerries (ed.), *Prelude to the Easter Rising*, memorandum of Boehm, 24 June 1915, p. 131.
35 Ibid., p. 20.
36 Ibid., p. 14.
37 Coates (ed.), *The Irish Uprising 1914–1921*, pp.61–3.
38 Doerries (ed.), *Prelude to the Easter Rising*, p. 18
39 Jeffery, *Ireland and the Great War*, p. 7.
40 Johnstone, *Orange, Green and Khaki*, p. 202.
41 *The Hibernian*, 25 September 1915.
42 *The Freeman's Journal*, 14 August 1915.
43 *The Hibernian*, 25 September 1915.
44 *The Tablet*, 23 September 1916.
45 Quai d'Orsay, Paris, vol. 545 Grande-Bretagne/Irlande, Cambon to Delcassé, 14 June 1915.
46 Johnstone, *Orange, Green and Khaki*, p. 218.
47 Philip Orr, *The Road to the Somme: Men of the Ulster Division tell their Story* (Belfast, 1987), p. 116.
48 Quai d'Orsay, Paris, vol. 545 Grande-Bretagne/Irlande, Cambon to Delcassé, 14 June 1915.
49 Alistair Horne, *The Price of Glory, Verdun 1916* (St Yves, 1993), pp. 273–4.
50 Ferguson, *The Pity of War*, p. 103.
51 Quai d'Orsay, Paris, vol. 545 Grande-Bretagne/Irlande, letter no. 7, de Longchamps to Ministre des Affaires étrangères, 18 April 1916.
52 Ibid., rapport d'André Géraud, pp. 130–1.
53 Ibid., p. 129.
54 Ibid., p. 141.
55 Ibid., p. 123.
56 Ibid., p. 126.
57 Ibid., p. 126.
58 Mac Giolla Choille (ed.), *Intelligence Notes 1913–1916*, p. 119 and 166–74.
59 ICR, Hagan papers, letter no. 110, Curran to Hagan, 30 September 1914.
60 Quai d'Orsay, Paris, vol. 545 Grande-Bretagne/Irlande, rapport d'André Géraud, pp. 133–4.
61 Ibid., rapport d'André Géraud, pp. 136–8.
62 Ibid., p. 142.
63 Ibid., pp. 141–50.
64 *L'Opinion* in *The Freeman's Journal*, 9 October 1916.
65 Quai d'Orsay, Paris, vol. 545 Grande-Bretagne/Irlande, rapport d'André Géraud, p. 165.
66 *The Freeman's Journal*, 5 October 1916.
67 Ibid., 6 October 1916.
68 Quai d'Orsay, Paris, vol. 545 Grande-Bretagne/Irlande, rapport d'André Géraud, p. 165.
69 NLI, O'Kelly papers, MS 27728(1), Curran's memoirs, p. 169.
70 *The Irish Catholic Directory*, 1917, p. 528.
71 *The Freeman's Journal*, 10 October 1916.
72 Ibid., 10 October 1916.
73 *The Irish Catholic Directory*, 1917, p. 528.

74 *The Irish Times*, 10 October 1916.
75 Quai d'Orsay, Paris, vol. 545 Grande-Bretagne/Irlande, rapport d'André Géraud, p. 177.
76 *The Freeman's Journal* in *The Tablet*, 14 October 1916.
77 *The Irish Times*, 10 October 1916.
78 ICR, Hagan papers 1916, letter no. 100, Curran to Hagan, 15 October 1916.
79 Quai d'Orsay, Paris, vol. 545 Grande-Bretagne/Irlande, rapport d'André Géraud, p. 176.
80 ICR, Hagan papers 1916, letter no. 100, Curran to Hagan, 15 October 1916.
81 *The Freeman's Journal*, 11 October 1916.
82 Quai d'Orsay, Paris, vol. 545 Grande-Bretagne/Irlande, rapport d'André Géraud, p. 167.
83 Ibid., p. 176.
84 Ibid., letter no. 178, l'Evêque d'Orléans to Président du Conseil, 25 October 1916.
85 Jean-Marie Mayeur, 'Les Catholiques Français et Benoît XV en 1917', in Nadine-Josette Chaline (ed.), *Chrétiens dans la Première Guerre Mondiale*, pp. 153–65.
86 Brigitte Waché, 'Un Parlementaire Catholique dans la Guerre', in Nadine-Josette Chaline (ed.), *Chrétiens dans la Première Guerre Mondiale*, p. 55.
87 Quai d'Orsay, Paris, vol. 545 Grande-Bretagne/Irlande, rapport d'André Géraud, p. 167.
88 Ibid., 169–71.
89 Mahon, 'The Irish Welter as I found it', p. 125.
90 Quai d'Orsay, Paris, vol. 545 Grande-Bretagne/Irlande, rapport d'André Géraud, p. 175.
91 Service Historique de l'Armée de Terre (SHAT), Vincennes, France, file 7N1261, de la Panouse to Clemenceau, 17 April 1918.
92 Quai d'Orsay, Paris, vol. 545 Grande-Bretagne/Irlande, rapport d'André Géraud, p. 177.
93 Julienne, 'La France et l'Irlande nationaliste de 1860 à 1890', pp. 128–9 and 130–2.
94 Doerries (ed.), *Prelude to the Easter Rising*, Von Bernstorff to Von Bethmann Hollweg, 17 May 1916, p. 219.

NOTES TO CHAPTER 5

1   Moody, Martin and Byrne, *A New History of Ireland*, p. 392.
2   Johnstone, *Orange, Green and Khaki*, pp. 235 and 253.
3   *The Freeman's Journal*, 13 November 1916.
4   Ibid.
5   Miller, *Church, State and Nation in Ireland*, p. 347.
6   Murphy, *Patrick Pearse and the Lost Republican Ideal*, p. 67.
7   *The Tablet*, 23 December 1916.
8   Murphy, *Patrick Pearse and the Lost Republican Ideal*, p. 74.
9   Maume, *The Long Gestation*, p. 191.
10 NLI, O'Kelly papers, MS 27728(1), Curran's memoirs, p. 173.
11 DDA, Walsh papers, 388I/1916, Walsh to the Lord Mayor of Dublin, 26 November 1916.
12 ICR, O'Riordan papers, no. 17, letter no. 227, O'Dwyer to O'Riordan, 14 December 1916.
13 Dangerfield, *The Damnable Question*, p. 251.
14 Boyce, 'British Opinion, Ireland, and the War, 1916–1918', *Historical Journal* XVII, 3(1974), p.584.
15 ICR, O'Riordan papers, no. 17, letter no. 228, Curran to O'Riordan, 16 December 1916.
16 Alison Phillips, The Revolution in Ireland, 1906–1923, p. 126.
17 ICR, O'Riordan papers, no. 17, letter no. 228, Curran to O'Riordan, 16 December 1916.
18 PRO, London, CO 904/157, see various reports.
19 Moody, Martin and Byrne, *A New History of Ireland*, pp. 392–3.
20 Miller, *Church, State, and Nation in Ireland*, p. 346.
21 PRO, London, CO 904/157, see various reports between 1916 and 1918.
22 Quai d'Orsay, Paris, vol. 545 Grande-Bretagne/Irlande, Cambon to Briand, 3 May 1916, p. 22, see chapter 3.
23 PRO, London, CO 904/157, Midlands & Connaught District report, November 1916, p. 204.

24   Ibid., 31 December 1916.

25   Alan J. Ward, 'Lloyd George and the 1918 Irish Conscription Crisis', *The Historical Journal* XVII, 1(1974), p. 108.

26   Dangerfield, *The Damnable Question*, p. 252.

27   David George Boyce, 'The Unknown Chief Secretary: H.E. Duke and Ireland, 1916–1918', *Irish Historical Studies* 79 (March 1977), pp. 306–7.

28   *The English Review* in *The Irish Nation*, 13 January 1917.

29   ICR, O'Riordan papers, no. 18, letter no. 10, Curran to O'Riordan, 15 January 1917.

30   O'Callaghan, 'Bishop Edward O'Dwyer and the Course of Irish Politics 1870-1917', p. 375.

31   NLI, Richard Mulcahy papers, MS 24357, O'Dwyer to INAVDF, 17 May 1917.

32   LDO, O'Dwyer papers, file M, Plunkett to O'Dwyer, 14 April 1917.

33   Alison Phillips, *The Revolution in Ireland 1906–1923*, p. 124.

34   Ibid., p. 125.

35   Dangerfield, *The Damnable Question*, p. 252.

36   Kenneth O. Morgan, 'Lloyd George and the Irish' in British Academy (ed.), *Ireland after the Union* (Oxford, 1989), p. 99.

37   ICR, O'Riordan papers, no. 18, letter no. 14, Curran to O'Riordan, 18 January 1917.

38   NLI, O'Kelly papers, MS 27728(1), Curran's memoirs, p. 182.

39   Ibid., Curran's memoirs, p. 182.

40   Rafferty, *Catholicism in Ulster 1603–1983* (Dublin, 1994), p. 199.

41   Murphy, *Patrick Pearse and the Lost Republican Ideal*, p. 75.

42   *The Irish Nation*, 20 January 1917.

43   Miller, *Church, State, and Nation in Ireland*, p. 350.

44   Denis Carroll, *They have fooled you again; Miceál O'Flannagáin* (Blackrock, 1993), p. 56.

45   Murphy, *Patrick Pearse and the Lost Republican Ideal*, pp. 75 and 79.

46   *The Freeman's Journal* in *The Tablet*, 10 February 1917.

47   *The Irish Catholic Directory*, 1918, pp. 507–9.

48   Moody, Martin and Byrne, *A New History of Ireland*, p. 392.

49   *The Freeman's Journal*, 8 February 1917 and *The Tablet*, 10 February 1917.

50   *The Irish Catholic Directory*, 1918, p. 509.

51   *The Freeman's Journal*, 20 February 1917.

52   ICR, O'Riordan papers, no. 18, Kelly to O'Riordan, 15 February 1917.

53   ACA, Logue papers, Lenten pastoral, 12 February 1917, p. 9.

54   Ibid., O'Donnell papers, Lenten pastoral, 1917.

55   O'Callaghan, *Bishop Edward Thomas O'Dwyer and the course of Irish Politics 1870–1917*, p. 373.

56   DDA, Curran papers, Lenten pastoral, Bishop O'Dwyer, February 1917, pp. 5–6.

57   Jeffery, *Ireland and the Great War*, p. 7.

58   LDO, O'Dwyer papers, file O, Fogarty to O'Dwyer, 19 February 1917.

59   W.E. Vaughan and A.J. Fitzpatrick (eds.), *Irish Historical Statistics: Population 1821–1971* (Dublin, 1978), p. 263.

60   *The Tablet*, 10 March 1917.

61   Moody, Martin and Byrne, *A New History of Ireland*, p. 393.

62   *The Irish Opinion*, 31 March 1917.

63   Alison Philips, *The Revolution in Ireland 1906–1923*, p. 115.

64   LDO, O'Dwyer papers, file M, Plunkett to O'Dwyer, 14 April 1917.

65   *New Ireland*, 14 April 1917.

66   Murphy, *Patrick Pearse and the Lost Republican Ideal*, p. 83.

67   Miller, *Church, State, and Nation in Ireland*, p. 352.

68   Carroll, *They have fooled you again, Miceál O'Flannagáin*, p. 66 and Murphy, *Patrick Pearse and the Lost Republican Ideal*, p. 86.

69   *New Ireland*, 5 May 1917.

70   NLI, Redmond papers, MS 15197, Redmond to Hoare, 25 April 1917, and Hoare to Redmond, 26 April 1917.

71   LDO, O'Dwyer papers, file O, Fogarty to O'Dwyer, 5 May 1917.

72   Miller, *Church, State, and Nation in Ireland*, p. 354.

73   Ibid., p. 355.
74   *The Irish Catholic Directory*, 1918, pp. 517–8.
75   NLI, O'Kelly papers, MS 27728(2), Curran's memoirs, 'Important Manifesto against Partition'.
76   *The Freeman's Journal* in *The Tablet*, 12 May 1917.
77   *The Evening Telegraph* in *The Tablet*, 12 May 1917.
78   Miller, *Church, State, and Nation in Ireland*, p. 356.
79   *The Freeman's Journal*, in *The Tablet*, 19 May 1917.
80   *The Freeman's Journal*, 25 May 1917.
81   Maume, *The Long Gestation*, p. 196.
82   PRO, London, CO 904/157, Northern District intelligence report, 31 May 1917, p. 152.
83   *The Freeman's Journal*, 25 May 1917.
84   *The Cork Examiner*, 26 May 1917.
85   Dangerfield, *The Damnable Question*, p. 256.
86   Alison Philips, *The Revolution in Ireland 1906–1923*, p. 122.
87   *The New York Times* and *The Washington Times* in *The Freeman's Journal*, 24 May 1917.
88   Miquel, *La Grande Guerre*, pp. 406–7.
89   *Le Figaro* in *The Cork Examiner*, 25 May 1917.
90   *The Tablet*, 2 June 1917.
91   ICR, O'Riordan papers, no. 18, letter no. 73, Curran to O'Riordan, 22 May 1917.
92   *The Irish Catholic Directory*, 1918, p. 522.
93   Miller, *Church, State, and Nation in Ireland*, p. 360.
94   *The Irish Catholic Directory*, 1918, p. 525.
95   ICR, O'Riordan papers, no. 18, letter no. 94, O'Dwyer to O'Riordan, 22 June 1917.
96   Ibid., letter no. 99, O'Dwyer to O'Riordan, 3 July 1917.
97   R.B. McDowell, *The Irish Convention 1917–1918* (London, 1970), p. 90.
98   ICR, O'Riordan papers, no. 18, letter no. 95, MacRory to O'Riordan, 24 June 1917.
99   Carroll, *They have fooled you again, Micéal O'Flannagáin*, p. 39.
100 *The Tablet*, 7 July 1917.
101 Ibid., 7 July 1917.
102 Cardinal Tomás O'Fiaich, 'The Irish Bishops and the Conscription Issue, 1918', *The Capuchin Annual*, 1968, pp. 367–8.
103 PRO, London, CO 904/157, Midlands & Connaught District intelligence report, July 1917, p. 144.
104 Murphy, *Patrick Pearse and the Lost Republican Ideal*, p. 88.
105 ICR, O'Riordan papers, no. 18, letter no. 94, O'Dwyer to O'Riordan, 22 June 1917.
106 The Earl of Longford and Thomas P. O'Neill, *Eamon de Valera* (Dublin, 1970), p. 5.
107 Miller, *Church, State, and Nation in Ireland*, p. 395.
108 Ibid., p. 393.
109 Murphy, *Patrick Pearse and the Lost Republican Ideal*, p. 89.
110 O'Callaghan, *Bishop Edward Thomas O'Dwyer and the Course of Irish Politics 1870–1917*, pp. 375–6.
111 Murphy, *Patrick Pearse and the Lost Republican Ideal*, p. 91.
112 *The Freeman's Journal*, 20 August 1917.
113 *The Tablet*, 25 August 1917.
114 *Nationality*, 25 August 1917.
115 *New Ireland*, 25 August 1917.
116 *The Catholic Bulletin*, September 1917, pp. 587–9.
117 *The 'Factionist'*, 23 August 1917 and 30 August 1917.
118 *The Limerick Leader*, 20 August 1917 (courtesy of Mr Tony Bonfield, Limerick).
119 *The 'Factionist'*, 23 August 1917 and 30 August 1917.
120 Morrissey, *Archbishop Walsh, Archbishop of Dublin 1841–1921*, p. 304.
121 Murphy, *Patrick Pearse and the Lost Republican Ideal*, p. 90.
122 Ellis, 'The degenerate and the martyr: nationalist propaganda and the contestation of Irishness, 1914–1918', *Eire Ireland* (autumn 2000–1), pp. 23–4.
123 Alison Phillips, *The Revolution in Ireland 1906–1923*, p. 116.

124 PRO, London, CO 904/157, Southern District intelligence report, 31 May 1917, p. 157.
125 *The Freeman's Journal*, 25 May 1917.
126 Fitzpatrick, *Politics and Irish Life 1913–1921*, p. 72.
127 *The Tablet*, 7 July 1917.
128 *Nationality*, 25 August 1917.
129 Maume, *The Long Gestation*, p. 54.
130 Kee, *The Green Flag*, p. 612.
131 *The Freeman's Journal*, 26 November 1917.
132 *The Tablet*, 25 August 1917.
133 ICR, O'Riordan papers, no. 18, letter no. 190, Logue to O'Riordan, 16 September 1917.
134 *The Freeman's Journal*, 22 October 1917.
135 Maume, *The Long Gestation*, p. 201.
136 Kee, *The Green Flag*, pp. 608–9.
137 *The Freeman's Journal* in *The Irish Catholic Directory*, p. 538c.
138 Morrissey, *Archbishop Walsh, Archbishop of Dublin 1841–1921*, p. 304.
139 PRO, London, CO 904/157, Midlands & Connaught intelligence report, September 1917, p. 118.
140 *The Irish Catholic* in *The Tablet*, 22 September 1917.
141 Murphy, *Patrick Pearse and the Lost Republican Ideal*, pp. 92–3.
142 PRO, London, CO 904/157, Midlands & Connaught intelligence report, 31 October 1917, p. 107.
143 Dangerfield, *The Damnable Question*, p. 262.
144 *Nationality*, 3 November 1917, 10 November 1917, 19 January 1918.
145 *New Ireland*, 6 April 1918.
146 *The Irish Catholic*, 10 November 1917.
147 Ryle Dwyer, *De Valera, the Man and the Myths*, p. 22.
148 *The Freeman's Journal*, 23 November 1917.
149 *The Irish Catholic*, 24 November 1917.
150 Alison Phillips, *The Revolution in Ireland 1906–1923*, p. 133.
151 *The Worker*, 9 January 1915.
152 *The Freeman's Journal*, 6 September 1915.
153 *The Freeman's Journal*, 26 November 1917.
154 NLI, O'Kelly papers, MS 27728(2), Curran's memoirs, 'Cardinal Logue comments on the dream of an Irish Republic'.
155 *The Freeman's Journal*, 27 November 1917.
156 *Nationality*, 8 December 1917.
157 *Nationality*, 22 December 1917.
158 *Nationality*, 10 November 1917, 26 January 1918, 22 December 1917.
159 Kee, *The Green Flag*, pp. 613–4.
160 McDowell, *The Irish Convention 1917–1918*, pp. 145–50.
161 ICR, O'Riordan papers, no. 18, letter no. 26, Kelly to O'Riordan, dated 1918.
162 McDowell, *The Irish Convention 1917–1918*, p. 155.
163 *The Tablet*, 9 February 1918.
164 ACA, Logue papers, Lenten pastoral, 5 February 1918.
165 *The Freeman's Journal*, 11 February 1918.
166 Ibid., 11 February 1918.
167 ACA, O'Donnell papers, Lenten pastoral, 1918.
168 ICR, Lloyd George to Plunkett, 25 February 1918.
169 NLI, O'Kelly papers, MS 27728(2), Curran's memoirs, 'Cardinal Logue comments on the "dream" of an Irish Republic'.
170 McDowell, *The Irish Convention 1917–1918*, p. 174.
171 Ward, 'Lloyd George and the 1918 Irish Conscription Crisis', *Historical Journal*, XVII, 1(1974), p. 114.
172 NLI, O'Kelly papers, MS 27728(1), Curran's memoirs, p. 250.
173 Philip Ollerenshaw, 'Businessmen in Northern Ireland and the Imperial Connection' in Keith Jeffery (ed.), *An Irish Empire? Aspects of Ireland and the British Empire*, p. 174.

174   Miller, *Church, State, and Nation in Ireland*, p. 389.
175   *The Freeman's Journal*, 14 December 1917.
176   Ibid., 11 February 1918.
177   *Nationality*, 2 February 1918.
178   PRO, London, CO 904/157, Southern District intelligence report, 28 February 1918, p. 62.
179   Quai d'Orsay, Paris, vol. 547 Grande-Bretagne/Irlande, letter no. 10, Blanche to Ministre des Affaires étrangères, 11 February 1918.
180   *New Ireland*, 6 April 1918.
181   *The Freeman's Journal*, 11 March 1918.
182   Ellis, 'The Degenerate and the martyr: nationalist propaganda and the contestation of Irishness, 1914–1918', *Eire Ireland* (autumn 2000–1), p. 22.
183   *Nationality*, 23 March 1918.
184   T.M. Healy, *Letters and Leaders of my Day* (London, 1928), vol. II, p. 592.
185   ICR, Bishop of Down and Connor to unknown addressee, dated 2 March 1918 [*sic*]. The date cannot be correct since Redmond died on 6 March 1918.
186   *The Freeman's Journal*, 7 March 1918.
187   *The Irish Catholic Directory*, 1919, p. 504.
188   Quai d'Orsay, Paris, vol. 547 Grande-Bretagne/Irlande, note no. 35, '*à propos de la visite de M. Géraud en Irlande*', 5 March 1918.

NOTES TO CHAPTER 6

1   Dangerfield, *The Damnable Question*, p. 270.
2   Correlli Barnett, *The Swordbearers*, (Reading, 2000), pp.304–8.
3   Johnstone, *Orange, Green and Khaki*, pp. 364–90.
4   Barnett, *The Swordbearers*, p. 317.
5   Ferguson, *The Pity of War*, pp. 103–4.
6   McDowell, *The Irish Convention 1917–1918*, pp. 185–6.
7   Foster, *Modern Ireland 1600–1972*, pp. 488–9.
8   Ward, 'Lloyd George and the 1918 Irish Conscription Crisis', *Historical Journal*, pp. 110–11.
9   Boyce, 'British Opinion, Ireland and the War, 1916–1918', *Historical Journal*, p. 587.
10   Dangerfield, *The Damnable Question*, p. 271.
11   Ward, 'Lloyd George and the 1918 Irish Conscription Crisis', p.110.
12   Ibid., p. 111.
13   Service Historique de l'Armée de Terre (SHAT), Vincennes, France, file 7N1261, de la Panouse to Président du Conseil, 17 April 1918.
14   General Sir Nevil MacReady, *Annals of an Active Life* (London, 1924), vol. I, pp. 294–5.
15   Ferguson, *The Pity of War*, pp. 269 and 274–5.
16   Boyce, 'The Unknown Chief Secretary: H.E. Duke and Ireland, 1916–1918', p. 307.
17   Ward, 'Lloyd George and the 1918 Irish Conscription Crisis', p. 113.
18   Dangerfield, *The Damnable Question*, p. 273.
19   Morgan, 'Lloyd George and the Irish', p. 99.
20   Ibid., p. 92.
21   Ward, 'Lloyd George and the 1918 Irish Conscription Crisis', p. 114.
22   Mahon, 'The Irish Welter as I found it' in Fitzgerald, *The Voice of Ireland*, pp. 127–8.
23   In Doerries, *Prelude to the Easter Rising*, letter from von Bernstorff to von Bethmann Hollweg, 17 May 1916, p. 219.
24   Ward, *Ireland and Anglo-American Relations, 1899–1921*, p. 163.
25   Boyce, 'British Opinion, Ireland and the War, 1916–1918', pp. 587 and 591.
26   ICR, O'Riordan papers, no. 18, letter no. 103, H. Stevenson (Prime Minister's office) to O'Riordan, 6 July 1917.
27   Thomas Jones, *Whitehall Diary* (London, 1971), vol. III: *Ireland 1918–1925*, pp. 3–4.
28   Tim Pat Coogan, *Michael Collins* (London, 1990), p. 85.

29   O'Fiaich, 'The Irish Bishops and the Conscription Issue 1918', *The Capuchin Annual*, p. 352.
30   NLI, O'Kelly papers, MS 27728(1), Curran's memoirs, pp. 252–3.
31   *The Freeman's Journal*, 10 April 1918.
32   Richard Mulcahy, 'Conscription and the General Headquarters' Staff', *The Capuchin Annual* (1968), p. 388.
33   Jones, *Whitehall Diary*, vol. III, p.2.
34   NLI, O'Kelly papers, MS 27728(1), Curran's memoirs, p. 253.
35   PRO, London, CO 904 161/4, 12 April 1918 and CO 904 161/4, 11 April 1918.
36   *The Tablet*, 13 April 1918.
37   *The Freeman's Journal*, 12 April 1918.
38   Morrissey, *William J. Walsh, Archbishop of Dublin 1841–1921*, p. 271.
39   DDA, Walsh papers, 1918, 390 I, Logue to Walsh, 13 April 1918.
40   Pauric Travers, 'The priest in politics: the case of conscription', MacDonagh, *Irish Culture and Nationalism 1750–1950*, p. 164.
41   *The Freeman's Journal*, 15 April 1918.
42   Ibid., 15 April 1918.
43   Ibid., 13 April 1918.
44   Ibid., 15 April 1918.
45   ICR, Hagan papers, 1918, letter no. 22, Harty to Hagan, 15 April 1918.
46   NLI, O'Kelly papers, MS 27728(1), Curran's memoirs, pp. 255–6.
47   Moody, Martin and Byrne, *A New History of Ireland*, p. 394.
48   Liam Deasy, *Towards Ireland Free* (Cork, 1973), p. 19.
49   *The Freeman's Journal*, 15 April 1918.
50   Imperial War Museum, London, French papers, F/48/6/7; letter no. 32, Mahon to French, 16 April 1918, and letter no. 31, French to Mahon, 17 April 1918. Courtesy of Dr Brian Murphy, Glenstal Abbey.
51   NLI, O'Kelly papers, MS 27728(1), Curran's memoirs, p. 257.
52   Imperial War Museum, London, French papers, F/48/6/7, letter no 30, French to Lloyd George, 18 April 1918. Courtesy of Dr Brian Murphy, Glenstal Abbey.
53   NLI, O'Kelly papers, MS 277281(1), Curran's memoirs, p. 261.
54   Ibid., pp. 261–2.
55   Ryle Dwyer, *De Valera, the Man and the Myths*, p. 23.
56   Lyons, *John Dillon*, p. 434.
57   ACA, O'Donnell papers, 'Ireland's Solemn League and Covenant', April 1918.
58   Miller, *Church, State and Nation in Ireland*, p. 404.
59   Ibid., pp. 404–5.
60   O'Fiaich, 'The Irish bishops and the conscription issue 1918', p. 356.
61   ACA, O'Donnell papers, 'Ireland's Solemn League and Covenant', April 1918.
62   NLI, O'Kelly papers, MS 27728(1), Curran's memoirs, pp. 263–4.
63   Mulcahy, 'Conscription and the General Headquarters' Staff', p. 392.
64   Colonial Office, CO 904/105 microfilm (Mary Immaculate College, Limerick), Inspector General to Under Secretary, April 1918.
65   *The Irish Independent*, 19 April 1918.
66   NLI, O'Kelly papers, MS 27728(1), Curran's memoirs, p. 264.
67   Ibid., pp. 264–5.
68   *The Irishman*, 27 April 1918.
69   *The Irish Catholic Directory*, 1919, p. 521.
70   ARA, O'Donnell papers, Page to O'Donnell, 1 June 1918.
71   *The Freeman's Journal*, 22 April 1918.
72   O'Fiaich, 'The Irish bishops and the conscription issue 1918', pp. 357–9.
73   NLI, O'Kelly papers, MS 27728(1), Curran's memoirs, p. 266.
74   Ibid., Curran's memoirs, pp. 265–6.
75   Ellis, 'The degenerate and the martyr: nationalist propaganda and the contestation of Irishness, 1914–1918', *Eire Ireland*, p. 26.
76   *The Tablet*, 27 April 1918.

77 Alison Phillips, *The Revolution in Ireland 1906–1923*, p. 146.
78 *The Freeman's Journal*, 22 April 1918, 23 April 1918, 26 April 1918, and *The Irish Independent*, 22 April 1918.
79 *The Freeman's Journal*, 22 April 1918.
80 Ibid., 23 April 1918.
81 O'Fiaich, 'The Irish bishops and the conscription issue 1918', p. 360.
82 *The Freeman's Journal*, 25 April 1918.
83 Ibid., 6 May 1918.
84 *The Freeman's Journal*, 23 April 1918.
85 Dangerfield, *The Damnable Question*, p. 281.
86 Ward, 'Lloyd George and the 1918 Irish conscription crisis', *Historical Journal*, p. 117.
87 Dangerfield, *The Damnable Question*, p. 287.
88 Séan Ó Lúing, 'The German Plot 1918', in *The Capuchin Annual* (1968), pp. 377–8.
89 *The Freeman's Journal*, 18 May 1918.
90 Ó Lúing, 'The German Plot 1918', pp. 380–1.
91 ICR, O'Riordan papers, 1918, Curran to O'Riordan, 18 May 1918.
92 *The Irish Times*, 28 May 1918.
93 *The Irishman*, 22 June 1918.
94 Jeffery, *Ireland and the Great War*, p. 7.
95 Boyce, 'British Opinion, Ireland and the War, 1916–1918', *Historical Journal*, p. 593.
96 *The Times* in *The Irish Independent*, 25 April 1918.
97 Archivio degli Affari Ecclesiastici Straordinari, Vatican, *The Times*, 22 April 1918.
98 *The Morning Post* and *The Daily Express* in *The Irish Independent*, 25 April 1918.
99 Travers, 'The priest in politics: the case of conscription', in MacDonough, *Irish Culture and Nationalism 1750–1950*, pp. 167–8.
100 NLI, O'Kelly papers, MS 27728(1), Curran's memoirs, p. 267.
101 *The Star* in *The Irish Independent*, 25 April 1918.
102 Archivio degli Affari Ecclesiastici Straordinari, Vatican, *The Daily Chronicle*, 2 May 1918.
103 Ibid., *The Catholic Herald*, 20 April 1918.
104 Harris, *The Catholic Church and the Foundation of the Northern Irish State*, p. 68.
105 Archivio degli Affari Ecclesiastici Straordinari, Vatican, *The Glasgow Observer*, 1 June 1918.
106 O'Fiaich, 'The Irish bishops and the conscription issue 1918', p. 362.
107 *The Irishman*, 4 May 1918.
108 All French newspapers in *The Freeman's Journal*, 4 May 1918.
109 *The Irish Times*, 1 May 1918.
110 DDA, Walsh papers, 1918, 390 I, Logue to Walsh, 2 May 1918.
111 *The Freeman's Journal*, 7 May 1918.
112 Ibid., 27 May 1918.
113 DDA, Walsh papers, 1918, 390 I, Amigo to Walsh, 3 May 1918, including letter from Amigo to Denbigh, 29 April 1918.
114 Morrissey, *William J. Walsh, Archbishop of Dublin 1841–1921*, pp. 312–13.
115 ICR, O'Riordan papers, no. 19, James Britten to O'Riordan, 17 May 1918.
116 O'Fiaich, 'The Irish bishops and the conscription issue 1918', p. 362.
117 PRO, London, CO 904/157, Midlands and Connaught District intelligence report, 31 May 1918, p. 28.
118 Ibid., FO 380/17, April–May 1918, and Archivio degli Affari Ecclesiastici Straordinari, Vatican.
119 ICR, O'Riordan papers, no. 19, Tomás De Bháll to O'Riordan, 1 July 1918.
120 Ibid., Fogarty to O'Riordan, 20 July 1918.
121 Ibid., letter no. 62, Logue to O'Riordan, 8 July 1918.
122 NLI, O'Kelly papers, MS 27728(1), Curran's memoirs, pp. 283–4.
123 ACA, O'Donnell papers, O'Riordan to O'Donnell, 26 July 1918.
124 PRO, London, FO 380/18, Gasparri to De Salis, 9 July 1918.
125 *The Irish Independent*, 25 April 1918, and *The Freeman's Journal*, 22 April 1918 and 8 May 1918.

126 Travers, 'The priest in politics, the case of conscription', in MacDonagh, *Irish Culture and Nationalism 1750–1950*, p. 172.
127 Harris, *The Catholic Church and the Foundation of the Northern Irish State*, pp. 66–7.
128 PRO, London, CO 904/157, Midlands and Connaught District intelligence report, 30 June 1918, p. 18.
129 *The Freeman's Journal*, 30 April 1918.
130 PRO, London, CO 904/157, Midlands and Connaught District intelligence report, 31 May 1918, p. 28.
131 *The Freeman's Journal*, 7 May 1918.
132   Ibid., 6 May 1918.
133 *The Evening Telegraph* in *The Freeman's Journal*, 6 May 1918.
134 *The Freeman's Journal*, 11 May 1918.
135 PRO, London, CO 904/157, Midlands and Connaught District intelligence report, 30 April 1918, p. 37.
136 Colonial Office, CO 904/105 microfilm (Mary Immaculate College, Limerick), Inspector General to Under Secretary, April 1918.
137 Travers, 'The priest in politics: the case of conscription', p. 175.
138 NLI, O'Kelly papers, MS 27728(1), Curran's memoirs, p. 278.
139 Ibid., Curran's memoirs, p. 290.
140 *The Freeman's Journal*, 2 May 1918.
141 Miller, *Church, State, and Nation in Ireland*, pp. 412–13.
142 Carroll, *They have fooled you again, Micéal O'Flannagáin*, p. 82.
143 Lyons, *John Dillon*, pp. 440–1.
144 NLI, O'Kelly papers, MS 27728(1), Curran's memoirs, p. 288.
145 Michael Laffan, *The Resurrection of Ireland, the Sinn Féin Party 1916–1923*, (Cambridge, 1999), pp. 162–3.
146 Carroll, *They have fooled you again, Micéal O'Flannagáin*, p. 83.
147 NLI, O'Kelly papers, MS 27728(1), Curran's memoirs, pp. 284–5.
148 Travers, 'The priest in politics: the case of conscription', in MacDonagh, *Irish Culture and Nationalism 1750–1950*, p. 176.
149 ACA, O'Donnell papers, Logue to O'Donnell, 20 July 1918.
150 *The Irish Times*, 4 June 1918.
151 Oliver MacDonagh, 'Irish emigration to the United States of America and the British colonies during the Famine', in R. Dudley Edwards and T. Desmond Williams (eds.), *The Great Famine* (Dublin, 1994), pp. 317–88.
152 Malcolm Campbell, 'Emigrant responses to war and revolution, 1914–1921: Irish opinion in the United States and Australia', in *Irish Historical Studies*, May 2000, vol. XXXII, no. 125, p. 76.
153 Francis Carroll, *American Opinion and the Irish Question 1910–1923* (Dublin, 1978), p. 89.
154 Campbell, 'Emigrant responses to war and revolution, 1914–1921: Irish opinion in the United States and Australia', pp. 77–8.
155 NLI, Redmond papers, MS 15236, Leslie to Redmond, 2 March 1916; Leslie papers, MS 22832, Redmond to Leslie, 27 November 1915, Leslie to Redmond, 11 November 1915 and 16 May 1916.
156 ACA, O'Donnell papers, Leslie to O'Donnell, 15 August 1916.
157 ICR, O'Riordan papers, no. 17, letter no. 241, Leslie to O'Riordan.
158 *The Freeman's Journal*, 22 February 1917.
159 NLI, Redmond papers, MS 15236, Leslie to Redmond, 10 November 1916.
160 *Ireland* in *The Freeman's Journal*, 14 November 1916.
161 ACA, O'Donnell papers, Leslie to O'Donnell, 24 November 1916.
162 *The Irish Opinion*, 24 February 1917.
163 ICR, O'Riordan papers, no. 16, letter no. 1, 'L'Appello del Santo Padre per la Pace', December 1915, from Bishop O'Dwyer; *Nationality*, 25 December 1915.
164 NLI, Leslie papers, MS 22832, Leslie to Redmond, 9 March 1917.
165 Saint Joseph's Seminary, New York, archdiocesan archives, AANY 1–23, O'Riordan to

Farley, 21 December 1916 and 22 December 1916. Research done for the author by Fr Oliver P. Rafferty (SJ).

166 *The Irish Opinion*, 24 February 1917.

167 Campbell, 'Emigrant responses to war and revolution, 1914–1921: Irish opinion in the United States and Australia', *Irish Historical Studies*, p. 84.

168 NLI, O'Kelly papers, MS 27728(2), Curran's memoirs, 'Longford election is fatal blow to Irish Party'.

169 Boyce, 'British opinion, Ireland and the war, 1916–1918', *Historical Journal*, p. 585.

170 Carroll, *American Opinion and the Irish Question 1910–1923*, pp. 90–1.

171 Ibid., pp. 94 and 102.

172 *The Freeman's Journal*, 25 May 1917.

173 Carroll, *American Opinion and the Irish Question 1910–1923*, pp. 103–4.

174 *The Freeman's Journal*, 20 December 1917.

175 Ibid., 18 January 1918.

176 Carroll, *American Opinion and the Irish Question 1910–1923*, pp. 108 and 240, footnotes 49, 50 and 51.

177 *The Freeman's Journal*, 29 April 1918.

178 Carroll, *American Opinion and the Irish Question 1910–1923*, pp. 112 and 115.

179 Quai d'Orsay, Paris, vol. 547 Grande-Bretagne/Irlande, note no. 35, Géraud to Ministre des Affaires étrangères, 5 March 1918.

180 *The Freeman's Journal*, 13 April 1918.

181 NLI, Joseph McGarritty papers, MS 17435, 'Speech by Mgr Gerald P. Coghlan at Philadelphia', 21 April 1918.

182 DDA, Walsh papers, 1918, 390 I, Kiely to Walsh, 19 May 1918.

183 Patrick Callan, 'The Irish Soldier, a propaganda paper for Ireland, September–December 1918', in *The Irish Sword*, no. 59, p. 74.

184 T.P. Coogan, *Michael Collins*, p. 91.

185 David Fitzpatrick, *Oceans of Consolation* (Cork, 1995), p. 7.

186 John Moloney, *A History of Australia* (Victoria, 1988), p. 218.

187 Niall Brennan, *Dr Mannix* (London, 1965), p. 89.

188 Dermot Keogh, 'Mannix, De Valera and Irish Nationalism' in John O'Brien and Pauric Travers (eds), *The Irish Emigrant Experience in Australia* (Swords, 1991), pp. 197 and 199.

189 D.J. Hickey and J.E. Doherty, *A Dictionary of Irish History 1800–1980* (Dublin, 1980), p. 353.

190 Moloney, *A History of Australia*, p. 221.

191 Campbell, 'Emigrant responses to war and revolution, 1914–1921: Irish opinion in the United States and Australia', *Irish Historical Studies*, pp. 79–80.

192 Ibid., p. 80.

193 Moloney, *A History of Australia*, p. 225.

194 Campbell, 'Emigrant responses to war and revolution, 1914–1921: Irish opinion in the United States and Australia', *Irish Historical Studies*, p. 81.

195 *The Freeman's Journal*, 29 June 1916.

196 LDO, O'Dwyer papers, file O, Fogarty to O'Dwyer, 5 May 1917.

197 *The Times* in *The Freeman's Journal*, 24 May 1917.

198 Campbell, 'Emigrant responses to war and revolution, 1914–1921: Irish opinion in the United States and Australia', *Irish Historical Studies*, pp. 85–6.

199 Moloney, *A History of Australia*, pp. 224–5.

200 Brennan, *Dr Mannix*, pp. 130–1 and 109–10.

201 Moloney, *A History of Australia*, pp. 224–5.

202 Campbell, 'Emigrant responses to war and revolution, 1914-1921: Irish opinion in the United States and Australia', *Irish Historical Studies*, p. 86.

203 PRO, London, FO 380/18, Balfour to de Salis, 26 July 1918, p. 4.

204 Moloney, *A History of Australia*, pp. 226–7.

205 Archivio degli Affari Ecclesiastici Straordinari, Vatican, Australia 1917, Blattaney to Vatican, 27 November 1917.

206 Moloney, *A History of Australia*, pp. 226 and 234.

207 Tim Pat Coogan, *Wherever Green is worn* (London, 2000), pp. 466–7.
208 *Nationality*, 1 December 1917.
209 Boyce, 'British opinion, Ireland, and the war, 1916–1918', *Historical Journal*, p. 584.
210 Ward, 'Lloyd George and the 1918 Irish conscription crisis', *Historical Journal*, p. 109.
211 *The Freeman's Journal*, 22 April 1918.
212 *The Irish Independent*, 22 April 1918.
213 *The Irishman*, 27 April 1918.
214 PRO, London, FO 380/18, Gasparri to de Salis, 22 August 1918.
215 PRO, London, FO 380/17, report of Henry Lambert for Arthur Balfour, 22 May 1918, p. 217.
216 PRO, London, FO 380/18, Gasparri to de Salis, 10 July 1918.
217 Ibid., Balfour to de Salis, 26 July 1918.
218 Ibid., 15 August 1918.
219 Ibid., Gasparri to de Salis, 22 August 1918.
220 Miquel, *La Grande Guerre*, pp. 406–24.

NOTES TO CHAPTER 7

1 Thomas Bartlett, *The Fall and the Rise of the Irish Nation, the Catholic Question, 1690–1830* (Dublin, 1992), pp. 17–29.
2 *The Catholic Bulletin*, 'Notes from Rome', Nov. 1918, pp. 514–15.
3 Denis Gwynn, *The Vatican and the War in Europe*, p. 92.
4 Mark Tierney, *Croke of Cashel: the Life of Archbishop Thomas William Croke 1832–1902* (Dublin, 1976).
5 Larkin, *The Roman Catholic Church and the Plan of Campaign 1886–1888*, (this book relates the Vatican's intervention in detail).
6 C.J. Woods, 'Ireland and Anglo-Papal relations, 1880–1885', *Irish Historical Studies*, 69, (March 1972), pp. 31–2 and 36–7.
7 Lyons, *John Dillon*, p. 94.
8 Dermot Keogh, *The Vatican, the Bishops and Irish Politics, 1919–1939* (Cambridge, 1986), p. 11.
9 Prill, *Ireland, Britain and Germany 1870–1914*, pp. 67–80.
10 Woods, 'Ireland and Anglo-Papal relations, 1880–1885', *Irish Historical Studies*, pp. 48–9.
11 Brian Murphy, 'J.J. O'Kelly and the Catholic Bulletin: Cultural Considerations – Gaelic, Religious and National, 1898–1926' (Ph.D thesis, NUI, 1986), p. 313.
12 *The Catholic Bulletin*, 'Notes from Rome', Nov. 1919, p. 570.
13 Catherine Shannon, 'The Legacy of Arthur Balfour to Twentieth-century Ireland', in Peter Collins (ed.), *Nationalism and Unionism: Conflict in Ireland, 1885–1921* (Antrim, 1994), p.26.
14 ACA, MacRory papers, O'Riordan to MacRory, 31 October 1916.
15 *The Catholic Bulletin*, 'Notes from Rome', Nov. 1919, p. 574.
16 Ibid., p. 576.
17 Ibid., p. 577.
18 Murphy, 'J.J. O'Kelly and the Catholic Bulletin', p. 306.
19 *The Catholic Bulletin*, 'Notes from Rome', Jan. 1913, pp. 32–3.
20 Murphy, 'J.J. O'Kelly and the *Catholic Bulletin*', pp. 313–14.
21 *The Catholic Bulletin*, 'Notes from Rome', Nov. 1919, p. 578.
22 Coates, *The Irish Uprising, 1914–1921*, p. 44.
23 Murphy, *John Chartres, Mystery Man of the Treaty*, p. 28.
24 William A. Renzi, 'The Entente and the Vatican during the period of Italian neutrality, August 1914–May 1915', *The Historical Journal*, XIII, 3, (1970, pp. 491–7, footnotes no. 92 and 106.
25 Ibid., pp. 492–3.
26 *The Tablet*, 9 January 1915.

27 NLI, Leslie papers, MS 22892, 'biographical study of Card. Gasquet'.

28 Ibid.

29 LDO, O'Dwyer papers, file N, Harty to O'Dwyer, 24 January 1915.

30 ICR, O'Riordan papers, no 15, Hagan to O'Riordan, 21 November 1914.

31 ICR, Hagan papers, 1914, letter no. 183, Curran to Hagan, 16 December 1914.

32 NLI, Leslie papers, MS 22892, 'biographical study of Card. Gasquet'.

33 Keogh, *The Vatican, the Bishops and Irish Politics, 1919–1939*, p. 22.

34 *The Catholic Bulletin*, 'Notes from Rome', Jan. 1915, pp. 7–8.

35 Murphy, 'J.J. O'Kelly and the Catholic Buletin', p. 138.

36 LDO, O'Dwyer papers, file 'O'Riordan to O'Dwyer 1887–1917', O'Riordan to O'Dwyer, 3 January 1915.

37 *The Catholic Bulletin*, 'Notes from Rome', Feb. 1915, pp. 98–9.

38 *Scissors and Paste*, 30 January 1915.

39 *The Catholic Bulletin*, 'Notes from Rome', Nov. 1919, p. 578.

40 Renzi, 'The Entente and the Vatican during the period of Italian neutrality, August 1914–May 1915', *The Historical Journal*, p. 505 and footnotes 106 and 107.

41 LDO, O'Dwyer papers, file 'O'Riordan to O'Dwyer, 1887–1917', O'Riordan to O'Dwyer, 23 April 1915.

42 Brigitte Waché, 'Un parlementaire catholique dans la guerre, Denys Cochin', in Nadine-Josette Chaline (ed.), *Chrétiens dans la Première Guerre Mondiale*, p. 53, footnote 14.

43 *The Catholic Bulletin*, 'Notes from Rome', Feb. 1916, p. 70.

44 Dom Benedict Kuypers, 'Cardinal Gasquet in London', *The Downside Review*, 134, (1929), p. 142.

45 Dom Urban Butler, 'Cardinal Gasquet in Rome', *The Downside Review*, 134, (1929), p. 150.

46 Murphy, 'J.J. O'Kelly and the Catholic Bulletin', p. 315.

47 Keogh, *The Vatican, the Bishops and Irish Politics, 1919–1939*, p. 16.

48 ICR, O'Riordan papers no. 16, letter no. 53, Leslie to O'Riordan, 3 April 1915.

49 Butler, 'Cardinal Gasquet in Rome', p. 151.

50 Shane Leslie, *Cardinal Gasquet* (London, 1953), p. 237.

51 ICR, Hagan papers, 1914, Hagan to Gasquet, 29 October 1914.

52 Ibid., Hagan papers, 1914, letter no. 136, Gasquet to Hagan, 30 October 1914.

53 Ibid., Hagan papers, 1914, letter no. 140, O'Riordan to Hagan, 6 November 1914.

54 Ibid.

55 Keogh, *The Vatican, the Bishops and Irish Politics, 1919–1939*, pp. 15 and 36.

56 ACA, O'Donnell papers, Hagan to O'Donnell, 14 April 1915.

57 LDO, O'Dwyer papers, file I, O'Riordan to O'Dwyer, 5 January 1916.

58 *The Tablet*, 20 November 1915.

59 Ibid., 18 December 1915

60 NLI, Leslie papers, MS 22892, 'biographical study of Cardinal Gasquet'.

61 *The Catholic Bulletin*, 'Notes from Rome', Nov. 1919, pp. 576–7.

62 Ibid., 'Notes from Rome', Nov. 1919, p. 578.

63 LDO, O'Dwyer papers, file O'Riordan to O'Dwyer, 1887–1917', O'Riordan to O'Dwyer, 3 January 1915.

64 LDO, O'Dwyer papers, file 'O'Riordan to O'Dwyer, 1887–1917', O'Riordan to O'Dwyer, 6 January 1915.

65 *The Irish Catholic Directory*, 1916, p. 502.

66 *The Freeman's Journal*, 15 February 1915.

67 *The Catholic Bulletin*, 'Notes from Rome', Nov. 1919, p. 580.

68 LDO, O'Dwyer papers, file 'O'Riordan to O'Dwyer, 1887–1917', O'Riordan to O'Dwyer, 20 March 1915.

69 Ibid., 8 April 1915.

70 Renzi, 'The Entente and the Vatican during the period of Italian neutrality, August 1914–May 1915', *The Historical Journal*, p. 505.

71 LDO, O'Dwyer papers, file 'O'Riordan to O'Dwyer, 1887–1917', O'Riordan to O'Dwyer, 6 June 1915.

72 Ibid., 6 June 1915.

73 Ibid., 26 June 1915.

74 Numerous letters and documents regarding the correspondence and chaplaincy crises can be read in the Limerick Diocesan Office (O'Dwyer papers), Ara Coelie Armagh (Logue papers), Irish College Rome (O'Riordan papers), Bishop's House Carlow (Foley papers), Dublin Diocesan Archives (Walsh papers) and Archives of the Archdiocese of Westminster. For further reading: Tom Johnstone and James Hagerty, *The Cross on the Sword: Catholic Chaplains in the Forces* (London, 1996). This book relates in detail the role of Irish Catholic chaplains in Irish regiments and one chapter is devoted to the quarrel between the Irish and English hierarchies about authority on the chaplains. However, Benedict XV's decisive intervention is not mentioned.

75 Leslie, *Cardinal Gasquet*, p. 248.

76 ICR, O'Riordan papers no. 16, letter no. 122, O'Dwyer to O'Riordan, 8 September 1915.

77 ICR, O'Riordan papers no. 16, letter no. 132, O'Dwyer to O'Riordan, 26 September 1915.

78 ICR, O'Riordan papers no. 16, letter no. 1, 'L'Appello del Santo Padre per la Pace', January 1916.

79 *The Catholic Bulletin*, 'Notes from Rome', Jan. 1916, pp. 14–15.

80 ACA, O'Donnell papers, Hagan to O'Donnell, 25 January 1916.

81 *The Freeman's Journal*, 11 May 1916.

82 LDO, O'Dwyer papers, file 'letters from Rome', O'Riordan to O'Dwyer, 12 May 1916.

83 PRO, London, foreign office index 1906–1919, old Irish reference 'Ireland 41 89 600/16'.

84 Quai d'Orsay, Paris, vol. 545 Grande-Bretagne/Irlande, de Longchamps to Ministère des Affaires étrangères, 18 April 1916.

85 NLI, O'Kelly papers, MS 27728, Curran's memoirs, 'May the 26th 1916'.

86 LDO, O'Dwyer papers, file 'letters from Rome', O'Riordan to O'Dwyer, 27 May 1916.

87 Leslie, *Cardinal Gasquet*, p. 247.

88 LDO, O'Dwyer papers, file 'O'Riordan to O'Dwyer, 1887–1917', O'Riordan to O'Dwyer, 10 June 1916.

89 Coogan, *Wherever Green is worn*, pp. 405–7.

90 *The Catholic Bulletin*, 'Notes from Rome', Nov. 1919, pp. 580–1.

91 LDO, O'Dwyer papers, file 'O'Riordan to O'Dwyer, 1887–1917', O'Riordan to O'Dwyer, 23 October 1916.

92 Saint Joseph's Seminary, Archdiocesan Archives, New York, Farley papers, AANY 1–23, O'Riordan to Farley, 21 December 1916. Research done for the author by Fr Oliver Rafferty (S.J.).

93 Archivio degli Affari Ecclesiastici Straordinari, Vatican, file Guerra anno 1914–1918, rubrica 244, fasc. 92, rubrica 244 D3, no. 43338, La Recente Insurrezione in Irlanda, September 1916. On 3 July 1933, this document was transferred by Cardinal Tardini, Secretary of State, from the archives of the Secretary of State of the Vatican to the Archives of Extraordinary Ecclesiastical Affairs during the controversy between Eoin MacNeill and Count Plunkett in Ireland concerning the latter's mission to the Vatican in April 1916. It is difficult to find copies of the 'Red Book'. The author found three: in Limerick, the Vatican and the Quai d'Orsay in Paris.

94 Ibid., *La recente insurrezione in Irlanda*, pp. 6–8.

95 John Pollock, *Kitchener* (London, 2001), pp. 379–80.

96 Denman, *Ireland's Unknown Soldiers*, pp. 21–3 and 34.

97 *The Catholic Bulletin*, August 1916, p. 408.

98 *The Cork Examiner*, 10 October 1916.

99 Archivio degli Affari Ecclesiastici Straordinari, Vatican, file 'Guerra anno 1914–1918', rubrica 244, fasc. 92, rubrica 244 D3, no. 43338, La Recente Insurrezione in Irlanda, pp. 21–2.

100 *The Catholic Bulletin*, 'Notes from Rome', March 1917, pp. 140–2.

101 Archivio degli Affari Ecclesiastici Straordinari, Vatican, file 'Guerra anno 1914–1918', rubrica 244, fasc. 92, rubrica 244 D3, no. 43338, La Recente Insurrezione in Irlanda', pp. 22–5.

102 Ibid., p. 38.

103 LDO, O'Dwyer papers, file 'O'Riordan to O'Dwyer, 1887–1917', O'Riordan to O'Dwyer, 23 October 1916.

104 Quai d'Orsay, Paris, vol. 545 Grande-Bretagne/Irlande, mission des évêques français en Irlande, pp. 173–4.

105 Leslie, *Cardinal Gasquet*, p. 249.

106 LDO, O'Dwyer papers, file 'O'Riordan to O'Dwyer, 1887–1917', O'Riordan to O'Dwyer, 22 January 1917.

107 PRO, London, FO 380/8, no. 86, Howard to Grey, 21 October 1916.

108 Catherine Shannon, 'The legacy of Arthur Balfour to twentieth century Ireland', in Peter Collins (ed.), *Nationalism and Unionism, Conflict in Ireland, 1885–1921* , pp. 18–19 and 23.

109 PRO, London, FO 380/9, telegram no. 35, Balfour to de Salis, 11 December 1916, p. 108.

110 Quai d'Orsay, Paris, vol. 545 Grande-Bretagne/Irlande, letter no. 187, French embassy Rome to Président du Conseil, 25 November 1916.

111 Ibid., French embassy Rome to Président du Conseil, 25 November 1916.

112 Westminister Diocesan Archives, London, Bourne papers, AAW B01/72, Long to Bourne, 8 May 1918 and Bourne to Long, 17 May 1918.

113 Denis Gwynn, 'Cardinal Bourne and Ireland', *Irish Ecclesiastical Record*, July 1940, vol. 56, p. 89.

114 Angus Mitchell (ed.), *The Amazon Journal of Roger Casement* (Dublin, 1997); discussion with the editor of this book.

115 René MacColl, *Roger Casement* (London, 1965), pp. 231–3.

116 Brian Inglis, *Roger Casement* (London, 1973), p. 368.

117 LDO, O'Dwyer papers, Gavan Duffy to O'Dwyer, 24 October 1916, (copy of Gavan Duffy to Daly, 17 August 1916).

118 Ibid., (copy of Bidwell to Gavan Duffy, 22 August 1918).

119 ICR, O'Riordan papers no. 17, letter no. 155, Curran to O'Riordan, 24 September 1916; Saint Joseph's Seminary, New York, Archdiocesan Archives, Farley papers, O'Riordan to Farley, 22 December 1916; LDO, O'Dwyer papers, Gavan Duffy to O'Dwyer, 24 October 1916.

120 D.J. Hickey and J.E. Doherty, *A Dictionary of Irish History 1800–1980*, p. 214.

121 Gwynn, 'Cardinal Bourne and Ireland', pp. 88–9.

122 Westminster Diocesan Archives, London, Bourne papers, AAW BO 3/5-11, Carey to Bourne, 17 July 1916.

123 Ibid., AAW BO 3/5–11, Bourne to Carey, 22 July 1916.

124 ICR, O'Riordan papers no. 18, letter no. 80, Farley to O'Riordan, 29 May 1917.

125 Westminster Diocesan Archives, London, Bourne papers, AAW BO 3/5–11, Bourne to De Lai, 4 January 1917.

126 Morrissey, *William J. Walsh, Archbishop of Dublin, 1841–1921*, p. 298.

127 Leslie, *Cardinal Gasquet*, p. 250.

128 Bishop's House, Carlow, Foley papers, box no. 13, file PF/MC, O'Riordan to Foley, 23 January 1916.

129 DDA, Walsh papers, 1918, 390 I, Kennedy to Walsh, 17 March 1918.

130 Ernest Oldmeadow, *Francis Cardinal Bourne* (1944), vol. 2, p. 122, read in Westminster Diocesan Archives.

131 LDO, O'Dwyer papers, file I 'letters from Rome', O'Riordan to O'Dwyer, 25 March 1917.

132 LDO, O'Dwyer papers, 'O'Riordan to O'Dwyer, 1887–1917', O'Riordan to O'Dwyer, 23 October 1916.

133 ACA, MacRory papers, O'Riordan to MacRory, 31 October 1916.

134 LDO, O'Dwyer papers, file 'O'Riordan to O'Dwyer, 1887–1917', O'Riordan to O'Dwyer, 6 December 1916.

135 Ibid.

136 Quai d'Orsay, Paris, vol. 546 Grande-Bretagne/Irlande, note no. 6, Degrand to de Margerie, 21 December 1916.

137 LDO, O'Dwyer papers, file 'O'Riordan to O'Dwyer, 1887–1917', O'Riordan to O'Dwyer, 21 December 1916.

138   *The Catholic Bulletin*, 'Notes from Rome', Jan. 1917, p. 10.
139   John Cornwell, *Hitler's Pope, the secret history of Pius XII* (St. Ives, 1999), pp. 60–61.
140   Moody, Martin and Byrne (eds), *A New History of Ireland*, p. 393.
141   ACA, MacRory papers, O'Riordan to MacRory, 1 May 1917.
142   LDO, O'Dwyer papers, file 'O'Riordan to O'Dwyer, 1887–1917', O'Riordan to O'Dwyer, 4 July 1917.
143   Ibid., 5 August 1917.
144   *The Tablet*, 8 September 1917.
145   *The Catholic Bulletin*, 'Notes from Rome', June 1917, pp. 352–3.
146   Keogh, *The Vatican, the Bishops and Irish Politics, 1919–1939*, pp. 35–6.
147   Murphy, 'J.J. O'Kelly and the Catholic Bulletin', pp. 322–3.
148   *The Morning Post* in *The Freeman's Journal*, 6 December 1917.
149   *Globe* in *The Freeman's Journal*, 15 December 1917.
150   Oldmeadow, *Francis Cardinal Bourne*, p. 110.
151   DDA, Walsh papers, 386 II, Bourne to Ward, 29 October 1914.
152   DDA, Walsh papers, 1918, 390 I, Amigo to Ministry of Information, attached to a personal letter from Amigo to Walsh, 3 May 1918.
153   DDA, Amigo to Ministry of Information, attached to a letter to Walsh, 3 May 1918.
154   Coogan, *Wherever Green is worn*, pp. 626–7.
155   DDA, Walsh papers, 1918, 390 I, Kennedy to Walsh, 17 March 1918.
156   *The Irish Catholic Directory*, 1919, p. 507.
157   *The Freeman's Journal*, 19 March 1918.
158   DDA, Walsh papers, 1918, 390 I, O'Riordan to Walsh, 24 March 1918.
159   Archivio degli Affari Ecclesiastici Straordinari, Vatican, file 'Guerra anno 1914–1918', O'Riordan to Cerretti, 6 June 1918 and 7 June 1918.
160   Keogh, *The Vatican, the Bishops and Irish Politics, 1919–1939*, p. 6.

NOTES TO CHAPTER 8

1   T.M. Healy, *Letters and Leaders of my Day*, p.598.
2   Service historique de l'Armée de Terre (SHAT), French Military Archives, Vincennes, France: the numerous reports of French generals in 1918 are very relevant on this topic.
3   Miquel, *La Grande Guerre*, p.532.
4   Ibid., p.531.
5   Gregor Dallas, *1918, War and Peace* (London, 2000), p. 47.
6   Ward, *Ireland and Anglo-American Relations, 1899–1921*, p. 163, footnote no. 63.
7   Dallas, *1918, War and Peace*, pp. 47 and 60–1.
8   Miquel, *La Grande Guerre*, pp. 531–2.
9   Westminster Diocesan Archives (AAW), Bourne papers, BO 1/72, O'Connor to Samuels (copy), 7 May 1918.
10   Murphy, *Patrick Pearse and the Lost Republican Ideal*, p.113.
11   NLI, O'Kelly papers, MS 27728(1), Curran's memoirs, pp. 291–2.
12   Kendle, *Walter Long, and the Union 1905–1920*, p.164.
13   S.J. Connolly (ed.), *The Oxford Companion to Irish History* (Oxford, 1998), p. 328.
14   Westminster Diocesan Archives (AAW), Bourne papers, BO 1/72, Bourne to Long, 17 May 1918.
15   Kendle, *Walter Long, and the Union 1905–1920*, p.168.
16   Boyce, 'British Opinion, Ireland, and the War, 1916–1918', *Historical Journal*, p.589.
17   Kendle, *Walter Long and the Union 1905–1920*, p.168.
18   *The Freeman's Journal*, 11 February 1918.
19   Westminster Diocesan Archives, Bourne papers, AAW BO 1/72, Logue to O'Connor (copy), 1 March 1918.
20   Ibid., O'Connor to Samuels (copy), 7 May 1918.
21   SHAT, Vincennes, attachés militaires, file 7N1261, de la Panouse to Clemenceau, 3 August 1918.

22 SHAT, Vincennes, attachés militaires, file 5N278, author and addressee unknown, 5 January 1917.
23 Horne, *The Price of Glory, Verdun 1916*, pp. 212–13.
24 NLI, Redmond papers, MS 15236, Leslie to Redmond, 10 November 1916.
25 Quai d'Orsay, Paris, vol. 547 Grande-Bretagne/Irlande, letter no. 8, Pichon to Tardieu, 8 February 1918.
26 Quai d'Orsay, vol. 546 Grande-Bretagne/Irlande, Blanche to Pichon, 11 February 1918.
27 Quai d'Orsay, vol. 547 Grande-Bretagne/Irlande, Blanche to French Foreign Office Secretary, 19 February 1918.
28 PRO, London, see files CO 904/157, CO 904/207 and CO 904/161.
29 Quai d'Orsay, Paris vol. 547 Grande Bretagne/Irlande, note no. 35 concerning Géraud's visit to Ireland.
30 Macready, *Annals of an Active Life*, pp. 294–5.
31 Dallas, *1918, War and Peace*, p. 47.
32 R.I.Q. Adams and Philip P. Poirier, *The Conscription Controversy in Great Britain, 1900–1918* (Macmillan, 1987), p. 236.
33 ACA, Logue Papers, report of J.S. Hay.
34 Ibid.
35 Ibid.
36 Ibid.
37 Ibid.
38 Quai d'Orsay, Paris, vol. 546 Grande-Bretagne/Irlande, report of Fr Flynn's mission in Ireland.
39 ACA, Logue papers, report of J.S. Hay.
40 Maison diocésaine de Paris, Amette Papers, série 4B1,6, Logue to Amette, 11 August 1918.
41 Ferguson, *The Pity of War*, p. 313
42 SHAT, Vincennes, Fonds Clemenceau, file 6N53, Amette to Clemenceau, 16 August 1918.
43 ACA, Logue papers, report of J.S. Hay.
44 Ward, 'Lloyd George and the 1918 Irish Conscription Crisis', *Historical Journal*, p.122.
45 ACA, Logue papers, report of J.S. Hay.
46 Ibid.
47 ACA, Logue papers, John Stuart Hay to Logue, 1 September 1918.
48 ACA, Logue papers, report of J.S. Hay.
49 Ward, 'Lloyd George and the 1918 Irish conscription crisis', pp. 122–3.
50 Maison diocésaine de Paris, Amette Papers, série 4B1,6, Amette to Logue.
51 Adams and Poirier, *The Conscription Controversy in Great Britain 1900–1918*, p. 241.
52 Dangerfield, *The Damnable Question*, p. 273.
53 Dallas, *1918, War and Peace*, p.47.
54 Ibid., pp. 60–1.
55 David Lloyd George, 'Citadel of Peace and Liberty', *International University Course*, section 3 (Nottingham and London), pp. 168–70.
56 Dangerfield, *The Damnable Question*, p.292.
57 Johnstone, *Orange, Green and Khaki*, p. 395.
58 Ibid., pp. 394–5.
59 Imperial War Museum, London, diary of General Sir Henry Wilson, courtesy of Mr Julian Putkowski, England.
60 Dangerfield, *The Damnable Question*, p.292.
61 Miller, *Church, State and Nation in Ireland 1898–1921*, p.422.

NOTES TO AFTERMATH

1 Stewart, *Edward Carson*, p. 95.
2 Foster, *Modern Ireland, 1600–1972*, p. 490.
3 Johnstone, *Orange, Green and Khaki*, p. 428.

4   David Lloyd George, 'Citadel of Peace and Liberty', *International University Course*, section 3 (Nottingham and London), pp. 168–70.

5   Kenneth O. Morgan, *The Age of Lloyd George* (London, 1978), pp. 86–100.

6   Jane Leonard, 'Getting them at last, the IRA and Ex-Servicemen' in David Fitzpatrick (ed.), *Revolution? Ireland, 1917–1923* (Dublin, 1990), pp. 118–19.

7   Gwynn, *John Redmond's Last Years*, p. 163.

8   Terence Denman, A Lonely Grave, the Life and Death of William Redmond (Blackrock, 1995), pp. 102–3 and p. 120.

9   Colvin, *The Life of Lord Carson* (Victor Gollancz, 1934).

10   Patrick Murray, *The Oracles of God: the Roman Catholic Church and Irish Politics, 1922–1937* (Dublin, 2000), pp. 112–13.

11   Earl of Longford and O'Neill, *Eamon de Valera*, p. 204.

12   Laffan, *The Resurrection of Ireland, the Sinn Féin Party, 1916–1923*, p. 124.

13   Morrissey, *William J. Walsh, Archbishop of Dublin, 1841–1921*, p. 319.

14   Ibid.

15   Ryle Dwyer, *De Valera, the Man and the Myths*, pp. 198–9.

16   LDO, O'Dwyer papers, file 'Irish politics, 1912–1922', Freedom of the City speech, 14 September 1916.

17   Morrissey, *William J. Walsh, Archbishop of Dublin, 1841–1921*, pp. 326–7.

18   Ibid.

Bibliography

Summary of abbreviations for reference purposes
ACA   Ara Coeli Armagh
SHAT   Service Historique de l'Armée de Terre
DDA   Dublin Diocesan Archives
ICR   Irish College Rome
LDO   Limerick Diocesan Office
NLI   National Library of Ireland
PRO   Public Record Office
CO   Colonial Office
FO   Foreign Office

INSTITUTIONAL ARCHIVES AND PUBLIC RECORDS

France

Service Historique de l'Armée de Terre, Vincennes
(French military archives)
File SN 278
File 7N1261 (attachés militaires)
File 7N1255 (attachés militaires)
File 6N155 (fonds Clemenceau)
File 6N53 (fonds Clemenceau)
File 6N162 (fonds Clemenceau)

Quai d'Orsay, Paris
(French Foreign Office archives)
Grande-Bretagne vol. 540
Grande-Bretagne vol. 544
Grande-Bretagne/Irlande vol. 545
Grande-Bretagne/Irlande vol. 546
Grande-Bretagne/Irlande vol. 547

Germany

Auswärtiges Amt, Bonn
(German Foreign Office archives)
File R21153 Krieg 1914
File R21154 Krieg 1914
File R21156 Krieg 1914
File R21157 Krieg 1914
File R21158 Krieg 1914
File R21160 Krieg 1914

Great Britain

Archives of the Archdiocese of Westminster, London
Cardinal Francis Bourne papers

Bodleian Library, Oxford
Matthew Nathan Archives (MS 468, MS 469)
Courtesy of Dr Colman Ó Clabaigh (OSB) Glenstal Abbey, Co.
  Limerick, Ireland

Imperial War Museum, London
Lord French papers
Sir Henry Wilson papers
Courtesy of Dr Brian Murphy (OSB) Glenstal Abbey, Co. Limerick,
  Ireland

Public Record Office, London
Colonial Office (CO 904/161/4, CO 904/157, CO 904/207)
Foreign Office papers (FO 380/8, FO 380/9, FO 380/17, FO 380/18)
Foreign Office Index 1906–1919 (old references: Ireland 41 89 600/16
  and Ireland 41 114046/115612)

Ireland

Ara Coeli Armagh
Cardinal Michael Logue papers
Cardinal Patrick O'Donnell papers
Cardinal Joseph MacRory papers

Bishop's House Carlow
Bishop Patrick Foley papers

Dublin Diocesan Archives
Archbishop William Walsh papers
Mgr Michael Curran papers

Limerick Diocesan Archives
Bishop Edward O'Dwyer papers

National Library of Ireland
Joseph Brennan papers (MS 26166)
George Gavan Duffy papers (MS 15439)
Shane Leslie papers (MS 22832, MS 22892, MS 22885)
Joseph McGarrity papers (MS 17435)
Richard Mulcahy papers (MS 24357)
John Redmond papers (MS 15236, MS 15188, MS 18290, MS 15197, MS 15180, MS 15172, MS 18291, MS 18292)
Seán T.O'Kelly papers (MS 27728, MS 27677)

Italy

Irish College Rome
Mgr John Hagan papers
Mgr Michael O'Riordan papers

San Isidoro, Rome
(church of the Irish Franciscans in Rome)
Church archives

United States

Saint Joseph's Seminary, Archdiocesan Archives, New York
Courtesy of Fr Oliver P. Rafferty (SJ)
Cardinal Farley papers

Vatican

Archivio Segreto
(Secret Archives)

Archivio per gli Affari Ecclesiastici Straordinari
(Archives of the Extraordinary Ecclesiastical Affairs)
Guerra anno 1914–1918, rubrica 244, fasc. 92, rubrica 244 D3
Files concerning Ireland: 15274, 15543, 16086, 16148, 43338, 62775, 62776, 62780, 63545, 63566, 63567, 63568, 63569, 63588, 91187

JOURNALS AND NEWSPAPERS

Archivium Hibernicum
The Bandon Opinion
The Catholic Bulletin
The Church of Ireland Gazette
Collectanea Hibernia
The Cork Examiner
The Downside Review
The English Review
Eire Ireland
The 'Factionist'
The Freeman's Journal
The Hibernian
The Historical Journal
The Irish Catholic

Irish Freedom
Irish Historical Studies
The Irish Independent
The Irishman
The Nation
The Irish Opinion
The Irish Times
The Irish Volunteer
The Irish Worker
Nationality
New Ireland
Scissors and Paste
The Spark
The Tablet
The Workers' Republic

REFERENCE BOOKS

Duffy, James (ed.), *The Irish Catholic Directory 1800–1980* (Dublin: Duffy, 1915–1919)

Coates, Tim (ed.), *The Irish Uprising, 1914–1921* (London: The Stationery Office, 2000)

Connolly, S.J. (ed.), *The Oxford Companion to Irish History* (Oxford: Oxford University Press, 1998)

Hepburn, A.C., (ed.), *The Conflict of Nationality in Modern Ireland* (London: Edward Arnold, 1980)

Hickey, D.J. and Doherty, J.E., *A Dictionary of Irish History, 1800–1980* (Dublin: Gill & Macmillan, 1980)

McGraw and Hill (eds.), *New Catholic Encyclopedia* (San Francisco: McGraw & Hill Books, 1967)

Macksey, Charles, 'Wars', *Catholic Encyclopaedia* vol. XV.

Mitchell, Arthur and O'Snodaigh, Pádraig (eds), *Irish Political Documents, 1869–1916* (Dublin: Irish Academic Press, 1989)

Moody, Martin and Byrne (eds), *A New History of Ireland*, Vol. VIII (Oxford: Clarendon Press, 1976)

The Sinn Féin Rebellion Handbook (Dublin: compiled by the *Irish Times*, 1916)

SELECT BOOKS

Adams, R.I.Q. and Poirier, Philip P., *The Conscription Controversy in Britain, 1900–1918* (London: Macmillan, 1987)

Alison Philips, W., *The Revolution in Ireland, 1906–1923* (London: Longmans & Co., 1923)

Asquith, Earl of Oxford, *Memories and Reflections*, vol. 2 (London: Cassell & Co., 1928)

Bardon, Jonathan, *A History of Ulster* (Belfast: Blackstaff Press, 1992)

Bartlett, Thomas and Jeffrey, Keith (eds), *A Military History of Ireland* (Cambridge: Cambridge University Press, 1996)

Beresford Ellis, P. *History of the Irish Working Class* (London: Pluto, 1985)

Bower Bell, J., *The IRA, the Secret Army from 1916* (Massachusetts: The MIT Press, 1979)

Brennan, Michael, *The War in Clare* (Dublin: Irish Academic Press, 1980)

Buckland, Patrick, *James Craig* (Dublin: Gill & Macmillan, 1980)

Buckland, Patrick, *Ulster Unionism and the Origins of Northern Ireland, 1886–1922* (Dublin: Gill and Macmillan, 1973)

Callanan, Frank, *T.M. Healy* (Cork: Cork University Press, 1996)

Carroll, Francis M., *American Opinion and the Irish Question* (Dublin: Gill and Macmillan, 1978)

Coates, T. (ed.), *The Irish Uprising 1914–1921* (London: The Stationery Office, 2000)

Collins, M. E., *New History in Context 2* (Dublin: Hodder & Stoughton, 1996)

Collins, Peter (ed.), *Nationalism and Unionism: Conflict in Ireland, 1885–1921* (Antrim: W. & G. Baird Ltd., 1994)

Colvin, Ian, *The Life of Lord Carson* (London: Victor Gollancz, 1934)

Coogan, Tim Pat, *Michael Collins* (London: Hutchinson, 1990)

Coogan, Tim Pat, *Wherever Green is Worn* (London: Hutchinson, 2000)

Dangerfield, George, *The Damnable Question* (London: Constable Ltd., 1977)

Deasy, Liam, *Towards Ireland Free* (Cork: The Mercier Press, 1973)

Desmond Williams, T. (ed.), *Secret Societies in Ireland* (Dublin: Gill & Macmillan, 1973)

Devoy, John, *Recollections of an Irish Rebel* (New York: Youngu, 1929)

Doerries, Reinhard R., *Prelude to the Easter Rising: Sir Roger Casement in Imperial Germany* (London: Frank Cass, 2000)

Dudley Edwards, Ruth, *Patrick Pearse and the Triumph of Failure* (Swords: Poolbeg Press, 1990)

Dudley Edwards, R. and Desmond Williams, T. (eds), *The Great Famine* (Dublin: Lilliput Press, 1974)

Fisk, Robert, *In Time of War* (London: A. Deutsch, 1983)

Fitzgerald, Desmond, *Memoirs of Desmond Fitzgerald, 1913–1916* (London: Routledge & Kegan Paul, 1968)

Fitzgerald, William G., *The Voice of Ireland* (Dulin and London: Virtue and Company Ltd, 1979)

Fitzpatrick, David, *Oceans of Consolation* (Cork: Cork University Press, 1995)

Fitzpatrick, David, *Politics & Irish Life, 1913–1921* (Dublin: Gill & Macmillan, 1977)

Fitzpatrick, David (ed.), *Revolution? Ireland, 1917–1923* (Dublin: Trinity History Workshop, 1990)

Foster, Roy, *Modern Ireland, 1600–1972* (London: Penguin, 1989)

Geary, Laurence M., *The Plan of Campaign 1886–1891* (Cork: Cork University Press, 1986)

Gwynn, Denis, *The History of Partition, 1912–1925* (Dublin: Browne & Nolan, 1950)

Gwynn, Stephen, *John Redmond's Last Years* (London: Edward Arnold, 1919)

Headlam, Maurice, *Irish Reminiscences* (London: Robert Hale, 1947)

Healy, T.M., *Letters and Leaders of my Day*, vol. II (London: Thornton & Butterworth, 1928)

Holmes, Richard, *The Little Field Marshal: Sir John French* (Milan: Credito Italiano, 1981)

Hornman, Wim, *Kinderen van Het Geweld* (Haarlem: Gorntmer, 1973)

Inglis, Brian, *Roger Casement* (London: Hodder & Stoughton, 1973)

Jeffery, Keith (ed.), *An Irish Empire? Aspects of Ireland and the British Empire* (Manchester: Manchester University Press, 1996)

Jones, Thomas, *Whitehall Diary*, vol. III: Ireland 1918–1925 (London: Oxford University Press, 1971)

Kassar, George H., *Kitchener: Architect of Victory* (London: Kimber, 1977)

Kee, Robert, *The Green Flag* (London: Weidenfeld & Nicolson, 1969)

Kendle, John, *Walter Long and the Union, 1905–1920* (Dun Laoghaire: Glendale, 1992)

Keogh, Dermot, *Jews in Twentieth Century Ireland* (Cork: Cork University Press, 1998)

Laffan, Michael, *The Partition of Ireland* (Dublin: Dublin Historical Association, 1983)

Laffan, Michael, *The Resurrection of Ireland, the Sinn Féin Party, 1916–1923* (Cambridge: Cambridge University Press, 1999)

Lawlor, Sheila, *Britain and Ireland, 1914–1923* (Dublin: Gill & Macmillan, 1983)

Lee, J.J., *Ireland 1912–1985: Politics and Society* (Cambridge: Cambridge University Press, 1989)

Longford, Earl of and O'Neill, Thomas P., *Eamon de Valera* (London: Gill & Macmillan, 1970)

Lyons, F.S.L., *Culture and Anarchy in Ireland, 1890–1939* (Oxford: Oxford University Press, 1982)

Lyons, F.S.L., *John Dillon* (London: Routledge & Kegan Paul, 1968)

McDowell, R.B., *The Irish Convention, 1917–1918* (London: Routledge, 1970)

McHugh, Roger (ed.), *Dublin 1916* (London: Arlington Books, 1966)

MacColl, René, *Roger Casement* (London: First Four Square Edition, 1965)

MacDonagh, Oliver (ed.), *Irish Culture and Nationalism, 1750–1950* (London: Macmillan Press, 1983)

MacEntee, Sean, *Episode at Easter* (Dublin: Gill & Son, 1966)

Mac Giolla Choille, Breandán (ed.), *Intelligence Notes, 1913–1916* (Dublin: State Paper Office, 1966)

Macready, Gen. Sir Nevil, *Annals of an Active Life*, vol. I (London: Hutchinson, 1924)

Mansergh, Nicholas, *The Unsolved Question* (London: Yale University Press, 1993)

Martin, F.X. (ed.), *Leaders and Men of the Easter Rising: Dublin 1916* (London: Methuen & Co., 1967)

Martin, F.X. (ed.), *The Irish Volunteers, 1913–1915* (Dublin: James Duffy, 1963)

Maume, Patrick, *The Long Gestation* (Dublin: Gill & Macmillan, 1999)

Mitchell, A. and O'Snodaigh, P. (eds), *Irish Political Documents 1869–1916* (Dublin: Irish Academic Press, 1989)

Mitchell, Angus, (ed.), *The Amazon Journal of Roger Casement* (Dublin: Anaconda Editions, 1997)

Moloney, John, *A History of Australia* (Victoria: Viking O'Neill Penguin, 1988)

Morgan, Austen, *Labour and Partition, The Belfast Working Class 1905–1923* (London: Pluto, 1991)

Morgan, Kenneth O., *Ireland after the Union* (Oxford: Oxford University Press, 1989)

Morgan, Kenneth O., *The Age of Lloyd George* (London: Allen & Unwin, 1971)

Morton, Grenfell, *Home Rule and the Irish Question* (Essex: Longman, 1994)

Murphy, Brian P., *John Chartres, Mystery Man of the Treaty* (Blackrock: Irish Academic Press, 1995)

Murphy, Brian P., *Patrick Pearse and the Lost Republican Ideal* (Dublin: James Duffy, 1991)

Nowlan, Kevin (ed.), *The Making of 1916* (Dublin: Stationery Office, 1969)

O'Brien, John and Travers, Pauric (eds), *The Irish Emigrant Experience in Australia* (Swords Poolbeg, 1991)

O'Broin, Leon, *Dublin Castle and the 1916 Rising* (Dublin: Helicon, 1966)

O'Broin, Leon, *Protestant Nationalists in Revolutionary Ireland* (Dublin: Gill & Macmillan, 1985)

O'Broin, Leon, *Revolutionary Underground* (Dublin: Gill & Macmillan, 1976)

O'Broin, Leon, *The Chief Secretary* (London: Chatto & Windus, 1969)

O'Hegarty, P.S., *The Victory of Sinn Féin* (Dublin: Talbot Press, 1924)

Owen, Frank, *Tempestuous Journey: David Lloyd, his Life and Times* (London: Hutchinson & Co., 1954)

Pakenham, Thomas, *The Boer War* (London: Weidenfeld & Nicolson, 1998)

Phoenix, Eamon, *Northern Nationalism* (Belfast: Ulster Historical Foundation, 1994)

Pollock, John, *Kitchener* (London: Constable, 2001)

Prill, Felician, *Ireland, Britain and Germany, 1870–1914* (Bristol: Gill & Macmillan, 1975)

Ryle Dwyer, T., *De Valera: the Man and the Myths* (Swords: Poolbeg, 1992)

Stewart, A.T.Q., *Edward Carson* (Dublin: Gill & Macmillan, 1981)

Stewart, A.T.Q., *The Ulster Crisis* (London: Faber & Faber, 1967)

Tierney, Michael, *Eoin MacNeill: Scholar and Man of Action, 1867–1945* (New York: Oxford University Press, 1980)

Valiulis, Maryann Gialanella, *General Richard Mulcahy* (Blackrock: Irish Academic Press, 1992)

Vaughan, W.E. and Fitzpatrick, A.J., *Irish Historical Statistics Population 1821–1971* (Dublin: Royal Irish Academy, 1978)

Ward, Alan J., *Ireland and Anglo-American Relations, 1899–1921* (London: Weidenfeld & Co., 1969)

Yeates, Pádraig, *Lockout, Dublin 1913* (Dublin: Gill & Macmillan, 2000)

Younger, Calton, *Arthur Griffith* (Dublin: Gill & Macmillan, 1981)

BOOKS ON THE FIRST WORLD WAR

Barnett, Correlli, *The Swordbearers; Supreme Command in the First World War* (Reading: Cassell & Co., 2000)

Chaline, Nadine-Josette (ed.), *Chrétiens dans la Première Guerre Mondiale* (Paris: Editions du Cerf, 1993)

Dallas, Gregor, 1918, *War and Peace* (London: John Murray, 2000)

Denman, Terence, *Ireland's Unknown Soldiers* (Blackrock: Irish Academic Press, 1992)

Denman, Terence, *A Lonely Grave, the Life and Death of William Redmond* (Blackrock: Irish Academic Press, 1995)

Falls, Cyril, *The History of the 36th (Ulster) Division* (London: Constable, 1996)

Ferguson, Niall, *The Pity of War* (St Ives: Penguin, 1998)

Fischer, Fritz, *Germany's Aims in the First World War* (London: Chatto & Windus, 1967)

Fitzpatrick, David (ed.), *Ireland and the First World War* (Dublin: The Lilliput Press, 1988)

French, David, *British Strategy and War Aims, 1914–1916* (London: Allen & Unwin, 1986)

Horne, Alistair, *The Price of Glory, Verdun 1916* (St Ives: Penguin, 1993)

Jeffery, Keith, *Ireland and the Great War* (Cambridge: Cambridge University Press, 2000)

Johnstone, Tom, *Orange, Green and Khaki, the Story of the Irish Regiments in the Great War* (Dublin: Gill & Macmillan, 1992)

Johnstone, Tom and Hagerty, James, *The Cross on the Sword: Chaplains in the Forces* (London: Geoffrey Chapman, 1996)

Leonard, Jane, *The Culture of Commemoration, the Culture of War Commemoration* (Dublin: Cultures of Ireland, 1996)

Liddell Hart, Sir Basil H., *Liddell Hart's History of the First World War* (London: Papermac, 1992)

MacDonald, Lyn, *1915, The Death of Innocence* (St Ives: Penguin, 1997)

Miquel, Pierre, *La Grande Guerre* (Saint-Amand: Marabout, 1983)

Miquel, Pierre, *Les Poilus* (Saint-Amand: Plon, 2000)

Moorehead, Alan, *Gallipoli* (Hertfordshire: Wordsworth, 1997)

Novick, Ben, *Conceiving Revolution; Irish Nationalist Propaganda during the First World War* (Bodmin: Four Courts Press, 2001)

Orr, Philip, *The Road to the Somme: Men of the Ulster Division tell their Story* (Belfast: The Blackstaff Press, 1987)

Taylor, A.J.P., *The First World War* (London: Penguin, 1966)

Terraine, John, *The Great War, 1914–1918* (London: Lake, 1965)

Tuchman, Barbara W., *August 1914* (London: Constable, 1962)

BOOKS ON THE CATHOLIC CHURCH AND ECCLESIASTICS

Bartlett, Thomas, *The Fall and Rise of the Irish Nation, the Catholic Question 1690–1830* (Dublin: Gill & Macmillan, 1992)

Begley, John, *The Diocese of Limerick from 1691 to the Present Time* (Dublin: Browne & Nolan, 1906)

Brennan, Niall, *Dr Mannix* (London: Angus & Robertson, 1965)

Canning, B.J., *Bishops of Ireland, 1870–1987* (Ballyshannon: Donegal Democrat, 1987)

Carroll, Denis, *They have fooled you again, Míceál O'Flannagáin* (Blackrock: The Columba Press, 1993)

Clifton, M., *Amigo, Friend of the Poor* (Leominster: Fowler Wright Books, 1987)

Connolly, Sean, *Religion and Society in Nineteenth Century Ireland* (Dublin: SIESH, Studies in Irish Economic and Social History, 1985)

Cornwell, John, *Hitler's Pope: The Secret History of Pius XII* (St. Ives: Viking, 1999)

D'Arcy, Charles Frederick, *The Adventures of a Bishop* (London: Hodder & Stoughton, 1934)

Fremantle, Anne (ed.), *The Papal Encyclicals* (New York: New American Library, 1956)

Gwynn, Denis, *The Vatican and the War in Europe* (Dublin: Browne & Nolan, 1940)

Harris, Mary, *The Catholic Church and the Foundation of the Northern Irish State* (Cork: Cork Cork University Press, 1993)

Inglis, Tom, *Moral Monopoly* (Dublin: Gill & Macmillan, 1987)

Joyce, P.J., *John Healy, Archbishop of Tuam* (Dublin: Gill, 1931)

Keogh, Dermot, *The Vatican, the Bishops and Irish Politics, 1919–1939* (Cambridge: Cambridge University Press, 1986)

Larkin, Emmet, *The Roman Catholic Church and the Creation of the Modern Irish State, 1876–1886* (Dublin: Gill & Macmillan, 1975)

Larkin, Emmet, *The Roman Catholic Church and the Plan of Campaign in Ireland, 1886–1888* (Cork: Cork University Press, 1978)

Larkin, Emmet, *The Roman Catholic Church and the Fall of Parnell, 1888–1891* (North Carolina: University of North Carolina Press, 1979)

Leslie, Shane, *Cardinal Gasquet* (London: Burns Oates, 1953)

MacDonald, Walter, *Reminiscences of a Maynooth Professor* (London: Jonathan Cape, 1925)

Miller, David W., *Church, State and Nation in Ireland, 1898–1921* (Dublin: Gill & Macmillan, 1973)

Morrissey, Thomas J., *William J. Walsh, Archbishop of Dublin, 1841–1921* (Dublin: Four Courts Press, 2000)

Murray, Patrick, *The Oracles of God; the Roman Catholic Church and Irish Politics, 1922–1937* (Dublin: University College Dublin Press, 2000)

Oldmeadow, Ernest, *Francis Cardinal Bourne*, vol. II (London: Burns, Oates & Washbourne, 1944)

Peters, Walter, *Benedict XV* (USA: Bruce, 1959)

Rafferty, Oliver P., *Catholicism in Ulster, 1603–1983* (Dublin: Gill & Macmillan, 1994)

Rafferty, Oliver P., *The Church, the State and the Fenians* (Basingstoke: Macmillan, 1999)

Tierney, Mark, *Croke of Cashel: the Life of Archbishop William Croke 1832–1902* (Dublin: Gill & Macmillan, 1976)

Walsh, P.J., *William J. Walsh, Archbishop of Dublin* (Dublin: Talbot Press, 1928)

ARTICLES

Boyce, David George, 'British Opinion, Ireland, and the War', *Historical Journal*, XVII, 3 (1974)

Boyce, David George, 'The Unknown Chief Secretary: H.E. Duke and Ireland, 1916–1918', *Irish Historical Studies*, 79 (March 1977)

Buckland, Patrick, 'The Southern Irish Unionists, the Irish Question, and British Politics, 1906–1914', *Irish Historical Studies*, 59 (March 1967)

Butler, Dom Urban, 'Cardinal Gasquet in Rome', *Downside Review*, 134 (1929)

Callan, Patrick, 'Ambivalence towards the Saxon Shilling', *Archivium Hibernicum*, 41 (1986)

Callan, Patrick, 'The Irish Soldier: a Propaganda Paper for Ireland, Sept.–Dec. 1918', *The Irish Sword*, 59

Campbell, Malcolm, 'Emigrant responses to war and revolution, 1914–1921: Irish opinion in the United States and Australia', *Irish Historical Studies*, XXXII, 125 (May 2000)

Denman, Terence, 'The Catholic Irish Soldier in the First World War: the "racial environment"', *Irish Historical Studies*, 27 (1991)

Fitzpatrick, David, 'The Logic of Collective Sacrifice: Ireland and the British Army, 1914–1918', *Historical Journal*, 38 (1995)

Gwynn, Denis, 'Cardinal Bourne and Ireland', *The Irish Ecclesiastical Record*, 56 (July 1940)

Gwynn, Denis, 'John Redmond', *Studies*, 180 (1956)

Julienne, Janick, 'La France et l'Irlande nationaliste de 1860 à 1890: évolution et mutation de liens multiséculaires', *Etudes Irlandaises* (spring 1999) 24–1

Kuypers, Dom Benedikt, 'Cardinal Gasquet in London', *Downside Review*, 134 (1929)

Lloyd George, David, 'Citadel of Peace and Liberty', *International University Course*, section 3 (Nottingham and London: Walter Black & Co., 1930s)

MacDonagh, Michael, 'Irish Catholic Chaplains in the War', *The Irish Ecclesiastical Record* (October 1915)

McCann, James, 'A Catholic Chaplain in the Great War', *Irish Monthly* (July 1940)

Mulcahy, Richard, 'Conscription and the General Headquarters' Staff', *The Capuchin Annual* (1968)

O'Callaghan, Edward, 'Bishop O'Dwyer and Bishop Foley on the Rising', *Collectanea Hibernia*, 18/19 (1976/77)

O'Fiaich, Tomás, 'The Irish Bishops and the Conscription Issue, 1918', *The Capuchin Annual* (1968)

Ó Luanaig, Dónall, 'Irishmen and the Franco-German War, 1870–1871', *The Capuchin Annual* (1971)

Ó Luing, Séan, 'The "German Plot" 1918', *The Capuchin Annual* (1968)

Rahilly, Alfred, 'The Catholic View of War', *Studies*, 26 (June 1918)

Renzi, William A., 'The Entente and the Vatican during the Period of Italian Neutrality, August 1914–May 1915', *Historical Journal*, XIII, 3 (1970)

Ward, Alan J., 'Lloyd George and the 1918 Irish Conscription Crisis', *Historical Journal*, XVII, I (1974)

Woods, C.J., 'Ireland and Anglo-Papal Relations, 1880–1885', *Irish Historical Studies*, 69 (March 1972)

THESES

Aan de Wiel, Jérôme, 'The Irish Reaction to World War One, 1914–1915' (Paris, Sorbonne Nouvelle, 1991) MA thesis

Aan de Wiel, Jérôme, 'L'Eglise catholique irlandaise et l'Eglise d'Irlande face à la Première Guerre Mondiale, 1914–1915' (Paris, Sorbonne Nouvelle, 1992) Pre-Ph.D thesis

Aan de Wiel, Jérôme, 'L'Eglise catholique en Irlande, 1914–1918: guerre et politique' (Caen, 1998) Ph.D thesis

Callan, Patrick, 'Voluntary Recruiting for the British Army in Ireland during the First World War' (Dublin, UCD, 1984)

Murphy, Brian P., 'J.J. O'Kelly and the Catholic Bulletin: Cultural Considerations – Gaelic, Religious and National, 1898–1926' (NUI) Ph.D thesis

O'Callaghan, Edward, 'Bishop Edward Thomas O'Dwyer and the Course of Irish Politics, 1870–1917' (UCG, 1976) MA thesis

Woods, C.J., 'The Catholic Church and Irish Politics, 1879–1892' (University of Nottingham, 1969)

Index

Page numbers in *italics* refer to illustrations or photographs